THE EARLY GROWTH OF LOGIC
IN THE CHILD

IN THE NORTON LIBRARY

BY JEAN PIAGET

Play, Dreams and Imitation in Childhood
The Origins of Intelligence in Children
The Child's Conception of Number
Genetic Epistemology

BY JEAN PIAGET AND BARBEL INHELDER

The Child's Conception of Space
The Early Growth of Logic in the Child

THE EARLY GROWTH OF LOGIC
IN THE CHILD

CLASSIFICATION AND SERIATION

BY

BÄRBEL INHELDER

AND

JEAN PIAGET

TRANSLATED FROM THE FRENCH BY
E. A. LUNZER and D. PAPERT

The Norton Library

W · W · NORTON & COMPANY · INC ·

NEW YORK

Translated from the French
LA GENÈSE DES STRUCTURES LOGIQUES ELEMENTAIRE

Books That Live
The Norton imprint on a book means that in the publisher's
estimation it is a book not for a single season but for the years.
W. W. Norton & Company, Inc.

ISBN 0 393 00473 2

PRINTED IN THE UNITED STATES OF AMERICA
4 5 6 7 8 9 0

CONTENTS

PREFACE

WE should perhaps apologize for inflicting another volume on the patient reader. And yet, in a sense, this work is long overdue. Elsewhere, in our discussions on the development of children's thinking in relation to problems of number, quantity and space, and again in dealing with the notion of chance and inductive reasoning, we have spoken of the formation of elementary logical operations. But the development of these structures as such deserves a separate study, and, from a logical point of view, we should have started with it. However, it often happens that questions which arise at the beginning of an investigation need to be deferred until a comparatively late stage.

Our second excuse is that we have often been accused of writing books and constructing theories on the basis of 10 or 20 individual cases. The present volume marks a departure, in that it includes detailed statistical tables and gives precise indications of the number of subjects.

A third point which we would emphasize is that the statement of our central theme will be found to be concise. The remainder of the work is designed to be used as reference material and not to be read *in extenso*. We shall therefore advise the reader to begin with the conclusions. The main body of the work can be consulted as he thinks fit, to find the justification for this argument or that. Finally (but only if he feels obliged to read the whole) he may turn to the introduction, to find out why these problems have been chosen. Indeed, we were tempted to begin with the conclusions and relegate the introduction to an appendix. But we might have been accused of having the conclusions in mind before collecting and analysing the data, where in fact these conclusions are the fruit of eight years' experimental work.

TRANSLATOR'S INTRODUCTION

The Early Growth of Logic in the Child differs from many of the authors' more recent publications in English in that the relevance of the actual experiments to the development of thought in real life situations may be less apparent to the non-specialist. A somewhat closer consideration suggests that it is in fact a most important contribution to the study of children's thinking, and one that is as far-reaching as any in its psychological and educational implications.

I. CLASSIFICATION AND INFERENCE

The sub-title of the book is *Classification and Seriation,* and its purpose is to examine the origin and growth of these two kinds of systematization in detail. The importance of consistent classification and categorization has been recognized by psychology for at least thirty years, and many of the relevant studies are referred to by the authors in their concluding chapter. The majority of these have also been well reviewed by Vinacke.[1] It remains that comparatively little has been done in regard to the study of the origins of classificatory behaviour in children. Even here most researches such as those of Hazlitt,[2] Thompson[3] and Annett,[4] have been limited to an empirical determination of the extent to which children are able to classify or cross-classify at different ages. By contrast the present authors seek to penetrate more deeply into the psychological mechanism underlying the development of classificatory behaviour in a large number of situations. In other words, where many of these works are concerned mainly with the *description* of children's behaviour, the present volume is the first attempt to offer a thorough-going explanation of such behaviour in developmental terms. At the same time, Inhelder and Piaget are particularly concerned to establish the precise relation between the classifications of children and the kinds of inferences that they make on the basis of these classifications.

In order to appreciate the part of unambiguous classification in inference, one might begin by considering the judgment that a chair would float or burn because it is made of wood. (Cf. the following

[1] Vinacke, W. E. *The Psychology of Thinking*, McGraw-Hill, 1952, ch. 7.
[2] Hazlitt, V. (1930), "Children's thinking", *Brit. J. Psychol.*, 20, 354–61.
[3] Thompson, J., (1941), "The ability of children of different grade levels to generalize on sorting tests", *J. Psychol.*, 11, 119–26.
[4] Annett, M. (1959), "The classification of four common class concepts by children and adults", *Brit. J. Educ. Psychol.*, 29.

example of reasoning from the records of Susan Isaacs[1] "Frank (5·7) dropped a pair of scissors from the gallery to the floor below. He said 'They didn't break—they're metal'.") Such an argument may represent an abstraction from the object as a given "use-object" of one of its properties, wooden, by virtue of which it is expected to share the properties of "all things wooden", however dissimilar. A corollary would be that a metal chair would be likely to sink, although its intuitive form as a functional constituent of experience is such as to link it far more closely with a wooden chair than a pair of scissors. But this is not necessarily so. The child may reason: wooden objects float, chairs are wooden, chairs float, metal chairs (insufficiently distinguished from other chairs) will float likewise. Verification might show that they do not. Nevertheless, the child may continue to argue that "all chairs float, only some do not". The following chapters, and Chapter IV in particular, abound with examples of how, in the thinking of young children, the use of "all" is consistent with exceptions.

Some kind of classification is implicit in a great many actions and in every judgment. For instance, if a child enters a room with a chair in it and names it "chair", or otherwise acts in a way which implies that he recognizes that it is a chair (by sitting down on it), then we as observers are entitled to infer that in one sense he has classified the object as a chair. But this kind of pre-classification is an ongoing part of ongoing behaviour. Piaget would term this "recognitive assimilation". By the same token the child might use the chair as a pedestal to stand on and reach onto a shelf. But the particular characterization of the chair as object to sit on or object to stand on, will be dictated by the needs of the moment. At no point is there simultaneous recognition of these two properties (uses) as characteristic of the same object. And by the same token, the assimilation of the chair to other chairs is no more than implicit to the child; it is explicit only to the observer who recognizes the similarities of his behaviour on successive occasions which involve different, but similar objects. It is explicit for the observer, because, in recalling these several occasions, he is uniting them within a single act of attention. For the child, it is implicit, because the several actions are successive in their occurrence.

Somewhat later we may find that the child will recognize that a chair is an article of furniture and may be bought from a furnishing store. Here the classification is a little more explicit, a little more dissociated from the action as a whole (e.g. of looking in shop windows). Yet taken by itself the judgment involves little *abstraction* from the concept of "chair" as evolved in the course of immediate practical experience.

In passing, we might note two points, first that the recognition that

[1] Isaacs, S. *Intellectual Growth in Young Children*, p. 146.

things may belong to categories of wider *generality*, e.g. chairs to furniture, apples to fruit, and so on, may occur very early. Indeed Brown[1] has argued very reasonably that the degree of generality which belongs to the first word that a child is given for an object is a function of the degree of specific discrimination required or expected of him in relation to the type of object. For instance, it is important to recognize dogs from cats, etc., and so he is likely to learn the word "dog" rather than "animal"; likewise, he will learn "money" rather than names of coins; but although "Fido" and "terrier" have less generality than "dog", these words (and categorizations) will generally be acquired later.

Second, the recognition that things may belong simultaneously to two categories, one of wider generality, the other of narrower, e.g. a thing is both a pear and a fruit, undoubtedly represents an advance on the mere recognitive assimilation considered in the last paragraph. Nevertheless, in and for itself, this kind of classificatory judgment is not sufficient to ensure a basis for correct inferences. Classifications of this sort can and do provide the basis for correct inferences and argument, but only on condition that there is adequate *abstraction* of the properties by virtue of which the elements of one class also belong to another, of higher generality, and not *vice versa*.

Overt classifications are comparatively rare in the reasoning of young children, and so, for that matter, in everyday adult reasoning. But the kind of analogy sometimes loose, sometimes precise, which directs our thinking, is itself a classificatory (or pre-classificatory) activity. Referring again to Susan Isaacs' accounts of incidental reasoning by children at Malting House, one might cite the following examples:

When Mrs. I. and the children were sharpening pencils with a knife, Dan (4·11) said, "Why can't we sharpen them like they were when we first got them, all round and smooth?" Then, after a moment—"I know, it's because they're not done with a knife, they're done with those things that you turn round!"[2]

Or again:

Looking at the picture of a whaling ship with smaller boats hung over the sides, one of the children said "Those are lifeboats". "No", said Paul (4·0), "lifeboats don't be on the side of the ship, they are on the cliff in a long shed".[3]

In the first case, the sharpening of pencils is assimilated by analogy to a similar action assumed to have been done when they were first manufactured, and this gives rise to dissatisfaction with the result. Here, the partial inadequacy of the analogy is then pinpointed. In the second case there is an almost explicit classification of lifeboats as

[1] Brown, R. G., "How shall a thing be called?" *Psychol. Rev.*, Vol. LXV, 1958, pp. 14–21.
[2] Isaacs, S. *Intellectual Growth in Young Children*, p. 147.
[3] ibid., p. 151.

housed in sheds, and a consequent rejection of the description of "lifeboats" on the deck of a ship.

The argument of Isaacs is that children, like adults, learn from experience. That they do can hardly be questioned, but the question that may be raised concerns the way in which they learn from experience, what sort of generalizations are made, and how far false generalizations are refined and corrected. The extent to which experience contradicts expectation brings about a change in the assimilatory generalizations or analogies that anteceded it depends on the analysis brought to bear on such experience. And this is a matter of substituting a precise differentiation for a loose assimilation. But the condition for a precise differentiation is the ability to "turn round on" the initial assimilatory generalization, and examine the criteria which motivated it.

Even if overt classifications represent a somewhat artificial type of situation, their interest lies in the fact that they are intimately linked with this ability to "turn round on a schema", *to abstract the criteria of generalization.*

It is true that the simplest kinds of sorting, e.g. sorting a collection of cards which are similar in every respect except colour, into red, yellow and blue, may be carried out without such abstraction, i.e. without the mediation of an awareness of the criteria of the sorting. But such a test represents a special case, and its bearing on everyday intelligent behaviour is almost notional. For in fact we are constantly interpreting new situations in the light of previous experience, and in the final analysis this means that we are grouping or classifying these diverse situations under the same heading. Only rarely, if ever, can the determinants or criteria of this grouping be wholly unambiguous. Often enough, the tendency to assimilate the new to the familiar will lead to false analogies, and predictions or solutions based on these will turn out at variance with the facts. The question then arises whether we can detect the error, and in order to do so, we need to be aware of the initial criteria which determined the analogy. We have to be able to retrace our steps, to go back on our reasoning.

The following pages show very clearly that the ability to do so argues a slow and gradual development. Young children undoubtedly try to organize their experience after a fashion, and in the same way, they are willing enough to impose some kind of an organization on an array of objects. But to begin with they fail to carry out the task in any coherent way because they deal with the objects one at a time, and the basis of their own behaviour eludes them. They cannot turn round on their own activity and abstract any single consistent criterion to govern the entire sequence. Although they might, perhaps, deal with the situation if the objects differed only in one characteristic, they cannot do so when the differences are more varied.

It therefore appears that if classificatory problems are somehow connected with problems of inference in general, it is because classifications depend on the abstraction and retention of clear and unambiguous criteria. When this restriction is not attended to, the results of classificatory experiments can just as easily mislead as clarify the processes involved in reasoning. There is an excellent example of "pre-classificatory" behaviour which may still lead to correct solution of a test in Chapter VI. Children are asked to complete a four-cell matrix similar to Raven's Matrices from a series of multiple choice items. Many of the younger ones are remarkably successful in certain cases. But they themselves have no idea why they choose the correct item, and when asked if another will do as well, they are more than ready to change their mind.

All of the foregoing may be summed up as follows: Classifications both covert and open play an important part in inference, but only insofar as (i) the subject can make such classifications unambiguous, and (ii) he is able to recognize the criteria of his own classifications, i.e. he knows wherein they are unambiguous. In other words, the sort of classificatory behaviour which is especially relevant for reasoning is the activity involved in the abstraction of the criteria of classification. It is this recognition which distinguishes the present account from the work of most other psychologists.

II. CO-ORDINATION

The argument thus far is that classification only becomes logical when it carries with it an explicit recognition of its criteria. We have called this an activity of abstraction. However, in order to appreciate the novelty and power of Piaget's analyses, we have to appreciate that there are two kinds of abstraction. The term "abstraction" is used most commonly to refer to a bringing together of common properties and relations inherent in different objects and events. Here the abstraction is an abstraction from the object, or the situations, as experienced. Abstracting the criteria of a classification involves a different kind of abstraction. It is a "turning round" on the actions of grouping and re-grouping, and the logical inferences which it generates depend on abstraction from the activity of the subject. Something more will be said of the first kind of abstraction in section III. But, first of all, we must see how, by his emphasis on abstraction from the actions of the subject, Piaget's analysis of reasoning represents an advance on the thinking of his predecessors. For it is this co-ordination of actions which, for Piaget, confers the element of necessity on the inferences which we draw. Logic itself, he argues, is not an innate characteristic of thinking, nor is it simply a mode of organization forced on us by the world as experienced. It is one that we construct by co-ordinating our own actions and abstracting the relations between them.

To take an example. In Chapter IV of this work, the authors show how a child of 6 or 7 persistently refuses to recognize that a bunch of flowers containing 4 primulas and 2–4 other flowers must contain more flowers than primulas because all the primulas are flowers and not all the flowers are primulas. Yet at 7 or 8 this is self-evident. The answers which are given by younger children show quite clearly that so soon as they begin to think of the flowers as primulas and others they are quite unable to retain a concept of the bunch (or class) as a whole. Hence, their reply invariably testifies to the fact that they are comparing one part with another instead of comparing one part with the whole.

Now this is not at all because they fail to understand the meaning of the terms "primulas", "roses", "flowers", etc. For their answers show quite clearly that they do. It is because the judgments which they are required to make correspond to actions that they might carry out. There are two sorts of actions which they can carry out. One of these is to take a number of primulas and add a small bunch of miscellaneous flowers to produce a large collection of flowers. This is an addition or "union". The other is to take the primulas from the bunch of flowers, leaving only the miscellaneous "remainder". Both are actions which they could carry out in practice and both are actions which they can entertain as virtual actions in their head. But the addition and the subtraction are not co-ordinated with one another. Taking away a part of the flowers has the effect of destroying the previous unity of the total. This would be the case if the action were carried out in practice and it remains so when it has the status of a virtual action, performed in "the child's head". In order to be able to compare the part with the whole, the subject must have in mind the addition or "union" even while performing the mental subtraction. This is not so much a matter of doing two things at once as doing the same thing in a different way. The difference, moreover, is twofold: in the first place, the possibility of reverting to the union is never lost sight of, so that the addition and the subtraction bear on one another; but, and this is the crucial difference, in the second place the act of addition is recognized as being the inverse of the act of subtraction. This is not just a matter of being aware of the fact that one might be able to perform another action and so revert to the point where one began; it implies that the subject realizes that this other action is bound to lead him back to the starting-point *because this action is the inverse of the other*.

Therefore, when the 7 or 8 year-old child recognizes implicitly that the whole is *necessarily* greater than (or equal with) any of its parts, the systematization which confers a logical character to his reasoning derives from the fact that he is aware of the relatedness of his own actions.

Many readers will recognize that the experiment on the primulas and flowers recalls a similar experiment, using brown and white beads. This is an experiment carried out long ago by Jean Piaget, and recorded in *The Child's Conception of Number*. Similarly, the experiments on seriation reported in the present volume recall the work reported in that volume. A part of Piaget's thesis is that a correct understanding of classificatory relations is essential to an adequate conception of number. Thus, the set of positive integers may be regarded as a hierarchical classification in which each successive number constitutes a class which includes all of its predecessors. Thus, the number 5 includes 4, 3, 2 and 1; and 4 includes 3, 2 and 1, etc. Similarly, having regard to the systematic ordering of serial relations, the same numbers may be regarded as forming a series in which any term is greater than any of those that precede it and lesser than any of its successors. These two characteristics of number are far from being of interest only to the logician. Any teacher is aware of the gain in understanding that results when a child realizes that it is impossible to subtract a larger number of concrete things from a smaller number; and he also knows how difficult it sometimes is for children to realize when a number is larger or smaller (quite apart from the added difficulties that arise in conjunction with our use of the decimal notation).

It is true that subsequent research has tended to show that children may have a partial understanding of number and of its importance before they have fully come to grips with the implication of class-inclusion. For instance, many children of 6 will be convinced of the necessary invariance or "conservation" of a row of objects (for example, a row of egg-cups) despite transformations of its arrangement (for example, shortening or lengthening the row by reducing or increasing the intervals between the cups). The same children may not be able to compare primulas with flowers or brown beads with beads until a year later. But this only means that a systematic co-ordination of all the relations involved in an operational understanding or number is a gradual process. It does not invalidate Piaget's thesis that an *adequate* understanding of number must involve an understanding of class-inclusion.

But even the partial understanding implied by operational or necessary conservation is intimately related to the kinds of co-ordination studies in the present volume.

For in order that a child accept the invariance of the quantity of a number of objects when the spatial appearance of the collection suggests that there are more or fewer than at the start, he must reject these perceptual cues in favour of a new criterion. If one row of objects, for example, egg-cups, was deliberately set out in such a way as to exhibit a one-one correspondence with another row, for example, a row of eggs, then, although the cups are subsequently moved, the child insists that the two collections are equal. He is therefore basing his judgment on his initial action in setting up the correspondence, and, more especially, on his understanding that whatever actions were taken in disturbing the correspondence, these may be cancelled by carrying out the inverse actions. In other words, instead of being swayed by a fluctuating criterion (whatever perceptual features of the set-up happen to predominate at any given moment), he deliberately selects a fixed criterion, and one which is invariant precisely because it is regulated by actions which he can control. Clearly the child can only reject one kind of criterion in favour of another to the extent that he becomes aware of the criteria which he uses and is able to retain the criteria which he chooses throughout the judgments that he makes.

The Early Growth of Logic contains a detailed study of the way in which children come to a gradual awareness of the criteria of their own actions, because classification is intimately bound up with the retention of unambiguous criteria in the definition of classes. But the selection and use of unambiguous criteria of definition underlies all of the behavioural developments studied by the authors in the course of their previous work. Thus, the conservation of number depends on adherence to a criterion of number based on the enumeration of objects by taking each once and once only, thereby setting up a one-one correspondence between the numbered collection and all other collections having the same cardinal value. Similarly, the conservation of length depends on adherence to a criterion of length based on the action of establishing an interval relation between two limit points. The conservation of weight argues a criterion based (initially) on the use of a balance. Each of these criteria involves an appeal to actions carried out by the subject, and the selection of such a criterion is attributable to the fact that such actions can be systematically related to one another—so that their effects can be anticipated. Thus, there is an intimate relation between the operational systematization of concepts and their operational definition. Only concepts that are operationally definable by reference to a precise set of actions are systematizable, and conversely, it is only because these actions are systematized that they can be used to define relatively invariant and stable concepts.

It should be added that this conception of operations as (mental) actions which bear on actions of the subject constitutes what is probably the most significant difference between Piaget's view on learning[1] and the view which is common to all other "theories of learning". Each of these sets out in its own way to account for the progressive adaptations

---

[1] See Piaget, J. "Apprentissage et Connaisance", *Etudes d'épistémologie génétique*, Vol. X (1959), pp. 159–88.

of behaviour by first showing how one particular action may be modified (by the operation of a "law of effect", or by a "law of proximity", or a "principle of need reduction", etc.), and then extending this to the co-ordination of sequences of such actions (as in Pavlov's "dynamic stereotypes", or Hull's "habit family hierarchies[1]"). But although this allows for the modification of individual actions by their association with other actions ("pro-action" and "retro-action") the actions still remain what they were: actions on the environment and reactions to the environment. None of these theories has been conspicuously successful in dealing with problems of conceptual learning. It is because Piaget's concept of an "operation" is a total departure from this approach[2] that his experimental studies have been more successful in this respect, while still remaining closely tied to a clear-cut theoretical formulation.

Readers who are particularly interested in the psychological mechanisms underlying this development, and one must presume that these will be the majority, will find Chapter VII particularly rewarding. Throughout the central chapters, the authors are at pains to bring out the characteristic features of children's reactions to each of their experiments at each of the several phases. Often these differences are subtle, so that it is not too difficult for the reader to imagine how any given phase will fade into its successor. This method of treatment is one that we have come to expect, for it is a characteristic of all their previous work. But perhaps the outstanding feature of the present book is the detailed consideration that is given to hindsight and foresight. Hindsight, or "retro-action", is the process whereby a subject is led to revise his earlier actions in the light of those that have followed: he goes back on his moves, or corrects his mistakes. Foresight or "anticipation" is the process of internally carrying out actions which will not be actually performed until a later stage, and thereby modifying the action that is in fact carried out in the present. The actual judgments made by the subjects or their arrangements of the material are not the same thing as the hindsight and foresight. The latter are underlying processes which the psychologist infers from such overt actions. If one considers only the judgments and motor behaviour of the subject, together with what they

[1] Despite the fact that Pavlov stresses the rigidity of the "dynamic stereotype", while Hull introduces the "habit family hierarchy" to account for the plasticity of behaviour. An adequate statement of theory will need to give an account of both types of behaviour. The fact that the Hullian account is *nearer* to what might be called "intelligent" behaviour is bound up with his use of the "fractional anticipatory response" (see next note).

[2] Hull's conception of a "fractional anticipatory response", and the "mediatory responses" of Miller, Mowrer and Osgood may be thought of as approaches to a similar concept, for these responses are held to act as stimuli for further responses. But the essential difference still remains that these further actions are still actions on the environment, on a par with any others, while "operations" are actions which bear primarily on other actions, and only secondarily on the environment.

imply about his *understanding* of the situations, one is led to infer a succession of *discontinuous* phases, each corresponding to a different degree of logical organization. But when we turn to consider the mechanisms that give rise to such overt behaviour, there is complete *continuity*. The one-directional pro-action, whereby actions already performed tend to influence those that succeed, passes insensibly into retro-action, and the latter in turn passes into foresight. Thus, the discontinuity of Piaget's "stages" is only relative; it is one part of the picture. The continuity of the underlying processsess that engender these stages is treated more fully in this volume, and especially in Chapter VII, than it is in any of the author's previous translated works.

III. TWO LEVELS OF INFERENCE

We have deliberately called the English version of this text *The Early Growth of Logic* to emphasize its connexion with *The Growth of Logical Thinking*. For it deals with only one part of logic, classification and seriation, and with only one part of reasoning, reasoning in relation to these. The earlier work deals with what is in fact the later development of reasoning, the formation of systematic hypotheses and their verification by a deduction of their implications. It bears on another branch of logic, the logic of propositions.

It is an essential part of Piaget's thesis that logical reasoning in relation to classification and seriation develops *before* the type of reasoning referred to in the previous paragraph. In order to bring out the distinction between the two, and at the same time to illustrate the importance of classificatory reasoning itself, I would refer to just one of the experiments recorded in *The Growth of Logical Thinking*. The experiment is one in which children of different ages are encouraged to discover as much as they can of Archimedes' law. The apparatus consists of several tanks containing water, some larger than others, together with a variety of miscellaneous objects, including a toy duck, a toy boat, a large block of wood, stones, a nail, a piece of wax, a metal can, etc. The child is first asked to sort out these various objects by saying which of them will float in the water and which will sink. He is asked why he thinks they will do so. Then he is encouraged to try them out in order to see whether his judgments were correct. If they were wrong, he is asked why, and encouraged to change his ideas, and, if possible, to test them again.

Children of 4 or 5 rarely justify their predictions: sometimes they refer to relevant experience (as when one child replies that he has seen a bit of wood floating), but more often they simply say of one object that it will stay up on top "and swim", while another will go to the bottom. If the prediction proves incorrect, they simply accept the fact or they may attempt to force an object to the bottom or hold it on the surface. A year later, they begin to adduce more reasons for their predictions, some of which will be rather global appeals to experience or sense of purpose (for example, a duck will float because ducks can swim), while others involve an unsystematic appeal to criteria. The latter tend to be contradictory (for example, a nail will sink because it is small but a piece of wood may float for the same reason). There may be confusion of small with light and of large with heavy, and both categories may be confused with strong versus weak.

At 7 or 8, these contradictions begin to be eliminated, with the result that children now discover that large objects may be light, etc. Because of this, they now begin to explain the floating or sinking by referring to a primitive conception of density: to begin with there may be some wavering between the absolute and relative uses of the words "light" and "heavy" (for example, a nail will be said to sink because it is heavy; and then, when the child is asked to compare the nail with a block of wood, he will refer the fact that it sinks to the material of which it was made; iron sinks). But by the age of 9 or 10, children are far more able to refer directly and unambiguously to the fact of things being light or heavy for their size, depending on the material of which they are made. But although this enables them to predict with more or less accuracy which of the objects will float and which will sink, it still leaves open the question why they behave as they do. Often children will refer to the water, as for instance when they explain that some objects sink because they are full of holes so that the water gets in. But this sort of explanation (based on an inadequate generalization from what they have observed in the case of hollow vessels) leads them into contradictions. For they also think of a material that is dense as one that is "full". They cannot therefore formulate a general law to explain the behaviour of bodies immersed in liquids. Even if this is explained to them, they cannot grasp the principle because they are unable to think in terms of the weight of an imaginary volume of water.

Yet, about the age of 13 they begin to compare the weight of the objects with the weight of the same volume of water (instead of merely referring to the water in the bath as strong enough or too weak to support an object). And by the age of 14 or 15, they begin to see their way to establishing the specific gravity of a substance by using a unit-measure consisting of a hollow cube which may be filled either with the substance itself or with water and weighing it.

There are two important features in the findings of this experiment. The first is that it is only because the child of 7 to 9 can group objects unambiguously by their size, weight, and substance, and because he can order them unambiguously as larger, heavier, etc., that he learns to avoid contradictions and arrives at the elementary notion of density. He reasons that not all large elements sink, not all light objects float, etc. And because he knows this, he finds a new way of classifying the material: light or heavy for its size. He may not achieve this at 7 or 8, preferring to speak of the substance of which it is made, this being an easier classification, since he is already familiar with a number of materials. At the same time, when he thinks of the substance, he has only to bear in mind the relative sizes of different objects, which he can do already, and this will lead him to anticipate that if an iron nail were as large as a wooden block it would be heavier.

The experiments in *The Growth of Logical Thinking* nearly all deal with real problems of induction and proof, and their relevance to the use of reasoning in school and in daily life is immediately apparent. The above is one example. Conversely, many of the experiments in the present work seem to be concerned with rather artificial problems, like the problem of deciding whether there are more flowers or more primulas. On the other hand, most of the discussion in the other work centres on the later evolution of reasoning. Yet, in every one of the experiments of which it treats, the role of classification and seriation is very clear. In each case, the development of these more elementary forms of reasoning brings about an important gain in understanding, even if it is not enough for the complete solution of the problem. The true significance of classification is the fact that the child who can classify can reason logically about the properties of things by adhering to unambiguous criteria.

The second feature of this experiment is that the 9 or 10 year-old is quite unable to arrive at a true understanding of specific gravity. There are two reasons for this. In the first place, the notion of specific gravity implies a comparison of the weight of an object with the weight of the same volume of water. Now children of 9 or 10 have no difficulty in fastening on to the idea of the relative weight of an object, and they are perfectly clear as to the criteria by which it is established. To this extent their reasoning is logical and systematic. The mental actions of which it consists are "operations". But the weight of an object still remains a property of *that object*. On the other hand, the weight of an equivalent volume of water is not a property of any object that one can see. At best it is a property of an object that one might deliberately *construct*. But it is one thing to be unambiguous about the several properties of an object when this is given, or even imagined as possible, and quite another to *construct an object out of its properties*. The latter demands a complete and deliberate *abstraction* of these properties.

In the second place, when the child of 14 or so deliberately fills (or thinks of filling) a given container with wood or wax or metal and another identical container with water, and then weighing them to establish their relative densities, he cannot be thinking exclusively of the substance and its relation to weight. He must be aware *at the same time*

that volume will affect weight, and it is this alone which leads him deliberately to construct the objects he wishes to compare in the way that he
does: deliberately holding the volume constant when comparing the
two substances. In other words, he is not considering only the one implication, that substance affects weight, he is considering two implications
at the same time, and co-ordinating their effects. That is why the
"propositional reasoning" studied by the authors in the earlier compan-
ion volume is so far in advance of the type of reasoning studied in
this.

The experiment on floating bodies is far from the best illustration of
the special characteristics of "formal" or "propositional" reasoning.
Inhelder's study of the discovery of the exclusive role of length in the
periodicity of a pendulum would have been far better. But there are
two reasons for selecting this experiment for the purpose of the present
introduction.

The first is that it brings out clearly the practical implications for
reasoning and learning of the earlier development of classification and
seriation, which are the concern of the present work.

The second is that it is fairly close to an experiment recorded in
Chapter III of the present volume. Children aged 4 to 9 are shown a
letter balance together with a collection of boxes. The balance is largely
concealed in a box (so that only the pan is visible), and the apparatus
is so rigged that when a certain weight is put on the pan, the pointer on
the dial protrudes through a slot at the side of the box, this effect being
heightened by a ball at the end of the pointer. The boxes are of two
weights and two sizes and two colours, so that there are 8 kinds of boxes
altogether. The problem is to find out which boxes make the ball appear.
The reader will wish to consult the text for a detailed description of the
several ways in which children try to solve the problem and answer the
questions they are put. For our purpose, we may anticipate by mentioning the one finding that even as early as 6, a majority of children can not
only find out for themselves that the heavy boxes are the ones they need,
but they can also *prove* that not all the large (or red, or blue, etc.) boxes
are heavy by correctly pointing to those of the required size (or colour)
which happen to be light.

On the face of it, this is a result which flatly contradicts the thesis that
hypothetico-deductive reasoning, by which we mean the framing and
testing of hypotheses, is a form of thinking that is not achieved until the
period of adolescence. For not only do quite young children discover
how to work the apparatus, but they can also disprove what amount
to incorrect hypotheses.

However, the juxtaposition of the two experiments shows what
profound differences there are as between the testing of hypotheses at
7 and at 12–15. We have only to recall the two distinctive features of

formal reasoning that we have just noted in connexion with the Archimedes experiment to establish that neither obtains in this.

In the first place, all the boxes are present and ready-made in the experiment. The subject has no need to abstract the properties of weight, colour, etc., and deliberately construct an event or an object out of its relations or its attributes. He has only to classify the material that is in front of him. This is very different from the (imaginary) construction of a volume of water equal to that of an object, and even more different from the deliberate construction of an arbitrary unit of volume to compare the specific gravities of different substances.

In the second place, the fact that the material is ready-made means that when the subject tests the hypothesis that "all the blue boxes are heavy", etc., this is the only hypothesis he needs to bear in mind. Conversely, whenever he is required to frame his own hypotheses and test them by deliberately constructing and comparing events in a manner designed to ensure that the relevant variables are controlled (by the method of "all other things equal"), the very fact of doing so means that in testing a given hypothesis, he has to simultaneously bear in mind a number of others. In other words, the procedures of formal reasoning imply a systematic, "operational" co-ordination of hypotheses. Any one of these, taken singly, already implies a systematic co-ordination of the actions entailed in grouping or classifying objects according to their attributes. The constituent hypotheses are themselves "operational". That is why the operations of formal reasoning are *second-order operations*.

Finally, the fact that the experiment of Chapter III uses two weights, two sizes and two colours tends to favour an early solution of the problem. There is no need to seriate and classify at the same time, as there is in the experiments on multiple seriation of Chapter X. At the same time the symmetries and dichotomous arrangements make the classification itself easier. That is why successful solutions are found right at the beginning of the phase of development at which children evolve (first-order) operational co-ordinations.

However, both experiments illustrate the important achievements in the field of logical reasoning that come about as a result of a systematic classification of attributes. They are instances of classificatory reasoning in a realistic context. The reasoning is systematic, and therefore logical. But the system to which it conforms is a classificatory system. Because this type of logical inference, together with the inferences that are based on the systematic ordering of differences, are evolved several years earlier than hypothetico-deductive reasoning, Piaget argues that there is a need for a logic which will codify these systems. Such a logic will be a partial system. The logic of propositions will then be a more complete system, but one which presupposes this partial system and contains it just as mathematics contains arithmetic (or just as the "ring" of numbers contains the two "groups" of addition and multiplication).

Manchester,
September, 1963

E. A. LUNZER

INTRODUCTION

THIS volume as a whole incorporates the results obtained from the examination of a total of 2,159 children. The introductory chapter which follows consists of a general outline of the problems to be discussed, a number of essential definitions, and, finally, a résumé of the previous research which led up to the present work.

We propose to study the formation of operations of classification (chs. I–VIII) and seriation (chs. IX–X). Although we already know something about the stages shown in their development, we know next to nothing about the mechanisms which account for this development. The study of these mechanisms was first undertaken by A. Szeminska, so that this is a continuation of her work.

The greater part of this volume deals with classification, because the problems which it raises are far more complex. But we cannot afford to neglect problems of seriation altogether. Had we examined only one of these structures, we might easily have been led to systematic errors of interpretation by exaggerating the role of some factors and underestimating others. Thus, the part played by language would seem greater for classification than for seriation, while perceptual factors are probably more important in seriation. By comparing the two situations, we can discover the mechanisms which are common to both. These we may justifiably regard as the essential formatory mechanisms.

In order to elucidate the causal mechanism of a given process, we must first discover the structures which are there to begin with, and then show how and why these structures come to be transformed. All development presupposes an initial structure. The development consists in the completion and differentiation of this structure.

How far back should the analysis reach? We cannot decide on the mode of interpretation *a priori*. In other words, we have no right to decide, before turning to the facts, which group of factors (linguistic, perceptual, etc.) should be included in the initial structures, and which should be given the role of transforming these into operational structures. All that we can do to begin with is to make a list of all the structural factors involved.

This requirement suggests four alternative hypotheses (1 to 4), generated by three successive dichotomies (I to III):

(I) Structures of classification and seriation may be imposed by language alone (1), or they may owe their origin, at least in part, to operations underlying language itself. In the latter case (II) these could be co-ordinations which develop independently of the environment (2),

1

due, for example, to the delayed completion of connections in the central nervous system, or else they are elaborated out of previously existing structures. If they are not purely maturational (III) they must originate out of perceptual structures (3), or out of the differentiation of the sensori-motor system as a whole (4). Any other possible source, such as the ability to anticipate classification and seriation by mental imagery, is reducible to one of these. Thus, in the final analysis, the image[1] itself must depend either on perception or on more complex sensori-motor mechanisms.

Taking each of these broad factors in turn, we propose first of all to list the various forms or structures which could provide a starting-point for the construction of classification and seriation. But we will also point out what they lack of the final structures which we wish to explain. In the main body of the book, we can then study the way in which the gap is bridged, bearing in mind whatever ideas we have gleaned from our analysis of these initial structures.

1. LANGUAGE

Both the syntax and the semantics of language involve structures of classification and seriation. That this is true of classification is immediately obvious. All nouns and adjectives divide reality into classes. Insofar as children use words with the same meaning as adults, these may be directly transmitted to them when they learn to talk. In any case, words inevitably force a beginning of classification on the child. On the other hand, seriations are rarely completely elaborated in any language (as they are for certain series like that leading from "great-grandfather" to "grandfather", "father", "son", "grandson", etc.). But seriations are sometimes suggested in a language by special grammatical forms like the comparative and the superlative.

One possible hypothesis would be to attribute the formation of classification and seriation exclusively to language. Alternatively, we could give language no more than an auxiliary role (e.g., that of an accelerator). We might even say that while language is necessary for the completion of these structures, it is insufficient for their formation. If this view were found correct, their formation would have to be explained by operational mechanisms which underlie linguistic activity but are themselves independent of their verbal expression.

A number of avenues of research seem open for deciding between these possibilities. These are (1) the study of the deaf; (2) an analysis of

---

[1] We cannot, here, give a detailed account of the role of images; but there is a series of experiments in progress on the subject to which we hope to devote a subsequent volume.

the first verbal patterns (or "preconcepts"); and (3) the study of certain operational patterns which occur in the everyday use of language.

(1) We have not ourselves carried out any research on the deaf. But the excellent work of P. Oléron,[1] together with the articles of M. Vincent[2] on the intellectual development of the deaf, suggest the following conclusions, which are further borne out by the research of our colleague, F. Affolter, who studied the development of operational structures among deaf children, following our own work with normal children:

(a) The development of seriation is not noticeably different in the deaf.

(b) Deaf children carry out the same elementary classifications as do normal children, but are retarded in their handling of more complex classifications (e.g., changing from one criterion to another, using the same elements). In other words, deaf children undoubtedly show signs of operational thinking, as we understand the term; and this may be due to the fact that they use symbols (e.g., sign language). So it looks as if the social transmission of spoken language is not essential for the formation of operational structures. But it certainly helps; and it may well be a necessary, although not a sufficient, condition for the completion of these structures in their generalized forms.

Piaget,[3] in his description of the first verbal patterns or "preconcepts" showed that learning how to talk does not imply that children immediately adopt the collective classifications embodied in their mother tongue. Language merely accelerates the formation of classes.

Children assimilate the language they hear to their own semantic structures, which are a function of their level of development. Adult language may help to modify these, in the long run, yet at any given moment, it is always interpreted in terms of them. Thus, the generality of a word (i.e., a noun or an adjective) may be very weak for a child, so that symbolically the word is closer to an image than a concept, or it may approximate to a true conceptual generality—and there is every shade in between. In other words, the fact that a child calls a cat a cat does not prove that he understands the "class" of cats. The name is borrowed from the language of adults (for whom it signifies the class of cats, included in that of animals, of living creatures, etc.); but, to a child, it may be the schematic equivalent of an image, which is half-way between the individual and the generic.

For instance, a child of 3–5 years will talk about the "wind" made by a fan and then be unable to decide whether this "wind" is the *same object* as the breeze which blows the leaves, or whether these are two

---

[1] P. Oléron, *Recherches sur le développement mental des sourds-muets*, Paris (C.N.R.S.), 1956.

[2] Enfance, 1951 (4), 222–38; 1956, 1–20 and 1957, 443–64.

[3] J. Piaget, *Play, Dreams and Imitation in Childhood*, Heinemann, 1951.

distinct terms belonging to the *same class*. (The child describes the current of air made by shaking a branch as "some shaky", and distinguishes between "white shaky" or transparent air and "blue shaky", being the blue sky!). In the same way, the shadow of a screen on a table is said to come from "the shade of the trees", etc. The child cannot choose between the individual (the same substance displaced) and the generic (the same category of phenomena). Similarly, children will often be undecided whether to speak of "the moon" or "a moon" (and even "the" slug or "a" slug).

From the beginning language favours a series of assimilations, and these imply a notion of similarity. (In the same way, unsuccessful attempts at assimilation create a notion of dissimilarity.) But for a long time these relationships cannot be made concrete and precise. Little children cannot arrange a set of objects in such a way as to bring out the relation of inclusion, which is a part-whole relation. Yet this relation is essential to an understanding of classification in the strict sense. We are bound to conclude that, although language is an important factor in building logical structures, it is not the essential factor, even for children with normal hearing.

We have made a closer study of the role of language in chapters III and IV, by analysing the operational schema involved in the correct use of the verbal quantifiers "all" and "some". This implies the quantification of inclusion: if all A are B and some, but not all, B are A, then B exceeds A. The main finding of these investigations may be stated thus: the fact that the language of adults crystallizes an operational schema does not mean that the operation is assimilated along with the linguistic forms. Before children can understand the implicit operation and apply it, they must carry out a structurization, or even a number of successive re-structurizations. These depend on logical mechanisms. They are not passively transmitted by language. They demand an active construction on the part of the subject.

What research has proved is that language accelerates the processes of classification and seriation and helps to complete them. We do not propose to study how it does so in detail. In the first place, the importance of language is a commonplace. Secondly, we have concentrated more on the formation of structures than on their end-state. But, even when we look at their end-state, we will see that the development of seriation is almost exactly parallel to that of classification, and tends to precede it step by step. This shows conclusively that the development of these operations is largely independent of language. For, while the structures of classification are largely mirrored by verbal structures, serial structures are far less closely connected with language.

4

2. MATURATION

If language is not the only cause of operational structures (even those of classification), these mechanisms could be no more than the result of maturation of the nervous system, acting independently of the environment.

The question is bound up with what is still one of the most difficult problems in genetic psychology. Although psychology has used and abused the concept of maturation at every level of development, neurology has had very little to say about the reality of this development, apart from certain changes in the first few months of life.

We may assume, with all due caution, that in all probability maturation does play a part in the remarkable changes which occur about the age of 7–8 years, to take but a single example. (In our own "civilized" societies, these changes are thrown into further relief by the beginning of primary education.)

But we do not, in fact, know anything about it. In particular, we do not know any cognitive structure which can be shown to be wholly maturational in origin. We might make a number of negative statements. Thus it makes some sense to attribute the absence of certain types of behaviour (e.g., the absence of hypothetico-deductive reasoning between 2 and 4 years) to deficiencies of the nervous system. But from the positive point of view, the maturation of the nervous system can do no more than create the conditions for a continual expansion of the field of possibilities. The realization of these possibilities demands not only the action of the physical environment (practice and acquired experience), but also the educational influences of a favourable social environment.

3. PERCEPTUAL FACTORS

If the operational structures of classification and seriation cannot be attributed exclusively to language and maturation, it follows that their origin must lie in the most elementary cognitive structures, i.e., perceptual and sensori-motor structures.

Long before they learn to classify objects or to arrange them in order, children perceive objects in terms of relations of similarity and dissimilarity. It is tempting to look for the origin of classification and seriation in these perceptual relationships. Psychologists to-day agree that the perception of relationships is elementary. Perception itself is not confined to isolated terms which must then be brought together by a higher mechanism (association, judgement, etc.). Classification implies a relation of resemblance between members of the same class, and one of dissimilarity between members of different classes. Seriation is the product of a set of asymmetrical transitive relations connected in series. Hence, one may reasonably ask how far purely perceptual relationships can provide a starting-point for these operations.

The fact that we ask the question does not imply that we accept the common hypothesis according to which all knowledge about objects originates in perception. In fact, two different hypotheses are possible. We need not decide between them for the moment; but it is essential to have them in mind. Otherwise we might easily be led astray in our search for possible analogies between perceptual structures and those of classification and seriation.

The first of the two hypotheses is that perceptual knowledge exists prior to any other form of knowledge and is independent of anything else. Perceptual knowledge is taken to be "elementary" (this would not imply sensory atomism; the same thing might also be expressed in terms of "Gestalt"). All intelligent structurization (sensori-motor intelligence, conceptual intelligence, etc.) is then a matter of extending these initial perceptual structures, or of expanding them and making them more supple. Alternatively, we can still allow that these higher forms of structurization involve new structures, but the content of these new structures will consist of perceptual data and these will be ready-structured. In other words, we will still refuse to allow that these undergo any substantial modification by virtue of their integration into structures of a higher order.

But there is an alternative hypothesis. This is to assume that, at every level, perception is bound up with action schemata of a higher order, and that these structures can influence those of perception. This would mean that knowledge of objects cannot be considered as being "first" perceptual and "afterwards" super-perceptual. All knowledge of objects is a function of those action schemata to which the object is assimilated; and these range from the earliest reflexes to the most complex elaborations acquired by learning. Perceptual structures are bound up with more extensive structures right from the beginning. If we adopt this second hypothesis, we might still begin our study with an analysis of perceptual structures, but only because these are simpler, and not because they are more "elementary".

The perceptual structures which interest us are those which change least with age and are relatively independent of other factors. These include simple geometrical shapes as well as certain visual structures which we shall call "primary"—"primary" because they operate within the field of one centration and do not involve an interplay of successive centrations. These perceptual structures include certain relations which are partly analogous to the operations of classification and seriation. But the analogy is only partial, and even if we assume that such relations are the forerunners of operations in perception, we are still left with the whole problem of how they develop into complete and co-ordinated operational schemata.

What kinds of perceptual relations are most relevant to this enquiry? To answer this question, we could begin by drawing up an exhaustive list of all the various ways in which perceptions are organized, and then select those that we need. But it is more economical to work backwards by first defining the most general relations involved in classification and seriation, and then seeking their nearest perceptual analogues.

A *Classes*. Classes may be defined both by their "intension" and by their "extension". This distinction is not perfected until the stage of equilibrium reached at 9–10 years. As far as intension is concerned, we know from the Binet and Simon test on definitions that children below this age tend to give definitions by use rather than definitions by genus and differentia. As far as extension is concerned, our experiments on "all" and "some" (chs. III and IV) show that younger children have an imperfect grasp of the quantitative relations involved.

We will therefore pose the following as criteria for the operational existence of classes: (1) The subject can give an intensive definition of a class in terms of a more general class and one or more specific differences. (2) He can handle their extension in accordance with the structure of inclusion, as shown by his mastery of the quantifiers "all", "some", "one" and "none".

We will begin by giving a definition of each of these terms:[1]

Definition 1. Given a family of classes, A, A' and B, such that $B = A + A'$ and $A \times A' = 0$ (A' being therefore the complement of A with respect to B, since A and A' are disjoint), the "intension" of a class is the set of properties common to the members of that class, together with the set of differences which distinguish them from another class.

Definition 2. We shall call "relations of resemblance" (a for the elements of A, and b for those of B) all those properties which are common to the elements of one class, even though the relation of resemblance as such is not explicit. Thus, the statement "All grasses (A) are green (a)" implies that they resemble one another in being green and so present a relation of "co-greenness".

Definition 3. The "complementarity" a' of a class A' is the sum of the differences between its members and those of another class A where A and A' also have similarities by virtue of their common membership of B. For instance, if A is a group of brothers, then A', the first cousins of A, are the grandchildren of the same grandfather (and therefore B), although they do not have the same father: i.e. $a' = b$ *not* a. Again,

[1] These definitions do not themselves contain any hypotheses. They simply specify how these terms will be used.

7

vegetables are living things which are not animal, where the difference, non-animal, is the complementarity.

Definition 4. To define a class by genus and specific difference is to characterize its members as: both *b* and *a* or both *b* and *a'*.

Definition 5. The "extension" of a class is the set of members (or individuals) comprising that class (as defined by its intension).

Definition 6. Intensive quantification is given by the use of one or more of the quantifiers "all", "some", and "none". Thus, the statement "All *A* are *B*" implies that there are more *B* than *A*, without specifying the quantitative relationships between *A* and *A'* (where $A' = B - A$).

Definition 7. The conditions of "class inclusion" are satisfied if and only if the following propositions both obtain: (1) All *A* are some *B*; (2) $A < B$. (Some subjects do not understand the second of these, although they appear to agree to the first.)

Definition 8. The relation of "class membership" (denoted by the symbol ε) is the relation between an element *x* and the class *A* to which it belongs. This relationship will be written as: $(x) \, \varepsilon \, (A)$. We distinguish this relationship from "partitive membership", in which an element *x* is only a spatial part or a "piece" of a continuous whole (as the nose is to the face), and also from "schematic membership", where an element *x* is identified with a perceptual or sensori-motor schema as a result of assimilation by recognition.

How far can these relations, so defined, be paralleled in perception? Such perceptual equivalents can be found, and one of the writers has called these "partial isomorphisms".[1] But in order to bring out their implications we must also point out the essential difference between perceptual sets or aggregates and logical classes. It is this. There is an exact correspondence between the predicates or intensive properties of a logical class and the extensive distribution of its elements. But perceptual aggregates do not require a regular correspondence between the perceived qualities of individual elements and their grouping in more or less extended totalities. The reason is that the extension of a perceptual set depends on spatial proximity (for visual and haptic perception) or temporal proximity (for auditory perception), while the extension of a logical class is independent of the proximity of its members. We may therefore note the following three points (taking visual perception as an example):

1. Perception allows the relation of partitive membership (but not that of class inclusion, def. 8), and even extends it to collections or collective objects which are united by their spatial proximity. Thus, in Fig. 1, the element *x* is seen as part of the total set, but only because it is close to

[1] J. Piaget and A. Morf, "Les isomorphismes partiels entre les structures logiques et les structures perceptives", in *"Logique et perception"*, *Etudes d'épistémologie génétique*, Vol. VI, ch. II.

the set, and because it supplies a gap in the general configuration of the set as a whole. If there were no gap and *x* were further removed, it would no longer be seen as a part of the set (see *x* in Fig. 2).

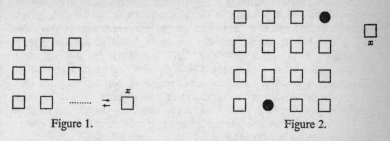

Figure 1.   Figure 2.

2. Perception also allows relations of similarity, whether it is applied to parts of the same figure which are perceived simultaneously (e.g. the sides of a square or the two black circles in Fig. 2), or whether it involves successive assimilations, as when we see the same object again after looking around, or when an object is presented several times in succession, or in general, whenever we recognize a shape from previous perceptual experience. Wherever there is perception of resemblance between objects seen successively, its occurrence involves an assimilation to a perceptual or sensori-motor schema (def. 8).

3. The relations of partitive membership and similarity do not always coincide. Thus, in Fig. 2, the black circles are seen as a part of the main collection, although they are different from the other elements, while the small outside square *x* does not seem to belong to it although it is similar to them.

It follows from (3) that perception does not recognize the relations of class inclusion (def. 7) and class membership (def. 8), since both demand the co-ordination of intensive and extensive properties. Hence, it makes no sense to speak of "perceptual classes".

Nevertheless, J. Bruner is not wholly wrong in maintaining that perception is an act of classification,[1] i.e. that its essential function is to identify an object by attaching it to a known class (for instance, "This is an orange"). In effect, he is doing no more than to emphasize the role of similarity in successive perceptions (see point (2), above).

But this does not mean that the class has been constructed by perception alone, nor that the subject perceives the class as such (as, for instance, the union of "all oranges"), nor even that he perceives a class membership. A class cannot be constructed by perception, for it presupposes a series of abstractions and generalizations, from which it

[1] J. Bruner, "Les processus de préparation à la perception", in "*Logique et perception*", *Etudes d'épistémologie génétique*, Vol. VI, ch. I.

derives its meaning or intension, together with additive operations, governing its extensive relations. A class can never be perceived as such, since it is generally of indefinite extension; and even when its extension is restricted, what the subject perceives is not the class itself but a certain spatial configuration of the elements which compose it. When we see an orange and say, "This is an orange", the connexion between the object and the class is not directly perceived. What we are doing is to assimilate the orange we see to a perceptual schema of the sort described by Brunswick as an "empirical Gestalt". The orange is perceived as presenting the familiar configuration of an ovoid with a corrugated skin and an orange colour. This configuration has acquired its stability as a result of previous perceptual experience. But it is closely linked to a number of sensori-motor schemata: peeling the fruit, cutting and chewing it, squeezing out the juice, etc.

The class of oranges is *based* on schemata of this kind, both perceptual and motor, and is further enriched by various botanical analogies. But what the subject *perceives* when he says: "This is an orange", is a "schematic membership" (def. 8) and not a class membership. For the adult, the first leads to the second through verbalization and the conceptual judgement that verbalization makes possible.

As for the schema itself, this is certainly not a class; it is not even a distinct perception which can be referred to a definite point of time, since it develops over a period, as a result of successive assimilations.[1]

Thus the only structures attributable to perception which come near to classificatory behaviour are (1) perceptual similarity in schematic membership—where the schema itself is not a product of immediate perception, and (2) partitive membership based on spatial proximity.

In neither of these structures is there co-ordination between intension and extension. Schematic membership is an intensive quality of objects in perception, and is quite separate from partitive membership which is an extensive property. Conceptual classification is developed out of the sensori-motor schema which governs the former, but, unlike perception, it involves the co-ordination of intension and extension.

B *Relations*. Although we cannot perceive classes directly, we do perceive relations. As stated above, we have an immediate perception of similarity, which is a symmetrical relation. But we also perceive differences (e.g. differences in size), which are asymmetrical relations.

Is there a difference between an operational structure of relations and the way in which they are organized in perception? To begin with, a

[1] When it is completed, such a schema can alter the way in which a single primary perception is organized. Nevertheless, its elaboration involves a succession of perceptions. Nor is this a case of passive perceiving, but of active assimilation, on the basis of perceptual activities, and of sensori-motor activity in general.

serial arrangement of a set of elements (e.g. strips of wood arranged in increasing order of length) is a "good" perceptual form. It is even "better" if the differences between elements are equal ($C - B = B - A$, etc. where $A, B, C, \ldots$ are the elements of the series). We may therefore ask what operational seriation adds to this perceptual configuration.

The difference is threefold. In the first place, operational seriation implies transitivity ($C > A$ if $B > A$ and $C > B$), while the perceptual configuration of a series is tied to the image. The transitivity of the image is a "pre-inference".[1] Second, there is no perceptual series unless the elements are arranged in a particular way. From the operational point of view, this graphic arrangement is not essential; it is no more than a symbolic representation of the series, in the same way as Euler's circles symbolize class-inclusions. Third, what makes seriation operational is the fact that it deals with the transformation of asymmetric transitive relations ($A < B < C \ldots$, implies $a + a' = b$, etc., if $a = A < B$; $a' = B < C$ and $b = A < C$)[2] and recognizes their reversibility ($b - a' = a$, etc.). For perception, only the results of these transformations are meaningful; the transformations themselves are simply a matter of the visible displacement of elements. The operation is an integrated whole involving both the various end states and the transformations leading from one to the other

Hence we shall find that it takes children nearly as long to achieve operational seriation on the basis of perceptual configurations as it does to achieve operational classification. Although perceptual anticipation is easier in seriation, the advantage accruing to *operational* seriation is comparatively slight.

4. SENSORI-MOTOR SCHEMATA

Clearly, there is a considerable difference between perceptual structures and the operational structures involved in classification and seriation. In fact the difference is even greater than would appear from the previous section. For we cannot assume that there is a linear evolution beginning with primary perception and ending with logical operations: primary perception → perceptual activities → sensori-motor schemata → pre-operational representation → operations. Field effects shown in primary perception may not be the "simplest" form of cognitive organization. There is certainly no proof that they represent the point of departure out of which higher forms are evolved. It is altogether more probable that these "good forms" are themselves the outcome of more

[1] J. Piaget and A. Morf, *Les préinférences perceptives*, "*Etudes d'épistémologie*", Vol. VI, ch. III, Paris, 1958.

[2] This may be read: ". . . if *a* is the increment from point *A* to point *B*; *a'* is the increment from point *B* to point *C* . . ." etc. (Translator's note).

complex sensori-motor schemata which are not confined to perception, and still less to immediate perception. We have to bear in mind our second hypothesis (page 6): that the operations of classification and seriation have their origin not in perception alone but in the development of sensori-motor schemata as a whole. We should then have to postulate a continuous modification of perception itself. The highest level of perception would then be a late development, and we would have to look for more primitive stages of perception corresponding with more primitive stages of intelligence.

We could take the perception of a square as an example of a "good form". Piaget and others[1] studied the resistance of this form at various ages. We found that the tendency to see a shape as a square was not constant but increased with age. The primary perception of the square is integrated into a schema of perceptual activity involving not only the immediate recognition of the square as a familiar shape, but a systematic comparison of sides and angles to see if they are equal. The application of the schema amounts to a transposition of exploratory movements, leading to the verification, for each perceived object, of the properties which constitute the intension of the class of squares. At the same time the extension of the class can never be realized in perception, since this would imply the simultaneous presentation of the set of squares, which is infinite. But the close parallelism between the perceptual schema and the class involves far more than primary perception. In older children and adults the perceptual schema is able to transform the character of primary perception by a process of active comparison based on transpositions and generalizations, which are wider than mere perception. The similarity of different squares (based on the equality of their sides, of their angles, etc.) is bound up with the similarity of the subject's exploratory actions. That is why, between the age of 5 and 9 or 10, there is a threefold increase in the stability of this "good form".

Any one sensory modality can operate only in close connexion with others. Visual perception is intimately bound up with haptic (or tactile-kinaesthetic) perception. The co-ordinations between sight and the action of gripping are established at about 4–5 months. From then onwards, if not before, the visual perception of objects is inextricably bound up with haptic perception: the meaning recognized in perception is a function of the entire sequence of actions. The perceptual schema is never independent; right from the start, perception is subordinated to action. It follows that, genetically, sensori-motor schemata are as elementary as primary perceptions. A schema is not just a rearrangement of past and present perceptions. Perceptions are no more than signals which enter into the construction of the schema (and they include

[1] J. Piaget, F. Maire and F. Privat, "La résistance des bonnes formes à l'illusion de Müller-Lyer", *Arch. de Psychol*, Rech. XVIII.

proprioceptive signals). As such, they are necessary but not sufficient. Nor can the schema be interpreted purely on the basis of exteroceptive and proprioceptive signals. The action itself which causes the signal is a vital factor in the organization of the schema as a whole. In other words, the subject does not perceive objects and his own movements separately; he perceives objects as things which are modified, or are capable of being modified, by his own actions. A cube is perceived as a thing which can be handled and turned over or turned round. Those portions which are invisible to the senses are still present in perception because of the way in which it is integrated with action. (The perceptual schema of a cube, even more than that of a square, is a function of exploratory actions on the part of the subject; it is not a datum in primary perception.) According to Janet, to perceive an arm-chair is to see an object in which one can sit. A still more forceful illustration is that of von Weizsäcker: to perceive a house is not to look at an image which has just got into your eye, but to recognize a solid shelter for you to get into!

We therefore come to our final hypothesis, that the origins of classification and seriation are to be found in sensori-motor schemata as a whole (which include perceptual schemata as integral parts).

Between the ages of 6–8 and 18–24 months, which is well before the acquisition of language, we find a number of behaviour patterns which are suggestive both of classification and of seriation. A child may be given a familiar object: immediately he recognizes its possible uses; the object is assimilated to the habitual schemata of rocking, shaking, striking, throwing to the ground, etc. If the object is completely new to him, he may apply a number of familiar schemata in succession, as if he is trying to understand the nature of the strange object by determining whether it is for rocking, or for rattling, or rubbing, etc. We have here a sort of practical classification,[1] somewhat reminiscent of the later definition by use. But this rudimentary classification is realized only in the course of successive trials and does not give rise to a number of simultaneous collections. However, even these latter are foreshadowed very early when children pile a number of similar objects together or when they construct a complex object. These two kinds of behaviours may be regarded as pre-verbal precursors of the graphic collections of ch. I.

As for seriations, some approximation to these can be found in various constructions. One such example is a tower made up of nesting boxes. To begin with, children may choose the boxes at random but in time they manage to arrange them approximately in order of decreasing volume.

The fact that we can observe various prototypes of classification and

[1] Cf. J. Piaget, *The Origin of Intelligence in the Child*, 1952, pp. 236–52.

seriation at the sensori-motor and preverbal stage of development proves that the roots of these structures are independent of language. Nevertheless, these elementary organizations are still far removed from the corresponding operational structures. A sensori-motor schema is the functional equivalent of a concept inasmuch as it results in intelligibility and generalization, but from a structural point of view the two are by no means identical. It is characteristic of the sensori-motor schema that its various possible applications cannot be realized simultaneously, so that "extension" and "intension" cannot be co-ordinated by reference to one another.

A sensori-motor schema consists of a stable pattern of movements together with a perceptual component geared to the recognition of appropriate signals. The schema can be applied to a series of new objects if these are sufficiently similar to one another, or to situations which are analogous with one another: e.g., swinging suspended objects, or obtaining an object on a sheet of paper or a cloth by pulling the support.

Following is an analysis of the intensive and extensive properties of a sensori-motor schema:

(1) From the intensional point of view, there is the construction of equivalence relations governing the properties of the various objects to which the schema is applied. The child recognizes that an object can be swung if he sees that it is suspended and that it can be pulled towards him if he sees it lying on a movable support which he can reach.

(2) The extension of a sensori-motor schema is the series of objects and situations to which it can be applied.

But from the point of view of the subject there is still no systematic correspondence between intension and extension because the elements to which the schema is applied do not form a simultaneous collection. Where there is operational classification, this condition is met by a material collection for a limited class of objects, and by a mental collection for open classes based on the manipulation of symbols. Properties (1) and (2) may be further analysed as follows:

(1a) Intensional properties which are internal relations of an object in perception (e.g. the relation of being suspended, of resting on a "support", etc.).

(1b) Relations of similarity between a perceived object and other objects to which the schema has been applied in the past.

(2a) Partitive membership relating a part of the perceived object to the whole.

(2b) Schematic membership relating the object actually perceived to the sensori-motor schema.

(1a) is an intensive property while (2a) is the corresponding extensive property. These two are integrated in the sensori-motor schema inasmuch as the potential uses of an object are seen as a function of the

14

relation of its parts to the whole. Similarly, the intensive property (1b) corresponds to the extensive property (2b). But these properties fail to coincide in the schema. Because there is no representation at this level, the child cannot evoke the set of objects to which the schema applies. Hence the similarity between the object actually perceived and the objects to which the schema has already been applied (1b) cannot be evoked, although the latent experience determines recognition. It follows that schematic membership (2b) cannot take the form of extensive inclusion. The predication of a given property to a particular object, which should establish an extensive relation between that object and the entire class defined by the predicate, is confined to the individual object and therefore remains intensive. At the very least, we shall say that there is a more or less complete lack of differentiation between extension and intension.

The rudimentary seriation shown at the sensori-motor level is less static and therefore closer to operational seriation than a perceptual configuration. But it has yet to achieve the complete mobility which engenders reversibility. Because there is no reversibility, the subject is unable to construct the series systematically by co-ordinating the relations $>$ and $<$.

In all likelihood, the nearest approach of these sensori-motor schemata to the structure of logical thinking is the differentiation of schemata into sub-schemata, with a resultant hierarchical organization. In this respect, the sensori-motor system foreshadows future operational hierarchies. Thus, the schema of pulling a support to obtain a coveted object will tend to the eventual differentiation of a sub-schema where the support is rigid like a plank: it can then be pivoted on its axis. The subject will then have a general schema of using a support to gain an object, subdivided into two sub-schemata, one of which consists in simply pulling the support while the other involves pivoting it or sliding it. However, both the differentiation and the hierarchical structure remain implicit. The situations in which the schema and sub-schema are appliable are not realized simultaneously either in practice or in principle. So once more there is no classification in the strict sense of the term.

The upshot of this chapter is to suggest that the origins of classification and seriation can be traced prior to the evolution of language and symbolic representation. The latter are necessary, but not sufficient, conditions for their development. While an early and rudimentary recognition of similarity and dissimilarity is highly suggestive of the "intensive" qualities of these later systems, "extension" is limited to the sublogical form of a spatial distribution of the parts of a single object, which may be collective. There is no extension as yet in the pre-logical form of a non-graphic collection or in the logical form of a class. The

15

central problem of classification must therefore be the differentiation and progressive co-ordination of extension and intension.

It will be apparent in the course of the next three chapters that this process is a complex elaboration and dependent on several interrelated factors. We will endeavour to study the problem in terms of the actions of the child at various levels of development in order to discover how he comes to construct the necessary operations by successive stages.

Chapter One

GRAPHIC COLLECTIONS[1]

THERE is a certain type of behaviour which is fairly common in young children and which throws a good deal of light on how classifications come to be formed. Children at stage I do not arrange elements in collections and subcollections on the basis of similarity alone. They are unable to overlook the spatial configuration of the objects, and what they do is to unite them in "graphic collections". The graphic collection stands midway between a composite spatial object and a class.

1. PRELIMINARY STATEMENT OF THE PROBLEM

As stated in the Introduction, a class involves two kinds of properties or relations. Both kinds are necessary; and at the same time sufficient to constitute a class:[2]

(1) (a) Properties which are common to the members of the given class and those of other classes to which it belongs.

(b) Properties which are specific to the members of the given class and which differentiate them from members of other classes.

(1a) and (1b) are intensive properties.

(2) Part-whole relations of class-membership and inclusion. These are conveyed by the quantifiers "all", "some" (including "one") and "none", when applied to the members of the given class and to those of the classes to which it belongs, insofar as they are qualified under (1a) and (1b). The relations described under (2) are extensive properties.

For example, cats have several properties in common, possessed by "all" cats, of which some are specific to cats while others are common to other animals.

This definition of a class can be applied to the classifications made by children above a certain age level. It does not involve the spatial configuration of the elements of a class. The spatial arrangement of individual cats does not affect properties (1) and (2) of the class of cats. It is true that relations of inclusion defined in (2) can be illustrated by a structure which is topological, and therefore spatial in character. But

[1] With the collaboration of G. Noelting and S. Taponier, who examined approximately 200 subjects for this and the following chapter.

[2] It will be noticed that the following definition cannot be applied to a single class in isolation, but only to a class which is included in others. We believe that a class cannot exist in isolation.

the spatial character is secondary, for it is a function of the isomorphism which obtains between the algebraic structure of class inclusion and certain topological structures. It is perfectly possible to give a complete description of the structure of classes without any reference to space.

The term "graphic collection" will therefore be used to describe a spatial arrangement of the elements to be classified where it seems clear that such a configuration plays an essential part in the eyes of the subject. In other words the child is clearly unable to divorce properties (1) or (2) from the graphic arrangement which he produces. Thus he may place a triangle above a square, because he thinks these two forms must be somehow related. The triangle reminds him of the roof of a house while the square can be the main part of the building. To him, this means that the triangle must be placed over the square and nowhere else. Here the spatial configuration plays an essential part in determining the intensive properties of the arrangement (1). Sometimes, however, we find that children use the words "some" and "all" in different ways, depending on the spatial arrangement of the parts of a collection. Here the arrangement is crucial to the determination of extensive properties (2).

But there are two preliminary problems. First, can one be sure that the child has understood that he is to classify a set of objects on the basis of similarity alone instead of making something meaningful out of them or simply grouping them at random? Second, can one be sure that the spatial configurations are not being used symbolically and that they do enter as an essential element in the construction of these "graphic collections"?

As far as the first problem is concerned (understanding the instruction), this is not the place to discuss the best ways of formulating the questions for young children. (The formulae used were: "Put together the things which are alike" or "things that go together", etc.) We hope to show that while the child of 2–5 cannot understand what a classification is in the same sense as one of 7–8 years, the way in which he interprets our instructions is the closest approach he can make towards this operational structure.

As to the second problem, it is true that whenever an adult (or even a logician) uses some kind of symbolical representation to describe a classification he is bound to think in spatial terms. We see examples in taxonomical "trees" or in the circles of Euler. Thus the relation of class-inclusion $(A < B)$ may be illustrated by two circles of which one (B) contains the other (A). This is a spatial figure: circle A is drawn inside B in order to show that A is a part of B. At the same time B is represented as larger than A because it contains additional elements besides those which belong to A. In much the same way, an older child who has outgrown the level of graphic collections, is likely to show a number of classes by making a number of "heaps", with little "heaps"

18

forming part of bigger "heaps". Here again an object is shown as forming a part of a "heap" or a "sub-heap" by the fact that it is inside it. But once again, the representation is simply symbolical. Euler's circles are merely transformed into collections.

In order to study the role of spatial relations in graphic collections, what we have to do is to decide whether the spatial arrangement is a spatial symbolism or whether it makes an essential contribution to the meaning of the classification itself (properties (1) or (2) of classes). In the case of taxonomical trees or of Euler's circles, the spatial figure is used only as a symbol for the set. The symbolical significance is limited to relations of class-inclusion or class-membership (extensive properties, 2). The symbolism depends on the isomorphism between classificatory structures and certain corresponding topological relations of inclusion. On the other hand, in the case of graphic collections, the spatial relations are *constitutive* and not symbolic. The proof is that they enter into relations between the members of a class. In other words they involve intensive properties (1) as well as class-inclusion and membership. What is more, by their very nature, extensive properties do not yet exist independently at the level of graphic collections because the differentiation between relations (1) and (2) is still incomplete.

In the case of a graphic collection the relations between the elements themselves inevitably lead to a certain graphic arrangement.[1] In the case of non-graphic collections or classes, the use of a figure is no more than a symbolic convenience which can be dispensed with if desired.

We can now formulate the following hypothesis about the formation of graphic collections:

(a) Classes (and classification) suppose the co-ordination of part-whole relations (properties 2) with those of similarity and difference (complementarity) which define the corresponding "intension" (properties 1).

(b) Now, while there are relations of similarity and difference at the level of graphic collections, these are always applied to objects in successive pairs and remain unconnected with part-whole relations. Such similarities and differences have their origin in practical schemata, which may be sensori-motor or verbal. They do not lead to the formation of a system which bears simultaneously on all the elements concerned. The latter is an essential characteristic of concepts, which can be defined by their extension as well as their intension.

(c) Again, while there are part-whole relations at this level, these are not yet applied to discontinuous sets or collections (class-inclusion and class-membership). They are always dependent on the perceptual configuration which means that they are limited to the field of what is

---

[1] We shall call a collection "non-graphic" if it does not yet constitute a class because it lacks the property of inclusion, while at the same time it is independent of its graphic representation with respect to properties (1) or (2); cf. ch. II.

continuous, i.e. spatial parts and wholes (subdividing a continuous figure and recomposing the whole out of the segments so obtained).

(d) Because he cannot co-ordinate intensive relations of similarity and difference (properties 1), with extensive part-whole relations (properties 2) the subject tends to construct graphic collections. When a child is given a set of objects to classify, he takes account of their qualitative properties (1) only insofar as these enter into the construction of one or more spatial wholes. He has yet to master class-inclusion and class-membership. In order to do so, he will need to be simultaneously aware of the similarities and differences involved instead of merely modifying his behaviour as a function of these at successive moments in time. Only then can part-whole relations be extended from the continuous to the discontinuous. And only then will the relations of class-membership and inclusion take their place beside that of partitive membership.

(e) What this amounts to is that the graphic collection constitutes the child's first attempt to co-ordinate part-whole relations with those of similarity and difference. This is rudimentary, (1) because relations of similarity and difference operate diachronically rather than simultaneously in the child's early schemata (perceptual and sensori-motor to begin with, later accompanied by imaginal schemata and the first verbal schemata); and (2) because the first intuition of part-whole relations is given perceptually in a spatial form.

What our experiments show in regard to graphic collections may be summarized in two broad conclusions:

(a) There is a stage of the graphic collection, which may be long or short depending on the materials used and the instructions given. This stage invariably precedes the stage of the non-graphic collection (this being a collection based on similarity and difference alone, so that class-membership is apparent while class-inclusion is not). True classification is later than either of these.

(b) There does not appear to be any definite sequence of sub-stages within the stage of the graphic collections. There are a number of different kinds of reaction which are easily recognizable, but these are overlapping rather than successive, and are a function of the experimental material and the way the questions are put. Following are the three main types:

(1) Laying the objects in line; the line may be continuous or discontinuous.

(2) Collective objects: graphic collections in two or three dimensions made up of similar elements, so that together they constitute an unbroken whole, this being a geometrical figure or pattern.

(3) Complex objects: unlike collective objects, these are made up out of heterogeneous elements. The end-product may be a geometrical figure, but it can also be descriptive or pictorial.

2. GENERAL RESULTS OBTAINED WITH FLAT GEOMETRICAL SHAPES

The first type of material consisted of square and triangular shapes, as well as rings and half-rings, some in wood and others in plastic. These shapes were of various colours. Occasionally, we included coloured letters of the alphabet. Using this material, we were struck by the large number of graphic collections of all types produced by children of $2\frac{1}{2}$ to 5 years. Non-graphic collections were rare below the age of $5\frac{1}{2}$, although in some cases they were found as early as $4\frac{1}{2}$. The most usual instruction was, "Put together things that are alike". But not infrequently this was further amplified; e.g. "Put them so that they're all the same", "Put them so that they're just like one another", or "Put them here if they're the same, and then over there if they're another lot different from this one but the same as each other". Following are typical examples of the various kinds of graphic collections listed above:

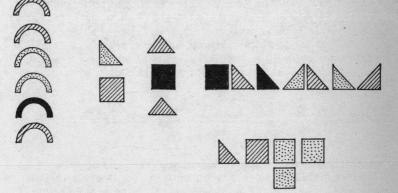

Figure 1.

I *Small partial alignments*—This response is a very primitive one. Instead of classifying all the objects in front of him, the subject is content to construct a number of independent arrangements with some of the things and does not bother to use the rest of the material. A striking peculiarity of these partial collections is that the arrangement is always linear. Later, we shall consider why this is so:

VIV (2; 6) looks first at the blue circle, then the red, and then the yellow, while saying: "*The same as that*" (successive similarities). She then constructs a row of circles, ignoring the other shapes. She is asked what goes with the yellow triangle: she points to the yellow circle and then to the blue square (which also has corners). She then places the triangle and the square in a small vertical line. Finally, she arranges a series of squares in a line (also vertical), saying, "*a tower*" (flat on the table).

Jos (3 ; 1) first places six semi-circles (two blue, two yellow, one red and one blue) in a line. Then she puts a yellow triangle on a blue square, and then a red square between two blue triangles with all three touching. She goes on to make a row of almost all the squares and triangles (touching one another still, but the shapes and colours taken haphazard). She now places a triangle and three squares in a line, and while doing so she decides that it is a house: she continues by adding a square below the three others. The last response therefore belongs to the category of "complex objects" (see Fig. 1).

NEL (3 ; 1) starts by constructing a row (oblique) of contiguous circles. Next she places some squares and triangles in a line but slightly spaced. Then she proceeds to a complex object (see III) and to total alignments (type II).

These partial alignments constitute the simplest form of classificatory combination. This does not mean that they belong to an earlier sub-stage, as there are subjects who start with complex objects, etc.

(1) The subject starts by establishing a similarity between the first element chosen and the second, and this is followed by a more or less independent relation between the second and the third, and so on. There is no preliminary plan nor does the subject set out to use all the elements. This is what Viv does before ever touching the circles, what Jos and Nel do as they handle them, and what all three subjects do in connecting squares and triangles because of their angles (independently of the number of angles).

Figure 2.

(2) The elements are connected by successive similarities between one object and the next; there is no anticipatory schema of the collection as a whole. Indeed such a schema does not even appear in the course of the behaviour, since the subject does not have to think of the first element when connecting the third to the second (the similarities being established successively). The subject finds a resemblance between one element and the next, and he makes it correspond with a part-whole relation. But this is easy enough since part-whole relations can themselves be created piecemeal. Without any preconceived plan of alignment, he places the second element next to the first, the third next to the second, etc., so constructing a linear sequence by successive one-dimensional vicinities—the simplest form of part-whole (spatial) membership.

(3) The alignment begins in this way, through the construction of successive similarities. After it has been built up, its underlying structure may sometimes become apparent even to the child. Then, and only then,

it becomes a schema capable of generalization and transfer. This is what we see in the second type of response.

II *Continuous alignments with fluctuating criteria*—Generalizing the alignment as such leads to a long line made up of sub-sets. But the latter are not constructed on the basis of an anticipatory plan, and the subject may not even be aware of their existence. They arise from the fact that the child forgets what went before as he moves from one element to the next, so that he changes the criterion of similarity involuntarily in the course of successive comparisons:

ALA (3; 11) places a blue triangle next to another and then continues with a blue square. The blue square is followed by a yellow square (a change from the criterion of colour to that of form), and then by red, yellow and blue squares. Since the last square is preceded by a yellow one, the child places a yellow triangle after it (probably guided by symmetry). This induces him to choose six more triangles, first two red, then two yellow, and finally two blue. —Ala later regresses to partial (and vertical) alignments, before switching to complex objects.

CHRI (4; 10) starts by aligning five rectangles, the fifth of which is yellow. This leads him to select four yellow triangles, followed by two yellow semi-circles. These in turn lead to five more semi-circles in different colours (see Fig. 2).

GAMB (5; 8) starts by aligning letters. The last, being yellow, is followed by a yellow circle, which is then followed by a sequence of circles of other colours, etc.

The change of criterion is the main characteristic of these continuous alignments. It testifies to the difficulty of co-ordinating relations of similarity with part-whole relations.

(1) At this level, similarities are established through relations which are successive in time. Children are unable to evolve a schema which is sufficiently differentiated to comprehend all the elements of a class simultaneously. Their nearest approach to such a schema is a graphic representation. But this is a far cry from a classificatory structure based only on the (extensive) quantification of elements defined by similarities and differences. It follows that part-whole relations are also successive in time, as well as being tied to a given arrangement in space. If the classification were adequate, these would follow automatically on the similarity and differences elaborated by the subject, their spatial representation being purely derivative. We have already seen how an alignment comes about quite naturally whenever the subject matches a chain of similarities found successively in time with a spatial succession of elements. But if he continues by prolonging the alignment as such, instead of making a series of independent sub-sets (1), he is bound to change his criterion as he goes along. The principle of succession,

23

whether spatial (as in the figure) or temporal (as in the series of similarities), is insufficient to represent a hierarchical class structure. The multiplicity of similarities and dissimilarities involved supposes a set of hierarchical inclusions rather than a linear succession.

(2) The changes of criterion are an indication of the leading role played by linear succession in space and time. When all the elements satisfying the initial criterion of similarity have been exhausted, the subject simply continues the alignment by looking for another similarity, which is how a second criterion emerges. But, at this point the first criterion is already forgotten, for the beginning of the alignment is distant both in time (memory) and in space (perception). In effect, these young subjects are limited to a series of two-term relations, these being the last item in the row and the one to be chosen next at any given moment.

(3) These continuing alignments do not represent a higher level of logical organization than the partial alignments described earlier—at least to begin with. The switch to an alternative sub-set and the switch to an alternative criterion are equivalent in that they both grow out of the limitations of successive two-term comparisons. Both reflect the same inability to co-ordinate the intension of a collection (similarities and differences) with its extension (class-membership), and (hence) the absence of hierarchical inclusion.

(4) However, once it has been constructed, the total series obtained by continuing an alignment may induce the subject to go back and inspect the figure as a whole. When this happens, the relations are seen simultaneously, and the alterations which follow now lead the subject to stage II, i.e. the juxtaposition of a number of qualitatively distinct logical collections. In this way, one of our subjects (Wal 4; 10),[1] starts with a continued alignment involving a succession of different criteria (first a line of squares ending with a yellow square, then yellow figures ending with a semi-circle, then semi-circles of which the last is blue, and finally blue squares), but he then goes on to move the blue squares from the end of the row to the beginning. He therefore finishes with three homogeneous linear segments (squares, triangles and semi-circles). In spite of the linear arrangement, these are not far removed from non-graphic collections.

III *Reactions intermediate between alignments and collective or complex objects*—Collective or complex objects are graphic collections in more than one dimension. Not infrequently, we find two types of construction which are not quite alignments and not quite collective or complex objects. The first of these consists of a number of partial alignments,

[1] See ch. II, §2, p. 51.

where several lines are constructed at an angle to one another. The second consists of figures which start as alignments but are later elaborated in two dimensions. Among these intermediate forms one might even include true alignments when these are rearranged to form some kind of symmetrical pattern. What began as a series of successive similarities here ends as a more or less consistent—but graphic—whole.

ALA (3; 11 already cited in II) constructs a sequence of five squares of which the middle one is red, the second and fourth blue and the two extremes yellow (two symmetries).

PONS (4; 6) carefully constructs a sequence of four coloured letters in the order blue—yellow—yellow—blue.

PAT (4; 0) constructs a symmetrical alignment of coloured rectangles and finishes it off at each end by a blue rectangle at right angles to the row. Seen again at 4; 5, he makes a large L shape, built up by successive similarities, with the criterion fluctuating between form and colour.

MIC (5; 0) constructs a vertical line of rectangles, and then continues at right angles with an assortment of circles and squares based on a criterion which fluctuates between form and colour. He ends with a horizontal row of letters.

NEL (3; 1 already cited in I) begins with a number of partial alignments, but goes on to place a yellow triangle next to a yellow square, followed by a red triangle below the yellow triangle and a red square below the yellow square. This gives a square figure which could be taken to represent a matrix composed of two rows and two columns. But she goes on to change the yellow square for a blue one, which proves that she has no thought of any logical arrangement and is merely switching from an alignment to a collective object. Later on the same child constructs a long continued alignment beginning and ending with squares, but with seven semi-circles in between: this she declares is "*a bridge*".

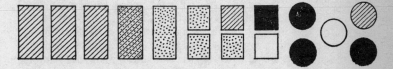

Figure 3.

PAT (4; 5) first forms symmetrical and right-angled alignments of the kind already described. In much the same vein, he constructs a row of three blue rectangles followed by a green one and a yellow one. Since there is not another yellow rectangle, he takes two yellow squares and puts one over the other to form a rectangle. This enables him to go on with a yellow square and a blue one, followed by a white one and a red one, then two circles and finally, three more circles. What began as an alignment ends as a two-dimensional figure (see Fig. 3).—Last of all, he builds another figure which is half-way between an alignment and a long surface, and calls this a "*long trolley-bus*" (see Fig. 4).

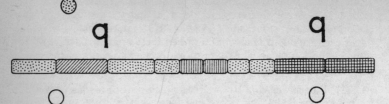

Figure 4.

BOR (4; 9) starts by arranging pairs of semi-circles which he matches for colour so that each pair forms a circle cut horizontally; he then goes on with a long row of unpaired semi-circles; finally, he constructs a pattern of squares in two dimensions.

These examples include one-dimensional symmetries (Ala, Pons, and Pat 4; 0); two or three rows forming right angles (Pat 4; 5 and Mic); and, finally, constructions which start off as linear but end as two-dimensional figures (Nel, Pat and Bor). They suggest the following interpretation. The initial alignment is a synthesis between the requirements of similarity and class-membership, but it is unstable inasmuch as both characters are apprehended only in terms of a succession of two-term relations. Because the resultant equilibrium is weak, the subject feels impelled to consolidate the synthesis. This he can achieve by strengthening the similarities between the elements in the row. He can also do it by accentuating their inclusion in the whole. In both cases, he is trying to substitute a simultaneous whole for a temporal series. But the two kinds of relations cannot yet be strengthened at the same time. Doing so would be equivalent to co-ordinating the "intension" of the collections (the qualitative similarities and differences involved) with their "extension" (relations of part to whole). Herein lies the whole problem of the formation of classes and hierarchical classification. At this level, children inevitably neglect part-whole relations when they reinforce similarities or else they neglect similarities when they reinforce part-whole relations.

When similarities are reinforced, the part-whole relation is left unaltered, being summed up by the fact that all the elements form part of one linear figure. What happens is simply that the child tries to improve the alignment, either by introducing small homogeneous series (continued alignments with changes of criterion), or by creating symmetries involving similarities between two or more sub-sets out of the total series.

When he wants to strengthen part-whole relations, the subject abandons one-dimensional inclusion (successive vicinities) in favour of a belonging in two dimensions. But these dimensions are graphic rather than logical, which is why we speak of collective or complex objects.

26

So what tends to happen is that by strengthening the inclusions, and making as many elements as possible belong simultaneously to an immediate whole, the subject tends to forget about the similarities between the elements. This is because the whole tends to acquire graphic properties of its own, which drive its classificatory function into the background. It follows that even when childen start out by constructing collective objects made up of homogeneous items, they readily transform these into complex objects comprising a heterogeneity of elements.

The transformation from a collective object to a complex object can happen in two ways. The arrangement may have a compelling geometrical shape as a result of which the subject forgets about the homogeneous elements of which he made it and goes on to add to it by using heterogeneous elements. This is what we see in Pat's long rectangular surface. Even more unambiguous are the responses classified as type V. Alternatively, and more frequently, the child decides that his arrangement represents an empirical object, which makes him lose sight of the original task — classifying the elements as such. This explains Pat's "bridge" or Nel's "long trolleybus". We shall come upon this sort of behaviour again when we come to type VI responses.

IV *Collective objects*—By definition, a collective object is a two- or three-dimensional collection of similar elements which together form a unified figure (cf. Nel's and Bor's square collective objects and Bor's pairs of semi-circles, both described under III). The collective object constitutes a response which can pass over into the more advanced behaviour shown in the non-graphic collection. A non-graphic collection differs from a collective object only in that the latter is tied to a definite shape. Both are composed of homogeneous elements. At the same time the collective object can grow out of or pass into either of the two modes of response already referred to: homogeneous linear segments and complex objects. Homogeneous linear segments are themselves linear collective objects, while complex objects differ from collective objects only in that they are composed of heterogeneous elements. From a developmental viewpoint, all these modes of response are equivalent. The tendency for a subject to add to a collective object by introducing heterogeneous elements is particularly widespread. That is why collective objects are unstable and occur far less frequently than complex objects. Following are a number of additional examples:

PIC (4; 6) constructs a matrix in which the determinants are crossed (cf. Nel, Section III). First he puts a large blue square above a small blue square, and, below these, a large blue circle above a small blue circle. Then, to the right of them, he puts a large yellow circle above a small yellow one, and, below, a large yellow square above a small yellow square. "*They're the same squares and the same circles!*"

BLU (5; 3) constantly wavers between a collective object (a large rectangle made up of six squares, in a criss-cross pattern of three blue and three yellow) and a complex object (a square surrounded by four triangles, which together form a large square lying on one vertex; the figure is further complicated by a small square placed at each angle). He also wavers between an alignment and a collective object. The first is a series of squares all the same size, while the second is an alignment made up of large and small squares alternately and ending in a row of large squares surmounted by a row of small ones.

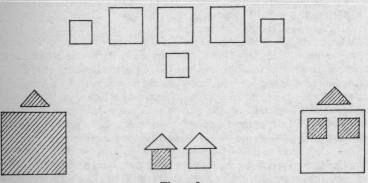

Figure 5.

BUC (5; 3) also wavers. First he makes a collective object (three large squares in a line and together forming a rectangle, but with an additional smaller square laid against three of its sides); then a complex object made up of squares and triangles (see Fig. 5).

V and VI. *Complex objects based on geometrical or situational content*— When the material is arranged to form a two-dimensional shape, part-whole relations are reinforced because the whole becomes a closed set. But collections in the form of a surface or a volume are more interesting than linear arrangements. As a result, children tend to be fascinated by the shape of the whole and forget about the internal relation of similarity and difference among its elements. In other words, the collection is still something more than a mere aggregate or "lot", as it will be at stage II, when objects are brought together simply by virtue of their similarity so that the child makes as many lots as he finds similarities. It is a "graphic" collection because the shape of the whole or set determines the placing of each element. Part-whole relations are therefore primary while those of similarity and difference are of secondary importance, which is why we find a predominance of complex objects as opposed to collective objects.

In type V responses the collection takes on a geometrical form.

Nevertheless, some of the internal relations between elements are preserved by the requirements of symmetry.

ALA (3; 11) puts two yellow semi-circles one below and one above a blue square, and two blue semi-circles one below and one above a yellow square.

JAX (4; 0) places a yellow cross in the centre of his figure, with four rays made up of three rectangles (two blue and one yellow) and a blue square.

Figure 6.

FRA (4; 0) arranges four blue and green rectangles to form a square enclosure, beneath which he makes a second enclosure out of five variously coloured squares.

CUR (5; 0) puts two blue rectangles side by side with a blue circle on the right and a blue square on the left (see Fig. 6).

Responses like these are legion. One is led to feel that the subject has lost sight of the initial purpose of the classification and interprets the instruction, "Put together what is alike", as no more than a request to make something. However, such an interpretation is insufficient. In the first place it can hardly account for the many transitional responses which are not quite alignments and not quite complex objects. In the second place we frequently find intermediate responses linking alignments and complex objects with non-graphic collections.

The same problem arises in the case of type VI responses, i.e. complex objects with a descriptive meaning. It is difficult to draw a hard and fast line between these responses and the preceding ones, partly because what looks to us no more than a pattern might be endowed with descriptive meaning by the child, and partly because very often the child starts with a geometrical pattern and then adds to it in such a way as to make it situational or descriptive.

FRA (4; 0) suddenly adds three circles underneath the rectangles and squares described in the last section and says, "*It's the Eiffel Tower*". (See also the example of Pat's trolleybus, III.)

Additional examples will be given in §4. As to their relevance to classification, we would point out in the first place that here again, these descriptive complex objects shade into non-graphic collections as children grow more mature, just as do the geometrical complex objects discussed above. These intermediate responses suggest a true filiation, i.e. graphic collections including complex objects are the real precursors of classificatory behaviour. These collections take on a collective character (either a pattern or a representative image) because children at stage I have no means of distinguishing between a collection and an object. They lack the operations necessary for the formation of inclusions (see below). As long as the relation of a component item in the collection of which it forms a part is sub-logical, i.e. spatial or partitive, the collection itself is an object. It ceases to be so only when the part-whole relation becomes one of logical inclusion or class-membership.

3. THE LINKS BETWEEN GRAPHIC COLLECTIONS AND CLASSIFICATION: FURTHER ILLUSTRATIVE MATERIAL USING GEOMETRICAL SHAPES

The mere describing of these six types of graphic collection is not enough. We have yet to examine the links between this mode of response and true classification in order to establish its relevance.

(1) The facts given above seem to show that the "intension" of these graphic collections is not exhausted by relations of similarity and difference, as in the case of logical classes. The intension includes relations of affinity or of belonging. This is how one might describe the relations governing the symmetrical placing of two circles on either side of a rectangle or the relation between a triangle and a square when the child puts them together to make a house with a roof. We would suggest the following hypotheses: (a) Young children are totally unable to differentiate between relations of similarity and those of belonging. Such lack of differentiation could be ascribable to the plastic character of sensori-motor assimilation. Sometimes an object is assimilated to an action schema by virtue of similarity alone (similarity between the object in question and other objects which induced the same action in the past); sometimes by virtue of a utilitarian belonging; and sometimes by a mixture of the two. (b) Children can differentiate between similarity and belonging as long as they are not constructing collections of objects, but not when doing so. Let us see how this could be. The intension of a logical class uniquely determines its extension. But in the case of graphic collections, extension is sometimes determined by intension (as long as the subject continues to collect "the same" elements), while at other times intension is determined by extension (when the collection acquires a shape which influences the choice). Since the child cannot tell which of these is dominant, he fails to differentiate between similarity and belonging when constructing such collections even though he can do so at other times. (c) All children can distinguish between relations of similarity and belonging at every level. If young children tend to switch from the first to the second it is only because they have not understood the instructions, or because they lose interest in classification when they

spot the interest of the complex object. (If this last hypothesis were correct, graphic collections would not represent a true stage in classification, but a sort of deviation of stage I.)

(2) The last hypothesis brings us back to the main problem, for which additional information is still needed. Do graphic collections constitute an essential stage in the formation of classifications, or do we find a mixture of graphic and non-graphic collections from the beginning? If so, one could argue that classificatory behaviour owes its origin to non-graphic collections alone. The occurrence of a series of transitional responses linking collective and complex objects with classifications would not be conclusive in establishing their importance, for it could well be due to a gradual merging between graphic and non-graphic collections.

To solve these problems, we carried out a series of experiments using geometrical shapes which fell into two large classes (curvilinear and rectilinear), each composed of smaller sub-classes or sub-collections (squares, triangles, semi-circles, circles, etc.). We also tried to reach back as far as possible (down to 1 year 11 months) by using very simple verbal instructions, "Put the same ones together", or even by giving children examples to imitate (the experimenter starts the classification and the subject has to go on, etc.).

Of the examples that follow, those marked (I) are spontaneous in the sense that the instructions were general and therefore liable to be interpreted by the individual after his own fashion; those marked (II) are either copied from the experimenter's model (even the action of imitating demands a measure of understanding), or else suggested by definite verbal instruction.

MON (1; 11). The experimenter starts by putting all the items in her hand one at a time to familiarize her with the materials.
I 1. She takes two rings, then starts collecting circles to which she adds a large square, then a large ring, then a small one, and finally a small square.
I 2. She makes a tower of four circles decreasing in size.
I 1. She begins another collection made up of two similar rings and a circle, but halfway through she stops to play with the elements.
I 3. She puts semi-circles together.
I 4. She places a triangle on a square, which could be a house.
II 1. "Put this (a circle) with something that goes with it." She merely piles things together at random.
II 2. "What shall we put in these boxes?" She makes up a random assortment, including a semi-circle, a circle, a ring and a small square, which she picks out anyhow.
II 3. The experimenter makes an alignment for her to imitate: she fails.

DES (2; 2). II 1. "Give me one like this (a ring)": he hands over the same ring. "And like that (a circle)": he hands over circles and semi-circles, and then triangles. He takes a small square, but puts it back saying, "*Not that!*"

II 2. "Give me some like that (the small square which he has just excluded)": he hands over three small squares and then, after some hesitation, two circles.
I 1. He takes a large square and puts it down, saying, "*There!*" Then he takes two medium-sized squares and tries to stand them on end. He then joins them to the large square which gives him an alignment or a collective object. "Carry on"; "*None left*". (But there are several left.)

II 3. After the subject has handled a triangle, the experimenter says, "Give me one like that". He hands over a semi-circle, then a triangle. "Any more?": he cannot find any more, although there are several left.

II 4. "Another one like this (a circle)": he gives the experimenter three circles, then says, "*Oh, none left*" (which is not true).

II 5. "Another one like this (a square)." He makes a pile of six squares in his hand before they fall over. "Put them in this box": he makes a line of two squares, then a triangle followed by another square.

MIC (2; 4). II 1. He picks up a square: "Put the same ones together." He makes a pile of two large squares, two small ones, a medium-sized one and a small one.

II 2. The experimenter mixes the material and repeats the same instruction. Mic picks up two large squares, two medium-sized squares and one small square, then a small circle, followed by the eighth (and last) square and a large circle.

II 3. He is given three boxes with the instruction, "Put only the same ones here. Afterwards you'll put the others there." He puts a large circle in the middle of the box, and surrounds it with almost all the squares, crying "*Closed!*" (= complex topological figure).

II 4. The experimenter puts two rings together and then two semi-circles over a circle. Mic takes a ring and puts it round his finger, then takes it off and fits all the rings together with the small circle in the middle.

II 5. "Give me one like that (a circle)": he hands over several circles, saying "*The same*".

II 6. *Idem* (a square): he produces other squares.

II 7. *Idem* (a triangle): he fails.

II 2. He then spontaneously places three small squares, then one large, one small and one medium-sized, all in a continuous row and says, "*That's pretty!*"

II 8. "Give me one like this (a triangle)": he produces a small square and a large one.

PAS (2; 9). "You put together all those which are the same." He first aligns two small squares, then two large ones, then a square and a triangle (edge to edge), and ends with two squares at right angles to the row. Next he makes a row of circles. He puts a small square between two large ones and covers each one with a circle. He finally piles all the circles on one of the large squares, several small squares on the medium-sized one, and a mixture of triangles and small squares on the second large square. Then he undoes the construction and piles everything on the two large squares.

After that he begins another collective object: two large squares followed by a medium-sized one, all edge to edge; he goes on to put a number of small squares all together in a corner of one of the big ones.

His final effort is a pile of circles.

MAR (2; 11). The instructions are identical. He begins with a pile of circles, then aligns a number of squares, continuing with semi-circles and circles.

A row of jumbled elements is: "*A train, ch, ch, ch!*"

JOU (3; 0), after being shown how, succeeds in separating red and black elements into two boxes (making two mistakes which he corrects); he also sorts out blue and yellow elements (with two uncorrected mistakes).

When shown how to put all the squares in one box and all the triangles and rhombi in the other, Jou does it with only one error.

UBE (2; 9 and 3; 2). At 2; 9, after being asked to "give me those which are the same" and being shown a circle, he takes three other circles and then the semi-circles. But he does not know what to do at first when asked to "put together those which are the same". When a rhombus is put on the table, he adds all the rhombi and triangles; then he stands the triangles up, one behind another.

At 3; 2, with the same instructions, he starts by collecting semi-circles and circles in his hands. "You can put them on the table. Take those which are the same." He takes semi-circles together with triangles, then makes a separate pile of squares. The experiment is repeated; this time he ends with three piles, one composed of triangles, one of circles and the last of semi-circles.

Further repetitions invariably lead to similar collections. But there are two innovations: the first is a series of squares in decreasing order of size (two large, two medium-sized, and four small ones), and the second is an alignment of almost all the elements in the form of a rotated L; except for a few errors all the items of one sort are juxtaposed in the alignment.

POU (3; 4) spontaneously puts all the large elements in the same box (rhombi, triangles and squares), but continues with arbitrary elements. "Are you going to put the big ones here and the small ones there?—(He does not understand.) — Do it like this (putting three large items in one box and three small ones in the other)." He continues correctly but without foresight. He has to look inside the box each time to make sure he has the right one, and now and again he puts an element in the wrong box before discovering his mistake.

CHRI (3; 5) starts with complex objects of 6–8 elements. She is given two boxes and asked to put "the same" elements together. Indicating the two boxes, the experimenter emphasizes "the same together". She produces two mixed collections, which are not wholly random since one is made up mostly of squares while the other has a majority of curvilinear elements.

We have made a point of giving a large number of examples so that our interpretations can be judged on the facts.

(A) We will begin by considering the second problem mentioned at the beginning of this section, i.e. the difficulty of deciding whether graphic collections are an essential step in classification or whether children can build non-graphic collections right from the start. The responses made by our youngest subjects suggest an obvious cause of the difficulty. They tend to concentrate at first on the action of collecting things and making a pile. Only later, if at all, do they become interested in the collection as such. In fact what we observe are two quite different kinds of response. One is to choose the elements, which means assimilating them to a functional schema; and the second is to build the collection. Mic, for example, was asked to "put the same ones together". On one occasion he collected eight squares and two circles in his hand (II 2): here the entire action may be summed up in their successive choice. But when he constructs a pile of squares or a topologically closed figure he is making a collective object (II 1) or a complex object (II 3). In much the same way, Mon collects semi-circles but does nothing with them (I 3), but the very same child can also be seen piling circles (I 2) or superimposing angular forms (I 4). We see a similar alternation in the behaviour of Des who makes alignments on one occasion (II 5) and collective objects on another (I 1).

Whether the collection is clearly graphic or apparently non-graphic seems to depend on which attitude is the prevailing one at any given moment. Where a child is choosing objects and piling them with the sole purpose of finding "the same ones" or of preparing a later collection, there is nothing graphic about what he is doing. One is therefore tempted to infer (whether rightly or wrongly) that he can make non-graphic collections. But the collection becomes graphic as soon as the child shows an interest in it as such.

The following interpretation seems the most plausible:

(1) The responses obtained at these early ages (1; 11 to 2; 11) represent compromises between sensori-motor assimilation, which is essentially successive (in time), and the representation of simultaneous collections (in space), because children cannot foresee the result they are aiming at while the action is in progress (cf. Pou at 3; 4 trying to imitate a two-way classification).

(2) While the factor of successive assimilation is dominant, the subject has no figure in mind and all he does is to make up a pile by picking up one object after another in such a way that each new object is similar to the one he took up last. To the observer these piles look like non-graphic collections. But the appearance is deceptive, for the attention of the child is centred on successive assimilations so that, from his point of view, there *is* no collection in the sense of something consciously constructed.

(3) However, as soon as the subject takes an interest in the collection as such, he gives it shape. It is then that we observe the various principal kinds of graphic collections: alignments (flat, or piled together vertically), collective and complex objects.

(4) In a sense, then, children can construct non-graphic collections from the start. But such collections are characteristically unpremeditated and cannot be used for the purpose of classification. Nevertheless, even now, children are not far from constructing non-graphic collections,

since they can imitate such divisions when the experimenter shows them how, although they do not make them spontaneously.

(5) Thus, in considering the genetic antecedents or *filiation* of classificatory behaviour we are led to the conclusion that graphic collections are an essential feature of this early stage, while at the same time recognizing that non-graphic collections in a primitive form co-exist with these from the beginning. Children cannot conceive an "extension" without the graphic structure. The primitive, diachronic, non-graphic collections reflect only the "intension" of the later classifications. We should therefore say that at stage I children are unable to differentiate between structures which are properly logical and those which are strictly sub-logical.[1] Because of this lack of differentiation their collections are not always purely graphic or purely non-graphic but frequently show a mixture of the two. What we call stage II is characterized by an incipient differentiation. Only then do children begin to look for new ways of co-ordinating extensive and intensive properties without falling back on graphic collections.

(B) The answer to the first of the two problems outlined earlier follows naturally from the above.

(6) When a child collects things by successive assimilations he is always showing some degree of generalization by equivalence—even when the assimilation is sensori-motor, as it usually is before the age of 3. Children do pass from a circle to a circle; but they can also pass from a triangle to a semi-circle or a square. How far the equivalence will carry depends on what the child has in mind and on the experimenter's instructions. The same child, on one occasion constructs a pile made up only of circles (Mon, I 2), and, on another occasion (when asked to put an element with "something that goes with it") heaps things together at random: here the relation "goes with", is assimilated to the act of collecting itself, so that it is just as much a matter of practical belonging as it is one of strict similarity.

(7) However, although there may be occasional confusion between similarity and mere belonging when the subject is making a series of successive assimilations, he is still in a position to differentiate between the two up to a point. It is when he begins to consider the collection itself that he is no longer able to do so and his collection tends to become graphic. For it is now the spatial extension of the collection that determines the belonging of its parts. When Mic surrounds a circle with squares (II 3) we are forced to interpret the relation as "belonging";

---

[1] Sub-logical operations are those which bear on the parts of a spatial continuum while logical operations bear on the relations between separate elements. The two sets of operations are isomorphic: subdivision corresponds to classification and spatial arrangement to seriation. See *The Child's Conception of Space*, 1956, ch. XV.

when he builds a pile of rings all round a small circle (II 4), we are tempted to think of their similarity: but it is doubtful whether he himself could differentiate between the two. In both cases, the relations he establishes are imposed by the shape (extension) of his complex or collective object, and not only by the likeness of elements (intension) as such.

4. "SIMILARITY" AND "BELONGING" IN THE GROUPING OF SMALL TOYS

The preceding facts still leave two questions unanswered: (a) Is it the geometrical character of the materials which induces children to make graphic constructions instead of classifying the pieces? (b) How far does the tendency to make graphic collections and to think in terms of "belonging" depend on the nature of the instructions? To answer these questions we varied the enquiry by using descriptive material instead of geometrical shapes.

Now the first point to notice is that although the use of geometrical shapes does favour collective or complex objects, using representational toys also leads children to construct complex objects. The main difference is that the latter now tend to be representative instead of being patterns.[1] What we find is that children group a doll with a cot, instead of classifying the baby with people and the cot with furniture. This is exactly what Binet found for his definitions: younger children give replies like: "A mother is for making supper" (or "for loving us", etc.), instead of defining the term by its genus and specific difference: "A mother is a lady who has children." The point is that in both cases, children are using pre-concepts and not true concepts. At that level, abstraction is still irreversible and non-operational, which means that the relation of class-inclusion eludes them. As far as they are concerned, if what is individual is a member of something more general, the relation must be one of subdivision in space. It follows that they do not see how the similarities and differences which determine the "intension" of a class generate a set of inclusions which form its "extension".

Here again we see the difference between similarity and "belonging". A cot "belongs with" a baby although it is not similar to a baby; and, similarly, making supper "belongs with" a mother although it is hardly an essential property which she shares with all mothers. True, most mothers make supper; and we could think of these "belongings" as similarities. But such similarities are accidental rather than essential, since not all mothers make supper and not all babies have cots. Now children do confuse "some" and "most" with all, and they do so

[1] In point of fact we started the investigation using representative material and then switched to the use of pattern shapes because of these complex objects.

precisely because they cannot co-ordinate intensive properties with extensive properties. But there is more to it than this. The child is not just classifying the baby together with "creatures with cots"; he is classifying the baby along with the cot itself. In other words he is lumping a not quite essential attribute along with the object it is supposed to define. Here we have an excellent illustration of the way in which part-whole relations tend to take the place of logical relations of class-inclusion. Once again we are reminded of the way in which the same thing happened when children made complex objects out of geometrical shapes.

The parallel is instructive, the more so as we can begin to see something of the differences between the kinds of response made to these and those made with geometrical shapes, as well as the analogies in the behaviour of our young subjects. Bringing out these analogies and differences should throw a good deal of light on what we now see as the crucial problem in the origins of classification—how to co-ordinate intensive and extensive properties.

We tried out various games with real objects, and we also used several different kinds of instructions. To describe every experiment in detail would be tedious. We shall confine ourselves to a summary description of two experiments which are typical of the rest. The first (I) consisted of presenting the child with a set of toy objects which could be classified according to similarity, but which could also be arranged to tell a story or grouped empirically and even topographically as a little village. The toys included 7 people, 8 houses, 9 animals, 4 fir trees, 7 fences, benches, fountains, motor cars, 2 babies and 2 cradles, etc. Instructions were of three sorts: (a) to arrange the objects in order, then (a second time) more in order, (b) to put things together where they go together, and (c) to put together things that are alike. In the second type of experiment (II) the experimenter emphasised the similarity as such, asking the child to put (a) "the same" objects or (b) "more or less the same" objects on separate sheets of paper. These could then be collected to allow for an analysis of the way in which the collections were formed.

I. The first technique was used with children of 2 to 9–10 years. The results testify to a lawful development which goes well beyond the stage under discussion (stage I). But it is sufficiently important to warrant a bit of discussion. The development is twofold. On the one hand, there is a progressive differentiation of sub-logical structures (these being composed of part-whole relations which form a spatial continuum) from logical structures (composed of relations entering in the construction of collections and classes). On the other hand, there is a sort of complementarity between these types of behaviour which reappears at every stage in spite of their growing differentiation. Without a proper appreciation of this twofold process, increasing differentiation being balanced by increasing complementarity, the sort of behaviour observed at stage I can give rise to considerable misunderstanding. The usual view is that logical structures are derived from the relations between concepts and statements, both of which are conceived of as essentially verbal in nature. In terms of this way of looking at things there is no connexion between classification and the structurization of space, since one depends on language while the other depends on geometrical intuition. However, if the origins of logical operations can be traced to pre-linguistic behaviour then these processes have a far wider import. The hierarchical structures found in the logic of classes and relations are determined by the exclusive play of relations between parts and wholes (as opposed to part-part relations). There is no reason to suppose that the various sets to which they give rise will be limited to a content which is discontinuous. Such sets as the addition or multiplication of classes and the addition or multiplication of relations can be paralleled by sets involving a continuous content. The operations which effect the various transformations of such sets will be identical except that they bear on spatial or spatio-temporal parts and wholes. Such operations have been called sub-logical elsewhere,[1] not because they are simpler than logical operations, but because in terms of Russell's theory of types they apply to a lower type than the individual object, which is of type O. The distinction between sub-logical and logical structures has no interest to the logician since what is sub-logical may always be described in the language and symbolism of logic. This is hardly surprising since the factor of continuity does not affect the structural isomorphism of logical and sub-logical sets. But the psychologist will look for two distinct constructions, each showing increasing differentiation and complementarity, evolving in parallel stages. With the present materials, it is only at stage III (7–8 years) that children are able to make classifications with hierarchical inclusions. At the very same stage they can also build a spatial model in strict conformity with a preconceived plan (the topography of a village). During stage II (5 to 7–8 years on the average) there is already a clear differentiation between the two structures, but there is always some measure of interference due to the inadequacy of the anticipatory schema. At this stage, although classificatory collections are no longer graphic, there is no hierarchical inclusion. In the same way, topographical constructions are based on spatial co-ordinations as distinct from logical similarity.[2] But the structure of these models is incomplete: we tend to find sections of the model, or sub-sets, juxta-posed instead of forming part of a co-ordinated whole. The analogy with the juxtaposition of non-graphic collections is very plain. But at

---

[1] *The Child's Conception of Space*, ch. XV.

[2] Children no longer put all the bridges together when making a village simply because they are all bridges (TN).

38

stage I, which is our present concern, children show little differentiation between the logical and the sub-logical. The instruction "Put together whatever is alike" gives a slight advantage to similarity relations of resemblance, but does not exclude spatial belonging, while the instruction "Put together whatever goes together" reinforces the latter without excluding the former. Here are a number of examples illustrating responses at stage I:

VIV (2; 6) first amuses herself by standing the objects up and moving them about without understanding the instruction "Arrange them in order". To "Put together whatever goes together", she takes a woman, finds a second woman, seizes a man and then a series of other men, by successive assimilations. "And this?": she takes the horse which she has been shown and seizes three others. She finally puts down a fir-tree (lying down), places a second on top of it and a horse above them.

IXE (3 years), with the same instructions, arranges the objects in pairs; two pairs of horses, to which he joins two rabbits and then two women. He grows enthusiastic about his classifying and shouts out joyfully: "*Same the same! The same women! There are three gee-gees.*" He puts two mice together, two men together, and the baby in the cradle. Then he starts constructing alignments of houses, horses, and fir-trees, followed by a series containing cats, women and men. He ends by making an alignment of these alignments, which implies a transition from successive assimilations to a simultaneous figure.

JOS (3; 10), with the instruction "Put together whatever is alike", starts with a continued alignment containing two dolls in a cradle, two wheelbarrows, a horse (which is finally placed in one of the wheelbarrows) and a series of animals. "What is like this (a cat)?"—(She produces cats, rabbits and turkeys)—"Give me something like this (a horse)"—(She hands over all the animals, and then a baby and two fir-trees). Finally she puts houses together, adds a cock, etc.

NIC (4 years) constructs alignments based on similarity: blue houses and a blue motor-car "*because it is blue*"; fir-trees in a row, "*It's the same colour*"; and then men: "*They aren't the same colour but they're all men.*" Then (with the same instruction "Put together whatever is alike"), he puts down a fence to fill an empty space, "*because it's almost the same size as the place*". Alignments based on similarity go together with arrangements based on size to form a collection which is more of a complex object than a model village.

YVE (4; 8) with the instruction "Put together whatever is alike", makes up a number of small collections, some of which are based on similarity (e.g. two fences) while others draw on empirical belonging: a woman next to a fir-tree, a bench against a house, and a church with a small tree and a motor-car. The juxtaposition of these collections betrays no clear plan, although it is not wholly random.

BER (4; 8) makes up a heterogeneous spatial group composed of short alignments and little collections: two turkeys, four horses, two chickens, two rabbits and a dog, etc. He is then given five sheets of paper to help him classify elements that are "alike". He puts the horses together, then the wagons, etc., but goes on to put the rabbits in with the prams "*because they sleep in the prams*", the women with the rabbits "*because they're looking at the rabbits*", and the cats with the horses and the ducks "*because they're the same*", etc.

The instruction, "Put together whatever goes together" leads to responses like these:

CUR (4; 2) puts the houses in a row with the church at some distance. He goes on to arrange the remaining objects, commenting: "*Here's a woman who's bringing in all the cows and the sheep and the horses and all the chickens.*" He places the sheep around the seated people whom he takes for fountains "*and a gentleman next to them to stop the sheep going away*". Finally: "*The bench in the middle and the trees all round just like my granny's.*"

BOJ (4; 6) forms an alignment of houses, men and fir-trees in order of size (a correct seriation of 4 elements), etc: "*Here are some animals, people, houses, trees, now comes a bench, and here's a thing* (a fence)."

AEB (4; 6). The arrangement is similar but based on colour.

The various kinds of behaviour shown in the handling of geometrical shapes are all found here, with the sole difference that complex objects take on an empirical character.

(1) The instruction "Put together whatever is alike" reinforces the tendency to group things by similarity, while "Put together whatever goes together" tends to lead to collections which "belong" together. But the connexion is far from universal. The first instruction also gives rise to associations of situational belonging (a woman next to a fir-tree, etc., in Yve's case; rabbits in Ber's prams, a horse in Jos's wheelbarrow, and so on). And the second instruction can result in groups based on similarity (Boj and Aeb).

(2) Collections based on pure similarity occur even in the responses of very young children, the underlying mechanism being that of successive assimilation (Viv). It is this which inspires Ixe's profound reflection: "Same the same!"

(3) But, as we saw in §3, a collection based on similarity may still be given a specific spatial form when the subject switches his attention from successive assimilation to the resultant whole. This explains why Viv ends with a vertical pile of two fir-trees and a horse, while Ixe makes alignments of his alignments.

(4) Partial and continued alignments echo those found with geometrical shapes, while collective objects are no less unstable.

(5) Complex objects are different in that they draw on representational meaning. Their very ubiquity testifies to the ease with which children slide over from a schema of similarity to one of belonging (see all the cases from Jos to Ber), because they are unable to differentiate the global notion of "alike".

(6) Finally, there is no clear differentiation between logical structures (graphic collections which are the precursors of true classes) and sub-

logical structures (which with this kind of material are topographical). Almost every subject changes from one to the other whatever instructions he is given.

II. In order to check these results and their interpretation, we made our questioning techniques more precise. We also asked subjects to separate their collections into boxes or on to sheets of paper. This is the technique II mentioned earlier in this section, but before describing our results we should like to describe what we found in a preliminary pilot run.

This was a test in which 16 objects were used: 4 animals, 4 human beings (a black baby, a man, a white girl and a cowboy), 4 kitchen utensils and 4 articles of furniture. Subjects were asked to classify these objects in open boxes with the instruction "Put together whatever goes together best". Results were: (a) Small children constructed series of alignments followed by heterogeneous collections when told to use the boxes. The principles governing them were generally clear and taught us nothing new. (b) At about 4–5 years we found the boxes being used to distinguish between separate collections. To begin with these collections themselves still showed a remarkable lack of differentiation between similarity and belonging; but there was also a progressive development towards non-graphic collections. We shall return to the second point in ch. II. But a few elementary cases are given here to illustrate the confusion between similarity and belonging:

PIE (5; 0) Box (A): "(Baby + chair + chair).—Why?"—(He puts the baby on one of the chairs, adds a man and says:) *The man is sitting with the baby.*" (He adds a pig) "*The baby is playing with the pig.*" (Then a pot) "*It's for the pig to eat out of.*" (Another man) "*The man is looking after the pig.*"

Box (B): "(Man + monkey:) "*The man is looking at the monkey*"; (a bird:) "*The bird and the monkey are playing*"; Later: "*The bird is drinking out of the pot; the man is sitting on a chair*; (a fish) *then he catches a fish.* (Monkey + pot) *The monkey is balancing on the edge*", and so on. Here we see only empirical belonging (except for the two chairs which could be held to argue similarity), and even the belonging becomes increasingly arbitrary.

GER (5; 6) shows rather more of an equilibrium as between similarity and belonging: (A) three men, a monkey and a pig: "*The gentleman is looking after the pig.*" (B) Two babies and a chair "*for the baby to sit on*". Three pots "*for cooking and fetching milk*". (C) Two men and a monkey. (D) Two chairs, a baby and a fish.

CHRI (5; 2) lies at the other extreme in the developmental series of which Pie is the least advanced, while Ger is somewhere in between. She first puts a pot and two pans in (A): "*They're for washing.*" Then she arranges chairs as though round a table (in B): "*They go together because they're all for the dining-room.*" She adds a fourth receptacle in (A) and says: "*All that is for the kitchen.*" In (C): a man and a pig, "*He's going for a walk and he has a pig farm*"; (she adds the monkey and the bird): *They're also in there.*"

41

These few examples are enough to provide the key to the problem of similarity and belonging.

(1) A number of groupings are pure similarity relations: two chairs (Pie), three men and a monkey, two pots and two chairs (Ger), etc.

(2) Many are pure cases of belonging (forming complex objects with an empirical meaning): a baby on its chair, a pig eating from a pot, a little man looking after a pig, a monkey balancing on the edge of a pot, etc.

(3) Some are intermediate and suggest a transition or compromise. Is the association of the man sitting down with the baby (Pie) governed by similarity or belonging? What of the man looking at the monkey? The answer seems to be: both.

(4) Finally, there is a true synthesis in Chri's case. The chairs around a table and the kitchen utensils are at one and the same time complex objects by virtue of their representational arrangement in space, and members of a pre-class defined "intensionally" by a common property: "all for the dining-room" or "all for the kitchen". These formulations are all the more remarkable in that they ensure a correspondence between the intension of the collection (based on similarity, but one which coincides with relations of belonging) and its extension (expressed by the word "all"). If these were translated in terms of Binet-Simon definitions, we should have here both a definition by use ("for" the kitchen or dining-room) and a definition by species ("all"). What is still lacking is the relation of class-inclusion, necessary to an adequate definition by genus and differentia.

When children base their collections on belonging (and similarly when they define words by use), the "belonging" relations and the complex objects to which they give rise are not accidental aberrations from what would be pure classifications. They arise out of the very same causes as the failure to achieve true classification. These are (a) failure to differentiate between sub-logical and logical structures, and (b) inability to co-ordinate intension and extension. (a) always implies (b) although (b) will persist when (a) has been overcome. Chri's success is, of course, exceptional; but all the more interesting because it shows the possibilities inherent in these elementary responses—usually these are not realized before the level of non-graphic collections.

Technique II also involved materials suggested by a village, but we now introduced three phases: (a) free preliminary handling of the objects,[1] then (b) classification of the "same" elements on to separate sheets of paper and finally (c) (by reducing the number of sheets) forcing the subject to unite the small collections. The conclusions arrived at in the last paragraph were confirmed. The interest of going on from a classification on several sheets of paper (b) to more extensive collections (c) is that phase (b) enables the child to show how far he can identify

[1] Phase 1 was only used with a special group of subjects.

the "same" elements by pairing them together on separate sheets, while at phase (c) he can either construct non-graphic collections, i.e., go on to stage II, or, if he remains at the level of stage I, he is bound to combine the objects in terms of concrete situations. Little by little we see him sliding over from the similarity relations used at phase (b) to those of belonging.

SAN (4; 2) starts in the usual way with partial or continued alignments. The sheets are introduced: (A) three trees including a fir-tree. "Are they alike?— *Yes, the same.*" (He adds a house)—"Are all those alike?—*Trees and a house.*— Are they all the same?—*Yes.*" (B) "What are you going to put?—*Two gentlemen and two ladies* (but he goes on to add two babies, a cradle and a wagon):— Are they all the same?—. . . . —I want them to be all the same.—(He takes the wagon away and puts it on sheet C with some trees, then he puts a house on it with the ladies and gentlemen!)—Is this pink house the same as the ladies?—(He changes the pink house for a red one).—Why do you put that there?—*There are some men in the house.*—Try keeping them the same.—(He puts the two houses together, but on sheet B. Then he picks up the fence.)— What will you put it with?—*With the trees.*—I want it to be with things that are the same.—(He takes the two fences and then puts them back with the trees. Then he takes a small horse).—Where are you going to put it?—*On its own.*—Is there nothing like it?—(He put it with the rabbits): *Because he's all alone, he doesn't like being alone.*" He then puts a flower on the sheet with the women and houses "*because that looks pretty*". And so it goes on. Later, of course, San can only put his small collections together by forming situational complex objects, since even the initial collections are a mixture of belonging and similarities. He will not allow the experimenter to make a class of all the vegetables (trees and flowers): "*No that's not right, it's prettier this way* (the way he had it originally)."

HES (4; 9), on the other hand, first puts only one object on each sheet. He is reminded that each sheet must have "all the things which are the same". He then groups them correctly by forming pairs of similar objects, but also introducing a few relations of belonging, such as the baby and the fountain, a fence with the fir-trees and the wagon with the horses. Finally, when he has to put the collections together, he continues with relations of belonging (the fountain with the fir-trees; the mother, the babies and the fences, etc.). He, too, refuses more general classes such as that of animals (rabbits and horses), because rabbits "*eat grass.*—And horses?—*They don't eat grass!*".

TAHI (5; 2), is first shown the material without sheets of paper and with no two objects exactly alike; he begins by aligning all the elements, leaving small spaces between segments of the "same things": a fir-tree and a tree, (space) a large horse and (after some hesitation) a rabbit, which he then puts a little further away in order to put a small horse in its place, (space) men, (space) a fence, the wheelbarrow with a flower in it (space), a cradle and a baby, etc. When the collections have to be brought together, he joins the animals to form a single alignment, then "*a little boy, a gentleman and a grandfather*", next, "*a lady and a lady, a grandfather, a musician* (= the policeman), *a baby and a cradle*", the flowers and the fountain, etc.

(1) When asked to classify the objects by placing them on separate sheets, children will either, like San, introduce relations of belonging mixed with those of similarity, or else take up a rigid attitude to the word "same", like Hes, who ends by putting one element only on each sheet.

(2) With the same general instructions, but without the sheets of paper, the usual alignments are found once more, often, as in Tahi's case, with confusions of similarity and belonging. The spaces between segments in his continued alignment are an unusual feature.

(3) Finally, when the collections have to be put together on fewer sheets of paper, the intrusion of belonging is more pronounced. Moreover, children refuse to accept more general classes based on similarity alone.

This control study parallels that described in §3 in relation to geometrical shapes, and the results obtained are practically identical. Whatever the material, the relation of similarity is dominant so long as the process is one of successive assimilation—but even here there may be instances of situational or representational belonging. On the other hand, no sooner does the subject cease to concentrate on the act of association in order to consider its result, than it is the graphic and representational properties which take over. The only difference is that instead of complex geometrical objects, we now find complex representational objects. In other words, because of the nature of the materials, functional belonging of the type baby + cradle, takes the place of perceptual belonging— e.g. triangle + square (although even this may at times include a representational meaning: house and roof).

5. CONCLUSION: GRAPHIC COLLECTIONS AS A FIRST ATTEMPT TO SYNTHESIZE INTENSION AND EXTENSION

The above account represents no more than a fraction of the work that went into our attempt to unravel all the features of graphic collections. But the main characteristics of these should now be apparent, and will help to clarify the further development of classificatory behaviour in young children.

We may recall that a system of logical classes involves a set of similarity and difference relations which, together, yield an intensional definition of every class and sub-class: (predicates such as "green" or "solid" are never absolute and invariably point to relations of similarity: "co-green" or "co-solid"). On the other hand, the elements or individuals qualified by these relations are quantified by means of extensive quantifiers "all", "some" (including "one") and "none". It is important to note that the intension of each class uniquely determines its extension. Thus intension and extension are always in correspondence, so that whenever one is known the other can be determined.

But at the level of graphic collections things are very different.

There is no question that children are perfectly well able to discover relations of similarity and difference by a process of successive assimilation. Nevertheless they are unable to avoid occasional lapses in the course of which other forms of association are substituted for the relation of similarity. In particular they are constantly misled by considerations of pattern or by the situational and descriptive properties of the material. Even more significant is the fact that because these assimilations are only successive, they cannot quantify their result. In other words the successive character of the assimilation is such as to prevent it from generating extensive relations. They cannot unite "all" the elements having a common property (similarity) to form a simultaneous whole (still less can they focus on "some" as a sub-class). The question is, therefore, what is it that determines extension at this level?

What children do is to allow themselves to be guided by what they can perceive. As a result they use spatial configurations like alignments and two- or three-dimensional collective and complex objects. It is at this point that the essential inadequacy of successive assimilation produces those features which go to define the graphic collection. The subject is unable to co-ordinate intension and extension because assimilations which are successive cannot give rise to operational quantifiers such as "all" and "some". And so we find him oscillating between extension and intension. Because they are unco-ordinated there is no perfect correspondence between them (as there is in the case of true logical classes). What is more, the two are undifferentiated so that the oscillation is unconscious. Such lack of differentiation was present to a lesser degree in the course of the initial associations, but it is considerably reinforced by the need to take a view of the whole. At one point a child will put "the same" elements together, so that intension determines extension as happens later in the logical classification; but he sometimes adds an element to a collection merely to complete the shape which it suggests: here it is the extension achieved so far which determines the action; in other words, extension determines the intension. This can happen in one of two ways: either the geometrical shape of the collection influences behaviour, so that an element will be added to others in order to complete the shape of the set as a whole, without there being any common similarity linking all its elements (geometrical complex object); or else, when representational objects are used, an element will be added to others to make up a coherent situation. In the latter case similarity is replaced by a relation of belonging drawn from the subject's past experience. However, the two forms are equivalent because in neither case do we find extension being determined by similarities and differences. Instead, the extension of the collection depends on its shape as a whole. It is therefore an indeterminate and arbitrary extension which frequently decides the intensive relations involved.

Thus both extension and intension exist in embryo, but they are neither fully differentiated nor completely co-ordinated with one another. However, there is a second lack of differentiation which is partly independent of the first, but which constantly interferes with it: lack of differentiation of the logical (or pre-logical) structures characteristic of discontinuous sets from the sub-logical (or pre-sub-logical) structures characterizing the subdivision of a continuous whole. It is partly independent because from the sensori-motor level onwards, children can be expected to be as familiar with the handling of discrete collections (piles, etc.) as they are with objects whose parts can be dissociated and reassembled. So it is that under the influence of perceptual configurations, they attribute shapes to discontinuous collections just as they do to continuous objects. Herein lies an initial reason for the lack of differentiation which continues through the present stage. For there can only be one way of clearly differentiating a collection of discrete objects from continuous wholes, and this is to impose some kind of stable structure on it which is quite independent of its disposition in space. In order to achieve such a structure the subject must first arrive at a clear differentiation between extension and intension, and, second, he must co-ordinate the two. Thus lack of differentiation between extension and intension is itself partly caused by a similar confusion between what is logical and what is sub-logical, but, at the same time, it helps to maintain that confusion. In other words the two failures in differentiation tend to sustain one another, yet they are not identical.

This somewhat complex situation is what leads to the kind of behaviour described in this chapter. The interpretation we have given will be further corroborated when we go into studying the difficulties which have to be overcome at stage II in order to make up non-graphic (i.e. pre-logical) collections. The difficulties of co-ordinating extension and intension become more apparent than ever. Indeed these latter are not overcome until stage III, and their solution evidently demands the elaboration of a proper operational structure based on class-inclusion.

Chapter Two

NON-GRAPHIC COLLECTIONS[1]

BETWEEN the first stage characterized by graphic collections and the third stage, that of hierarchical classification based on logical operations, we find a second stage in which the characteristic response is the non-graphic collection. We use the term "collection" rather than "class" in the strict sense, because the former term carries no implication of a hierarchical structure of class-inclusions. However, these collections are no longer graphic, and objects are assigned to one collection or another on the basis of similarity alone. Nevertheless, these several collections are simply juxtaposed, instead of being used as the basis of a hierarchical class structure. As we saw in ch. I, non-graphic collections are already foreshadowed in the successive associations of stage I, since very often they engender a series of similar objects, i.e. a non-graphic collection *in posse*. But it is unusual at this stage to find the similarity being respected when the subject turns to a consideration of the collection as such. During the course of stage II, non-graphic collections become more and more the rule, and it is important to see why. Anticipating the results and their discussion, we shall simply note that their growing predominance is largely due to an increasing differentiation of intension and extension, and hence a greater co-ordination of the two. We can hardly attempt a complete analysis of the process involved without first considering the quantitative relations to which it gives rise, and this forms the chief topic of ch. III, where we shall be studying the question of how children eventually come to differentiate "all" and "some". For the present, we will have to confine our account to a broad general description of the way in which classifications are evolved.

1. STATEMENT OF THE PROBLEM: CRITERIA OF AN ADDITIVE CLASSIFICATORY STRUCTURE[2]

The reaction characteristic of this stage may be described as a quasi-classification, as distinct from those of the preceding stage, which could hardly be said to amount to more than a pre-classificatory or a para-classificatory form of behaviour. But it is also very different from the true logical classification of stage III. The criteria of such a classification

---

[1] With the collaboration of Vinh-Bang, G. Noelting and S. Taponier.
[2] Additive as opposed to multiplicative classifications (see ch. VI).

form an essential prerequisite to an understanding of its development Now these criteria cannot be decided on wholly *a priori*; they are norms of reasoning to which the subject himself conforms as soon as he has mastered reversible operations and applies them to problems of classification. From this point of view, the characteristics of classification appear to be the following:

(1) There are no isolated elements, i.e. elements not belonging to a class. This amounts to saying that all the elements must be classified, and that, if an element (x) is the only one of its kind, it must give rise to its own specific (but singular) class: (x) ε (A_x).

(2) There are no isolated classes, i.e. every specific class A characterized by the property a, implies its complement A' (characterized by not-a)[1] within the closest genus B $(A + A' = B)$.

(3) A class A includes all the individuals having the property a.

(4) A class A includes only individuals having the property a.

(5) All classes of the same rank are disjoint: $A \times A' = O$ or $An \times Am = O$.

(6) A complementary class A' has its own characteristics a_x (thus $A' = A_x$), which are not possessed by its complement A: the individuals having the property a are thus not-A_x, just as individuals having the property a_x are not-a.

(7) A class A (or A') is included in every higher ranking class which contains all its elements, starting with the closest, B: $A = B - A'$ (or $A' = B - A$) and $A \times B = A$, which amounts to saying that "all" A are "some" B.

(8) Extensional simplicity: the inclusions in (7) are reduced to the *minimum* compatible with the intensional properties.[2]

(9) Intensional simplicity: similar criteria (e.g. colours) distinguish classes of the same *rank*.

(10) Symmetrical subdivision: if a class B_1 is subdivided into A_1 and A'_1 and the same criterion is applicable to B_2, then B_2 must likewise be subdivided into A_2 and A'_2.

This table allows us to distinguish stage II from stages I and III. We notice immediately that none of these properties is universally present at stage I, not even the first two. Children who are busy making graphic collections, do not feel in any way compelled to use all the elements (7) nor do they feel it incumbent on them to form several

---

[1] "Not-a" is a difference relation characteristic of a complementary class A', and shared by all the elements of a higher-ranking class B not included in a given class A (over and above the similarity b common to members of A and those of A'). Thus a might be the property of having a particular father and b the property of having a particular grandfather; first cousins would all share the negative property *not-a* to distinguish them from brothers, who are also b. (See *Traité de Logique*.)

[2] "To make the fewest possible piles", as one subject said, aged 5; 11.

collections (2). They may well construct a single complex object only, neglecting some elements (which are therefore unclassed). This complex object need not inspire the construction of another (as the construction of a class implies its complementary by way of negation, 2). Even a "collective object" which contains only elements with the same property a (cf. 4) does not necessarily contain them all (cf. 3). Moreover, the collective object is never the sole principle of classification for any one subject: complex objects which are almost always observed alongside the collective object, do not satisfy condition 4. As for properties 5 to 10—these have no meaning for subjects at stage I.

On the other hand, the non-graphic collections which characterize stage II do have some of the properties in the table (which is why the table is given now). But they do not have them all, and it is this which allows us to distinguish between stages II and III. Generally speaking, there is a steady growth in the extent to which each of these properties is recognized in the course of stage II; but there is also one very important exception: there is no inclusion (cf. 7).

As the following results testify, children at stage II understand the need to class all the elements which they are given (cf. 1); they invariably divide them into two collections or more (cf. 2); each of these contains all the elements of a kind (3) and no others (4). Not infrequently, there is a partial complementarity (cf. 2 and 6); collections of the same rank are disjoint (5); finally, there may be an attempt to find simplifications (8 and 9) and symmetries (10). Yet that which distinguishes the non-graphic collections of stage II from classes in the strict sense always remains the fact that there are no class-inclusions (7).

We must first of all find a psychological criterion of class-inclusion based on the actual course of mental development shown in children's behaviour, as opposed to an *a priori* criterion based on logical analysis. Let us suppose that a particular child classes squares (B) and circles (B') in two separate boxes; next he divides the squares B into red ones (A) on the left and blue ones (A') on the right; he then goes on to do the same with the circles. He is applying properties 1 to 6 and 8 to 10. But is he also applying property 7? It certainly looks that way: judging by the criteria of adult logic (or those of stage III), we should say that the fact that he has constructed collections having the structure $A + A' = B$ (and $A_2 + A_2' = B'$ or B_2), is sufficient proof that this child thinks of the red squares (A) and the blue ones (A') as subcollections "included" in the class of squares. Nevertheless we shall assume that this is not necessarily the case: we will draw a distinction between the subdivision of collections and class-inclusion in the strict sense, even if the distinction is not always easy.

The essential difference is that, in the case of true inclusion, B, the larger class does not exist only when its constituent parts, $A + A'$, are actually united (whether in the shape of a spatial collection or by means of an intuitive "bond"[1]). It continues to encompass them, and it conserves its identity, even when these are dissociated. In other words, the subject is able to reason in the form $A = B - A'$. On the other hand, the essential characteristic of a collection as distinct from a class is that it exists by virtue of the union of its elements in space, and ceases to exist when its sub-collections are dissociated. It follows that, so long as the sub-collections are united in the form $A + A'$, the subject does connect them with the whole, B $(A + A' = B)$; but once they are dissociated, be it in space or even in thought, he no longer connects the sub-collections with the whole collection: in other words, the operation $A = B - A'$ is beyond him. An operation being, by definition, reversible, we conclude that, since there is no inverse operation, $A = B - A'$, the union $A + A' = B$ cannot be a direct operation at stage II, however much it may resemble one. It is in fact no more than an intuitive union because it is contingent upon a temporary differentiation of the collection B into the sub-collections A and A'.

Obviously it cannot always be easy to decide whether or not there is inclusion in this sense, simply by looking at the way in which a subject structures a varied set of objects into collections and sub-collections. It is quite possible to find one who constructs a fairly subtle hierarchy and is still unable to reason in the inverse direction, $A = B - A'$. That is why the findings of the present chapter are not intended to provide conclusive evidence in their own right. These data need to be compared with the control experiments reported in chs. III and IV. Ch. III deals with the way in which children handle the key concepts "all" and "some" (criterion 7, p. 48). Even without destroying the union $B = A + A'$, we shall say that a child understands inclusion if he is capable of grasping that "all" the A are "some" of the B, while we do not have inclusion if the child understands the statement "All the A are B (or are b)" (for instance, all the circles are blue) as being equivalent to "All the A are all the B". (Thus a child will deny that all the circles are blue "because there are also blue squares".) The basic technique of ch. IV consists in presenting the child with a collection of items, B, made up of two sub-collections, A and A', such that $A > A'$ (i.e. there are more A than A'), and asking whether there are "more of A" or "more of B". Where there is no class-inclusion, children inevitably reply that there are more A than B, (i.e. the part is greater than the whole). The fact that A and A' are dissociated in imagination destroys the whole, B; and B is then reduced to A'.

[1] E.g., the imaginary bunches of flowers in ch. IV, or the imaginary necklaces of *The Child's Conception of Number*, 1952. (E.A.L.)

2. NON-GRAPHIC COLLECTIONS AS SEEN WITH GEOMETRICAL SHAPES

These are the reactions that follow genetically on the graphic collections described in ch. 1, §§2 and 3. But the transition is not abrupt, for non-graphic collections are still subordinate to the principle of spatial proximity between elements, even though they are free of the condition of a definite aggregate shape (as opposed to a mere "heap"). We therefore find all kinds of behaviour which shade between "partitive membership", characteristic of graphic collections, and class- (or pre-class-) membership, being a relation of belonging which subsists between an element and a collection independently of form. (We recall that such membership is not an inclusion, because, by definition, membership is always a relation between an element x and a collection or class, A, of the form $(x) \varepsilon (A)$, while an inclusion is a relation between one class, A, and another class, B, and is written $A < B$.)

We start with a number of transitional cases, the first few of which feature a sort of segmented collection which has not entirely shed the graphic characteristics of an alignment.

RAPH (4; 9) starts with two superposed alignments, each containing triangles, squares and semi-circles. The lower alignment is symmetrical: there are squares in the middle, with triangles to left and right, and up-ended semi-circles at each end constituting a neat closure. Afterwards Raph groups all the semi-circles together (out of both alignments); all the triangles (half superposed: "*That, that's a staircase*"); and all the squares (in a row: "*That, that's my name*"). His solution is half-way between a set of "collective objects" and a number of non-graphic collections. Both are homogeneous but the collective object is graphic, while the non-graphic collection is not.

WAL (4; 10) starts with a large continued alignment featuring a number of redundancies, but goes on to eliminate them. By way of example, he moves all the blue squares from one end and joins them to those at the other end, and so on.

SIM (5; 3), like Raph, builds up two alignments one above the other; here, the upper one is entirely blue and the lower entirely red. The two rows are carefully matched: two blue squares face two red squares, two blue circles face two red circles, etc.

The second transitional form substitutes a number of small collections for collective and complex objects. The graphic arrangement begins to drop out, and the elements of a collection are usually all of a kind. Sometimes this sort of response is spontaneous, but not infrequently it is helped by the form of the instruction ("Put all the same things together"). Similarly, the level of response depends a good deal on whether the collections are exhaustive, both individually and taken as a whole.

DAN (4; 5): "You try putting these things in order properly." (The objects are geometrical shapes and coloured letters.) She begins with a general alignment, starting with letters, and passing from *p* s to small circles, then rectangles, squares, and finally large circles. "Can you do it even more properly?" She breaks up her alignment by separating these segments. Each of these is now made the basis of a separate oblique alignment, of which there are seven in all: (1) letters of different kinds, (2) *p* s, (3) small circles, (4) rectangles, (5) one capital *F*, (6) squares and (7) large circles. "Now try putting together those which are really the same:" three horizontal rows (a) letters without the *p* s; (b) the *p* s; (c) circles, rectangles and squares.

PAT (4; 8) (whose reactions at 4; 0 and 4; 5 were reported in ch. I §2), to "arrange the things properly, with all the same things together", constructs five alignments on the basis of colour: (1) yellow elements (letters and squares), (2) a single white rectangle ("*I'm going to put this one all by himself because there aren't any others the same*"), (3) green elements (letters and a rectangle), (4) blue elements (letters, squares and rectangles) and (5) red ones (circles and letters).

CUR (5; 2), to "arrange the things properly", constructs 12 small collections, of which one is a complex object but all the others are either mere "lots" or else short alignments. Although no element is omitted, the basis of classification is a shifting one: blue objects occur in two different collections, as also do yellow objects and rectangles.

ZIM (5; 9), using the material of ch. I, §3, and told to "put the same things together", immediately takes the rings one at a time ("*That's a ring*", "*Another ring*", etc.) and piles them all in one lot (with no shape). Then he puts the triangles over the squares, "*That's a house*", and so on. Finally, he puts all the semi-circles together, calling them "*boats*". This yields two non-graphic collections (a "lot" of rings and a "lot" of "boats") together with a third collection made up of complex objects!

ENG (4; 4), although younger, starts with complex objects when given the same materials, and ends with three non-graphic collections. Even when the instruction is merely to "arrange these things properly", he divides them up into (1) squares, (2) rings, arcs and semi-circles, and (3) triangles.

There are innumerable examples of this kind of intermediate reaction between 4; 6 and 5; 6, with transitions from alignments to segmented collections, or from collective and complex objects to small collections juxtaposed. We could quote hundreds of cases covering all the possible combinations. Nevertheless, these few examples sufficiently illustrate the two conclusions given below. For whatever the materials and whatever the instructions, we always find: (a) transitions from graphic collections to non-graphic collections, (b) partial reversions from the latter to the former, and (c) mixtures of the two.

(1) These facts confirm the hypothesis that graphic collections constitute an elementary form of classification. The crucial consideration is that non-graphic collections are a direct lineal development out of

graphic collections, as is evident from the existence of a complete spectrum of transitional behaviour.

(2) There is no sudden leap from graphic collections to classification. The non-graphic collection itself is not a true classification. Its appearance points to the fact that the principle of similarity and difference tends, in time, to prevail over that of shape or belonging. But like the graphic collection, the non-graphic collection is bound by the condition of spatial proximity. That is why it is a "collection" and not a class. This condition constitutes a limiting factor throughout stage II, because it cannot be outgrown until there is some alternative to proximity to provide a cohesive bond between the elements in a whole. The structure of class-inclusion is such an alternative, but it depends on the clear differentiation of "all" and "some" which is not elaborated before stage III.

We may now go on to give a number of examples of pre-logical collections which are entirely non-graphic. The most elementary forms are mere juxtapositions which are not even exhaustive. The most advanced forms are so differentiated and hierarchized as to resemble class-inclusions:

(1) The simplest type consists of a number of small collections based on different criteria, together with an unclassified heterogeneous remainder.

JUD (5; 7) makes up six collections: 5 rectangles, 4 squares, 3 letters a, 3 letters of the same colour (m,p,t), 4 large circles and one small one. But he leaves a residue of various letters with different colours.

PIC (5; 6): 3 rectangles, 5 squares, 4 as and an n, 5 ds, 4 large circles, and a residue formed of various letters and a small circle. There is an n in the residue as well as the n in the third collection.

(2) At a slightly higher level, we may find small collections still based on a multiplicity of criteria, but without remainder and without overlap.

FON (5; 6) constructs nine collections: the circles, the squares, the rectangles, the ns, the as and bs, an x, the ps, a g and $m + t$.

MAR (5; 7): eight collections of the same kind.

(3) The next development consists in eliminating the fluctuations of criterion, without losing the gains of (2).

PAT (4; 8), whose earlier responses were intermediate (see p. 52), ends with five collections based on colour.

ONE (4; 6) starts by classing the materials (those of ch. I, §3) in four boxes by colour: blue, yellow, red and green. He then takes three boxes and puts all the squares and triangles in one, and all the circles, arcs, semi-circles, etc., in another, leaving the third box empty.

BEC (4; 8) has the same materials. His instructions are: "Put these things in the boxes to make them right": (a) squares, (b) circles, (c) sectors and (d) triangles. Given additional items, he puts the squares in (a), the arcs and small circles in (b), the rings in (c), and the semi-circles, sectors and triangles in (d).

JAC (5; 11) starts with six collections, and then reduces them by making colour the sole criterion.

(4) Finally, the most highly developed type consists in starting as in (3) but then proceeding to internal differentiations of a lower rank.

PIB (5; 10) starts with a juxtaposition of small piles. When given three boxes, he puts the circles, sectors, arcs and triangles in (a), the squares arranged in three collections of similar elements in (b), and the rings, semi-circles and circles in (c). After a series of tentative efforts, he succeeds in introducing a dichotomy: (a) all curvilinear elements, with sub-collections (the rings are separate, etc.) and (b) all the rectilinear elements with two sub-collections: the squares arranged in three pyramids, and the triangles all stacked together.

GIL (6; 4) constructs three collections: (a) all the letters except for p and q, (b) all the ps and qs, (c) geometrical shapes. The last of these is divided so as to form three stacks containing squares, rectangles and circles respectively.

KER (6; 4) starts with thirteen piles, of which one is an enclosure made up of all the squares. After a number of tentative attempts, he ends with two boxes, one containing all the rectilinear forms (with the squares and the triangles both separated from the rest), and the other containing all the curvilinear forms, these being further subdivided into circles, sectors, etc. There is one stray triangle among the sectors.

These subjects are forming three or even two large collections, and then dividing these into sub-collections. This amounts to a pre-operation of the form $(B_1 = A_1 + A_1') + (B_2 = A_2 + A_2')$. It is therefore reminiscent of the direct operation in the additive grouping of classes. Nevertheless it cannot be equated with that operation since the inverse operation, $A = B - A'$, is still absent. As we pointed out earlier, the true criteria by which we can distinguish such pre-operations from true classification are the ability of the subject to appreciate the relations of "all" and "some", and his power to reason correctly that $A < B$ (see chs. III and IV). Nevertheless the way in which children react in the present experimental conditions can often provide us with a fair indication as to whether they are classifying the material hierarchically or whether they are simply making up a number of collections and sub-collections. The following three cases show how children approach the situation at stage III:

BAER (7; 11), given materials consisting of geometrical shapes and letters, begins by putting the former on one side and the latter on the other. Then he subdivides the letters into five sub-classes: the bs, the as, the ds, the ns and mtx. Geometrical shapes are then divided into rectangles, squares and circles.

CHEN (8; 6) with the same materials, makes up three large classes: the rectangles and squares (forming two sub-classes), the circles (subdivided into large and small) and the letters (subdivided according to the different kinds).

Rob (8; 2), given the materials of ch. I §3, starts with four classes: (a) the circles, semi-circles and sectors, (b) the triangles, (c) the squares and (d) the rings. Then he unites (b) and (c), saying "*all the squares and triangles*", (i.e. rectilinear shapes, but he keeps them separate in the one box) and (a) and (d), "*all the rounds*" (= curvilinear forms) which are also subdivided according to variety.

There is no doubt that the transition from graphic collections to non-graphic collections and the subsequent elaboration of the latter is a very gradual process, so that the kind of behaviour proper to stage III is itself no more than the final term in a continuous development. Is the distinction between the type 4 collections of stage II and those of Baer, Chen and Rob (which we call classes) purely artificial?

Even though the only decisive criterion is that of quantification (chs. III and IV) there is still a relative discontinuity in the development outlined above. At stage II each component of the total response is a reaction to an immediate and partial problem: there is no over-all plan to begin with. So much is obvious enough in the type 1 response, when criteria are unstable and collections do not exhaust the elements. However it is not long before subjects are able to revise their criteria and to use up all the objects (type 2). At first this is no more than a series of groping attacks aided by hindsight (retroaction). But these in turn lead to partial anticipations occurring in the course of the behaviour itself. So it is we find a principal criterion tends to emerge (type 3), and later still, the collections so arrived at may be further subdivided (type 4).

Thus the advances made during stage II can be thought of in terms of retroaction and anticipation. In other words, they are a part of the gradual adjustment proper to all trial-and-error behaviour. It is only by trial-and-error that subjects like Pib (5; 11) and Ker (6; 4) finally arrive at an overall dichotomy of the material. But although anticipation is partial at first and no more than a by-product of hindsight, the natural line of its development ensures that in due course it will appear right from the start. It is then that adjustments cease to be successive and take on the character of logical transformations. That is why we feel entitled to speak of a relative discontinuity. Every one of the three subjects cited on the previous page forms a plan before he starts (or very soon after); what is more the plan enables them to pass freely from whole to part and vice versa. In other words their behaviour has the mobility to combine an upward process (uniting) and a downward process (subdividing). In fact, these three subjects differ from all the preceding ones because they have a plan. We may therefore state as our hypothesis (which will be developed in the sequel) that the inclusion of classes depends on an anticipatory schema (the same schema as that which underlies the transition from the direct operation $B = A + A'$ to its inverse $A = B - A'$, so that the latter ceases to be a contingent result of hindsight and becomes a necessary inverse operation). We believe that such a schema is essential, not only for reversibility, but also for the use of "all" and "some" and for the understanding of quantitative relations of the form $B > A$. In terms of this hypothesis, subjects at stage II remain at the level of non-graphic collections (even when these are differentiated). Because they lack such an anticipatory schema the mechanism of class-inclusion is still beyond them.

3. NON-GRAPHIC COLLECTIONS AS SEEN WITH ARBITRARY OBJECTS

The development of behaviour in this sort of situation is very similar when representative objects are used instead of geometrical shapes. Hence our account will be rather briefer than was necessary in ch. I, §4.

Once again the first few examples are transitional. If we bear in mind that with this kind of material it is situational belonging instead of patterns that determines the character of complex objects, we find a similar tendency for children to start with complex objects and gradually revise their conception until eventually similarity and difference become the sole criteria of grouping.

ELI (5; 6) begins by constructing a number of complex objects, but these are already based partly on similarity: three men; a negro, a little girl, a pig and a crow. He has various stories to explain why the elements are being put together in this way (but similarities of form and colour undoubtedly play a part). However, he then goes on to make collections based on similarity alone: the fish with the birds, etc. "*because they're all animals*", then the people, then pots, etc. "*because they're all things for making supper*".

VIV (6; 6) starts like Eli: a stool with a baby on it + a saucepan + a small chair + a basin + a fish, etc.: "*The bench is for the baby to sit on, the saucepan is for making his supper, the basin is for washing him, the fish is for him to play with and the little chair is for putting things on*:—Can you arrange them differently?—*Yes* (she puts the animals together with the man, and then takes him away): *Like that, they're all animals.*" Then she puts all the kitchenware together, etc. But a number of objects are left near the baby because they "belong".

GIN (5; 6), using the village material, begins with a continued alignment containing all the objects, with segments differentiated by similarity. She is then given five sheets of paper on which to "arrange things properly". Gin starts with small collections: (1) the houses and the men, but she takes these away: "*No, they have legs, and houses don't have legs*"; (2) two men; (3) two women; (4) the babies; (5) the cradles. She asks for more sheets of paper, but these are refused. So she puts the men with the babies "*because those have two legs*"; then the women "*with the prams*"—Do those go well together?—"*No* (she puts them with the men and the babies). *They all have two legs.*" She puts the fir-trees with other trees, but explains "*Those are fir-trees. They aren't the same: there are some which are bent* (tapered?) *and others which are round.*" Then: "*Here they're all animals.*"

Here we find much the same mixture as in the previous section, and the interpretation is identical. The only difference is that the influence of situational belonging is often harder to shake off than that of pattern. From what we know of the persistence of definition by use (see ch. I, §4), this is hardly surprising.

Passing to the stage of non-graphic collections proper, we find the same four types of solution as we did with geometrical shapes. However, there is no need to exemplify them in detail and the examples below merely illustrate the trend from juxtaposed collections to quasi-hierarchical grouping:

Mon (5; 3) starts with all the furniture. "Will you put anything else with them?—*No.*—Go on.—(He puts people, babies and a monkey together, and then makes a third collection of pots and pans.)—What about these (the monkey and the men), do they go together?—*Yes, it's a joke.*—What if you weren't joking?—*Then it goes with the animals.*"

Ed (5; 6) rapidly constructs the same four collections and explains: "*These* (1) *are all little men; those* (2) *are all for sitting on; those* (3) *are all for pouring into* (= vessels) *and those* (4) *are all animals.*—Very good. Can you arrange them again in another way?—*Yes, these* (a pile) *are all of wood, and those* . . . (all the rest)."

Van (6; 3), given elements consisting of 15 people, starts with 8 small juxtaposed classes: (1) two boys going to school; (2) two little girls; (3) two women; (4) two men; (5) a little brother and sister, etc. Try making four lots: (1) a policeman, a man in a dress-suit and three women; (2) a clown; (3) three boys with school bags and four girls; (4) a skier, a boy running and another one playing with a kite. "Now make two lots": (1) the boys and girls, (2) all the rest. "Could you do it differently?—*Yes, I could put all the gentlemen and the boys together, and all the girls and the ladies together.*" Van then constructs these two collections, subdividing each into adults and children.

Bac (6; 5) is given people, animals, plants, buildings and vehicles. "What could we put together so that they're alike?—*All the gentlemen, all the cars* . . . *I'm going to put the houses in another lot* (*the church doesn't go there because it isn't a house*), *then we can have flowers, trees, prams, animals.*" He continues in this way to form small collections, even distinguishing "*birds*" from "*animals*". Each lot is placed in a separate bag. Afterwards the experimenter gives him larger bags in which the first ones can be brought together. Bac groups adults and children under the heading "*people*", then chickens with animals "*because chickens are also animals*", then fir-trees and trees, to which he adds flowers "*because a tree is also a thing like the flowers* . . . *plants which grow*", and then "*the cars with the prams because they're things which roll*".

Cla (7; 0). Like Bac, first juxtaposition and then reduction: two cars, an engine and two prams "*because they all roll*"; two horses, two owls and two chickens[1] "*because they're all animals.*—If you wanted to write what there is

---

[1] We should explain that these are small wooden toys and not pictures.

inside, what word would you use?—*Six animals* . . . (she hesitates whether to write 'six chickens', but decides not to) *because they're all animals and because there aren't six chickens.*—Are there more animals or more chickens?—*More animals, because* . . . *no! more chickens!*—Why?—*Because there are three birds* (forgetting an owl), *yes that one too* (i.e. four)—Then are there more chickens or more animals?—*More chickens.*"

On the whole, the development of collections containing representative objects is exactly the same as that of collections made up of geometrical shapes. The process consists of starting with a large number of small juxtaposed collections, and gradually grouping them together through a series of comparisons involving both retroaction and partial anticipation, until one obtains a few large collections differentiated into sub-collections (cf. Van, Bac and Cla). Very striking in these progressive reductions is the increasingly frequent use of the quantifier "all" (cf. Ed, Van, Bac at the beginning, and Cla with cars and particularly with animals). Clearly enough, as children come to differentiate a collection of objects and to organize a large number of small "lots" into two or three larger ones, so they achieve a greater co-ordination of intension and extension. More particularly is this so when the large collections are further subdivided, so that the smaller ones are not lost in the process of reduction. Hence the use of the word "all" when constructing the larger collections.

Once again we may ask whether differentiated collections of this kind do not already constitute true classes, so that the dividing line between stages II and III is artificial. The example of Cla is highly instructive and the questions and answers lead naturally to the problems raised in chs. III and IV. What they show is that the use of the word "all" does not necessarily imply that the subject appreciates the quantitative relation between a sub-collection A and the total collection B. Twice Cla declares that horses, owls and chickens are "all animals", and that two horses, two owls and two chickens make "six animals" and not six chickens; yet she still concludes that there are more chickens than animals in this collection of six animals: because there are four birds. The next two chapters deal with the reasons underlying this type of error, and the way in which the appropriate relations are eventually mastered.

Chapter Three

"ALL" AND "SOME":
CONDITIONS OF CLASS-INCLUSION[1]

ALL that we have seen so far suggests that the key problem which arises in the construction of classes is that of co-ordinating extension and intension. In order to tackle this question directly we tried to devise experiments bearing directly on the problem of class-inclusion, i.e. the fundamental extensive relation which subsists as between a subclass (= "some") and an enveloping class (= "all"), where both are fully determined by a number of intensive relations or qualities.

The key question is what Hamilton, the logician, calls the quantification of the predicate. Psychologically speaking, this can only be resolved by the co-ordination of intension and extension (which ensures the quantification of the term to which the predicate applies). It is this co-ordination which subjects seemed to lack at stage II. According to Hamilton, "All the *X* are *y*" signifies "All the *X* are some of the *Y*", i.e. the class of *X*s is included (in extension) in that of *Y*s qualified by *y*. If we can translate this abstract relation into concrete terms suitable for children of 4 to 7–8, we should be in a position to see whether the problems it raises are sufficient to account for the fact that children find so much difficulty in proceeding from juxtaposed pre-logical collections to hierarchical constructions. Various methods were tried. Anticipating the results which follow, we may say that they confirm the hypothesis. In spite of the somewhat abstruse nature of the problem as presented here, the basic technique is simply to ask the subject whether "all the *X* are *y*". As an example, we may have a collection made up of blue circles and blue squares with a number of red squares thrown in: we then ask children whether all the circles are blue. Their answers show clearly enough that their quantification of the predicate is false. The "all" which belongs to the subject—circles—is assimilated to the predicate—blue. Here we have direct confirmation of our hypothesis: if children have difficulty with class-inclusion, it is because they find it difficult to adjust their use of "all" and "some" to the intensive properties of the elements to which these quantifiers are being applied.

---

[1] With the collaboration of A. Etienne, B. Matalon, A. Morf, H. Niedorf and S. Taponier.

1. "ALL" AND "SOME" APPLIED TO SHAPES AND COLOURS[1]

The child is presented with a series (I) of 8 to 21 counters consisting of red squares and blue circles; more often a few blue squares are added, thus giving series II (see Fig. 7). Several kinds of question may then be put. With the rows directly in front of him, the subject may be asked for a series of judgments: "Are all the squares red?", "Are all the circles blue?", etc. In order to see whether the subject's reply involves his power of representation and is more than a matter of perception (reading off

Figure 7.

what he can see in front of him), he can be asked to answer the same questions from memory. In this case, he is first shown the row and the experimenter then conceals it and checks to make sure that he remembers its exact composition. He is therefore told to reproduce the hidden row either by choosing the necessary counters or by indicating how many he would take from each of the four boxes provided (red squares, red circles, blue squares and blue circles). The reproduction of the rows, whether directly or by means of the boxes, still gives no indication of how the child understands inclusion. Success or failure in this part of the experiment tells us nothing about a child's understanding of class-inclusion and quite a number can reproduce the rows correctly although their attempts at classification amounted to no more than the juxtaposition of several small collections. But the answers they give show that even when children can learn the composition of the row by heart, they may still be unable to deal with the questions on "all" and "some". This clinical method was used to begin with and the results are shown in Table I. We went on to a more systematic enquiry involving three stages: (a) direct reproduction, (b) reproduction from memory (yielding results which differed but little from those of (a)), (c) a standardized set of questions. The results of this are shown in Table Ia.

To begin with, here are some examples from stage I, when even series I (blue circles and red squares) is sometimes too difficult:

PIE (5; 0) is shown five blue circles with three red squares. The red squares are scattered in the row: "What boxes do you need to remake this?—*Red circles and blue circles*.[2]—Are you sure?—*Yes*.—What is this?—*One of those*

---

[1] This work was started in 1939–40 with the collaboration of Käthe Wolf during her stay in Geneva.

[2] English children would probably talk about "red round ones" and "blue round ones" but we feel such a translation of *ronds* would put an unnecessary burden on the reader. (E.A.L.)

(red squares).—And this?—*Blue circles.*—Well, look, are all the circles here blue?—*Yes . . . no.*—Why?—*There are red ones.*—Where?—*There are red squares and blue circles.*—Are all the squares red?—*Yes.*"

Series II (three red squares, two blue squares, two blue circles): "Are all the circles blue?—*No, there are only two.*—Are all the squares blue?—*No.*— And all the circles are blue?—*No, there are blue and red ones.*—What are the red ones like?—*Square.*"

TIN (5; 1). Series I: "Which boxes do you need?—*Red squares and blue squares.*—(The two collections are partially separated by moving the blue circles slightly upwards.) And like this?—*Red circles and blue circles.*—(The two collections are now completely separated by putting the five blue circles on the right of the row and the three red squares on the left.) And like this?— *Red squares and blue circles.*—And now (alternated irregularly as before)?— *No.*—Why?—*I don't know. Because there are also blue ones* (= other counters which are blue without being squares!)—And are all the circles blue?—*Yes.* (There is no difficulty, for they form the majority.)—And all the squares are red?—*No!* (confidently)."

IRE (5; 5). Series I: "Are all these squares red?—*I don't know.*—Why?— *There are circles as well.*—But the squares are all red?—*Yes.*—And all the circles are blue?—*Yes.*—(a blue square is added to form the beginning of series II). And are all these squares red?—*No, because there is a blue one.*— And are all the blue ones circles?—*Yes.*"

Here are examples from stage II where the initial difficulties no longer arise (except residually as in the case of Jac, 5; 8):

BAR (5; 0). (The experimenter starts with a row (I) of 6 blue circles and 2 red squares (inserted after the 2nd and 5th circles). After looking at the row, Bar declares that she needs only the boxes containing red squares and blue circles to remake it. She puts aside the other two boxes and reproduces the row correctly. The experimenter goes on to series II, rows made up of 7 blue circles, together with a varying number of red and blue squares, 1 or 2 red, 1 to 5 blue.) Bar remembers the rows exactly every time; she puts aside the box of red squares, keeps the three others, and reproduces the rows correctly. She is asked the following questions about the last two:

(IIA).[1] "Are all the squares red?—*No.*—Why?—*There are red ones and blue ones* (Right)—Are all the blue ones circles?—*No.*—Why?—*There are circles and squares* [which are blue] (right).—Are all the red ones squares?—*Yes, because there were blue squares and red squares* (right).—Are all the circles blue?—*No* (wrong).—Why?—*Because there were* [blue] *squares and circles.*— Are all the squares blue?—*No* (right) *because there were* [blue] *circles and* [blue] *squares.*"

With the last row (IIB): "What did we have?—*Blue circles and red and blue squares* (right).—Are all the circles blue?—*No* (wrong), *because there are* [blue] *squares and circles.*—Are all the blue ones circles?—*No* (right), *because there were* [blue] *squares and circles.*—Are all the red ones squares?—*Yes, because there were only the squares.*—Are all the circles blue?—*No* (wrong), *there were circles and squares* [blue]."

[1] Series IIA and IIB differ only in the number of elements.

VER (5; 7) reproduces the initial row (I) of blue circles and red squares from memory. Two blue squares are then added, and the experiment is continued by direct inspection of row (II) which remains visible throughout: "Are all the circles blue?—*Yes . . . ah! no, because there were blue squares too* (!)—Are all the squares red?—*No.*—Are all the squares blue?—*No, there are red ones too* (right).—Are all the red ones squares?—*Yes* (right)."

BAL (5; 7) correctly reproduces the initial row as well as that containing blue squares. "Are all the squares red?—*No, there were blue ones* (right).—Are all the circles blue? *Yes* (right, but with a false reciprocity).—Are all the blue ones circles?—*Yes* (wrong).—All those which were blue were circles?—*Ah no, there were squares* (right).—Well, what were the squares like?—*Red and blue* (right).—Are all the circles blue?—*No, there were blue squares also* (!)—Are all the circles red?—*No, they were blue* (right).—Are all the red ones squares?—*No, there were blue squares as well* (!)"

JAC (5; 8) already has difficulty with the initial row of six blue circles and three red squares in front of him. "Are all the squares red?—*No, because there are* [blue] *circles.*—Are the blue ones squares?—*No.*—Then the squares are red?—*Yes.*" With three blue squares, a red square and three blue circles: "Are all the squares blue?—*No, there is a red square.*—Are all the circles blue?—*No, there are reds* [squares].—Are the red ones circles?—*No, they* [the circles] *are blue.*"

ARI (6; 0) has a row in front of him made up of 14 blue circles together with a few squares, two blue and three red: "Are all the squares red?—*No, there are blue ones* (right).—Are all the circles blue?—*No, there are two blue squares.*—Are all the red ones squares?—*Yes,* (right)."

BUR (6; 4) first reproduces a row of blue circles and blue and red squares. "Are all the squares red?—*No, there were blue and red ones.*—Good. And are all the red ones squares?—*No, they are blue and red.*—Listen carefully. Are all the red ones squares?—*No.*—Why?—*Because there were blue squares.*"

THI (6; 7) correctly reproduces the row of blue circles and blue and red squares from memory. "Are all the red ones squares?—*No, because there are blue ones too* (wrong).—Are all the blue ones circles?—*Yes* (wrong).—Are all the circles blue?—*Yes.*—Are all the squares red?—*Yes, with two blue squares* (!)"

FAB (6; 7). The same situation. "Are all the red ones squares?—*No, because some are blue too.*—Are all the blue ones circles?—*No, because there are squares too* (right).—Are all the circles blue?—*No, because there were also blue and red squares.*"

KUR (6; 8). The same situation with six blue circles, two blue squares and a red square. "Are all the blue ones circles?—*Yes . . . no, not all, there are six blue circles and two blue squares* (right).—But are the circles all blue?—*No, there are six blue circles and two blue squares.*—And are all the red ones squares?—*No.*—Why?—*Because there are only two red squares* [and the others are blue]."

DUP (7; 6). The same situation. "Are all the squares red?—*No.*—Are some of the blue ones squares?—*Yes* (right).—Are all the blue ones squares.—*No* (right).—Are all the red ones squares?—*No* (wrong).—Why?—*There are blue ones too.*"

All the above examples are taken from stages I–II. They may be compared with two examples of completely correct answers (stage III):

Cor (6; 8) "Are all the red ones squares?—*Yes.*—You are sure?—*Yes.*—Are all the blue ones circles?—*No, not all. There are also* [blue] *squares.*—Are all the squares blue?—*No, there are also red ones.*—Are all the circles blue?—*Yes.*"

Oec (7; 9). "Are all the circles blue?—*Yes.*—Are all the squares red?—*No, not all.*—Are all the red ones circles?—*No.*—Are some of the blue ones circles?—*Yes.*—Are all the squares blue?—*No, not all.*—Are some of the squares blue?—*Yes.*"

Finally, here is a table giving the percentage of correct answers to the four questions asked on the composite series (IIA and B), with the answers afterwards arranged in groups of two ($A < B$ or $B < A$), depending on whether the question was whether all the elements of a part A had the properties of the whole B (correct answer: yes), or whether all the elements of the whole B had the properties of the part A (correct answer: no). In the last two columns, the four questions are grouped according to whether the predicate bears on colour or on shape.

Table I. *Percentage of correct answers given to four questions bearing on the use of "all" (series II)*[1]

CB = Are all the circles blue?
RS = Are all the red ones squares?
BC = Are all the blue ones circles?
SR = Are all the squares red?
AB = Are all the *A*s *B*s? (if $A < B$) = CB and RS
BA = Are all the *B*s *A*s? (if $A < B$) = BC and SR
$+$ = correct answer to AB and BA

Age (and no. of subjects)	CB	RS	BC	SR	AB	BA	+	Mean CB+SR	Mean BC+RS
5 (23)	82	57	69	70	42	39	9	76	63
6 (31)	63	58	60	79	35	48	13	71	59
7 (14)	64	68	73	88	43	57	21	76	70
8 (10)	80	90	85	95	73	81	45	87.5	87.5
9 (8)	81	81	81	100	71	81	50	90.5	81

Since the results shown in Table I may be attributed to fatigue or inattention, a control experiment was undertaken in which questions were limited to those shown in these tables. The results of this experiment are shown in Table Ia. None of these 52 children had taken part

[1] The percentages which figure in tables I to III should not be taken as norms, since they are largely dependent on the particular form of questioning which is used. Their chief interest lies in the comparisons which they afford among the 4 questions.

in the previous testing sessions and the materials were plainly visible to each subject throughout the questioning.

Table Ia. *Percentage of correct answers given to the four questions bearing on the use of "all"*

Age (and no. of subjects)	CB	RS	BC	SR	AB	BA	+	Mean CB+SR	Mean BC+RS
5 (12)	67	54	79	66	42	58	8	66	66
6 (10)	90	55	80	80	45	70	20	85	67
7 (10)	100	70	80	90	70	70	50	95	75
8 (10)	100	80	100	90	80	88	70	95	90
9 (10)	100	85	100	90	80	90	80	95	92

(1) In columns 1–4 an answer is considered correct if the subject gave the right answer immediately. Such an answer is scored 1. If he corrected an initial error immediately the question was repeated; that item is scored $\frac{1}{2}$. The last two columns are the means of columns 1 and 4, and 2 and 3, respectively. (2) In columns AB, BA and $+$, a positive score represents a set of *perfect* answers, the maximum score of 1 having been awarded to both, or all 4 of the relevant questions. Allowing for a slight increase in the percentage figures due to the elimination of fatigue, the second set of results is in general agreement with the first, and they merit a close study. The following discussion bears on the qualitative illustrations as well as the figures shown in the above tables.

A first point is that subjects' replies are by no means always consistent. Children quite often give a correct answer to one question of a given type followed by an incorrect answer to another. There is even less consistency when all four questions are considered together. Thus the percentage of correct answers to individual questions ranges from 55 to 90 for the two 6-year-old groups, but when these questions are paired (columns AB and BA) these figures fall to 35–70%, while only 13–20% answer all 4 questions correctly. Now it is perfectly true that, however expert the experimenter (and he needs to be expert), the situation is not stimulating. The inconsistency could therefore be due to distraction or fatigue. It could, however, be due to the fact that the subject cannot handle the quantifier "all" in a coherent manner, but can still answer one or two questions correctly by guess or by chance. The argument that fatigue or lack of interest is not the sole factor requires some corroborative evidence, and we present such evidence in §§2 and 3.

However, what we have said about lack of interest does not mean that the distribution of successes and failures is random.[1] A number of trends

[1] It is possible to calculate the values which might be expected to appear at each age in columns AB, BA and $+$, on the assumption of complete lack of correlation between success in any one of the questions and success in any or all of the

emerge clearly enough. Thus not all subjects are as successful in dealing with questions of the form "Are all the As Bs?" as they are with those of the opposite type. "Are all the Bs As?" (See §3). Or again we can compare the last two columns. Here the average for $CB + SR$ is often better than that for $BC + RS$ and never worse. What this means is that the question tends to be easier (or at least, not more difficult) when the collection as a whole indicated by the word "all" is defined by shape than when it is defined by colour. In other words the "all" is not a true logical quantifier but an intuitive referent which gains in precision when it denotes a better graphic collection. Bearing in mind the conclusions we reached in our study of graphic and non-graphic collections, we are inclined to suggest the following three hypotheses. Together they account not merely for the partial successes but also for the distribution of failures.

(1) At the level of graphic collections, children try to make up some kind of a collective object (e.g. an alignment or a complex object) in order to envisage "all the Xs". Having done so, they can then answer the question "Are all the Xs y?" by deciding whether the collective object is wholly y. They can do this without bothering about other collective objects and graphic collections. The only one with which they are concerned is that made up by the Xs. They can forget about other objects which are also y, because they are not led to make up a second collection of Ys and to compare the extension of the two, Xs and Ys. All that we know about graphic collections makes it plain that the only one involved is that of the Xs. The only source of difficulty at this level is therefore that which is entailed in perceiving the Xs as a graphic whole.

(2) The problem becomes more complicated at the level of non-graphic collections, so long as children lack the ability to construct hierarchical systems, together with its correlative, the operation of logical subtraction. A non-graphic collection, it will be remembered, is still an intuitive set and not a true class. The question "Are all the Xs y?" no longer induces children to make up a collective object out of the Xs. Having passed beyond the level of graphic collections they are in a position to reason about "all the Xs" which are scattered about the table in front of them (which is still not the same thing as the class of Xs). But for this very reason, they are no longer able to ignore Ys which are not Xs when thinking about the applicability of property y. Instead of answering in terms of a single graphic collection (Xs), they are bound

others. In point of fact the *obtained* values are quite close to those we would expect on the basis of such an assumption. It is difficult to avoid the conclusion that the absence of correlation is itself a measure of lack of understanding, *particularly* at the younger age level (since the range of *possible* values for AB, BA and $+$ tends to decrease as the values for the first 4 columns *increase*, so that the *actual* values are then less significant).

to construct two non-graphic collections, one of Xs and the other of Ys, and to compare "all the Xs" with "all the Ys". Now, in order to decide whether "all the Xs" are "some of the Ys", we have to reason in terms of a schema of class-inclusion, and this is precisely what these children lack. The net result is that it is only at this level that children first come up against the problem of the quantification of the predicate, and at this level they cannot yet solve it. All they can do to decide whether all the Xs are y is to ascertain whether or not the collection of Xs coincides with that of Ys, which is as much as to reduce the question "Are all the Xs y?" to "Are all the Xs all the Ys?", instead of "Are all the Xs some of the Ys?", which is what it properly signifies. It follows that at the level of graphic collections the problem of "all" seemed simple (because the subject over-simplified it) while at the level of non-graphic collections it no longer admits of universal solution. Later on we shall see that the question "Are all the As Bs?" is harder than "Are all the Bs As?" (where $A < B$).

(3) Nevertheless the opposition of graphic collections to non-graphic collections is always a matter of degree. Even an older child will be better able to focus on a collection of elements scattered about the table (or scattered at random in a heterogeneous row, as in the present experiments) if these elements have some "graphic" property in common. This is true in spite of the fact that he is no longer constructing artificial "complex objects". The question we ask is: "Are all the Xs y?" Sometimes, but not always, the subject translates this in terms of purely extensive relations as "Are all the Xs Ys?" Whether or not he does depends in part on the properties which define the Xs and Ys, which may be shape or colour or size or weight. When x is a highly graphic property and y is less graphic (and especially when it is much less graphic) the situation tends to be exactly what it was at the previous level: the Xs are thought of in terms of extension and y remains an intensive property, so that it is easy enough to answer the query whether "all the Xs are y". But when properties x and y are equally graphic, and more especially where property y is more graphic than x, the older subject is much more inclined to translate "Are all the Xs y?" as "Are all the Xs Ys?", and then it becomes crucial whether, for him, the latter question means "Are all the Xs all the Ys?" or "Are all the Xs some of the Ys?"

Taken together, these three hypotheses would go far to explain the apparent contradictions of Tables I and Ia. In other words they would account for the fact that a given subject sometimes answers a question correctly while other questions of the same form are liable to lead to systematic errors. But we have yet to see whether a qualitative analysis of the schema underlying these children's answers supports these hypotheses.

(1) At the level of graphic collections we should expect the question, "Are all the Xs y?" to be relatively easy in principle. But the correctness of its solution depends on the extent to which the Xs can be envisaged as a graphic collective object; for it is about such an object that the judgment is made: "All the Xs" is equated with "the whole of X". Now the experimental set-up was deliberately contrived to make the construction of a collective object difficult. Hence we tend to find two trends which are specific to stage I. Both concern the quantification of the logical *subject*, not that of the predicate, as at stage II. In the first place, children find it easier to answer the question when the logical subject denotes a majority of the elements in front of them, these being the blue circles; the few red and blue squares which are scattered among the blue circles are less easy to intuit as collective objects. This explains why CB (Are all the circles blue?) is easier at 5 (67–82%) than SR (Are all the square ones red?) 66–70%; and, rather more telling, BC (Are all the blue ones circles? 69–79%) is consistently easier than RS (Are all the red ones square? 54–57%). A second feature is the fact that younger children frequently refer the argument to the entire collection, "all" in an absolute sense, instead of focussing on the sub-collections defined as "all the reds" or "all the squares", etc. Sometimes, but by no means always, this tendency is so strong that the subject cannot even select the boxes he would need to reproduce the row in front of him. More often, children think of "all" as the whole row instead of limiting it to those elements defined by the property mentioned. The first tendency is illustrated by Pie, who asks for boxes of red circles and blue circles to reproduce a row made up of blue circles and red squares; Tin asks for red squares and blue squares. The second difficulty is again apparent in Pie's response: he hates to admit that all the round ones are blue because what he sees is a graphic collection which includes red squares. Later on, when shown series II, he resolutely denies that all the round ones are blue, because "there are only two" (in a collection of 7, 2 fail to rate the quantifier "all"!). The sequel shows us that he is well aware that the red objects are square, but he still insists that not all the circles are blue when the collection as a whole includes "blue and red ones". Tin is another who will not allow that "all the square ones are red" when the red squares are interspersed with blue circles. Ire makes the same mistake at first, yet he finds no objection to the suggestion that "all the blue ones are round" even though he has just observed that the collection includes a blue square. To sum up, the errors made at stage I are due less to difficulties in deciding about the properties of a graphic collective object than to those entailed in the construction of such an object out of a row of jumbled elements. The reader can now appreciate why we were unable to obtain results from 3 and 4 year olds: they simply could not dissociate the collections we wanted to talk about.

(2) The pattern of successes and failures which supervenes at stage II is very different. The principal feature is that which separates the questions of the form "Are all the As Bs?" from those having the form "Are all the Bs As?" (bearing in mind that $A < B$). The development has both a positive aspect and a negative one. (a) The positive gain lies in the improved handling of the quantifier "all" which appears when the question takes the second form. The subject is shown two sub-collections, A and A', their differential properties being a and a'; together they form the collection B, and the question is: "Are all the Bs a?" or "Are all the Bs As?" More often than not at stage II he replies in the negative, and the reason he gives is that some are A's (or a'). (b) The negative aspect is that questions of the form "Are all the As b?" which should properly be answered in the affirmative are in fact answered in the negative also—and once again the subject explains his answer by reference to the A's which are also b.

Let us examine these two aspects separately before we consider what their implications may be when both occur together.

(a) With the material we used, we can either take B as the squares with a as red and a' as blue, in which case $A =$ the red squares and $A' =$ the blue squares; alternatively, B are the blue beads, in which case $A =$ those which are round and blue while $A' =$ those which are square and blue. Now the question whether all the squares (B) are red (a) or whether all the blue beads (B) are round (a) often elicits a correct negative answer (see Ver and Jac, and more especially Ari, Bur and Dup when B are the squares, and Bar, Bal, Fab, Kur and Dup when B are the blue beads).

However, incorrect answers are by no means rare. There are two sources of error. The first harks back to the graphic collection of stage I. Thus Jac, even at 5; 8 is unhappy when asked to admit that the squares in series I (red squares and blue circles only) are all red because he sees them as part of a graphic whole which includes blue circles. For series II, Thi is prepared to allow that all the squares are red "with the blue squares". His answer can only mean that the set of squares taken as "a whole" has two colours, so that either can be said to belong to the "whole": although this "whole" has less internal solidarity than a true collective object it has more than a non-graphic collection.

But the second type of error is more frequent and more interesting: it arises from the confusion of the expression "all the Bs are a" with the expression "all the As are b" (or, more precisely, of "all the Bs are As" with "all the As are Bs") these being regarded as equivalent. For example, Bal and Thi allow that "all the blue elements are circles" because they identify this with "all the circles are blue", and this reaction is very widespread. Is the confusion due to mere lack of concentration or is there a difficulty of logical understanding? (Even adults are apt to grow confused when asked several successive questions of the same kind involving changes or permutations of the subject and object.) If there is a logical difficulty it is that of class-inclusion. To distinguish between "All the *B*s are *a*" and "All the *A*s are *b*" is to understand that "All the *B*s are some of the *A*s" is incompatible with "All the *A*s are some of the *B*s, as the inclusion $B < A$ is incompatible with $A < B$; to confuse the two expressions amounts to reducing one to the other: "All the *B*s are all the *A*s" (therefore $B = A$, substituting identity for inclusion). It is undeniable that lack of attention may play a role here. But there is a decisive reason for believing that this type of reply, which is extremely common, owes a great deal to the tendency to substitute identity for inclusion: in general, the same subjects who translate "All the *B*s are *a*" as "All the *A*s are *b*" also translate "Are all the *A*s *b*?" as "Are all the *A*s all the *B*s?". This brings us to the second aspect.

(b) Once again, $A =$ the circles, $B =$ the blue objects ($b =$ blue) and $A' =$ the blue squares; or, alternatively, $A =$ the red squares, $B =$ the squares and $A' =$ the blue squares. But this time the question is whether all the *A*s are *b* (or are *B*s). Now the answer is more often false, and the argument on which it is based is always essentially the same: all the *A*s are not *b* (or are not *B*s) because the *A*'s are also *b* (or are also *B*s). In other words, one cannot affirm that "all" the circles are blue, because the blue squares (or some of the squares) are blue also! The difficulty of "all" and "some" is most evident in this type of answer, which highlights the thought processes of children at stage II; and quite often the very same children can give right answers when the form of the question is "Are all the *B*s *A*s?".

We may begin with the question "Are all the circles blue?". Here a majority of our subjects are fairly explicit. So Bar, who denies that all the circles are blue because there are "squares and circles" which are blue. Or Ver, who hesitates at first, but who subsequently, rejects the "all" "because there are blue squares too". Bal uses the same phrase, "There were blue squares as well." Jac's thinking is at a slightly more elementary level in spite of his final answer: he cannot wholly separate the blue circles from the row as a whole. Ari's argument is the usual: one cannot say that "all the circles are blue" because "there are two blue squares"! So also Fab: "No, because there were also squares." And Kur: "No, because there are six blue circles and two blue squares." Thi is the only child we have cited who accepts that all the circles are blue; but he also maintains that the reciprocal is true, i.e. all the blue ones are circles. Although his answers are opposite to those of the others, the underlying reasoning is identical.

There are no more than 6–8 round beads and every one of them is blue. Now each of our subjects is perfectly aware of this and when asked to reproduce the row he can do it correctly. Yet each one of them insists that not all the round beads are blue—because they are mixed in with a couple of blue squares. We are bound to conclude that to the child's mind, to say: "All the round beads are blue" is equivalent to saying: "All the round beads are all the blue beads", instead of: "All the round beads are some of the blue beads." This explains why Thi is the only one who tells us that all the round beads are blue: his admission is no more than the result of a momentary error, namely the belief that all the blue beads are round. When we go on to the question, "Are all the red beads square?" Thi denies this for the usual reason—there are two blue squares as well.

It looks as if the child's thinking is conditioned by a need for symmetry: the extension of the predicate "blue" must be the same as that of the subject "round". But the symmetry in question should not be taken in the sense of a reciprocity, i.e. "All the round beads are blue" = "All the blue beads are round". Other studies have shown that at this level children have considerable difficulty in handling judgments involving true reciprocity (the distance from A to B may be thought different from the distance from B to A; or a child may recognize that A is to the left of B without admitting that B is to the right of A; or again, he knows that so and so is his brother but refuses to admit that this brother has a brother—himself). The symmetry which is involved is a more primitive notion, and is tied up with graphic symmetry. What our subjects are doing is to assimilate the expression "All the Bs are a" to the expression "All the As are b". In other words they substitute equivalence $(A = B)$ for class-inclusion $(A > B$ or $B > A)$ which is exactly what we said earlier (2a). In a way, we ought to expect their answers to be paradoxical, for on the one hand they may admit that "All the Bs are a", having assimilated the question to "Are all the As b?", while on the other hand they may deny that all As are b having noted that all the As are not all the Bs—and this is exactly what does happen in the case of Thi. However, we have yet to see why questions of the form BA tend to present less difficulty at stage II than questions of the form AB (see Tables I and Ia). Where even the easier question is answered wrong, we are bound to infer that the statement "All the blue ones are round" is taken as equivalent to "All the round ones are blue". The only effective judgments being made are tautological judgments, e.g. "All the blue circles are round (or blue)", the reason being that these young subjects are still unable to envisage the total collections of "blues" or "circles". But at stage II they do abstract these total collections, which helps them to understand that "All the blues are round" is false. Yet for all that, they refuse to admit that the reciprocal assertion "All the round ones are blue" is true. As far as they are concerned, this would be tantamount to saying, "All the round ones are all the blue ones", which is manifestly false. It therefore looks very much as if the true

70

explanation is that at stage II children extend the quantifier "all" to the logical predicate of the sentence as well as to its logical subject.

This interpretation is further borne out by the answers to question *RS* (Are all the red counters square?). Almost all the subjects concerned recognize at once that "All the squares are red" is false, since two or three of the squares are blue; yet five out of eight deny that all the red elements are squares, although they know very well that there are no red circles (they say so, and prove it in their reproductions). Once again, the reason is that they cannot admit that "all the red elements are squares" without being able to justify their version, which is: "All the red elements constitute all the squares"—and this mistranslation is false as two or three of the squares are blue. Thi denies that all the reds are squares and gives as his reason: "No, because there are blue ones too." Bur, Fad, Kur and Dup are all equally explicit. Only Bar, Ver and Ari give the right answer, and Bar gives her reason: ". . . because there were only the squares" (which were red).

The facts are clear enough: if $B = A + A'$ children find it easier to answer correctly that all the *B*s are *A*s is wrong than to recognize that all the *A*s are *B*s is right. Our interpretation is that their quantification of the predicate is faulty: instead of taking the question "Are all the *A*s *B*s?" to mean "Are all the *A*s some of the *B*s?" they take it as meaning "Are all the *A*s all the *B*s?". The question is why.

Now the first point about which it is important to be clear is that even when the question "Are all the *B*s *A*s?" is answered correctly in the negative, this does not imply that the subject has avoided the sort of mistranslation to which we refer. He may say quite rightly: "No, all the squares are not red, because some are blue" and still be saying to himself "I have to see whether all the squares are all the reds" (or "Are all the blues all the circles?"). The answer which he produces will still be the right one although all he is doing is to establish whether or not the two collections "reds" and "squares" (or "blues" and "circles") coincide.

In effect, it is just as difficult to deny that "All the *B*s are *A*s" as it is to recognize that "All the *A*s are *B*s"—or would be if we could insist on the question being properly understood. But since we cannot, we have to recognize that to read "All the *B*s are all the *A*s" instead of "All the *B*s are some of the *A*s" will still produce the correct answer. The subject can see the *A*'s (blue squares) right in front of him, so he knows perfectly well that *B* does not coincide with *A*. And this may be why he gives the right answer. On the other hand, it is possible that he has established that *B* does not coincide with *A or any sub-set of A*, which would be the right answer again, but for the right reason. The experiment, taken by itself, is not decisive.

In spite of the fact that more children solve the question "Are all the *B*s *A*s?" than "Are all the *A*s *B*s?", we are quite deliberately supposing

71

the two questions to be basically equal in difficulty. This is far more than a logical quibble; it brings us to the heart of the psychological problem, which is to decide when we have sufficient evidence to accept that a subject understands the relation of class-inclusion. Supposing the (tacit) quantification of the predicate to have been false even in relation to the question "Are all the Bs As?", we infer that the child has not understood the relation of class-inclusion. Nevertheless his answer is correct because all he needed to do was to see whether the two collections A and B coincided. This makes far more sense than to assume that his quantification of the predicate was correct (i.e. "All the Bs are neither all the As nor some of the As"), for on this assumption the same child understands class-inclusion in one setting and fails to grasp it in another which is just as simple, i.e. when answering question AB (Are all the As Bs?).

This brings us to the main point: Why is there this false quantification of the predicate? Why is the statement "All the As are (some of the) Bs" interpreted as "All the As are all the Bs", and what is the relationship between this very common reaction and the problem of inclusion?

In ch. II we saw that at stage II children can differentiate a collection ($= B$) and recognize potential sub-collections (A and A'). They see these latter as "bits" of what amounts to an intuitive object. (It is true that B is not a graphic whole at stage II as it was at stage I; but it is still not an operational "class". It is a quasi-object because although it is seen as a set, the recognition is still intuitive.) However, these children do not see A and A' as "included" in B. The distinction is this: A child can form an impression of the total collection $B = A + A'$ even though he differentiates the two sub-collections, A and A'. Such an impression may be pre-operational if it is merely visualized, or seen. It is operational only if it carries with it the reverse implication: $A = B - A'$. But the inclusion of A in B implies this inverse operation: once a child has already divided B into its sub-classes A and A', he cannot recognize that A is a part of B unless he understands that $A = B - A'$. This understanding is much more difficult than forming the simple union $B = A + A'$. The point is that B no longer exists as a visible collection once A is separated from it (actually or mentally). It exists only as an abstract class because perceptually, it has been dissociated. Therefore, to establish a relation between A and B, the child must ignore the perceptual dissociation of B and reason in terms of its abstract invariance.

We now see why the quantification of the predicate tends to be incorrect at stage II. To accept the statement "All the As are Bs" as equivalent to "All the As are some of the Bs" is to reason in terms of an inclusive relation: $A = B - A'$. Conversely, to take it in the sense "All the As are all the Bs" is to reason in terms of a mere equality: $A = B$. The possibility of class-inclusion is left out of account. (Needless to say, little children are innocent of the subtleties of logicians, to whom equivalence itself is reducible to reciprocal inclusion: $[A \geqslant B] + [B \geqslant A] = [A = B]$.) In other words, the false quantification of the predicate at stage II derives from the difficulty of mastering inclusion. The underlying problem is identical.

As we saw earlier, when the question takes the form: "Are all the Bs As?" the quantification of the predicate is irrelevant. The subject simply inspects the collection B, and he sees that it has two parts, $B = A + A'$. The inverse operation is unnecessary. In other words, the right answer does not necessarily imply the presence of class-inclusion. Usually this form of question is solved quite easily at stage II, and the chief danger is that the child will invert the question "Are all the Bs a?" and think of it as "Are all the As b?"

In a way, we could extend this argument and reason as follows: Regardless of the form of question (which may be AB, are all the As b; or BA, are all the Bs a), the youngest subjects (who are 5) will invert it 50% of the time. Having done so, they answer the question correctly in terms of what they see—all their errors are due only to the inversion. From 6 to 9 the tendency to invert declines because children are beginning to get a grasp of class-inclusion, and therefore more of their answers are right. Most of the results in Tables I and Ia could be accounted for on the basis of this simplified hypothesis. The argument still depends on the fact that inclusion is a difficult relation while dispensing with any mention of quantification.

However, unless everything is to be explained by inattention, this hypothesis does not explain why it is that even young subjects who can read perceptual data correctly should invert the questions asked 50% of the time; i.e., why it is that they should be insensitive to inclusion. Now, in the first place, being unaware of the inclusion $A < B$ implies difficulty in quantifying the A with respect to the B or vice versa, i.e., difficulty in quantifying predicates. Moreover, a tendency to confuse questions of type AB with type BA is simply a tendency to identify the A and the B, and this again means interpreting a question like "Are all the As Bs?" as "Are all the As all the Bs?" (and just the same is true of the inversion of the opposite question).[1] In other words, the simplicity of the suggested hypothesis is a surface simplification. The quantification of the predicate is not side-stepped but simply masked.

(3) The phenomenon just described is only one aspect of stage II. It may be strengthened by perceptual or graphic factors or they may counteract it. Generally speaking the subject does tend to interpret "All the As are b" as "All the As are all the Bs"; but he will do so more

[1] Cf. the cases given in §3 to illustrate the relative use of "some". The case of Gra is particularly explicit and instructive.

or less readily, depending on the perceptual properties a and b which determine the As and Bs. These properties may be strong enough to encourage the establishment of a collection of Bs alongside one of As or they may be so weak as to make it particularly improbable. A child will not read "All the circles are blue" as "All the circles are all the blue beads" unless, for him, the collection of "all the blue beads" is just as obtrusive as that constituted by "all the circles". By looking at Tables I and Ia, we can see that usually this is not the case. Looking at the last two columns, we see that the mean percentages of correct answers given to $CB + SR$ are almost all higher than those given to $BC + RS$. This amounts to saying that it is easier for a child to form a non-graphic collection on the basis of shape than of colour. (There is a graphic factor even though the collections are non-graphic. They are non-graphic because the subject is no longer literally constructing figures and complex objects to give substance to his collections. Nevertheless the relative ease with which a given determinant can give rise to an imaged collection is very much a factor even when the collection is united only in the mind of the subject.)

We will come back to this factor in discussing the next experiment, when the virtual collections have to be constructed on the basis of colour and weight. There, the contrast in imaginal potential is a great deal stronger.

2. "ALL" AND "SOME" APPLIED TO TESTS OF EXCLUSION

Although the preceding experiments are relevant to the problems of classification, they have the obvious defect of having no interest or use for the child himself. It is hardly exciting for small children to spend twenty or thirty minutes looking at little circles and squares and saying whether they are "all" red or blue. Even though the situation was presented as a game, we could not but admire the youngsters of 5 and 6 years who still found this game absorbing! We thought it essential to check these results by means of an experiment in which the "all" and the "some" would have a functional significance. The experiment to be described is not directly concerned with pure classification, but the variables need to be quantified in terms of "all" and "some" in order to arrive at a satisfactory proof.

The idea behind the experiment is this. The subject is asked to find out the cause of a certain event. In order to solve the problem he will need to make a spontaneous classification of the variables, using general classes for statements like "All the x's produce a given result y" as well as sub-classes for statements like "Some (but not all) of the x's produce y".

If a subject wants to show that the y's are produced by the x's, he has to use an "all", but this "all" may be implicit and not clearly distinguished from "some". But in order to demonstrate that the *y*'s are not produced by the *x*'s, he must use sub-classes. He has two possible lines of attack of which one is based on the conjunction of (not *x*). (*y*) and the other is based on that of (*x*) (not *y*). He can disprove the statement "All the *x*'s are accompanied by *y*" by showing the existence of "some" *x*'s which are not accompanied by *y*. Likewise he can disprove "All the

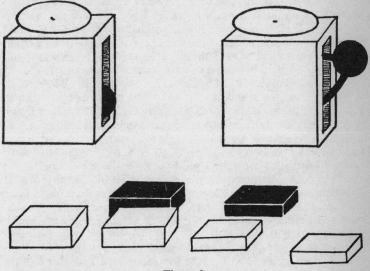

Figure 8.

y's go with *x*'s" by showing "some" *y*'s which do not. It is only at the level of formal reasoning that children carry out propositional operations, and only then are they in a position to follow all the possible combinations. The sort of experiment we will be describing does not call for such reasoning. But it does demand an adequate handling of "all" and "some" because it depends on the inclusions and intersections of the various classes of objects. At the level of formal operations, the subject will be able to foresee the various combinations, and he will use propositional operations to solve the problem. At 7 or 8 his solution is based on the inclusions and intersections of straightforward classes, but these do require a sufficient mastery of "all" and "some".

The apparatus,[1] we chose consisted of an ordinary balance like those used for weighing letters, but we added a counter-weight in the shape

[1] See Fig. 8 for the apparatus.

of a ball. This was hidden in a box which had a slot on one side. In addition there were a number of boxes to be put on the scale. These were in two weights. The heavier weights made the ball appear through the slot whereas the lighter did not. The child was shown the apparatus together with a collection of boxes varying in colour, size and weight. (The sizes were chosen in such a way as to minimize the effect of the "size-weight illusion" on estimates of weight.) He was asked to predict which of the boxes would make the ball come out of the slot, and then told to classify them on that basis. He was also asked for his reasons for each classification, the experiment being repeated as often as necessary.[1] In the end, he was asked how he would prove what he had found out (weight is a determinant while colour and size are not). Last of all, we put questions like "Are all the red boxes heavy?", introducing "all" and "some" in relation to his own classes and sub-classes.

Sub-section I deals with the results on 82 subjects using all 8 combinations of colour, weight and size. To make these results comparable with those of §1, we carried out a second experiment, on 30 additional subjects, in which only two factors were involved at any one time (i.e., colour and weight or size and weight), and one sub-class was always missing (e.g. both heavy and light boxes were red but the blue boxes were all light). This experiment will be described in sub-section II.

I. The main experiment involves eight possible sub-classes (heavy or light × red or blue × small or large). The solution of the problem takes the form of an equivalence between "heavy" and "makes the ball come out" and another between "light" and "does not make it come out".

From the point of view of "all" and "some", we again encounter problem (1) exactly as we did in §1: "Are all the Bs As (if $B = A + A'$)?" For example, if the child is asked (or asks himself) whether "all the blue boxes make the ball come out (or are heavy)" he is faced with this kind of problem (1): some of the blue boxes do make the ball come out and others do not. But the advantage of this functional situation is that the child can show his understanding by his actions as well as by his words. When he has to find a proof or a "counter-example"; he can show that all the blue boxes do not cause the ball to emerge, by looking for one which does not and putting it on the balance to prove that it does not.

Problems of type (2), i.e. "Are all the As Bs?" (if $B = A + A'$) could not be put directly since all the eight sub-classes or intersections were non-empty. But what is more striking is that although the children were

---

[1] The classification results in a division of the boxes into light and heavy (two classes whose elements all have the same weight). When the child is questioned at the end of the experiment, the boxes are mixed together but remain in front of the child. The classification is therefore in terms of light boxes and heavy boxes. Within these two classes all the boxes are identical in weight.

always faced with problem (1), they often gave similar answers to those given in §1 to problem (2): all the As are not Bs because there are also A's. Owing to their tendency to invert "Are all the Bs As?" into "Are all the As Bs?" accompanied by a false quantification of the predicate, they finish up by asking themselves the question "Are all the As all the Bs?" Now the original question was a type 1 problem: "Are all the Bs As?", e.g. "Do all the blue boxes make the ball come out?". The answer we may receive is "No, because some red ones do", i.e. it invokes the existence of B's (which, of course, proves nothing), instead of the A's (blue boxes which are light). But the reasoning behind this sort of answer is equivalent to the error made in relation to problem (2) as it appeared in §1. Here it reappears even though the problem is of type 1. These results are particularly convincing because, in spite of the fact that the subjects are motivated to solve a concrete problem, we still find erroneous proofs showing inversion of the question and incorrect quantification of the predicate.

There is a third type of problem which occurs in the context of the present experiment and does not figure in §1. If the subject is asked whether all the heavy boxes make the ball come out, or if he asks himself the same question in order to solve the puzzle, the logical form of the question is: "Are all the Bs all the As?" In this case the two categories are indeed equivalent, since all the heavy boxes are in fact all those which make the ball come out. Because the relation is one of equivalence and not one of inclusion, the question is easier than the others. In general, problems of weight are not solved early, the reason being that children fail to dissociate weight from volume. Here, the difficulty is circumvented by the fact that there is this simple relation of equivalence between the heavy boxes and those which work the apparatus. But even in this situation the problem remains insoluble until the subject can construct a class consisting of "all" the heavy boxes. In other words it is solved at stage II, but remains unsolved at stage I.

It may therefore be interesting to begin with a few examples of stage I, before proceeding to stage II with which we are more directly concerned in this chapter.

At stage I, children are prepared to allow that size or colour can be determining factors in spite of the exceptions. They do not rule out the quantifier "all" in the face of these exceptions. As a result, they fail to discover that weight is the sole factor.

IRO (4 years) refuses to make any predictions, but he does try a few of the boxes out, and this leads him to collect a number of small heavy boxes: "*The small boxes make the ball come out.*—Why?—*Don't know.*—See if it's true. (He constructs two piles; one consisting of the large boxes with one small one and the second of the remainder. He then predicts:) *Those in the first pile will make it come out.* (He tries a large light box.) *No,*" etc.

CHRI (5; 0) tries large and small boxes as well as light and heavy ones, and notes what happens. She then classes the boxes into small and large, and says of the former: *"Those don't make the ball come out.*—Try it and see— (She takes a small heavy one.) *It comes out.*—Then tell me which ones make the ball come out.—(She points to the large ones): *Those."* After several more attempts, the boxes are reshuffled and Chri is asked for a new classification. In spite of all the exceptions she still maintains her original dichotomy of large and small boxes, insisting that the former make the ball come out while the latter do not.

RAP (5; 2) divides the boxes into two classes: those which make the ball come out *"because they are big"* and those which do not *"because they're a little bit thinner.*—See if that's right.—(He tries a large light box on the scale.) *Oh! It's those* (the small ones) *which make the ball come out, not those* (the large ones). He takes a small heavy one and weighs it in his hand: *"Small and heavy, not much."* He tries it on the scale and, sure enough, the ball comes out. But Rap denies it: *"That doesn't make it come out much.* (He reverts to his original idea:) *It's these* (the small ones) *which don't make the ball come out and those* (the large ones) *which do.*—Can you show me if that's right?—(He tries two small heavy ones in succession and then sits dumb.)— One boy told me that it was the large boxes which made the ball come out. Is that true?—*It's not true that it's the large ones.*—Can you show me that it isn't true?—*Yes* (he puts a large heavy one on the scale). *I'm right about the small ones, and he's right about the big ones. He's quite right about the big ones, and me too, I'm right about the small ones!"* Then: *"He wasn't right about that one* (a large heavy box)."

CAT (5; 6) offers no predictions. She tries each of the boxes and divides them correctly into two classes. Now she explains that the ball does not come out with the little boxes but only with the large ones. "Can you show me that you're right?—(The experiments she makes contradict her statement and her classification is correct.)—Well why do those make the ball come out?— *Because here there are big boxes and little ones.*—Then why don't these make ti come out?—*Because here there are little boxes and big ones."*

BER (6; 6) also gives an explanation based on size. "Are you sure?—*Yes.*— Try—(A small heavy one.) *No.* (A large light one.) *It's less heavy!"* But he falls back on the factor of size. "One boy told me that it's the red ones. Was he right?—*Yes, with some boxes he's right and with some boxes he's wrong.*— What was it he said?—*He said the blue boxes don't make it come out, and the red ones do.*—Can you show me if that's true?—(A large heavy red one.) *Yes, he is right. It's about the blue ones he's wrong.*—One boy told me that it's the large ones?—*No, there are large ones which don't make it come out also.*— Well, was he right or not?—*Yes.*—Sure?—*Well not quite right because there are large ones which don't make it come out."*

All the above examples belong to stage I. They illustrate the difficulties which children experience in evolving the notion of "all", i.e. in abstracting a quality which is common to all the elements of a class. The same difficulty appeared in ch. I, where inability to abstract such a quality precluded the co-ordination of intension and extension, so that the little children we examined constantly made up what we called graphic collections instead of grouping objects into classes. The reader will no doubt recall from §1 that at stage I children frequently showed confusion in their answers to questions dealing with a row of beads made up exclusively of red squares and blue circles. Because the two types of counters were jumbled together, they were unable to abstract the class of "all" the squares, or circles, etc. Here, again, the type 1 problem is too difficult—i.e. children cannot be sure that "all the Bs are not As". We should add that the construction of the correct class of "all" the heavy boxes is more difficult in any case, since the criterion is weight. In short, one key to the problems of stage I is failure to abstract.

We note that none of our subjects succeeded in classifying the boxes correctly without first weighing each one. They did not discover that weight was what counted after one or two trials. Ber is the only one who ever came near to the correct criterion, for one brief moment ("because it is less heavy"), and even he assimilated "heavy" to "large" and "light" to "small". Once every box had been tried the classification was often correct. Yet none of these subjects could formulate the criterion of this classification, i.e. describe the qualities common to all the elements in the two collections he had made (even though the defining quality of the A' collection was simply the negation of that of the A collection).

Let us study these examples. Iro generalizes what he has learnt in the first few trials by the rule: "The small boxes make the ball come out", and then makes two piles in which one small box is added to the large ones. Chri thinks the same, and calmly ignores the exceptions. Rap thinks that one can be right in asserting simultaneously both that the large boxes make the ball come out and that the small ones do. Yet all the time he is using the word "all" and not "some". In other words he can see no contradiction; he is attributing one and the same effect to two quite opposite causes. We see the same reasoning in the replies of Cat; the boxes in collection A make the ball come out "because there are big boxes and little ones" and those of collection A' do not make it come out for what amounts to the same reason: that "there are little boxes and big ones". (The inversion of the order in the second sentence is most illuminating!) Even Ber argues on similar lines, in spite of the fact that he has once mentioned weight.

It is very tempting to translate what these children have to say in such a way as to make it conform with our own logical structures, and what is more, we can do this very nicely by quietly making one or two tiny alterations. There is nothing wrong with saying: "Some large boxes make the ball rise and so do some small ones; but some large ones do not make it rise, and there are some small ones which do not do so either." Expressed in this way, the children's statements would simply show that they had failed to isolate the factor of weight (and we already know the difficulty of dissociating weight from volume). Their statements might be "tautological" but they would not be contradictory. But things are not quite so simple, or we should be quite unable to account for the difficulties raised by problem (2) ("Are all the *A*s *B*s?") at stage II. Above all, we have to remember that at stage I children cannot make a straightforward classification and cannot even construct non-graphic collections.

As a matter of fact, the failure to find the correct rule, the tendency to ignore exceptions and the use of two arguments which are mutually contradictory, are all expressions of a systematic difficulty in distinguishing between "all" and "some". At a deeper level, the problem is to distinguish between the extension of collections and their intension. When a large box makes the ball emerge, the child deduces a causal relationship involving size. Size then becomes one of the characteristics to be incorporated into the "intension" of the collection of "boxes which make the ball come out". It is now one of the properties of the collective object constituted by this collection, instead of being a property common to all of its individual elements. This kind of property exists on a different level from "all" and "some"; it belongs to a purely intensive collection which is not a class or a grouping of individuals, but an aggregate into which these individuals are incorporated. If other boxes belonging to the same aggregate fail to confirm a causal relation between size and the appearance of the ball, this only affects these exceptional boxes, not the collection as such. We believe that some such reasoning as this lies behind the replies which we have quoted.

The difference between these reactions and those of stages II and III is the following. At the level of logical classes (stage III), a quality is not chosen as constituting the intension of a class unless it applies to "all" its members, and "all" is itself determined by a quality of this kind. Intension and extension are differentiated, but at the same time they are in exact correspondence with one another. On the other hand, at the level of graphic collections (i.e. stage I), the qualities of a collection are not chosen with due regard to "all" of its elements, and its extension is not determined by properties which they have in common. It follows that "all" and "some" do not yet have the meanings which they will bear at a subsequent stage. This explains why these children systematically fail to use these quantifiers.

Now, turning to stage II, we may note three interesting developments which help to account for what we saw at stage I, just as the latter make them a good deal clearer. In the first place, children now succeed in distinguishing between light boxes and heavy ones. They can therefore apply "all" to weight and solve problem (3): all the boxes which make the ball emerge are all the heavy ones. In the second place, they are partially successful in solving problem (1): "Are all the *B*s *A*s (if *B* = *A* + *A'*)?" Insofar as their handling of "all" and "some" is intuitively correct, they argue with impeccable logic: "All the *B*s are not *A*s because there are *A'*'s" (e.g. "all the red ones (*B*) are not heavy (*A*) because there are light red ones (*A'*)"). But even with questions of type (1), success is far from universal. Frequently they invert the question and this happens especially when the "all" is applied to weight rather than size or colour. They may also introduce a false quantification of the predicate ("Are all the *B*s all the *A*s?"). In other words, we may hear an explanation on these lines: "Are all the light ones blue?—No (correct), because there are red ones which are light (or even, because there are blue ones which are heavy!)"

Most of the following are examples of stage II, but the first few cases are transitional.

TAHI (4; 2) classes the boxes into large and small ones, predicting that the former will make the ball emerge and that the latter will not. He weighs a small heavy box and tries to minimize the exception: "*It made it come out a little bit.*" But he takes it into account and adopts a classification into light and heavy boxes. It is this which distinguishes stage II from stage I.

"A little boy told me that all the red ones are heavy. Is he right?—*No. These* (the heavy pile) *make it come out a lot, those don't.*"—Well?—*He isn't right, because there are red ones which don't make the ball come out.*—Show me.—(He takes a light red one): *There.*—What about all those which do make the ball come out?—*He's right.*—Show me.—(He takes a light red one and rejects it.) *I don't want that one.* (Then he puts on three heavy red boxes in succession): *There.*—Have you tried all the red ones?—*Yes.*—Was that little boy right?—*No.*—Why?—*Those* (the heavy red ones) *make the ball come out and those* (the light blue ones) *don't.*—But what about the red ones?—*Not all of them, because there is one which is light.*"

"Do all the blue ones make the ball come out?—*No, there are some which don't.*—One boy told me that all the large ones make the ball come out.—*He's right, that's true.*—And he says that the small ones don't make it come out.—*He's right.*—About all of them?—*No, not all.*"

ROM (4; 5) first divides the boxes according to colour, without weighing them. She then starts to weigh them, and re-divides them into large and small. Finally, she weighs them all and then re-divides them according to weight, without showing any explicit awareness of what she has done. "Do all the large ones make the ball come out?—*No.*—Why?—*There are some like this too* (pointing to the small heavy ones!)—(She is shown a heavy blue one.) What's this one like?—*Blue.*—One little girl told me that all the blue ones are light. Was she right?—*No.*—Why?—*Because here* (pile of light ones, *there are* (also) *red ones* (!)—She says that all the small boxes are light.—*No, there are some small ones here* (among the heavy ones).—Do all the red ones make the ball come out?—*No, because there are red ones here* (the light ones)."

Questioned again at 5; 10, Rom solves problem (1) in the same way. But she no longer makes a false quantification of the predicate, as she did at 4; 5.

GEN (5; 5) succeeded very quickly in classing the boxes into light and heavy ones, and in explaining the mechanism by weight. "Are all the red ones heavy?—*No, because there are some red boxes and some blue ones* (in the pile of heavy boxes!)—All the blue ones make the ball come out?—*That's wrong. Some of them are not heavy, and some of them are heavy.*"

FRA (5; 6) first explains the difference by size and then, after experimenting, by weight. "A little girl told me that all the red ones are heavy.—*That isn't true. There are red boxes and blue ones* (in the pile of heavy boxes!). *A red one is heavy, and a blue one, that's heavy too.*—What did the little girl say?— *She said they were all red, the heavy ones* (translating 'All the *A*s are *B*s' into 'all the *A*s are all the *B*s' by extending 'all' the red ones to 'all' the heavy ones!).—How would you show me that she's wrong?—(She indicates a large heavy blue box, a choice which is perfectly justified, if one agrees to her translation.)—But what was it that she really said?—*That the red ones make the ball come out.*—Can you show that that's wrong?—*Yes, with the blue one* (putting a heavy blue box on the scale, in spite of the fact that the second verbal formulation no longer alters the quantification of the predicate!) —A boy told me that all the large ones make the ball come out.—*No, there are small ones too* (just as before! She indicates a small heavy box).—Is there some other way you can show he's wrong?—(This time she points correctly to a large light box.)—*That's a large one which doesn't make the ball come out.*—Good. What did the boy tell me?—*That it was only the large ones which made the ball come out* (once again extending 'all' to the predicate!).—Well? —*I'm showing him that it's large and that it doesn't make the ball come out* (but this is no longer correct on the basis of 'only the large ones')."

FAC (5; 6) makes up two correct piles without a word of explanation. "Do all the red ones make the ball come out?—*No, these don't and those do. There are some red ones which don't make it come out.*—What about all the large ones?—*No, there are some big ones like that* (pile of light boxes) *too, and they don't make it come out.*—Well, one boy told me all the blue ones are light, and don't make it come out. Is that true?—*No, because there are some big red ones too which don't make it come out* (!).—What about all the small ones?—*No, there are small ones which do make it come out.*"

ROC (5; 10) quickly gives an explanation based on weight. "Are all the heavy ones large?—*No, there are some light ones which are large too* (!).—Are all the light ones small?—*Yes.*—Are all the large ones light?—*No, there are large ones which are heavy too.*—Are all the small ones heavy?—*No, because they are light,* [but] *there are some heavy ones.*"

BOR (5; 11) also understands the role of weight. "Are all the red boxes heavy?—*No, because the blue ones are heavy too* (!).—Are all the blue ones light?—*No, because there are two which aren't heavy and are red* (!)."

GRO (6; 10) immediately discovers the importance of weight. "Are all the blue ones heavy?—*No, there are light ones also, like this one for instance.*— Are all the red ones light?—*No, because there are blue ones which are light too* (!).—Are all the blue ones light?—*No, not all; the red are light as well* (!).— Are all the red ones heavy?—*No, that one is heavy, that one is light.*"

Finally, here are a few examples of the sort of replies we are given at stage III, when the necessary structures have been perfected. These children were right in their answers to the questions about the beads in §1, and, here too, their demonstrations are perfect and unhampered by false quantifications of the predicate.

DUB (7; 0): The ball emerges "*because they are heavy and not when the boxes are light.*—See if that's true.—(He places large light boxes and small heavy ones on the scale.)—One boy told me that they made the ball come out because they were red.—*No* (he places a light red box on the scale, followed by a large heavy blue one): *There is a large red box which does not make the ball come out and a blue one which does make it come out.*—Is that because it is large?—*No, it comes right out with both of them, the large boxes and the small ones* (placing them on the scale)."

STA (7; 2) demonstrates the effect of weight by putting on first a large light box and then a small heavy one. "Isn't it because they are large?—*No, there are* (among the large boxes) *heavy ones and light ones* (he places a small heavy one on the scale).—One boy told me that all the red ones make the ball come out.—*No* (he indicates a light red box).—And he said the small ones don't make it come out.—*No* (he places a small heavy box on the scale).—He also said blue boxes didn't.—*No* (he puts a heavy blue one on the scale)."

Table II shows the percentage of children at each age who give no proof whatever, those whose proofs are wrong at least part of the time (All the Bs do not cause A because there are B's as well), and, finally, those whose demonstrations are correct:

Table II. *Adequacy of demonstrations at ages 4 – 9+*

Age	N	No proof given	Demonstrations wholly or partly incorrect	Correct Demonstrations
4 years	6	66%	33%	0
5 & 6 years	31	13%	29%	58%
7 & 8 years	20	10%	15%	75%
9–13 years	8	0	0	100%

The examples representing stage II are worth considering from two different points of view. In the first place, they need to be examined from the standpoint of the three possible relationships involved: $A = B$ (problem 3), $B > A$ (problem 1) and $A < B$ (problem 2); in the second place, they are instructive in that they bring out the imaginal qualities which facilitate a correct use of "all", and those which retard it.

As far as the relation $A = B$ is concerned, we can see that at this stage all our subjects understand that the emergence of the ball depends on weight and not on volume, in spite of the fact that, for most problems,[1] the dissociation of weight and volume is a very much later

[1] Cf. J. Piaget and B. Inhelder, *Le développement des quantités chez l'enfant* Delachaux et Niestlé.

development. We can think of two reasons for the relative precocity of this dissociation in the quite atypical setting of the present experiment. First, there is the fact that the distribution of variables is uniform throughout (there are two colours, two sizes and two weights), which makes it easier to separate them in perception. And second, there is the fact that "all" the heavy boxes (A) are "all" those (B) which make the ball come out. Thus $A = B$, which does not involve an asymmetrical relation of inclusion.

Children at stage II are frequently successful in solving problem (1): "Are all the Bs As (if $B = A + A'$)". provided that the question is correctly understood as being of this form. Even children of 5–6 years argue correctly 58% of the time. Tahi, who is intermediate between stages I and II, is still inclined to accept the use of "all" where he can see exceptions. But when discussing whether the red boxes (B) are those which cause the emergence of the ball (A), he still replies correctly: "Not all, because there is one (A') which is light." Nor is he the only one who shows that he can rule out a false assertion: All the Bs are not As because there are Bs which are not-a ($= A'$s). However, as we saw in §1, the reason that this type of argument is accessible at stage II is that it is based on the perception of B as a sum: $B = A + A'$ and it does not imply the inverse operation, $A = B - A'$, which is the hallmark of operational inclusion.

On the other hand, there are some results which strikingly confirm those of §1, in spite of the fact that the problems are set in a realistic and functional context instead of being posed in terms of pure classification. All the questions we put belong to type (1): "Are all the Bs As? (when $B = A + A'$). Nevertheless, one after another, we found children who answered: "No, because there are B's (i.e. there are Cs which are not-B, where $C = B + B'$)."[1]

The underlying reasoning again involves the false quantification of the predicate, which we know to be characteristic of stage II, although it is more frequent in answer to problems of type 2 (see §1). In effect, the child is saying: "All the Bs are not Cs (gratuitously translated as 'all the Cs') because there are some B's as well." This is an exact replica of what we saw in §1: "All the As are not ('all the') Bs because there are some A's!"

Here are a few cases in point. Rom is asked "Do all the large ones (B) make the ball come out ($=$ are A)?" and he answers "No, because there are small heavy ones (B') which also make the ball come out ($= C$ which also includes A)". When asked whether all the blue ones

---

[1] It should be noted that the classes dealt with here have non-empty intersections, unlike most of those occurring in §1. Thus B (e.g., large boxes) contains or includes A (the large, heavy boxes), but A is also included in C (heavy boxes), and C also includes B' (the small heavy boxes).

are light, Rom does not answer "No, because there are heavy blue ones" but rather "No, because there are also light red ones". Gen and Fra give similar answers (heavy, red boxes) and so does Roc (large, heavy ones). So also do Bor (heavy, red; and light, blue) and Gro (light, red). The reason for all these incorrect arguments, is that the child turns "Are all the Bs As?" into "Are all the Bs all the As?" by extending the "all" to the predicate. Fra is quite explicit: having heard "All the red ones are heavy" she repeats this as "They were all red, the ones which were heavy"; and "All the large ones . . . , etc." becomes "only the large ones".

Now it goes without saying that this sort of reaction is by no means universal in the present experiment, because no subject is compelled to extend a type (1) problem to a type (2) relationship by inverting the question. What is remarkable is that the extension occurs spontaneously and fairly frequently, as may be seen from the number of type (2) arguments which are adduced. All of which confirms our interpretation of the errors which were noted in §1, with questions of type (2), e.g. "Are all the circles blue?" We now see very clearly that these were not mere verbal confusions but genuine pointers to the complexity of class-inclusion for children at stage II.

There is also a second reason that incorrect quantification of the predicate is not universal in the weighing experiment. Perceptual and imaginal factors are more important here than they were in the experiment of §1. They help to decide when "all" will be used correctly and when it will not. The two questions "Are the heavy ones red?" and "Are the red ones heavy" are very different in difficulty, because it is far easier to group elements together in one's mind so as to form a non-graphic collection based on colour than it is to group them by their weight. The difference in imaginal potential is greater than that between colour and shape which figured in §1.

This brings us to the next experiment in which we again used the letter scale, but in which the experimental design is an exact parallel to that of §1, so that the two sets of results are more strictly comparable.

II. In this experiment we questioned an additional 101 children of all ages ranging from 5–9. But this time the only two variables were colour and weight, and these were distributed so as to create one empty intersection. In other words, the logical structure of the variables was identical with that used in §1. The boxes were either light and red, or light and blue, or heavy and red; the heavy boxes being those which made the ball appear out of its groove. There were no heavy blue boxes, just as in §1 there were no round, red beads.

We asked four questions and these were strictly analogous to the four questions of §1: (1) "Are all the heavy ones red?" (which we will refer to as HR); (2) "Are all the blue ones light?" (BL); (3) "Are all the red ones heavy?" (*RH*); and (4) "Are all the light ones blue?" (*LB*). *HR* and *BL* are of type (2), or *AB*, i.e. "Are all the *A*s *B*s (where $A < B$)?" (the correct answer being "yes"), *RH* and *LB* are of type (1) or *BA*, i.e., "Are all the *B*s *A*s (where $A < B$)?" (the correct answer being "no").

Because the logical structure of these questions is exactly parallel to that of those asked in §1, the results we obtained were also parallel. But whereas in §1, the decisive difference was that between the type (1) group (*BA*) and the type (2) group (*AB*), here we find a far greater difference between questions in which the word "all" is applied to a collection defined by its colour (*BL* and *RH*) as opposed to those in which the collection is defined by its weight (*HR* and *LB*). *BL* and *RH* are very much easier than *HR* and *LB*.

Here are a few examples of the replies we obtained at stage II:

PAR (5; 11): "Are all the red boxes heavy?—*No*.—Why not?—*There are light red ones* (correct).—Are all the blue ones light (type 2)?—*Yes* (correct).—Are all the light ones red (type 2)?—*No, some are heavy and some are light* (he answers as though he had been asked; are all the red ones light, or are all the light ones all the red ones?).—(Same question.)—*No*."

GIR (5; 6): "Are all the heavy ones red?—*No, there are some* (red boxes) *which are empty and some which are heavy*.—Are all the blue ones light?—*Yes, all of them*.—Are all the light ones blue?—*Yes, all of them* (assimilating this to the previous question).—Are all the red ones heavy?—*Not all. Some are heavy and some are light*.—Are all the light ones blue?—*Yes* (inverting the question)."

DEN (5; 7): "Are all the red ones heavy?—*No, not all. That one is heavy, and that one too*.—What do you have to show?—*All*. (He tries all the red boxes.) *There are no heavy blue ones*.—Are all the heavy ones red?—(He points to all the red boxes, of which some are light and some heavy.) *No*.—But are all the heavy ones red?—*There were red ones which weren't heavy* (!)—Are all the blue ones light?—(He indicates the blue boxes.) *No, all the blue ones are not light* (they are). *I made a mistake about all the blue ones being light*."

MUL (5; 8): "Are all the blue ones light?—(He tries them.) *Yes*.—Are all the light ones blue?—(He tries all the blue boxes again.) *Yes, they are light* (!)—Are all the red ones heavy?—(He tries them.) *No* (correct.)—Are all the heavy ones red?—(He tries all the red boxes again.) *No, only three are*.—Are some of the heavy ones red?—*Yes, there are some*.—Are some of the blue ones light?—(He indicates all the blue boxes.) *Yes*.—What did you show me?—*The light ones*."

JAC (6; 0): "Are all the heavy ones red?—*No, because those* (light red boxes) *are not heavy*.—Are all the blue ones light?—*No, some are light and some heavy* (wrong).—And are all the light ones blue?—*No* (right, but he tries to prove this by pointing to the heavy red ones!)."

ROT (6; 9): "Are all the heavy ones red?—*No, there are light ones as well* (which are red). *Those are heavy and all the others are light*.—But I asked whether all the heavy ones were red?—*No, not all the red ones are not heavy. There are some heavy ones too* (!)"

86

GIL (7; 9): "Are all the heavy ones red?—*No, three are heavy and three are not heavy.*—Are all the light ones blue?—*Yes*—(He is shown a light red box.) Well, are all the light ones blue?—*Yes.*—Really?—*No, there are three red ones and six blue ones.*—Is it the same thing to say 'All the heavy ones are red' and 'All the red ones are heavy'?—*Yes.*"

EUG (8; 1): "Are all the heavy ones red?—*No, there are some light blue ones as well . . . no, yes, they are all red.*—Are all the light ones blue?—*Yes.*—Which ones should you be looking at?—*The blue ones.*—Is it the same thing to say 'All the light ones are blue' and 'All the blue ones are light'?—(She considers the question for a long time.) *Yes.*"

FEL (8; 6): "Are all the heavy ones red?—(He touches each of the red boxes in turn.) *No.*—Show me all the heavy ones.—(He indicates the three heavy red boxes.)—What was it I asked?—*Are all the red ones heavy?*"

Here, now, are just two examples of stage III:

AUD (6; 6): "Are all the red ones heavy?—*No, there are three heavy red ones.*—Are all the heavy ones red?—*Yes.*—Why?—*They are all red, the heavy ones. But not all the red ones are heavy; three of them are heavy and three are light.*—Are all the heavy ones red?—*Yes, three, and they're red; none are blue, only red.*—Are all the blue ones light?—*Yes.*—Are all the light ones blue?—*No, there are three light red ones and three light blue ones.*—Which is it better to say: 'All the blue ones are light' or 'Some of the blue ones are light?'—*All.* What about 'All the red ones are heavy' or 'Some of the red ones are heavy?'—*Some.*"

PAT (7; 3) still shows a trace of stage II. "Are all the red ones heavy?—*No, not all.*—Are all the heavy ones red?—*No, not all, because all the red ones aren't heavy.*—Is it the same thing to say that all the red ones are heavy and that all the heavy ones are red?—*Yes . . . Oh no! Because all the heavy ones are red and all the red ones aren't heavy.*—Are all the blue ones light?—*Yes.*—Are all the light ones blue?—*No, not all. There are light ones there also* (pile of red boxes)."

From a qualitative point of view, these reactions closely parallel those of §1. Yet here the children are genuinely interested in these questions of "all" and "some", because these terms are now being applied to an absorbing puzzle. This is particularly true inasmuch as they themselves work out their preliminary classification by colour and weight after trying out the various boxes on the scale to see whether the little ball will come out or stay put.

Once again, we are faced with the crucial question: why do so many children invert the question they were asked so that "Are all the *X*s *y*?" becomes "Are all the *Y*s *x*?". (When the question is "Are all the light ones blue?" the five-year-old group invert it 80% of the time; and when it is "Are all the heavy ones red?" they still do so 65% of the time.) We can no longer explain the result away by talking about lack of concentration because we know these children were interested in giving the right answers. Now it can be argued that the inversion does not imply a false quantification of the predicate. In other words, the subject knows that "All the Xs are y" means "All the Xs are some of the Ys", while "All the Ys are x" means "All the Ys are some of the xs", but nevertheless he cannot avoid mixing them up. An alternative interpretation is that he does not distinguish between them and simply assimilates them to an expression of identity: "All the Xs are all the Ys" (and, of course, vice versa). In order to decide between these alternatives we asked several children point blank whether the two questions are the same (cf. Gil, Eug and Pat). A dozen children were asked this question at stage II, and every one of them replied in all confidence that the two questions were the same (and Eug did so after prolonged thought on the matter). Naturally enough, those at stage III replied that the two were different. It is interesting to watch Pat making the transition by first assimilating the two questions, and then discovering quite suddenly that they are not the same. The fact that there is this assimilation at stage II should convince us that the inversion which goes with it does indeed derive from a false quantification of the predicate.

But if the two questions are identical to the child, why should he invert them as often as he does? This question is easily answered in terms of the lay-out of the experiment. If he can choose freely whether to think about a collection defined by colour or by weight, he chooses the former because it is easier.

Table III. *Four questions involving "all" in a realistic context; % correct replies at ages 5–9[1]*

Age and no of subjects.	HR	BL	RH	LB	AB	BA	+	Average for weight (HR+LB)	Average for colour (BL+RH)
5 (20)	35	82	100	20	35	20	5	27·5	91
6 (20)	40	91·5	100	53	36·5	53	17·5	46·5	95·5
7 (25)	47	100	100	44	47	44	28	45·5	100
8 (20)	67·5	97	100	55·5	65·5	55·5	41	61·5	98·5
9 (16)	89	98	100	62	89	62	62	75·5	99

Like Tables I and Ia, Table III illustrates the failure of younger children to quantify the predicate correctly with any consistency. But

[1] HR = Are all the heavy ones red?
  BL = Are all the blue ones light?
  RH = Are all the red ones heavy?
  LB = Are all the light ones blue?
Column AB shows the percentage who were right for both HR and BL (type 2). Column BA gives those who were right for both RH and LB (type 1). Column + shows the percentage % of subjects whose answers were all correct. The last two columns give the means for HR/LB and BL/RH respectively. The marking scheme was identical with that used for Tables I and Ia.

over and above this general feature, which is common to both sets of results, we find a particular feature which here assumes an overriding importance. It is the striking difference between columns *HR* and *LB* as compared with *BL* and *RH*. Up to and including the age of seven, the number of correct answers given to questions in which the "all" refers to the weight of the boxes ("Are all the heavy ones . . ." or "Are all the light ones . . .") is less than half what it is for questions in which the "all" applies to their colour! Tables I and Ia show a slight advantage to categorization by shape as against categorization by colour. But the difference is only slight.

Here we see that when "all" is used for "blue boxes" and "red boxes", its meaning is usually interpreted correctly, but when it is used for "light boxes" and "heavy boxes" it is very often misinterpreted. Thus *BL* receives between 82 and 100% correct answers while *LB* is answered correctly only 20–62% of the time. This has nothing to do with the fact that all the blue ones are light whereas not all the light ones are blue. As a matter of fact questions of type *BA* are in principle easier than those of type *AB*. The true explanation is that in the question "Are all the blue boxes light?", the "all" conjures up an intuitive non-graphic collection. Because of this factor, we see that column *BA* is irregular.

The importance of the intuitive or imaginal potential of the property qualified by "all" was apparent even in the results of the previous experiment, where the various factors were combined in every possible way. It was particularly evident when we studied the proofs which the subjects were using. A few control experiments, carried out in addition to the free interrogations, showed that among a group of subjects all of whom argued correctly (i.e. gave correct counter-examples) when dealing with "Are all the small (or large) ones light?" only 67% argued correctly when dealing with "Are all the light ones small (or large)?". Similarly, among a group of whom 67% dealt correctly with "Are all the large ones heavy?" only 25% did so with "Are all the heavy ones large?" But such imaginal factors are less important when all four classes are present than when one of them is missing, perhaps because the symmetrical distribution of properties tends to cloud the issue. Symmetry is itself a quasi-intuitive attribute at stage II. Our conclusion is therefore that the development of understanding in relation to the true meaning of the quantifier "all" is very much bound up with imaginal properties in general.

3. THE ABSOLUTE AND RELATIVE USES OF "SOME"[1]

§§1 and 2 deal with the relationship between "all" and "some" by means of questions involving the use of the word "all". We now know that

[1] This part of the investigation is based on 31 subjects.

children at stage II misinterpret the sort of question we have designated as type 2: "Are all the *A*s *B*s?" is taken to mean "Are all the *A*s all of the *B*s?" whereas its true meaning corresponds to "Are all the *A*s some of the *B*s?".

To begin with we tried to find out just what children understand by the word "some", without regard to the specific case in which the elements of a collection *A* are both "all" of the *A* and "some" of the *B* (*A* < *B*). What we wanted to know was the precise significance which this word "some" conveys to a child in a relatively unstructured situation. All that happens is that he is faced with a variety of objects and asked to hand over "some blue counters" or "some yellow flowers" and so on. We tried this with various types of material, i.e. (1) the counters of §1 (blue circles and red and blue squares), (2) drawings of flowers (white and yellow roses, white and yellow tulips) and (3) drawings to be coloured in (fruit, trees, landscapes with houses, etc., in which "some" of the elements had to be coloured, but not all). The subjects were also asked, to compare "some" and "all", or else to define the word "some", or occasionally to compare it with other expressions of his own choosing (such as "almost all" etc.).

Generally speaking, at stage II, children are aware that "some" has a different meaning from "all", but at the same time they cannot fix on a stable meaning for the word. Especially at the beginning of this stage, they vacillate about what it means. This vacillation harks back to stage I when they saw no difference between "all" and "some". The following is an example of stage I.

Jac (5; 2). Counters as in §1. "Can you give me some blue ones?—(He gives one.)—Is that some or one?—*One*.—Now 'some'.—(He takes one.)—Now all the blue ones.—(He takes one.)—All the squares.—(He takes two.)—All the circles.—(He takes all of them.)—Some of the blue ones.—(Two, then three, then all of them.)"

At stage II some distinction is made between "some" and "all", either in the verbal definition or in practice. Interestingly enough, the practice is not always co-ordinated with the definition.

Kar (5; 4). Counters: "Give me some blue ones.—(He gives four out of six.)—Some of the squares.—(He gives both of them; these are subsequently put back, this being standard practice after each question.)—Give me all the squares.—(He gives back the same two squares.)—Just now, you gave me the same thing for 'some'. Is it the same?—*No*.—What does 'all' mean?—*A lot*.—And 'some'?—*One or two*." A new row (five blue circles, two blue squares and two red ones): "Give me some of the blue ones.—(He gives the five circles.)—Could one do it otherwise?—*Yes* (he gives the last two).—Would a circle and a blue square do for 'some blue ones'?—*Yes*.—Give me some of the squares.—(He gives one blue and one red square.)—Some of the circles.—(He gives three of them.)—Some of the red ones.—(Gives the two red squares.)—And all the red ones?—(Gives the same.)—Are you right both times?—*Yes, not very.*—What is not very right?—*One ought to give one* (= some) *or several* (= all).—Some of the blue ones.—*Circles?*—Just as you like, provided they're blue ones.—(He takes two blue circles and makes as if to take a blue square, but puts it back.)—Would it have been right to give me that one too?—*Yes.*"

MAR (5; 6). Counters: "Give me some of the blue ones.—(Takes them all, squares and circles.) *A lot!*—Is that 'some' or 'all'?—*All*—But what would you give if I just asked for some?—*The circles.*—Would only two circles do?—*Yes.*—Give me some of the squares.—(He gives them all, red and blue.)—Is that some?—*Yes.*—What are you giving me there?—*Squares.*—Is it more correct to say 'some' or 'all'?—*Some.*—Would it also be correct to say 'all'?—*That's* ['All' is] *for the same colour.* (!)—Give me some of the circles.—(Takes them all.)—Is that some?—*Yes.*—And all the circles?—*That's all the circles.*—And some?—*That's the blue ones* (= the same!)."

TER (5; 2). Counters: "Some of the blue ones.—(Gives one.)—All the blue circles.—(Gives them all.)—Some of the squares?—(Gives a red one.)—Could you give more?—*Yes, two.*—And like that (two red squares and a blue one, one blue square being left out?)—*No, that isn't the same colour.*—Give me some of the circles.—(Takes them all.)—Some of the blue squares.—(Takes them all.)—Is that some or all of the blue squares?—*There are only three blue squares* (some and all are identified because of the insufficient number of objects).—Is that some or all?—*All.*—Supposing I put in these as well (adding three), how many would you give me for 'some'?—*Three.*—Could you give four?—*Yes.*—And five?—*No.*—Why?—*Because there are five* (in fact there are six; but, thinking that there are five, Ter refuses to give the last one, which would mean giving 'all')."

RUS (5; 3). Counters: "Give me some of the blue ones.—*Circles?*—Whatever you like.—(Gives a blue square and a blue circle.)—Some of the red ones.—(Gives three out of four.)—Some of the circles.—(Gives all but one.)—Some of the squares.—(All the blue squares.)—Would it have been all right to give me both the blue squares and one red one (out of two)?—*No, they're not the same colour.*—All the circles.—(Gives them all.)—Is 'all' the circles the same as 'some'?—*No, because some doesn't mean all.*"

It looks as if Rus has some appreciation of the relativity implied by the use of "some". Yet this fails to appear when he is questioned about the flowers (3 white and 3 yellow tulips, 3 white and 4 yellow roses). "Some of the yellow tulips.—(Gives them all.)—And some of the white tulips.—(Two out of three.)—Would it do to give me that one too (the last)?—*Yes, it's the same.*—Give me some flowers.—(Gives several.)—And if I add these?—*No, that isn't some.*—All the flowers.—(Gives them all.)—If I left one out, would it still be 'all'?—*No.*—Some white tulips.—(Gives two of them.)—And another one (the last)?—*No.*—Why?—That would be *'a lot'*.—Is some a number?—*Yes, three.*—Only three?—*Two or three.*"

REM (5; 8) Flowers: "Some yellow tulips?—(Gives all three.)—And all the yellow tulips?—(The same.)—Is all and some the same thing?—*Yes.*" "Some tulips.—(Gives the white ones.)—And with that one (yellow), would that also be some tulips?—*No, because it's yellow.*—All the tulips.—(Gives them.)—

And like that (with one less)?—*No, because there's one missing.*" Later: "Some yellow tulips. (Takes all three, and puts one back.)—Why do you put it back?—*Because otherwise there would be none left.*—And all?—(Takes the one which he had put back.)"

The remaining examples belong to the latter half of stage II. Although there is some progress in the differentiation of "all" and "some", they still fail to grasp the essentially relative meaning of "some".

CHA (5; 6). Counters: "Give me some blue counters.—(Gives all but one.)—All.—(Gives them.)—Some of the [four] square counters.—(Gives two red and one blue.)—Some of the blue counters.—(Gives them all.)—And some circles.—(All again.)—Is that some or all?—*All. I must take some away.*—Is it still right when you give me all?—*No, 'some' is half.*—Exactly half or about half?—*Exactly.*—How many is half of six?—*It's four.*—And of four?—*Four.* —Give me some squares.—(He gives all four, and they are then put back in place.)—And half of four?—(Gives them all.)"—The only progress here is that "some" is defined as being "half" but even "half" is still not a relative term so far as Cha is concerned!

LIS (5; 8). Counters: three blue circles and seven red squares. "Some blue ones.—(Gives them all.)—Some squares.—(Gives four and leaves three.)—Some red ones.—Gives three, after some hesitation.)—Some circles.—(Gives two and leaves one.)—How can you tell what to do when I say 'some' and what to do when I say 'all'?—*'Some' means that it isn't a lot.*—Would this be some blue counters?—*No, that's a lot.*"

BON (5; 11).—"Some blue circles.—(Gives three out of eight, but also agrees to four, five, etc.)—And the last one?—*No, because that would be 'all'.*—All the blue ones.—(Takes all the blue squares and circles.)—Some pink squares.—(Two out of three.)—And that one?—*No, because there wouldn't be enough.*" This expression occurs again when flowers are used: "Some of the roses" = the three white roses, leaving the three yellow ones. "Can I take that one (one of the three yellow roses)?—*No, because there wouldn't be enough.*" Thus "some" still means "a few".

BERT (5; 11). Correct on the whole. Yet at one point having given all of a small collection, she was asked whether that was "all" or "some". "*It's a few tulips,*" she explained.

CAS (6; 1). For eight squares, "some" = one, then two, then three. "Till how many?—*Up to four.*—And like that (five)?—*No.*—Why?—*It's a lot.*"

FAB (6; 10). "Some" is "*several*". One or two do not constitute "some", but any number from three to a hundred does. On the other hand:

FRA (7; 4). Ten squares. "Give some of them.—(Seven).—Is four some?—*Yes.*—Five?—*Yes.*—And eight?—*No, that is more.*—After what number can one say "some" (in descending order)?—*After seven.*—Is some and all the same thing?—*No, some is less than all.*"

In spite of the vagueness and variability of the answers there are three points which emerge quite clearly. In the first place, all the subjects—including those at the beginning of this stage—distinguish between "some" and "all". But few can formulate the distinction verbally. There are occasional momentary lapses when a subject seems unable to distinguish between the two words, and now and again, one may go so far as to say that they mean the same (cf. Rus and Rem when confronted with the three yellow and white tulips). But it is significant that the confusion is limited to the analysis of small collections numbering two or three (we shall see the reason for this presently). Rus, for example, identifies "all" and "some" when dealing with three white tulips; yet she refuses to give all the flowers for "some flowers"; what is more, she will not even give all but a few, since "that isn't some". Incidentally children never react differently to "some A" (e.g. "some blue ones") and "some of the As". We deliberately alternated between these forms because we wished to find out whether or not they conveyed any subtle differences of meaning to our subjects.[1] From the semantic point of view, the only general form of definition available to this group of subjects is that offered by Rus (in spite of identifying some and all for three white tulips): "Some doesn't mean all!"

These observations lead to a second conclusion, which is this: even in the second half of stage II, "some" has an absolute meaning which is bound up with the number of elements instead of pointing to a relation between part and whole. Thus Kar contrasts "all = many" with "some = one or two", and returns to this distinction with "one = some" and "several = all". Mar is less clear about the number involved, because he emphasizes a range of quality. This leads him to various confusions based on the notions "some = a few of different kinds" and "all = many of a uniform type". Ter, on the other hand, is quite explicit: for sufficiently large collections (the circles) "some" is taken to mean one or two, while "all" implies the whole set; but for small collections (the three blue squares) all and some merge into one another, because "some" means a small number. By way of control: if three blue squares are added to the others, "all" and "some" become distinct once more, and "some" now denotes any collection of up to n-1 squares. For Rus, "some" cannot mean "many", and tends to denote quite simply: "two or three". Cha and Fra each have their own quantitative definition (half, several, etc.).

Finally, we come to the third feature of these reactions. This is far more obscure than the others, and is based on the relative failure to differentiate between extension and intension. When a collection B (with b as common characteristic) contains two different sub-collections A and A' (whose characteristics are a and a', e.g. the squares (B) can be red (a) or blue (a')), then the term "some" is often limited to one of the

<hr>

[1] One of the authors had already noted in 1921 that children had verbal difficulties in mastering the relation of the part ("some of" etc.) to the whole. Cf. J. Piaget, "Essai sur quelques aspects du développement de la notion de partie chez l'enfant", *Journ. de Psychol.*, 1921 (XVII), pp. 449–480.

sub-collections (generally the smaller, as with Ter, for whom "some squares" cannot mean a mixture of red and blue); in other cases, "some" is freely applied to heterogeneous sets, while "all" is limited to a homogeneous collection (e.g. Mar, for whom all is "for the same colour"). In short, the meaning of "all" and "some" is not restricted to the extension of collections defined by common characteristics (intension); instead we find that its meaning also includes some reference to the homogeneity of these characteristics. This feature of our observations becomes less apparent by the second half of stage II.

Thus although children may begin to differentiate as between "all" and "some" by the beginning of stage II, they have a great many complications to overcome, so that confusion between these terms is still prevalent when the collections involved are too small or when they contain sub-collections. It is only "all" that has a constant meaning at this stage (where at stage I even this did not hold, since "all" often admitted exceptions—as though to prove the rule!). At stage II, "all" is the set of elements of a collection, without exception. As for "some", the term may denote an absolute quantity, i.e. "few" as opposed to "many", or again it may connote one of a variety of relations of "intension". As a result it is often confused with the whole, at least in "extension". We are now in a better position to understand the incorrect quantification of the predicate discussed in §§1 and 2: a subject has difficulty in understanding that "All the As are Bs" means "All the As are some of the Bs" and not "all the Bs", for he does not distinguish systematically between "some" and "all".

We now turn to a consideration of the essentially relative connotation of "some". In this connexion we examined 32 children aged from 6–9. The subject was seated at a table on which were 5 white tulips, 4 yellow tulips, 4 white roses and 5 (or 6) yellow ones. By way of introducing the linguistic distinction involved, the subject was first asked (A) for "some" of the "tulips", "all the white roses", etc. We then proceeded to the central question (B): Are "all the tulips" and "some of the flowers" the same thing? Can a given bunch (that the child or the questioner has made) be called "all the tulips" and "some of the flowers" at the same time? To elucidate the meaning of answers given to this crucial question, the following questions were asked (using an appropriate bunch of flowers for each question): (1) If X (the name of a playmate) said that "All the tulips are flowers" and you said that "Some of the tulips are flowers", who would be right? Why? (2) If you said "Some of the flowers are tulips" and X said "All the flowers are tulips", who would be right? (3) Which is more correct: "All the flowers are tulips" or "All the tulips are flowers?" (4) "All the yellow tulips are flowers" or "All the flowers are yellow tulips?", etc. Finally, we asked a number of questions involving the quantification of inclusion (a topic to which we will return in ch. IV): Are there more tulips or more yellow tulips in this bunch? Are there more flowers in this (mixed) bunch or more yellow roses? etc.

Here are a few replies illustrating stage II.

BEN (6; 1) Quest. 1: "*It is I who am right* [= some of the tulips are flowers] *because all the flowers are not tulips.*" Quest. 2 to 6: correct. Quest. (*B*): Ben will not allow that a bouquet consisting of all the tulips is also a bouquet of "some" or "some of the" flowers, on the grounds that the latter description demands additional varieties.

GRA (6; 2): "Are all the tulips flowers or only some?—*All the tulips . . . No, some of the tulips because that's not all the flowers.*—But are all the tulips flowers?—*No.*—Why?—*Because there are other flowers.* (! cf. "All the *A*s are all the *B*s")—Are some of the flowers tulips or are all the flowers tulips?—*Some of the flowers are tulips, because there are other flowers.*—Are all the tulips flowers?—*Some flowers are tulips and some tulips are flowers.*—Then what are the other tulips, if they aren't flowers?— . . . —Can't we say that all the tulips are flowers?—*No, there have to be other flowers.*—Have you got some of the flowers?—*No.*—What have you?—*Tulips.*—But aren't all the tulips some of the flowers (quest. *B*)?—*No, this is all the tulips. You have to take one tulip away* [to have "some of the flowers"].—Why?— . . . —What must we do then?—(She removes the white tulips.)—Well, is this bunch some of the flowers?—*No, they're all tulips.*" Yet when asked "Are some of the flowers yellow tulips, or are all the flowers yellow tulips?" Gra accepts that "*some of the flowers are yellow tulips*", because he rejects the alternative. We continue: "Can one say that all the yellow tulips are flowers?—*No, because there are other colours and other flowers.*"

LIC (6; 4) makes up a bunch using all the roses. "All?—*Yes, there are none left.*—Can one say that I have some of the flowers here?—*No, it's some of the roses.*" A little while later, Lic makes the same bunch once again: "Can one call this bunch some of the flowers?—*One says some of the roses.*—But is it some flowers?—*Yes, because if you find them in a field and there are others, then it's some* [i.e. without the others]. *But if there are none left, then it's all.*—And if I take all the tulips, is that some of the flowers?—*Yes.*—And are all the roses some of the flowers?—*If you put all the flowers together, it's all the flowers. If there are only roses it's 'some', and if you take all the roses, then it's 'all the roses'*—But would that be 'some flowers'?—*When you take all the roses I think that's the same as when you say 'some flowers'* (but she does not sound convinced)."

MUR (6; 7). "Are all tulips flowers or are some of the tulips flowers?—*All the tulips is better, because all the tulips are together.*—Well, are some of the flowers tulips or are all the flowers tulips?—*All the flowers are tulips.*—Really?—*No, because there are others also.*—Are all the tulips some of the flowers?—*No, all the tulips are flowers.*—Can't we say that all the tulips are some of the flowers?—*No, because the tulips are flowers and not some of them.*—Give me all the yellow roses.—(She puts them all in a bunch.)—Is that all the yellow roses or some of them?—*Some.*—Give me some of the flowers.—(She selects two tulips and two roses.)—Have I more flowers or more roses?—

It's the same.—How many flowers have I got?—*Four.*—How many roses?—*Two.*—And tulips?—*Two.*—Have I more flowers or more tulips.—*It's the same.*"

We conclude with two examples of stage III:

BRA (8; 1): "Give me all the yellow flowers.—(He makes a bunch of them.)—Do I have all the yellow flowers there or some of them?—*All.*—Is that also some of the flowers?—*Yes, of all the flowers that is some.*" "Are all the tulips flowers or are some of the tulips flowers?—*All.*—And are all the flowers tulips or some of them?—*Some of the flowers are tulips.*" "Give me all the tulips.—(He does so.)—Is it more correct to say 'all the tulips' or 'some of the flowers?'—*One can say both!*—Is it the same thing?—*Yes.*"

ROS (9; 2): "I asked a boy for a bunch of all the tulips, then I asked him for a bunch with some of the flowers. He gave me the same bunch both times. Was he right?—*Some of which flowers? Those flowers over there?*—Yes.—*Yes, he was right.*"

These results on the relative connotation of the word "some" are in line with all that we have already learnt of stage II: they confirm the systematic failure to understand the inclusion implicit in "All the *A*s are *b*", i.e. "All the *A* are some of the *B*s". Thus Ben and Gra obviously think that "some" flowers and "some of the" flowers refers to the intension of a collection instead of its extension (we also find this in Gra when the question is simply, "Are all the tulips flowers?"). To have "some flowers", other varieties must be added. ("There have to be other flowers" because all the tulips are "tulips".) Gra concludes that "Some tulips are flowers and some flowers are tulips". When Mur explains that "the tulips are flowers and not some of them", she, too, implies that the word "some" denotes variety (which is why she selects two tulips and two roses to illustrate what she means). Lic, after considerable suggestion, managed to admit without conviction, that "all the tulips" = "some flowers"; but she too begins by objecting that "some of the flowers" can be used for a part of the flowers in a field, while all the roses are "some of the roses" and not "some flowers", etc. And once again, we repeatedly encounter the familiar incorrect quantification: "All the *A*s are *b* = All the *A*s are all the *B*s" (as with Gra and others who deny that "all the tulips are flowers").

As to the quantitative distribution of successes and failures, the central question, "Are all the tulips (or roses) some of the flowers?" led to an immediately correct reply in only 21% of all subjects aged between 6 and 8. An additional 30% accepted the right answer after some hesitation and some reformulation; 49% persistently denied it. For question 1 (Are all the tulips flowers?), which corresponded to problem 2 (all the *A*s are *B*s, where *A* < *B*) of §§1 and 2, the percentage of correct answers amounted to 47, again with subjects of 6–8 years. Question 2 (Are all the flowers tulips or are some of the flowers tulips?) which corresponded to problem 1 (All the Bs are *a*, where $A < B$), gained a correct percentage of 81. This discrepancy confirms the difference between the two types of question which we emphasized in §1. To understand why only 21% of the subjects accept that "All the tulips are some of the flowers", while 81% accept the logically identical statement that "Some of the flowers are tulips", we need only remember from §1 that a child can see that the collections *A* and *B* do not coincide, and will therefore refute the statement that "All the Bs are *a*", even if he understands this as meaning "All the Bs are all the As". That is why 81% of the answers are correct. The statement "All the As are *b*" is a better index to the understanding of inclusion.

Finally, we may note once again the importance of intuitive or imaginal factors. If the questions are altered so as to weaken the cohesion of the *A* class, e.g. "Are all/some of the flowers yellow tulips?" and "Are all/some of the yellow tulips flowers?" then only 68% of answers to the first question (Are all the Bs As?) are correct (between 6 and 8) and only 37% to the second (Are all the As Bs?).

As to the last question of all, questions involving the quantification of inclusion (Are there more tulips or more flowers in this bouquet? Are there more flowers or more yellow roses in this one?) received no more than 33% correct answers from subjects of 6–8 years. We shall return to this question in ch. IV.

4. CONCLUSIONS. "SOME" AND "ALL", INCLUSION AND THE RELATIONS BETWEEN INTENSION AND EXTENSION

The results of these experiments are, on the whole, fairly coherent. They show, first of all, that there is no systematic co-ordination of "all" and "some" at stage II. "Some" still has an absolute connotation (it means a small number), and when the collection is very small "some" merges into "all". Nor is the usage of "all" invariably correct, even when the problem is of our type 1: "Are all the Bs As (with $B = A + A'$)?" Our results also show that, in tackling a type 2 problem: "Are all the As Bs (where $A = B - A'$)?" a child at stage II will extend the reference of "all" to cover the predicate ("Are all the As all the Bs?"). And the reason is, first, that he cannot understand the relative character of the implicit "some" ("All the As are some of the Bs") and, second, that he cannot use the inverse operation $A = B - A'$. What follows is a systematic failure to grasp the relation of inclusion. Psychologically as well as logically, error in handling "all" and "some" entails error in handling inclusion.

To conclude chs. II and III, we have yet to elucidate the nature of these difficulties, and in so doing, we shall, in effect, be providing a general characterization of stage II. Once again, we shall look to the nature of the distinction between extension and intension and the kinds of relation which exist between them from the point of view of a child who still thinks in terms of non-graphic collections.

Now the non-graphic collection does mark a clear-cut advance as compared with the earlier graphic collections; the "intension" of the former is no longer dependent on its shape as a whole or on the special arrangement of its elements. In other words a non-graphic collection is something very different from a collective or complex object. It is a mental "pile" or heap of things, the shape of which is irrelevant. But a non-graphic collection is still a "collection" and not a "class". This means that its constituent elements need to be perceptible and that they have to be fairly close together. Moreover, they are held together in the child's mind only by virtue of a qualitative criterion and this must be reasonably intuitable, i.e. graphic in character. The union of such elements is therefore a static form of representation, for it lacks the reversible mobility of an operational class. If we want to find out why these children find it difficult to handle "all" and "some" correctly, our starting-point must be this residual wholeness of non-graphic collections. A non-graphic collection is still a qualitative entity and its properties belong to it *as a whole*.

The basic question is whether stage II subjects understand "all" as referring to extension alone, or whether the differentiation of intension and extension—which was totally lacking at stage I—is still incomplete at the level of non-graphic collections.

At the operational level, intension is the set of characteristics common to the members of a class, and extension is the set of members themselves. In other words, extension involves considering a class as a union of elements, while the intension is given by each individual member *qua* representative of the common characteristics of the class. This, of course, is only true once the class has been established and clearly defined. To know whether a given property forms part of the intension of a class is to know whether "all" the members of the class possess it (i.e., whether it is "general"). Intension thus implies extension, just as extension implies intension. But, once the class exists, any one member will suffice to represent its intension, yet one member gives no information whatever concerning its extension, of which it is only an unknown fraction: $1/x$.

On the other hand, the child at the pre-operational level reasons only in terms of qualified collections, and extension can only apply to such collections. "All" refers to properties of a collection in much the same way as intensional properties are assigned to particular individuals. Insofar as a collection is itself an intuitive entity (because the young child cannot differentiate between the logical relations of classes of individuals and the sub-logical relations of part and whole) its general properties belong to the collection as a whole and not separately to its individual members. When the word "all" is applied to a collection, it introduces a property which the collection possesses as an entity (see §1, p. 65 and §2, p. 80). Moreover, the property, must be sufficiently graphic or intuitive for the child to be able to elaborate the statement: "All the . . .". Thus "All the circles are blue", means that the collection, as a whole, is *exclusively* and *entirely* blue and made up of circles, just as a particular object must be entirely blue, as well as circular, to be called a "blue circle". If the collection of "blue" counters contains both squares and circles, it is easy for the child to say that "All the blue ones are not circles", because the collection of blue counters does not coincide with that of circles. But he will often deny that "All the circles are blue", because the collective property "blue" is not possessed by "circles" exclusively, so that the two collections of circles and blues do not constitute one and the same doubly defined collection.

In short, the pre-operational use of "all" follows from the lack of differentiation between intension and extension (and this in turn follows from the relative lack of differentiation between class and object which points to the intuitive character of a pre-logical "collection"). This, of course, does not mean that "all" has nothing to do with extension, for lack of differentiation does not always mean the primacy of intension. But, in so far as it refers to a total and, usually exclusive property, "all" represents a characteristic of a collective entity instead of being a pure quantification of its members. That is why the quantitative difference between "some" and "all" (§3) presents such difficulty. The term "all" has not yet attained the character of a purely quantitative (albeit logical and not numerical) symbol; and this means that "some" is bound to be a vague concept, because the true quantificatory meaning of "some" is functionally related to the quantifying "all". Finally, because there is this lack of quantification, the relation of inclusion is devoid of any possible meaning, and in its place we find what is no more than a qualitative differentiation of the whole.

Thus the varied reactions of stage II subjects show a deep-lying unity. This unity would not have been obvious had we confined our analysis to elementary classificatory behaviour. There are hidden mechanisms underlying the difficulty of class-inclusion, and these are bound up with the problem of co-ordinating the extension and intension of non-graphic collections.

Chapter Four

CLASS INCLUSION AND HIERARCHICAL CLASSIFICATIONS[1]

THE non-graphic collections of ch. II are the immediate precursors of classes involving a structure of inclusion. The construction of such classes implies a thorough grasp of "all" and "some", no mean achievement, as we saw in the course of the last chapter. We can now turn to a discussion of stage III, which is characterized by class inclusion, and we shall be describing new experiments bearing on the transition from stage II to stage III.

Knowing what difficulties the child encounters in co-ordinating extension and intension, we shall not restrict ourselves to analysing his classificatory behaviour. We shall also try to elucidate how he understands the extension of a class (or collection), i.e., how far he succeeds in quantifying the extension. But this time we will avoid questions of "all" and "some". These would be tedious for the reader and tiring for the children (as a matter of fact, that problem of ours was the only one in which our subjects failed to show a genuine interest!). We therefore chose the following form of question: suppose one class A to be included in another class B, without being equal to the whole of B, are there more As than Bs or more Bs than As?

The question can be made very concrete. The last subject in ch. II (Cla at 7; 0), told us that six small toys consisting of four birds (A) and two horses (A') were "all animals" and that that made "six animals" (B). Nevertheless, he said that there were more birds than animals, i.e. $A > B$ instead of $A < B$! Now this sort of problem forms the topic of an earlier experiment, with beads.[2] It is all the more interesting to see whether the fact that the present subjects carry out their own classifications spontaneously will materially affect the results.

But there is a small paradox which we ought to clear up first to avoid possible misunderstandings. We have seen that "All the As are Bs" tends to be understood at stage II as "All the As are all the Bs". We now propose to ask whether there are more As than Bs or less As than Bs taking it for granted that "all the As are b". But this is precisely what a child is denying when he answers the questions of ch. III, §2: "Are all the circles (A) blue counters (B)?—No, because there are also blue squares (A')." We expect our stage II subjects to say that there are more As than Bs (if $A > A'$), although by rights

[1] With the collaboration of Vinh-Bang, B. Matalon and B. Reymond-Rivier.
[2] J. Piaget and A. Szeminska, *The Child's Conception of Number*, ch. VIII.

they ought to say that there are the same number or less if their answers are to be in line with those they gave in ch. III. So there would seem to be a contradiction between the answers given to questions about "all" and "some" as described in ch. III, and the basis of our questioning when dealing with the quantitative relations between A and B.

But the contradiction is purely formal. In neither case should the children's statements be taken literally; and in both it is the negative aspect which is significant. When answering "Are all the As Bs?" the child at stage II does not see the relation. "All the As are some of the Bs", which is why he fails to understand inclusion. When answering "Are there more of the As or of the Bs?" he cannot compare the As with the Bs, and he compares them with the A's, precisely because he cannot handle class-inclusion. When he evaluates the Bs correctly, he is unaware of the As and A's (so that "all" is then applied correctly to B without reference to its divisions). Alternatively, he can compare A and A' forgetting about B (so that "all", and even "some", are applied correctly to A). But he cannot compare A and B. He cannot think simultaneously of the part and the whole (precisely because he cannot deal with inclusion), and this is reflected both in the incorrect usage of "all" and in the false quantifications. Thus the child will readily agree to a qualitative demonstration that all the As are b, even though he is perplexed when the problem is presented in purely quantitative terms "Are all the As Bs?" just because his grasp of the term "all" is lacking in precision.

1. CLASSIFICATION OF FLOWERS (MIXED WITH OTHER OBJECTS)

In this experiment 20 pictures were used, of which 4 represented coloured objects and 16 represented flowers. Eight of these were primulas, four being yellow and the others being of four different colours. This arrangement gives rise to the following sequence of inclusions:

A (yellow primulas) $< B$ (primulas) $< C$ (flowers) $< D$ (flowers and other objects). Beads were used as well, to allow of comparisons with the earlier experiment already mentioned. The beads consisted of the following classes: A (red square ones) $< B$ (red beads, round and square) $< C$ (wooden beads with various colours) $< D$ (wooden beads and glass ones).

The following problems were put and will subsequently be referred to by the appropriate Roman numeral:

(I) Spontaneous classification. (II) General questions on inclusion: If you make a bouquet out of all the primulas, will you use these (the blue primulas)? (III) Four types of question all bearing on the quantification of inclusion: (IIIA) Is the bunch made of all . . . [e.g. the yellow primulas] bigger or smaller or the same as the bunch of all . . . [e.g. the primulas]? (IIIB) Are there more . . . [primulas] or . . . [flowers]? (IIIC) If you take all the . . . [primulas], will there be any . . . [flowers] left? (IIID) If you take all the . . . [flowers], will any . . . [primulas] be left?

Here are some examples of stage I and stage II, when subjects fail all the questions in group III. Usually they will either fail the simpler type II questions as well, or else they cannot co-ordinate their answers to the thinking required for later questions (type III).

GAE (4; 9). I. He puts four yellow and two blue primulas in Class *A*, adding the other blue flowers; a pink primula, another pink flower and a cherry then form *A'*: *"The pink ones go together"*; the lily of the valley and green hat go in *C'* (he remarks on the lily's green stalk): *"The colours go well."*

Questions II: "Can one put (this) in the bouquet made of (these)?" Whatever the question his answer is always "Yes". This means that the *A*s can be part of the *B*s (= *A* + *A'*), the *A'*s are part of the *A*s, while the *B'*s are part of the *A*s as well as the *A'*s, etc.

Questions III are not understood in any of the three forms.

FAV (5; 4). I. All the primulas go to *A*, together with other yellow and orange flowers; the rest of the flowers from *A'* and the other objects make up *B'*. Questions II: all the answers are negative. Questions III: "Are there more primulas or more yellow primulas?—*More primulas*.—And are there more primulas or more flowers among all these?—*More primulas*."

TER (5; 8). I. He first classifies the objects by their colour, and subsequently puts the primulas in *A*, the remaining flowers in *A'*, and the other objects in *B'*. II. "Can I put an (*A'*) in (*A*)?—*Yes, it's a flower*.—And an (*A*) with the (*A'*)?—*Yes, it's also a flower*.—And is a pink flower (*A'*) one of the primulas (*A*)?—*Yes, you can put all the flowers together*." Thus Ter accepts the fusion of Class *A* and Class *A'*, but fails to understand the inclusion relation *A* < *A* + *A'*. Questions III: "Are there more yellow primulas or more primulas?—*No, there are more yellow primulas*.—And are there more primulas or more flowers?—*More flowers* (but he points to *A'* and not to *A* + *A'*)."

BREG (6; 2). I: All the primulas go to *A*, the remaining flowers forming *A'* (but they are carefully grouped around the primulas to make the colours match); the other objects then form *B'*. II: No to all questions. III: "A little girl takes all the yellow primulas and makes a bunch of them, or else she makes a bunch of all the primulas. Which way does she have the bigger bunch?—*The one with the yellow primulas will be bigger* (he counts the others). *Oh no, it's the same thing* (4 = 4).—And which will be bigger: a bunch made up of the primulas or one of all the flowers?—*They're both the same*. (He compares the 8 *A*s with the 8 *A'*s.)"

RAP (6; 4) puts the yellow primulas and the other yellow flowers in Class *A*, the blue primulas and the other blue flowers in *A'*, the cherries and the rest of the flowers in *B'*, and the other objects in *C'*. "Show me which flowers are exactly alike.—(He points to the four yellow primulas.)—And which ones are nearly alike?—(He points to the other four primulas.)—Show me all the primulas.—(Right)—And all the flowers.—(Right.)"

Questions II: "Is this (pink) primula one of these (yellow primulas)?—*No, it isn't yellow*.—And is this one (a yellow primula) one of these (all the primulas)?—*Yes, it's a primula too*.—If a little girl makes up a bunch out of all the flowers, can she put the primulas in it?—*Yes*.—And could she put this (pink tulip) in a bunch of primulas?—*No*."

102

Questions III: "Then are there more flowers or more primulas?—*Both the same*.—And more primulas or more yellow primulas?—*Both the same*."

RIC (6; 6) puts all the primulas and the yellow flowers in A, the rest of the flowers (grouped according to colour) in A', and the other objects in B'. He then transfers the other yellow flowers to A'. Questions II: "Can I put an (A') in (A)?—*No, it isn't a primula*—And is an (A) one of these $(B = A + A')$? —*Yes, a primula is a flower too*.—Does that mean I can put primulas in a bunch of flowers?—*Yes, you can put a primula in the big bunch*." Questions III: "How would I be making a bigger bunch, by taking the primulas or by taking the yellow primulas?—*They're both the same*.—And a bunch of flowers or a bunch of primulas?—*It's the same*."

In the simple classification of problem I, there is a continuous development towards logical arrangements. The most immature of these subjects, who is Gae, can manage no more than four little parallel collections and his criteria tend to fluctuate. (Although he puts the primulas together, he adds other blue flowers to the blue primulas, while another of his collections is based on colour alone, and so on.) Fav also arranges the flowers contiguously. But, starting with Ter, we find all our older subjects, at their first or second attempt, are spontaneously able to construct collections which are clearly differentiated by logical criteria: $A =$ the primulas; $A' =$ the other flowers; B $(= A + A') =$ all the flowers; $B' =$ the other objects; and C $(= B + B') =$ all the objects. Our problem is to decide whether this classification amounts to a true "grouping", comprising both inclusion and reversibility $(A = B - A'$, etc.) or whether it is no more than a set of non-graphic collections because there is no class-inclusion.

The type II questions give some information on this point, in that the answers obtained are not up to the apparent level of the classifications. We can distinguish three phases. During the first, everything is a part of everything else (Gae) or nothing is a part of anything else (Fav and Breg, although Breg's spontaneous classification suggested a higher level). In the second phase (Ter), the subject agrees to combine A and A' to obtain B, but without understanding that, although all the As are Bs, not all the Bs are As. In the final phase (Rap and Ric), he seems to understand the relations of class-inclusion. For example, when Ric says that a primula "is also a flower", he seems to have constructed the relation $A < B$; and his answer to the next question (is an A' one of the As?) appears to confirm this.

Nevertheless, the type III questions show that none of these subjects can make a genuine quantitative comparison of the part A and the whole B. The reason is that in order to compare A and B, they would need to separate B into A and A' and still retain its identity. In other words, the relation $A < B$ implies the inverse relation $A = B - A'$, so that the whole B continues to exist even while its components A and A'

are separated in thought. But as soon as these are separated, our subjects lose sight of B, which is why they compare A and A'. Some (like Far) decide that there are more primulas A than flowers (meaning $A' =$ the other flowers), others that there are more A' than A (Ter), and others again that they are the same (Breg, Rap, Ric).[1]

This reaction is quite characteristic of stage II, but what is interesting here is that the type II questions precede the type III ones, and ought to make them easier. Moreover, the present experiment differs from the earlier experiment with beads in that A and A' are numerically equal. (In the earlier experiment these classes were in the ratio of 10 to 1 or 2, as compared with our four yellow primulas and four of other colours, etc.) Why is it then that so many subjects (e.g. Rap and Ric) succeed with type II questions and fail with type III? We cannot accept the answer that they did not understand the language we used. In every single case we took good care that they did.[2] On the other hand if there was a systematic verbal misunderstanding this would itself require an explanation in terms of logical structures. The results of ch. III suggest that when a child at stage II gives the right answers to the type II questions his thinking is qualitative, or at most it is half-way to quantitative thought: the yellow primulas belong to the primulas because "they are primulas". Spatial extension is the only kind of extension available to our subjects ("you can put a primula in the big bunch"). As we saw in ch. III, "all" then becomes an intensive quality which belongs to the whole taken as a unit. When he has to deal with extension in the strict sense, the child is lost, which means that his achievement in solving questions of type II is strictly limited. Type III questions are not answered in terms of extension. And this is crucial, because the essential characteristic of class-inclusion is the fact that this relation generates a hierarchical nesting structure which is extensive. It is therefore quite different in scope from a mere qualitative differentiation.

However, the situation is paradoxical in one respect. Between 50% and 90% of these subjects (ages 5–7) who fail questions IIIA and B, answer IIIC and D correctly. Thus the same child will tell us that there are more primulas than flowers in a bunch, while admitting that there would still be some flowers left in a garden if he picked all the primulas) but if he picked all the flowers there would be no primulas left.

THE (5; 6). "If I make a bunch out of all the primulas, and you make one out of all the flowers, which will be bigger?—*Yours*.—(Four primulas and four other flowers are chosen, and the question is repeated.)—*They'd be the same* $(A = A')$.—If you picked all the primulas in a field, would there be

---

[1] A and A' can, of course, be replaced by B and B' (included in C), etc.

[2] The experiment with beads has been repeated by educational psychologists in Paris, who obtained similar results using bunches of grapes ("are there more grapes or more black grapes?" etc.).

any flowers left?—*Yes*.—Now supposing you picked all the flowers would there be any primulas left?—*Yes . . . no*.—Why?—*Because you're taking all the flowers*.—All right, if you pick all the yellow primulas, will there be any primulas left?—*Yes, the purple ones are left*.—And if you pick all the primulas, will there be any yellow ones left?—*No, because you're taking all the primulas and there are none left*." Nevertheless, questions on the quantification of inclusion are still unsolved.

AUB (6; 9). "Are there more primulas or more flowers in this bunch?— *More primulas, because here there are two* (other flowers) *and here there are three* (primulas).—And are there more yellow primulas (2) or more primulas (3) in this one?—*More yellow primulas. There is only one purple one*.—You pick all the primulas in a field. Are any yellow primulas left?—*No*.—And if you pick all the yellow primulas, are any primulas left?—*No*.—And are there more primulas or more yellow primulas in this bouquet?—*More yellow ones, because there are two yellow ones and there is one purple one*."

DEM (6; 6), "Say you pick all the flowers in a field. Are there any primulas left?—*No, I've picked them all*.—And if you take all the yellow primulas, will there be any primulas left?—*Yes*.—If you take all the primulas, will there be any flowers left?—*Yes, some daisies, a rose . . .* —If you make a bunch out of all the flowers and I make one out of all the primulas, which will be bigger? —*Yours*."

Although some of these answers are still wrong (e.g. Aub with primulas and yellow primulas), they are usually right, although the very same subjects consistently deny that a collection ("all the flowers") is bigger than a sub-collection ("all the primulas"). At first sight, this would seem to contradict our assumption that they cannot compare a sub-collection A with the collection B without destroying B (so they compare A and A'). Indeed, it would seem to contradict all the findings of ch. III. One is tempted to argue that not only the wrong answers given to questions IIIA and B, but also the errors found in relation to "all" and "some", are all instances of verbal misunderstanding. When questions are formulated in a concrete and familiar way the subject seems perfectly capable of handling class-inclusion, and he also seems to understand the subtraction $B - A = A'$ (the flowers minus the primulas = the other flowers).

We find the same thing with beads.[1] We show a child a box containing red beads, some round and some square, and ask him: "If you take all the red beads from this box, will there be any square ones left?" Naturally enough, he answers "No". When we ask him: "If you take the square beads, will there be any red beads left?" he usually answers that the round ones would be left. This does not stop him from saying that

[1] We shall not weary the reader with the details of the bead experiment. The stages observed were the same as in the experiment with flowers, and they occurred at the same average ages. The quantification of the inclusions $A < B$ and $B < C$ (only $A < B$ had been studied previously) was also similar. The beads were, if anything, a shade easier.

the square beads are as numerous as the round ones or even outnumber them, in spite of the fact that he can see for himself that all the beads are red and says so explicitly.

In effect, the two statements (1) "If one takes away all the primulas (B), there will be no yellow primulas (A) left" and (2) "If one takes away the yellow primulas (A), the purple ones (A') will be left", should express the operations $A + A' = B$ and $B - A = A'$ applied to the classes A, A' and B. Is this true of the child? To prove that it is, one would have to show that B is retained in the child's mind, i.e. that the apparent logical subtraction really is the inverse of the apparent addition. Now all we know from (1) is that B (the primulas) has two different parts A (yellow) and A' (mauve), and taking the whole means taking both parts. (2) merely implies that the part A' remains when the part A is taken. It does not necessarily imply that in spite of that separation B retains its identity as the union of these two parts. The union $A + A' = B$ can exist without (a) mobility of parts, (b) reversibility of the transformations ($+$ and $-$), or (c) preservation of the whole (B). But unless all these are present in thought, such a union is tantamount to an intuitive apperception of the fact that the given collection consists of unlike parts. Only when all three are present can we legitimately speak of operational addition. The only decisive test is to ask the subject to compare the extension of B with that of A. If he recognizes that there are more primulas (B) than yellow primulas (A) in a bunch, he must be aware of B as the sum of $A + A'$ and he must simultaneously be aware of A as the difference $B - A'$. Such simultaneous awareness, which is characteristic of operational thinking, implies the conservation of the whole B. It is not surprising that a subject at stage II can be intuitively aware that the whole is the union of its parts (statement 1), and that one part is distinct from another, even though he cannot compare the extensions of the part and the whole. For this comparison is not implied by statements 1 and 2. The fact that the subject only succeeds in comparing A and A' (for B is momentarily non-existent) shows that statement 2 does not express the logical subtraction of classes, but only a simple intuitive separation of A and A'.

When the problem of inclusion cannot be solved, the most frequent error is to compare A and A', instead of A and B. But it is not the only one possible. The reduction of B to A' is not always automatic and unconscious; it may be motivated by the fact that one cannot use the same elements in two different ways. A child, for example, may say: "If I make a bunch out of the primulas (A), the bunch of flowers (B) will no longer contain any primulas because these will be in the first bunch". (B is then reduced to A' by the conscious subtraction of A.) We might add that where there are more A's than As the subject often appears to be giving the right answer, although in fact when he tells us that there are more Bs than As, what he means is that there are more A's than As and he is simply calling the A's Bs.

Rather more interesting are the following two sorts of answers. The first reply appears to be right, and in fact is wrong. The subject agrees that $B > A$ on the ground that B, represented by A', is more heterogeneous than A ("there is more than one colour"). This, of course, is not inclusion, even if the whole class B is intended; for instead of being thought of as a higher ranking class it is simply being looked on as a variegated unit. Finally, in some cases, when a child replies: "They're both the same" to the question "Are there more As or more Bs?", he is not thinking of the A's: he says they are the same because he thinks that "if all the As are Bs" then "all the Bs are As". This is a clear instance of the incorrect quantification of the predicate discussed in ch. III, §§1 and 2.

Here are two examples of subjects who decide that A and B are equal.

PER (8; 3) has already constructed three classes: yellow primulas, primulas and flowers. "Can one put a primula in the box of flowers (without changing the label)?—*Yes, a primula is also a flower.*—Can I put one of these flowers, say a tulip, in the box of primulas?—*Yes, it's a flower like the primula.*" When the experimenter does so, she changes her mind, and puts it back with the other flowers. "Can one make a bigger bunch with all the flowers or with all the primulas?—*It's the same thing. Primulas are flowers, aren't they?*—Suppose I pick all the primulas, will there be any flowers left?—*Oh yes, there will still be violets, tulips, and the other flowers.*—Well, suppose I pick all the flowers, will there be any primulas left?—*No, primulas are flowers. You're picking them too.*—Are there more flowers or more primulas?—*The same number. Primulas are flowers.*—Count the primulas.—*Four.*—And the flowers? —*Seven.*—Are there the same number?—(Astonished.) *The flowers are more . . .*"

PAG (8; 11). "Could you make a bigger bunch out of all the primulas or out of all the yellow primulas?—*It comes to the same thing.*—What do you mean? The same number?—*Yes, primulas are also flowers.*"

Both these cases support the interpretation of the results obtained with "all" and "some", given in ch. III, §1.

We now give a few examples of stage III.

VIB (6; 11) immediately constructs the classes: A = the yellow primulas; A' = the other primulas (below A); B' = the other flowers (by the side of A and A', showing that B is the class of primulas); C' = the cherries (beyond the flowers); D' = the other objects (these being placed apart, showing that C is the class of flowers and D is the class of flowers and fruit). Questions II: "Can one put an (A) among the (Bs, indicating $A + A'$)?—*Yes, it's a primula.* —And a primula (B) among the flowers (C)?—*Yes, it's a flower.*" Questions III: "Who will have the bigger bunch: a boy who takes all the flowers or one who takes all the primulas?—*The one who takes all the flowers* (pointing to the set $C = A + A' + B'$).—What about one who takes the yellow primulas

107

and one who takes the primulas?—*The one who takes these* $(A + A')$; *he'll have all the primulas.*"

DID (7; 5) first classes the objects as follows: A = the yellow primulas; A' = the other primulas and an orange flower; B' = the other flowers; C' = the other objects. "Is that right?—*No, this one* (the orange flower in A') doesn't really fit in (he puts it in B'). Question III (given before II): "If one boy wanted to pick all the flowers and another boy wanted to pick all the primulas, who would have more?—*Both the same: they're both 8.* (This shows residual traces of stage II, as does the initial error in classification.)— How about one who wants to pick all the primulas and another who wants to pick the yellow primulas?—*The one who takes all the flowers; because he takes the yellow primulas as well.*" Questions II: "Can one put an (A) among the (Bs)?—*Of course, it's a primula.*—And this one (an orange primula) among the (As)?—*No.*—Could you put the primulas in a bunch made up out of all the flowers?—*Yes.*—And this one (a blue flower)?—*Of course.*—And can I put this lily of the valley among these $(A + A')$?—*No, it isn't the same.*" Question III (repeated): "All the flowers or all the primulas?—*The one who takes all the flowers takes the primulas too, so he'll have more.*"

GIL (7; 6). A = yellow primulas; A' = other primulas; B' = other flowers; C' = other objects. Questions II: "If you make a bunch out of the primulas, can you put an (A') in it too?—*Yes, that's a primula too*—An (A') in the (B's)?—*No, those don't grow together.*—Can you put the (As) in a bunch made out of all the flowers?—*Of course, they're flowers.*" Questions III: "More flowers or more primulas?—*More flowers. These* $(A + A' + B')$ *against these* $(A + A')$.—More primulas or more yellow primulas?—*More primulas. These* $(A + A')$ *against those* (A).*"

RIE (8; 2) classes the objects exactly as did Gil. Questions II: "Can one put an (A) among the (Cs)?—*Of course, it's a flower.*—And an (A') among the (As)?—*No, it isn't yellow.*—And a (B') among the (Bs)?—*No, it isn't the same kind of flower.*—And a (B) among the $(C = B + B')$?—*Yes, a primula is still a flower!*" Questions III: "More primulas or more flowers?—*There are more flowers.* More primulas or more yellow primulas?—*More primulas.*"

TREV (8; 6). As above; and questions II correct. Questions III: "Which will be bigger: a bunch made out of all the primulas or one made out of all the yellow primulas?—*The one with all the primulas.*—Why?—*Because it's all the primulas.*—Suppose you make a bunch out of all the flowers and I make one out of all the primulas. Whose will be bigger?—*Mine.*—Which ones will you take?—(Correctly indicates $A + A' + B'$): *All those.*—Are there more flowers there (indicating all the objects) or more primulas?—*There are more flowers, yes.*—What about in the wood, (a new question not previously asked) are there more flowers or more primulas?—*More primulas.*—Suppose someone picks all the flowers, will there be any primulas left?—*There won't be any left.*—So are there more flowers or more primulas in the wood?— *More primulas.*—Show me all the flowers here.—(He now indicates the B's alone!)—What if I take all the yellow primulas and you take all the primulas, who will have more?—*Me. I'll have all the primulas here* (A) *and there* (A'). Count them.—*No* (as much as to say, it isn't worth it), *there are more primulas!*"

AR (9; 2) classes and answers questions II correctly. Questions III: "Which would make a bigger bunch: one of all the primulas or one of all the yellow primulas?—*All the primulas, of course. You'd be taking the yellow ones as well!*—And all the primulas or all the flowers?—*If you take all the flowers, you take the primulas too.*"

Needless to say questions IIIC and D were always answered correctly.

Among 69 subjects, aged from 5–10 years, the following percentages of answers were correct. The column heading $A < B$ denotes the question: "Are there more primulas or more yellow primulas in this bunch?" and $B < C$ the question: "Are there more flowers or more primulas?"

Table IV. *Percentage of correct answers to questions on the inclusions of classes of flowers*[1]

Ages (no. of subjects)	5–6 (20)	7 (19)	8 (17)	9–10 (13)
$A < B$	30	38	67	96
$B < C$	46	47	82	77
Both questions	24	26	61	73

The following results were obtained with questions IIIC and D. $\bar{B}A$ denotes: "If all the Bs are picked, are any As left?"; $\bar{A}B$ denotes: "If all the As are picked, are any Bs left?"; and $\bar{C}B$ and $\bar{B}C$ denote the corresponding questions for B and C.

Table V. *Percentage of correct answers to questions $\bar{B}A$, $\bar{A}B$, $\bar{C}B$, $\bar{B}C$*

Age	$\bar{B}A$	$\bar{A}B$	$\bar{C}B$	$\bar{B}C$
5–6 years	71	83	71	71
7–8 years	66	75	85	88

We note that subjects aged 8 years and above differ markedly from those at stage II (5–7). Not only do they classify correctly in the form of additive groupings, but they recognize the inclusions implied by that structure. ($A + A' = B; B + B' = C; C + C' = D.$) Questions of type II no longer present any difficulty whatever. What is more, in this situation, as in that of ch. III (§§1 and 2), subjects at stage III can compare the extension of a part with that of the whole. This means that the whole retains its identity although it is conceptually separated into its component parts. Most of the answers are quite explicit. Did, for example, says "The one who takes all the flowers, [will have more] because he takes the primulas as well." Extension is at last co-ordinated with intension!

[1] The total number of answers varied slightly from one subject to another.

Nevertheless there are times when the reasoning of these subjects lags far behind. A subject like Trev may reason perfectly correctly with the objects right in front of him, yet one has only to ask him to apply the relation of inclusion to the flowers and primulas "in a wood" to find the same incorrect reasoning as before! Although Trev tells us without the slightest hesitation that "there are more flowers than primulas" among those in front of him, he compares the primulas growing in a wood with the other flowers (not primulas), and cannot compare the class of primulas with the higher ranking class of flowers which includes it. Nonetheless he can tackle question IIIC: "Suppose somone picks all the flowers (in the wood), will there be any primulas left?" This raises a problem which will be taken up in the next section.

2. CLASSIFICATION OF ANIMALS

The three kinds of questions (see 1) were put to another group of children, numbering 117 in all, with the only difference that we used pictures of animals instead of flowers. Ages ranged from 7 to 13 or 14 years. The reason for presenting these results separately is that they systematically lag behind those already given, even though the stages are basically the same. We have here a remarkable instance of the way in which the emergence of concrete operational reasoning depends very closely on the intuitive character of its content. We have to ask why this is so. It does not appear to be true of formal operations, so long as they are elementary.

That different results are obtained when animals are used must be due to the fact that these classes are more remote from everyday experience and therefore more abstract. It is true that circles and squares, or primulas and flowers, are designated by words which evoke verbal concepts of a general kind and are therefore abstract. But children do play about with circles and squares between the ages of 5 and 9; and unless they are city dwellers they often pick flowers or just primulas either in their gardens or when they go for a walk. Now using pictures of ducks and other birds and animals should make precious little difference if the questions are still confined to the actual pictures on the table. Each one of these represents a perfectly familiar object and there is no difficulty about naming them. There is certainly no explicit reference to the highly generalized conceptual structure which lies behind this nomenclature. But in fact (this is our *a posteriori* explanation of the results), a child cannot say that ducks are birds and birds are animals by simply relying on experience drawn from his own actions, as he can for squares and circles which he has drawn and for flowers which he has picked. He is compelled to rely far more on purely linguistic concepts and he may need to structure and develop these in the course of the actual experiment. This explains the time lag. In effect the problem we are faced with is this: What is the effect of introducing this kind of material, which is finite and perceptible but relies on a more abstract kind of knowledge? More particularly, how will hierarchical classification and the quantification of class-inclusion differ as compared with the previous situation where the objects could readily be handled.

Figure 9.

The following objects were used for this part of the study: (1) series I contained three or four ducks (class A), three to five other birds (class A': cock, sparrow, parrot, etc.), and five animals other than birds (class B': snake, mouse, fish, horse, poodle). This series is illustrated in Fig. 9. The primary classes[1] were ducks (A), birds (B) and other animals (C).

[1] The primary classes are those which define the sequence of inclusions: $A < B < C < \ldots$, and the secondary classes are the complements defined by this sequence: $A' = B - A, B' = C - B, \ldots$

111

(2) Series II consisted of three ducks (A), four other birds (A'), four winged animals which were not birds (B': bee, butterfly, dragon-fly and bat), and three inanimate objects (D'). The primary classes here were ducks (A), birds (B), flying animals (C), animals (D), and the universal class (E). We used transparent boxes of different sizes (these were kept transparent so that the relationships would remain perceptible), which fitted inside one another to correspond with the primary classes A, B, C, etc. As each class was named by the subject, so this name was written on the appropriate label-card. The procedure for the interview was identical with that used for the flower experiment (cf. the beginning of §1). The question "Has one the right to put A in B or B in A?" was particularly emphasized.

We found that neither the hierarchical system ($A < B < C$, etc.) nor the quantification of inclusion were properly understood until the second half of stage III. A number of subjects were nearly at the stage of formal operations by the time they showed such understanding. Subjects who answered other questions at the level of stage III often gave replies equivalent to those of stage I when dealing with animals. We shall denote the stages found in the animal experiment by DI, DII, DIII,[1] these being stages which lag behind those found in other situations.

DI, then, is the stage at which the preliminary classification is inadequate and there is no understanding of relations in terms of extension; there may, however, be some partial successes with questions IIIC and D.

PIE (7; 11). Series I. "This one is one of the . . . —*Animals.*—Can you make two piles?—(She puts the ducks on one side, and the other animals on the other.)—Now can you make two new piles with these (the other animals)?— *Yes, birds and animals* (as though birds were not animals).—Are the ducks birds?—*Yes . . . no.*—They all have feathers?—*Yes.*—If I put them all in this box, what would you write on the label?—*Animals.*" Pie puts the ducks in A and the other birds in B. "Are the ducks animals?—*Yes.*—Are the birds animals?—*Yes*—Can one put the ducks (A) in (B)?—*No, they aren't birds.*— Can one put them in (C)?—*No.*—What is (C)?—*All the animals.*—So can one put the ducks (A) in (C)?—*No.*"

"If a fox killed off all the ducks, would there be any other feathered animals left?—*Yes, the birds.*—If he killed the ducks, would there be any other animals left?—*Yes, the birds, the cat,* (*etc.*)—If one killed all the animals, would any ducks be left?—*Yes . . . no, they'd all have been killed.*—If one kills all the animals, will any feathered animals be left?—*No, because one kills all the animals.*"

"Are there more birds or more animals in this box?—*More birds.*—Why?— *No, it's the same thing.* (Four birds and four other animals.)"

---

[1] The symbols DI, DII, DIII have no connexion with the class D. The letter D stands for the French "décalé" i.e., delayed. (E.A.L.)

Esc (7; 6) puts all animals with open wings in group (1), all those with closed wings in (2), and those without wings in (3). When given the boxes, he puts the birds in box *A*, the three insects and the sea-gulls in *B*, and the animals without wings in *C*. "Is it all right to take this away (the partition between *A* and *B*)?—*Yes, because they have wings.*" But he refuses to put the sea-gulls among the birds, and insists that ducks have no wings.

He agrees that the birds are animals. "Are there more birds or more animals in this box?—*More animals, no, more birds.*"

Mey (8; 10). "Make separate piles with the animals which are like each other.—(Four piles: (1) ducks; (2) other birds; (3) a cat and a mouse; (4) a horse and a cat.)—Can one put (1) and (2) together?—*They're all birds.*— And (3) and (4)?—*They're all animals.*" Given the boxes, Mey puts the ducks in *A*, the other birds in *B*, and all the rest in *C*. The experimenter then asks (using the movable partitions): "Can one put everything in (*C*)?—*Yes, then it's all the animals.*—Are the ducks birds?—*Yes.*—Are they animals?—*Yes.*— Can one put them in (*B*)?—*Yes.*—And in (*C*)?—*No.*—Can one put the horse in (*A*)?—*No, it's just as if I put a bird in* (*C*) (note the false reciprocity).— Why?—*The horse isn't a duck.*—But can one put the ducks in (*C*)?—*Yes, they're animals.*"

"If a fox killed all the ducks, would any birds be left?—*Yes.*—What about any other animals?—*Yes.*—If he killed all the birds, would any ducks be left?— *Yes.*—What if one killed all the animals, would there be any birds left?—*No, they're all animals.*"

"Are there more ducks or more birds in this box (four ducks and four other birds)?—*Both the same*—Try and count all the birds.—*With the ducks?* (agreeing that the ducks are birds).—All the birds.—*There are eight* (correct). —And the ducks?—*There are four* (correct).—So are there more birds or more ducks?—*Both the same* (!)"

Stod (8; 11). Series II: divides the pictures into animals and inanimate objects. "*You can also put the wild animals together against the tame ones. Or you can put them so that they get bigger and bigger.*—Put some in box (*A*); they must go with box (*B*) when 1 takes away the partition; etc.—(*A*) *Dragonfly, bee, spider, butterfly;* (*B*) *the smaller animals and the ducks;* (*C*) *birds and frogs;* (*D*) *the large animals.*" "If a hunter managed to catch all the birds, would there be any animals left?—*No.*—And any mosquitoes?—*Oh yes; if you just killed all the birds, and there would be butterflies left as well.*—Are there more animals which fly in the world or are there more animals?—*I don't know.*—What about in this box (4 out of 8)?—*The same.*"

These replies are very much of a piece with those given by children of 4–6 years, for the problems of flowers and geometrical shapes. Yet there is no doubt that these same subjects, had they been given that material, would have been able to reason correctly in terms of a hierarchical classificatory structure using the relations of class-inclusion.

Yet here they cannot even answer questions IIIC (If one took away all the *A*s would there be any *B*s left?) and IIID (If one took away all the *B*s would there be any *A*s left?). One is therefore not surprised to find that they cannot quantify the relations of inclusion.

Their difficulty in comparing the part with the whole in this domain must be due to the fact that zoological classes are not very clearly defined for them. Ducks, for Pie, are not birds; for Esc, ducks do not have wings and sea-gulls are not birds, etc. Spontaneous classifications are frequently made in terms of more familiar properties instead of the abstract verbal categories of birds and animals. Stod, for instance, suggests classifying the animals as wild and tame, or as large and small. Esc can find no surer criterion than to examine the cards to see whether the creatures are depicted with open wings (giving a class which includes insects and sea-gulls), or with closed wings. The most frequent classification is into animals that fly and animals that walk. But one sometimes finds very strange mixtures; Stod, for instance, begins with a class of insects, but goes on to put the ducks with the mice ("fairly small animals"), and the birds with the frogs.

One does no better by inducing the subjects to construct inclusion relations with boxes. There is the occasional glimmer of a generalization, as when Esc talks of "animals that have wings" $(A + A')$. But again and again the difficulties found at earlier ages seem to persist with the present material. Mey rightly refuses to put a horse with the ducks, but he finds it equally absurd to put a duck in the class of all animals (he does finally agree to this, but his first thought is undoubtedly that class-inclusion is a reciprocal relation: all the As are Bs = all the As are all the Bs). Pie opposes the birds to the animals, as though there were no such thing as inclusion; and Stod fails to construct any of the inclusions in the hierarchy $A < B < C < D$.

These results prove once again that there is no formal mechanism underlying this sort of classification. That is why we call it a concrete operation. The level of reasoning varies with the character of the content to which it applies. Unless the objects fall easily into a nesting set of classes each of which is readily distinguishable by virtue of an obvious perceptual criterion, the classification breaks down. Instead of trying to use the structures which they could apply with an easier material, children now fall back on classification by juxtaposition, and they make the same systematic mistakes which are so characteristic of earlier stages.

A second stage, DII, is suggested by certain developments occurring between the ages of 9 and 12. It forms a gradual transition between the outright failure of stage DI and the complete success of stage DIII.

Lou (9; 11) first forms a number of collections of equal rank which show no coherent structure (cf. stage DI). But when given the boxes, he puts the ducks in A, the other birds in B, the other flying animals (insects) in C, and all the remaining animals in D. "Is it all right to remove this partition (between A and B)?—*Yes, they're the same animals* (birds).—And is it all right to take away this one (between B and C)?—*Yes* (doubtfully). *They're all animals that fly.* (He removes the spider and puts it in D.)—And if I add the

114

fish, where will you put it?—*In* (*D*)." "Are there more animals that fly in the world or more birds?"—*I don't know.*—If you make a collection of animals that fly, and I make one of birds, who will have more?—*The collection of animals, because there are more animals than birds.*—Could one put the birds in the collection of animals?—*No.*—But are they animals or not?—*Oh, yes.*"

JAC (9; 1) puts the hens in box *A*, the "*ducks of all kinds*" (ducks and turkeys) in *B*, and the "*animals of all kinds*" in *C*. "Could I put the hens in the middle box too (*B*)?—*Yes, it's also a bird.*—And in the big box (*C*)?—*Yes, it's an animal.*—What about the cat, can I put that in (*B*)?—*Yes, it's also an animal.*—Why?—*Oh, no! It's an animal but it isn't a bird.*—Are there more hens or more birds in there (in box *B*)?—*The same number* (four hens and eight birds).—And are there more birds or more animals here (*C*)?—*More birds . . . Oh, no! More animals. The hens are also animals.*—Well are there more hens or more birds in that tray?—*More birds, because the hens are also birds.*—If a fox killed all the hens, would there be any birds left?—*No . . . yes.*—If he killed all the birds, would there be any animals left?—*No, yes, the dog.*—Well if one killed all the animals . . . —*No, nothing.*"

FRA (10; 2) classes the animals into "*those that fly*" (*B*) and "*those that stay on the ground*" (*B'*), and subdivides the birds into "*those that fly well*" (*A*) (parrot and finch) and "*less well*" (*A'*: ducks and a cock). "What can we call them altogether (box *C*)?—*Animals.*—Can I take away this partition (between *B* and *C*)?—*No, those aren't all poultry . . . yes, they're all animals.*—May I put the snake in (*B*)?—*Yes, it's also an animal . . . no, it isn't poultry.*—Could I put the cock in (*C*)?—*Yes, they're all animals. The snake isn't poultry, but the cock is an animal.*" Questions III C and D ("If one took away the *B*s would any *A*s be left? etc.") were all answered correctly. "Are there more poultry or more animals in the world?—*More animals, because poultry are animals as well.*—And, outside, is there more poultry or more poultry that doesn't fly?—*I don't know. There's a lot of both kinds.*—(The question is repeated.) Can one tell?—*One can tell, but it's difficult . . . Oh! they're all poultry. So there are more poultry.*"

CHAS (10; 2) reacts in the same way as Per and Pag in §1. "Are there more ducks or more domestic animals?—*Both the same. Ducks are also domestic animals.*—Are there more domestic animals or more animals?—*The same. They're animals too.*—All domestic animals are animals?—(He looks at one of the cards:) *That one is an animal, that one too, that too. Yes, they all are.*—And are all animals domestic animals?—(He looks:) *I see! No, not the snake.*—Are there the same number of animals and domestic animals.—*There must be more animals.*"

NOV (11; 5) classes series II into non-living (*D'*) and living things (*D*), then into animals that do not fly (*C'*) and animals that do (*C*), and then into insects (*B'*) and birds (*B*), the birds being subdivided into ducks (*A*) and others (*A'*). He agrees to remove the partition between *A* and *B*, to give all the birds, etc. "Are there more birds in these boxes, or more ducks?—*More birds.*—Are there more animals that fly or more birds?—(He looks at the numbers in *B* and *B'*.) *They're the same.*—(The question is repeated.)—*Oh, no! There are more animals that fly, because birds are animals that fly.*"

MERM (12; 9), to the same question: "*More birds, because there are more different types . . . Oh no! More animals that fly.*—More animals or more animals that fly?—*More animals, because the animals include all the other kinds.*"

We see that, alongside the progressive development of hierarchical classification, there is a correspondingly greater facility with the quantification of inclusion. But at stage DIII, correct replies are given immediately.

PAT (10; 2) classes series I into ducks (*A*), flying animals (*B*), and *"mixed"* animals (*C*). Refuses to put a dog in *B*, but agrees to put ducks, cocks, etc. in *C*. "Are there more animals or more flying animals in the world?—*More animals, because there are a greater number of them.*—And more animals or more birds?—*More animals.*"

JEL (10; 11) classifies series II in the same way as Nov. "Are there more animals or more birds in the world?—*More animals, because the birds are all animals.*—And more birds or more animals that fly?—*More animals that fly, because there are insects as well as birds.*"

DET (11; 11). Divides series II into ducks (*A*), other birds (*A'*), a sheep, a horse and an elephant (*C*), and inanimate objects (*C'*). "Can one take away this partition (between *A* and *A'*)?—*They're all birds (B)*—And (between *B* and *B'*)?—*They're all animals (C). All those are alive.*" The insects are added: *"One should have another section for the flying insects and the bats."* "Are there more flying animals or more birds?—*More flying animals.*"

TRA (12; 4) begins by putting the ducks and frogs in *A*, the birds and bats in *A'*, and the insects and other animals in *B'*. But he decides to start again, putting the insects in *A*, after first removing the spider, the birds and bats in *A'* (so that *A + A' = "animals that fly"*), and the other animals in *B'*. "Are there more insects or more flying animals?—*More flying animals because the insects are all flying animals.*—More flying animals or more animals?—*More animals, because those that fly are still animals.*—More flying animals or more birds?—*More flying animals, because there are birds and insects.*"

Table VI shows the frequency of correct replies to our various questions between the ages of 8 and 13. These figures refer to series I and are drawn from a total of 117 subjects.

Table VI. *Percentage of correct answers to questions on the inclusions of classes of animals*

Ages (no. of subjects)	8 (17)	9 (22)	10 (14)	11 (17)	12–13 (47)
A < B	43	50	50	46	67
B < C	38	66	62	82	75
Both	25	27	42	46	67

The corresponding results from questions IIIC and D, in the forms $\overline{BA}, \overline{AB}, \overline{CB}, \overline{BC}, \overline{AC}$ and $\overline{CA}$ (cf. Table V, §1), were as follows:

Table VII. *Percentage of correct answers to questions $\bar{B}A$, $\bar{A}B$, $\bar{C}B$, $\bar{B}C$*

Ages (no. of subjects)	$\bar{B}A$	$\bar{A}B$	$\bar{C}B$	$\bar{B}C$	$\bar{A}C$	$\bar{C}A$
7–8 (14)	75	94	75	90	100	88
9 (13)	94	100	100	100	100	88
10 (10)	100	100	90	100	100	100

There were no errors on these questions above the age of 11, these being much easier than those on class-inclusion.

Wrong answers continue to be given to a later age when animals are used instead of flowers. The most probable answer, which we have already indicated, is that the classification is more difficult because it does not correspond with a classificatory action like picking flowers to go into a bunch. This sort of action can be imagined as easily as it can be performed. But the actual animals could not be collected and classified even if the pictures can, and this would seem to be the reason that the hierarchical inclusions and their quantitative expression are so much more difficult.

It is legitimate to conclude that the schema of class-inclusion is a genuine logical operation and not a question of mere verbal facility. A number of writers found that children of 2–4 would tell them that a dog was an animal, a lady was a person and a daisy was a flower. They concluded that these children had reached the level of hierarchical classification.[1] To this we cannot agree. What these facts indicate is that, given certain familiar elements, these tiny children can reach beyond the level of graphic collections, and the corresponding linguistic schemata are structured into parts and wholes. But the structure is not that of an operational classification. It is that of a non-graphic collection, which is perfectly consistent with the degree of differentiation shown. The present results indicate that it is one thing to carry out the union expressed by $A + A' = B$ and quite another to understand that it is logically equivalent to its inverse $A = B - A'$, which means that the whole, B, retains its identity and that the entire relation can be quantitatively expressed in the form $A < B$. The conservation of the whole and the quantitative comparison of whole and part are the two essential characteristics of genuine class-inclusion; and it is worth stressing that this kind of thinking is not peculiar to professional logicians since the children themselves apply it with confidence when they reach the operational level. Inclusion, in this sense, has not been acquired merely because the child talks correctly and uses verbal concepts which reflect the inclusions implicit in the language of adults. On the contrary, inclusion has an essentially

[1] Cf. L. Welch and L. Long, *J. of Gen. Psychol.*, 22 (1940), 359–378; and *J. of Psychol.*, 9 (1940), 59–95.

operational character. That is why it is the basis of any classification which really does order classes, instead of only differentiating between them.

In order to study how children make the transition from the intuitive union $A + A' = B$ to the inverse $A = B - A'$, we should have to study the progressive co-ordination of ascending methods of classification (where the subject starts with small collections and constructs large ones) and descending methods (where he starts with large collections and then subdivides them). This amounts to the study of retroactive and anticipatory mobility, and forms the subject of ch. VII. But we prefer to postpone that enquiry until we have examined the development of the notion of a complementary class (ch. V), and that of intersecting classes (ch. VI).

Chapter Five

COMPLEMENTARY CLASSES[1]

WE now propose to study the development of the notion of a complementary class. A complementary class is one which may be combined with a given class, *A*, *B*, or *C* to yield the next higher ranking class *B*, *C*, or *D*. For example, if *A* is the class of ducks, *B* that of birds and *C* that of animals, their respective complementary classes are those which we called "secondary" when describing "elementary groupings": *A′* (birds other than ducks) is the complement of *A* relative to *B*, *B′* (animals which are not birds) is the complement of *B* relative to *C*, etc. (Such classes are called "complements of the first kind" in lattice theory.) The importance of this relation lies in the fact that it raises the more general problem of negation. Given a class *A*, the class not-*A* is the complement of *A* relative to *Z*, being the largest class in the system, (i.e. the universe of discourse: $Z - A = $ not-*A*, or $\bar{A}$). The psychologist wants to know how children understand the class not-*A*. Does a child think of the class of not-ducks as including pebbles, stars and fairy-tale characters; or does he usually connect it with other birds (*A′*) or other animals ($C - A = A' + B'$)?

It is obvious that the problem of finding a complement of a class is not unrelated to the problems of order-relations and class-inclusion. These relations are logically prior to that of the complementary class, which is why we studied them first. But it may be that the idea of a complementary class is a more elementary notion psychologically, either in the form of a specific complement (*A′*, *B′* etc.) or in the form of a general negation ($Z - A$).

Again, the idea of a complementary class links up with a number of quite specific problems such as that of the singular class, the null class, the role of absolute number both in the complementary relation and in classification generally, etc. All these problems are themselves connected with the problem of whether the method used in classification is an ascending method, proceeding by successive combinations, or a descending one, proceeding by successive subdivisions.

The lay-out of this chapter is based on the fact that two preliminary questions ought to be clarified, before discussing complementary classes as such. The first is that of the singular class, which can be introduced in terms of a situation in which the subject has to discover a rule (§1), the second is that of the part played by the numbers involved in a classi-

[1] In collaboration with A. Etienne, F. Frank, J. Maroun, B. Matalon, A. Morf and B. Reymond-Rivier.

fication (here again we meet up with the singular class when $N = 1$, but in the context of classificatory behaviour proper) (§2). After this we turn to the problem of "secondary" classes or complements of the first kind (§3), and this leads into the study of negation (§4), to the law of duality (if $A < B$, not-$B <$ not-A) (§5), and, finally, the null-class (§6).

1. THE SINGULAR CLASS IN A PRACTICAL CONTEXT

We shall see that up to the age of 8 or 9, children find it difficult to recognize a set containing a single element (called a "singular class" in logic, e.g., "the" sun, "the" moon, etc.) as forming a class or a separate intuitive collection. On the other hand, a large number of papers have been published on the problem of the "unique specimen" or "the one that is different", particularly in animal psychology.[1] Given sufficient motivation, an ape or a young child can pick out an object which is the only one of its kind, from among several other objects, even when the unique object is never the same on two occasions. How is this sort of behaviour related to the mechanisms of classification? In order to find out, we tried to discover just what a child understands of the relationships that enter into the situation, when reaching a practical solution, as he does. The success could be due in the first instance to sensori-motor learning together with the differentiation of perceptual signals, and still lead eventually to an understanding of classificatory structures and, in particular, of a singular class.

The material we used consisted of a number of triangles which varied from 3 to 6. In some cases we added one or more diamonds. The problem was to guess which of these objects had a cross on the other side. This one was always recognizable since it was always the only one of its kind. The use of six elements instead of three was helpful to some children because it heightened the perceptual contrast (the remaining five objects being exactly similar while the one with the cross was different). However, others found the task easier with only three. To try to gauge what the child had understood, we first of all asked him the reasons for his choice, and then told him to make up a similar puzzle of his own without actually using the same items and arrangement as we had done.

Three stages were observed. In the first, corresponding to stages I and II and ages 5–7, there was a 50% level of success, but either no understanding of the system, or only a partial understanding. These successes were entirely due to sensori-motor learning. At stage IIIA, corresponding to ages 7–9, there was a 75% level of success, combined with understanding of the system. At stage IIIB, corresponding to ages of 10–12, the percentage of success fell to 33% because of a tendency to

[1] The problem is often referred to as "the oddity problem".

introduce imaginary complications. Table VIII shows the frequency of successful solutions for each of these age-groups.

Table VIII. *Percentage of successful solutions to problems of finding "the one that is different"*[1]

Age group	N	2 v. 1 Successes	+	–	=	5 v. 1 Successes	+	–	=
5; 2–6; 7	18	55	55	27	18	48	50	41	9
7–9	14	76	78	14	8	66	70	22	8
10–12	12	33	—	—	—	—	—	—	—

Columns headed + show the percentage of children with more successes than failures, those headed – show those with more failures than successes, and those headed = indicate the percentage whose successes exactly balance their failures.

Subjects of stages I and II either fail to solve the problem, or else their success is not accompanied by an understanding of the system.

Following are a few examples:[2]

MOR (6; 0) provides a good example of an intuitive solution without understanding. With Y Bk Bk, he takes Bk 1. With B Y Y he points to Y 1 and then Y 2: "*Oh! Then it's there.*" (B). With Bk Bk Y, he takes Bk 1, then Bk 2 and then Y. With Y Bk Y, R Bk Bk and B.B.G, he takes Bk, R and G. "How did you know?—*Because each time you put it here, here or here* (indicating the positions 1, 2, 3, but not in the order in which we had varied them).— Well, look (Y R Y Y Y Y)—(He takes R) *because there were lots of yellow ones and one red one.*" But with Bk Bk Bk G Bk Bk Bk, he tries Bk 1 before choosing G. In copying the situation himself, he does construct 2 A + 1 A'; but he deliberately puts A' first on the left, then in the middle, and finally on the right. "How did you do it?—*Because it keeps going this way* (indicating the order of the three positions, which we too had varied, but at random).— Which one is it always?—*Sometimes it's a red one, sometimes a black one.*" He cannot be made to say that it is always the unique element which has the cross, even though his actual behaviour shows that he is subconsciously aware of it.

AGA (6; 3). Y Y R: takes Y 1, then Y 2, then R. Bk Y Bk: he tries the last one again. "Why?—. . ." Y Y G: takes G. B Y B: takes Y. He is then asked to make up a similar situation: he gives us R B R with the cross under R 1. We try once more. With B R B B B B he tried each of the Bs before taking R, but for Y Y B Y Y Y he takes B straight away. "Do you see how it's done now?—*Yes.*" We try him with G Bk Bk Bk Bk Bk, and he chooses G straight

---

[1] The number of presentations was 110 for the first series and 61 for the second, for subjects of 5–6 years, 59 and 9 for subjects of 7–9 years; and 23 altogether for those of 10–12 years.

[2] The letters Bk, B, G, R, Y stand for the colours black, blue, green, red, yellow.

away. But, asked to construct them himself, Aga produces R Bk R Bk with the cross under Bk 1, and then R Y B Bk with the cross under Y. He has not understood. He is deliberately shown Y G Y Y with the cross under G, but he still gives us Bk R Y Y with the cross under R!

REY (6; 3). Y Y R: tries Y, then Y, then R. For R B R, he points to B. "Why?—*I knew the colour* (!)—And like this (G Bk Bk)?—(He takes G.)—How did you know?—. . ." His own constructions: Bk Y G with the cross under Bk, then R G Bk with the cross under R, and Y Bk Y with the cross under Bk. "Why?"—*They're all the same colour.*" The game is resumed and he rediscovers the rule, but he still cannot explain it.

The following are intermediate between stages II and III, in that they reach a partial understanding of the principle. They do not reproduce the situation correctly at first, but in the end they succeed.

BOT (5; 6) With Bk Bk G, Y Bk Y. Y R R, his choices are always correct; but still he does not succeed in constructing a row of the form $2A + 1A'$ with the cross under A'. The game is resumed: Bk Bk R (correct). "How did you guess?—. . . —Y B Y (he takes B twice in succession).—Why that one?—*Because there are two others.*—And now (Bk R Bk)?—(He takes R) *because there are two black ones.*—And (B B G B B B)?—(He takes G) *because there is only one green one.*" Bot has chosen the unique element right from the start and has always found the cross. He carried on doing so without any real understanding at first, and he was unable to reproduce the situation. He seems to have discovered the principle eventually, but it may be no more than a mere description of the configuration, which is by no means the same thing as a classificatory schema.

MAT (6; 8). Y R Y: he takes R. "Why?—*I thought it would be red.*—And here (Bk B B):—(He takes Bk.)—(Y Bk Y)?—(He indicates Y 1, then Bk.)—And here (G R G)?—(Indicates R.)—Why?—*That's how I do it*—(G Y Y)?—(Points to Y 2, then G.)—How did you know?—*I don't know.*—And here (Bk Bk Bk Bk R Bk)?—*That one* (R).—Why?—*I don't know how I do it.*" His own constructions: Y Y Y Y with the cross under Y 2. "Can you make it easier? —(Bk B Bk with the cross under B): *I've used different colours. One blue and two black.*" Then B Bk B with the cross under Bk. "Why is it there?— *Because they aren't all the same colour.*"

These examples are extremely interesting, because they show that learning can take place in spite of the failure to understand the classificatory schema. Thus Mor needs only four trials before choosing the unique element every time, but he still thinks his choice is governed by position. His constructions take both factors into account. Only one of these is conscious and in point of fact he did not use it when solving ours; the other was unconscious but faithfully observed. Aga claims to have understood the principle, but he cannot reproduce the situation. Rey does reproduce it correctly, but says that the elements with the cross are always the same colour. Bot is probably a little less advanced than Rey. He happens to make the right choice to begin with, and he holds on to the right principle from then onwards. Yet he cannot reproduce the situation, and it is only right at the end of the session that he offers a correct formulation of the principle. Mat finds the principle fairly quickly and reproduces the situation correctly, but he cannot offer a general formulation.

This is not the place to offer a theoretical interpretation of this kind of learning; no doubt it involves the transfer of a perceptual contrast on the basis of reinforcement by success. Nevertheless, we have to recognize that solutions which are partly sensori-motor and partly intuitive persist throughout the stage of non-graphic collections (and as we have pointed out in ch. III, this sort of pre-classification itself is to some extent a function of intuitive and imaginal factors). The following examples illustrate stage IIIA (when children can construct a hierarchical classification and also show some understanding of class-inclusion). They are markedly different from those already given, although, as in ch. IV, §1, several of the subjects are less than 7 years old.

Dom (5; 6). Y B Y: chooses Y, then B. Y B B and B B R: straight away takes Y and R. "Why?—*Because I knew, I thought about it.*—(Bk B B)—(takes Bk).—Why?—*I thought about it.*" His own constructions: R Y Y, R Bk Bk and B Y Y with crosses under R, R, B (correct). "How do you do it?—*I put the cross there* (the unique element) *every time, and not under the others.*"

Cra (6; 11). "(R B B.)—*Here* (R).—(G G Bk.)—*Here* (Bk) *because it's a different colour.*—(Y R R.)—*The red one, not the yellow, because it's always another colour.*" B G B and R R B are both solved. His own constructions are correct: Bk R Bk and Y B Y, with crosses under R and B. With six elements (3 B, G and 2 B) he indicates G "*because it's a different colour from the others*". With 5 Y and R, he indicates R.

Ali (7; 7). Y G Y: he first tries Y 1, then G. Bk R R: takes Bk. Y Y R: takes Y 2, then R. Bk R Bk Bk Bk Bk: takes R. "Is that easier?—*Yes, because there are lots of black ones and only one red one.*—(B B B B Y B.)—*It's the yellow one, because there's only one that is yellow.*" His own constructions are correct, both with 3 and with 6 elements. "*There are two which are the same colour, and one that's a different colour.*"

Lem (7; 11). Right every time "*because it's always a different colour*".

Wil (8; 3). Y B Y, G B B, R Bk Bk and Y G Y: indicates B,G.R and G. "Why?—*Because it's the only green one.*—(5 Y and 1 R.)—*It's the red one, because the others are yellow.*—Which is easier: this one or (Y R Y)?—*It's the same thing, because they are all yellow except for one.*"

Dan (8; 4). Right every time "*because there's only one colour*". His own constructions are all correct.

Lac (8; 6). "*You only put down one black one, and all the rest were yellow. This time they're all yellow, with one green one!*" His own constructions are correct.

Lor (9; 0). After a few trials: "*Those which are the same colour don't have the cross, and those which are not the same colour do have the cross.*"

Gil (9; 2): "*Because it's the only one. I didn't understand it at first.*"

Cog (9; 5): *"Because there is only one of one colour," "because it's all alone."*
Riv (9; 5). G Bk Bk: *"It's the green one.—How did you know?—*(shrugs his shoulders).—*And here* (Y R Y):—*It's the red one because there is always one* (this being the second presentation!) *which is a different colour."*
Zep (9; 6). *"It's always the other colour. They're all black and the yellow one is different."*
Mos (9; 9). *"You always take the one which is by itself."*

In nearly every case, the subject states a rule and generalizes it as being "always" true. This is the essential criterion whereby we can recognize the underlying classificatory schema as distinct from mere collections which are always partially dependent on imagery, even when they are not strictly "graphic".

The outstanding case is Riv, who needs only two instances to conclude that the rule is "always" true. What is more, the rule itself must involve the mechanism of class-inclusion because its full expression would include some such phrase as Wil's "all except one".

These findings are truly remarkable because the classificatory mechanism involved is relatively complex. Since the colours are varied every time, the subject must do more than merely class the elements into A and A'. He has also to transpose the form of this classification from A_1 versus A_1' to A_2 versus A_2', A_3 versus A_3', and so on. It amounts to a generalized sort of alternation—generalized because instead of operating within the confines of a particular set it operates on a succession of different sets each of which exhibits a common framework.

There are two arguments that the child may use, and both are based on the complementarity of A and A': (1) The primary class A is the singular class, and "the others" form the secondary class A'; e.g. one black and "all the rest" (Lac), "It's the red one (A) because the others (A') are yellow" (Wil).

(2) Alternatively, the primary class A is that which contains several elements, in which case the secondary class A' is the singular class. This is the more usual form (examples being Cra, Ali, Lem, Lor, Riv and Zep).

At this level the notion of a "unique specimen" is structured by the operations of classification. It therefore takes on the character of a singular class (whether primary or secondary) because of the systematic complementarity which is involved. This is indicated by expressions such as "the others" or "different", these being generally of a positive kind, although they may also be negative, e.g. "not of the same colour" (Lor).

We have yet to say something of stage IIIB, which corresponds to the ages of 10–12. Curiously enough, there is an apparent regression at this stage. But this has nothing to do with the mechanisms of classification, and simply means that children tend to expect more complicated "puzzles" than the one which is actually set.

BAL (10; 2). Y Bk Bk: tries first Bk 2, then Y. R B R: tries first R 2, then R 1 and then B. B R R: tries first R 2, then B. "What are you doing?—*I'm just picking one by chance.*" Bk G Bk: Bk 2, then Bk 1 and then G. Y Y G: he takes G. "Why?—*I told you, I haven't got the hang of it yet.*" His own constructions: a series of wrong attempts, then Bk G Bk with the cross under G. "*Oh, I see! It has to be the one which is just one colour.*"

FRE (11; 0). Y R R: takes Y. Bk Bk R: tries Bk 1, then Bk 2 and then R. B Y Y: tries Y 1, then Y 2 and then B, etc. He suggests a rule: "*First it's on one side, then on the other, and then it's in the middle.*" Succeeding presentations do not confirm this, and he tries another rule based on position. Finally: "*Oh! It's because there's only one.*"

Bal tries to find a rule by starting with the last element, then choosing the first and finally the middle one. In point of fact he follows this procedure five times although he still says he is just picking at random.

Fra is another who tries to find a positional rule. They seem to try out several such hypotheses before considering the true hypothesis, which is also the simplest. The evidence points to the progress which has been made in the direction of combining hypotheses. In other words, there is more flexibility. But so far as this very simple problem is concerned, we do not find a more adequate use of intelligence because the artificial complications merely cloud the issue. Nevertheless this substage does introduce a higher level of performance in the case of hierarchical classifications, as we saw earlier (ch. IV, §2).

2. CLASSIFICATION AND THE RELATIVE SIZE OF CLASSES

The following experiments were undertaken with two aims in view: first, to find out whether children construct singular classes just as readily as they do classes containing several elements; and, second, to see how far classifications are affected by numerical disproportion.

I. The first question takes us back to the problem of a "unique specimen". The difference is that instead of asking for the solution of a practical problem we are now requiring each of our subjects to make up a classificatory system. He is shown the apparatus which consists of four large blue squares (5 cm. × 5 cm.), four small blue squares (2·5 cm. × 2·5 cm.), three large blue circles (diameter 5 cm.), four small blue circles (diameter 2·5 cm.) and a large red circle (diameter 5 cm.). We then proceed through the following questions: (1) the subject is told to classify these objects as he likes; (1b) if he has not done so already, he is told to divide the objects into two classes only; (2) he is asked to redivide them into two classes using a different criterion. (3); he is urged to do the same again, using a third criterion; (4) three red objects (a large square, a small square and a small circle) are added, a new classification being required.

What we wish to find out is whether or not the child uses colour in any of the first three classifications, because doing so would involve constructing a singular class with the large red circle. In general, young children use shape and colour about equally often when making spontaneous classifications, and size is not used until later. Thus the probability of using colour would be the same for classifications 1 and 2, were it not for the problems involved in the construction of a singular class. If we find that our subjects choose shape as the basis of their classification, and ignore colour, it can only mean that they refuse to admit that there is such a thing as a singular class. Adding three red objects should lead to a large number of classifications based on colour. If it does not, it may mean either that the inhibition created by the previous situation of colour spreads over to the new situation, or that perseveration rather than active inhibition is responsible for the continued neglect of the colour criterion.

The results were unambiguous, in spite of the small number of subjects involved (36 subjects aged 5–9 years). (1) Of the first set of classifications 22 were based on shape, 3 on size and only one on colour. Besides these, we were offered four complex objects by subjects of 5–6 years, while an additional six subjects failed to produce any classification. (1b) The first division of the objects into two classes gave 28 classifications based on shape, 4 based on size, 1 on colour, and 3 failures. (2) The second gave 17 classifications based on size, 4 on shape, 1 on colour, 6 complex objects and 8 failures. (3) The third gave 5 classifications based on colour (all on the part of subjects aged 7–9 years), and 6 based on size, while the remainder of the results consisted in complex objects and refusals. The addition of new red elements produced as many continued refusals as acceptances of classes based on colour!

It is clear that children have a strong tendency to avoid singular classes, and that it is only about the age of 7 or 8 that they begin to construct such divisions. The most frequent reaction of children at stage I is to neglect the properties of the unique element (the red circle), and to treat it as though it were just like the others.

KNA (5; 3) puts all the squares over to the left, with the small ones in the upper half and the large ones in the lower half. The circles are arranged in the same way on the right, the red circle being mixed with the three large blue ones. *"These are all the circles and those are all the squares.*—Can one mix all the circles together, will they go together?—*Yes.*—Do you have any other ideas?—(She constructs a row of squares, with all the large ones first and the small ones at the other end, and facing this, a similar row of large and small circles. She then puts all the large elements—squares and circles—on the left and all the small ones on the right, once again treating the red circle just as if it were blue.)" She is asked for a third arrangement, and this time she produces a complex object, a pattern of squares and circles, but with the

126

red circle still mixed in among the blues. Finally, the three red elements are added, and Kna constructs a new complex object with alternating groups of blue and red elements. The experimenter then puts all the blue elements in one compartment, and all the red ones in another. "Will this do?—*Yes, all the blue ones are here and all the red ones are there.*"

SPA (5; 10) classes the objects by their shape "*because all the ones here are circles and all the ones there are squares*". On being asked for a second classification, he continues to go by shape: "No, you find another way of doing it. Why did you put these like this?—*The small circles, the small squares, the large squares are all the same colour. The large circles are all the same colour, but one of them is red.* (Thus Spa has noticed the unique element, but he decides to ignore it as such.)—Well, what would be another way?—(He classes the elements correctly according to size.) *I've put all the big ones on one side, and all the small ones on the other side.*—Are they all alike?—*The big red circle isn't like the others.*—Well then, try and find a third way of arranging them—(He again classes the objects according to size.)—What have you done that's different?—*It's just like it was before, except for the red circle* (he means: excepting that I don't know what to do with the red circle).— Well, try another way.—(He classes them again by their shape.)—What have you done?—*It's just like it was at the beginning.*" The experimenter tries to suggest classifying the elements by their colour, but Spa resists this. "*The blue ones don't go together very well, but they do go a little because they're all the same colour.*" As for the red circle: "*You can't arrange them properly* (according to colour) *because there is only one* (that is red)." When more red elements are added, however, Spa accepts the classification based on colour.

BUR (6; 1). Like Spa, Bur first classes the elements by their shape and then by their size, ignoring the red circle. With the other red elements added, she starts constructing a complex object with alternating colours, but she does accept the classification by colour when this is suggested to her. The experiment is resumed with the original elements, and the experimenter now proposes a classification putting all the blue ones together on the left with the red circle on the right.—"Is that all right?—*No, there's only one there.*— (A second red element is added.) And like this?—*No.*—(A third is added.) Like that?—*No, there aren't enough.*—How many would we need?—(She counts the others.) *Nine.*"

The following subjects, who are slightly more advanced (stage II), spontaneously adopt a classification by colour after the additional red elements have been brought in, but not before.

MIL (6; 10) first classes the elements by shape and then by size, but does not succeed in finding a third criterion. A red square is then added, and she puts a blue square and a blue circle in the right-hand compartment, with a red square and circle in the left-hand compartment. When told to add the remaining elements she reverts to classification by shape.

FON (7; 3) classes the elements first by shape and then by size; he tries to find a third criterion but without success. When the three new red elements are added, he asks: "*Can one put all the blue ones on one side and all the red ones on the other?*"

127

GOB (7; 6) also has no difficulty in classing by shape or size, but fails to find a third criterion. As soon as the other red elements are added, he classes the objects by their colour: "Why didn't you do that before?—*I don't know.*"

JAC (7; 9). Ditto. "Why didn't you do that before?—*I don't know, because I didn't think of it. I never saw it.*"

GUY (8; 4). Ditto. "Why not do that before?—*Because I didn't have enough red ones.*" The new red elements are removed, and Guy decides that the classification according to colour (15 blue elements against 1 red one) will not do "*because there aren't enough here and there are a lot there*".

The reason for neglecting the red circle is quite clear: classifying consists of constructing collections, and a single red circle cannot form a collection. At stages I and II children refuse to construct singular classes or collections. This is in line with the way in which they relied on imagery to solve the problem of the "unique specimen", instead of applying a classificatory schema. On the other hand, just as they were able to extend the notion of complementarity by the age of 7 or 8, and apply it to a singular class, so, in the present situation, the capacity for generalization shown by 7 and 8 year-olds greatly exceeds that of the previous subjects.

URS (6; 11). Urs is one of those subjects who classes the elements according to colour at his second attempt. He starts with shape. Then: "Can you find another way?—(He puts all the blue elements on the left and the red circle on the right.) *I've put the red ones* (!) *in one box and the blue ones in the other.*" Only then does he go on to the criterion of size.

ISO (7; 4) and SEL (7; 4). Colour is chosen quite spontaneously after shape and size.

LIL (8; 4): "*Because those are blue and this one is red.*"

AM (8; 7): "*The blue ones together and the red one on the other side.*"

ROC (8; 10): "*I've put all the blue ones together and the red one apart.*"

FAB (8; 11) spontaneously selects colour as his first criterion: "*I've put the red ones* (!) *here and all the others in the other box.*"

For these subjects, complementarity overrides numerical extension. Several of them (e.g. Urs and Fab) even talk about "the red ones", rightly considering that the fact that there is only one red counter is immaterial to the validity of redness as an intensive property, and is nothing but an artefact of the experimenter's selection.

1b. Because we were aware of the fact that the content of a problem is a critical factor at the level of concrete reasoning, we carried out a similar investigation with a different content. Instead of the red circle and the blue shapes we used pictures of people: three women, two men and a boy. We were aware (cf. ch. VI, §4) that children class people by age just as frequently as by sex. We could therefore anticipate that if the two classifications did not occur equally often in this situation, it

128

was because the boy would constitute a singular class. In fact, 20 subjects aged 7–8 years produced 10 spontaneous classifications based on sex, none based on age, and 10 narrative arrangements (parents with children, etc.). When compelled to dichotomize, 15 based their classification on sex and none on age. The corresponding numbers, with subjects of 9–10 years, were 7 and 2. But when two girls were added to the collection, more than half the subjects accepted a classification based on age (in spite of the fact that even now the pictures of adults far exceeded those of children, the operative point being that these now numbered more than one). We also tried the experiment using five animals and one plant, the class represented by the singular element being far more heterogeneous than in the previous cases. In this case, one third of the subjects of 7–8 years spontaneously classed the objects as animals (a mouse, a giraffe, a snail and two birds) and plants (one tulip); a third did so after four more plants had been added, and the remaining third refused this dichotomy even then. At 9–10, two-thirds separated the cards into animals versus plant before the addition of the other flowers.

These two experiments point to the importance of content, but they also confirm the resistance to singular classes.

II. Experiments bearing on the role of number proved negative. The objects again consisted of geometrical shapes, as in I. There were 16 squares and 8 circles, of which 12 were large (5 cm.) and 12 were small (2·5 cm.). 12 of these objects were red and 12 were blue. We wished to see whether there would be a tendency to avoid using shape as a basis for classification, because of the numerical asymmetry this would yield. What we found with subjects of 5–8 years, was that shape and colour were used equally often. We have already shown that shape and colour are normally used with equal frequency by young subjects, while size is seldom chosen until a later age. It follows that the smaller number of circles did not affect our results.

3. THE "SECONDARY" CLASS IN A FORCED DICHOTOMY

We may now turn to the central problems of complementarity and negation. We begin with "complements of the first kind" or "secondary" classes.

Suppose that A is a class included in the class B, defined by its genus b and the specific difference a. Then, unless A is equal to B, there is a class $A' = B - A$, which can be defined negatively as the class of Bs which are not-A. Under certain special circumstances, it can also be defined positively by its own specific difference, a_2, where the first class A_1 is defined by its specific property a_1; this would apply where the extension of B is exhausted by two component classes, so that $B - A_1 =$

$A_1' = A_2$ and $B - A_2 = A_2' = A_1$.[1] There is a relation of "otherness" between A and A', in that the A's are the elements of B which by virtue of being different from the As, are "the others", although they share the generic property b. The property of otherness is one which depends on A, and on the property a characterizing its elements. We shall say that a subject is aware of "secondary" classes if he can group the A' elements together, once B and A are given. This means that he can think in terms of complementarity which is the extensive aspect of such a dichotomy and also in terms of otherness which is its intensive aspect.

The specific problem we wish to consider is the relation between secondary classes and class-inclusion. In the sense in which we have just defined secondary classes, they obviously suppose inclusion, for they depend on the inclusion of A in B and on the inverse operation $A' = B - A$. But we have seen (ch. IV, §§1 and 2: questions III C and D, Tables V and VII) that it is very much easier for a child to understand that there will be flowers left in a field if all the primulas are picked, but that no primulas will be left if all the flowers are picked, than it is for him to make quantitative comparisons between wholes and parts, as in the judgment "There are more flowers than primulas" $(B > A)$. This means that there is an intuitive or imaginal sort of complementarity, which precedes the mastery of inclusion at an operational level. In the same way, there may be an intuitive or pre-operational idea of "otherness", expressed by words like "the others", and corresponding to the pre-operational complement expressed by the phrase "all the rest". We shall try to trace the stages through which the idea of a secondary class is elaborated, in order to see which aspects of otherness precede the mechanism of class-inclusion and why this latter is essential to a complete understanding of secondary classes.

Two experiments were carried out. In I we used the same objects as in a previous experiment on inclusion (ch. IV, §1): pictures representing primulas of different colours, a pansy, a rose, a tulip and a lily-of-the-valley. The child was asked to divide these pictures into two classes, an available dichotomy being between the primulas and the other flowers. In II we used several apples, one or two pears, a couple of cherries, a banana, a melon, a bunch of grapes, an orange, etc. The child could, therefore, divide the elements into apples and other fruit. Additional fruits can be introduced after the classification is made, and the results can be most illuminating. Some children will accept any fruit for membership of the secondary class, since this can include any fruit "other than apples"; but many of the younger subjects refuse to allow any variety not represented in the original class A'.

There were four steps to the experiment. (1) The child is first asked to

[1] Thus the set of shapes B might be composed exclusively of squares = A_1 = A_2' and of circles = $A_2 = A_1'$.

130

divide the elements into two classes. Various formulations are allowed, e.g., "Would you make me two piles with all these?"—"Would you make me two piles by putting together the ones which belong together?" or "There are some pictures which belong together. Can you put all these pictures into two piles?" The child is then asked the reason for his choice. (2) Further elements are added, or else some of those present are removed. This might result in leaving only two apples and one each of several other varieties of fruit, or it could produce four apples together with a pear, a grape, a cherry and a melon. (3) By way of control, the experiment might be done with just one apple, but several pears. (4) Finally, once the elements are classified, the child is asked how the first box should be labelled and he readily gives the answer: "primulas", or "apples". We then ask him how to label the second box in one or two words—we don't let him list all the varieties.

In this experiment the child is forced to carry out a dichotomy, which he might possibly not do spontaneously. This is a disadvantage; but the method also has its advantages. It allows us to see whether the dichotomy leads to a classification, or whether it simply results in an arbitrary distribution of the elements between the two boxes. Where there is classification, we can see whether both classes are defined positively, or whether one is defined positively and the other negatively. In the latter case, we have to determine whether the negative definition expresses a relation to the class which is positively defined. Finally, we have the difficult task of deciding whether or not the definitions of A and A' are related to the whole B.

Out of a total of 63 subjects aged 5–10 years, only 7 resisted a dichotomy, and two of these were mentally retarded. We shall not again describe the elementary reactions of constructing graphic collections or small sets placed in juxtaposition (cf. ch. I and ch. II, §2). When subjects at this level are obliged to construct a dichotomy, they construct an arbitrary one in which no rules of classification are observed, i.e. one which is either not exhaustive or has similar objects in each of the two collections. For example, there might be one apple, the grape, the lemon and the melon in one collection, and two apples, the cherries, the banana and the pear in the other. At stage II, i.e. from the age of 5–6 onwards, we no longer find any refusals. The reactions to this task now fall into one of two categories. A number of children divide all the objects fairly rapidly into two collections, and go on to define one of these positively and the other negatively. The remainder usually try to find positive definitions for both collections. In any case they fail to give a negative characterization of the second by invoking the character of "otherness". The first group seems to have progressed further towards an operational understanding of complementarity and secondary classes in terms of class-inclusion, and as a matter of fact we find children in this group exemplifying every possible shade of transition. The second groups appears less advanced. Their reactions do not shade into stage III, and indeed they point to something midway between a true dichotomy and a set of small collections in juxtaposition. We shall therefore begin with examples of this second group.

Reb (5; 8) begins with three small collections of yellow, mauve and pink primulas. When two lots are asked for, he puts all these together and puts the other flowers in a second pile. "What shall I write on the labels?— *'Primulas' here, and here I don*'t *know what it is really: a rose, a pansy, a tulip* . . . —Can you put it all in one word?—*Perhaps 'Tulips'*.—But suppose that someone wants to find a rose.—*'Flowers.'*—Could one put primulas in the box of flowers?—*Yes* . . . *no.*—What about this anemone, where would that go?—(Puts it with the primulas, then:) *Perhaps on its own.*"

Fruit. First he produces a collection of pears and apples. Then he makes three lots: (1) Pears and apples, (2) a lemon, and (3) all the rest.

Ver (6; 1). Two lots: (1) the pink daisy and the pink primulas, and (2) the other primulas, the rose, etc. "Do they belong together?—*No* (puts all the primulas together and the rest apart).—What shall I write on these labels?— *Here: 'primulas'.*—And there?—*Roses, daisies* . . . —Can you put it in one word?—*Daisies.*"

Mau (6; 3) first forms pairs, and then puts the primulas together in one lot and all the rest in the second collection. He writes "primulas" for the first box, but will only accept an enumeration for the second.

Fruit: (1) Cherries, apples, strawberries; (2) the other fruit and the green and yellow apples. "Why are these (1) together?—*Because they're red.*—And supposing I add an orange?—*That goes in the second pile because there's no red fruit, because there's more yellow* (than other colours in 2)."

It is, of course, natural that a child will try to find positive characteristics for the second collection. And, as we have said, it may be artificial to make children construct dichotomies when they have not shown a spontaneous tendency to do so. But, given the dichotomy, it is perfectly legitimate to ask for a definition of the residual class, in order to see whether the reply involves the recognition that it has two general properties: (a) that of being a fruit or a flower, and (b) that of being a fruit other than an apple, or a flower other than a primula. Even though the problem may be slightly formal, the answer is a completely natural one, and stage III subjects give it quite spontaneously.

It is interesting that the subjects who do not define the second class by referring to the first one, are those who find it difficult to carry out the initial dichotomy. Some define the second class by genus alone (e.g. Reb, who defines it as "flowers"), without realizing that this definition applies to the first class as well; others define it by one of its elements (Ver defines it as "daisies"); others again define it by a property which is widespread but not general among its members (Mau, for instance, says that it has "more yellow ones"). These reactions are a long way from inclusion. This is brought out by the fact that the easiest question of all, i.e. that of defining the whole class obtained by combining the two sub-collections, is not always answered correctly. Although some subjects will name this class correctly as "fruit" (B.G. 6; 10), or "all the flowers" (J.P. 6; 2), others continue to refer to some representative kind of fruit or flower. They may call the class "pears" (E.V. 6; 9) or "bananas" (P.J. 6; 2); or they may say "apples and fruit" (B.O. 6; 2), using both terms together as if one did not include the other.

From about 5; 11, however, we begin to find dichotomies consisting of one relatively homogeneous collection of several elements and a second collection which is defined by reference to the first. The reference may be explicit ("The others") or implicit (it may be called "A mixture" in contrast with the first class). Here are some examples to illustrate the way in which "otherness' begins to be recognized well before there is an understanding of class-inclusion.

GUB (5; 11) first classes a yellow pansy and all but one of the primulas in (1), and the rest in (2). He corrects himself, however, and arranges all the primulas in (1) and the others in (2). "Why did you do it this way?—*They're the same here* (1), *they're primulas.*—And there?—*They're the others.*—If I want to write out a label for this box, what do you suggest I put down?— *Primulas.*—And there?—*The others.*—If I add a daisy, where would you put it? —*Here* (2).—And a tulip?—*That too.*—And this (a pansy)?—*That too.*—And this (a blue primula)?—*Here* (1).—Could one put the primulas in (2)?—*No.*"

"Could you arrange all these differently for me?— . . . —Suppose we put the roses here (1) and all these (indicating the rest) in (2), what should we write on the boxes?—*Here* (1) *they're roses.*—And here (2)?—*I don't know . . . the others!*"

Fruit: "*I've put the apples here and the others there.*—Suppose I add an apricot?—*Here* (2), *because it isn't an apple.*—Could you arrange them differently?—*Yes, the pears here* (1) *and the others there* (2).—And in yet another way?—*Yes, the grapes and the cherries here* (1) *and the others there* (2)," etc.

OBR (6; 2). "*I've put the primulas here and the other flowers here.*—You tell me what to write on these labels?—'*Box of primulas,*' and '*Box of other flowers.*'—Where would you put a chrysanthemum?—*There* (2)—And a jonquil?—*There also,*" etc. "Could you arrange them differently?—*Yes, the violet here* (1) *and the other flowers there* (2).—Can you arrange them like that with any flower you like?—*Yes.*—And if you put them all in the same box, what would you put on the label?—*Flowers.*"

Fruit: The apples in (1) and "*here* (2) *the box of lots of fruits.*—Suppose I add some cherries?—*You can put them there* (2), *because there are some there already.*—And strawberries?—*Also* (not represented initially).—If you put them all in the same box, what would you write?—*I'd put: apples and fruit.*— If both piles were inside, wouldn't one word be enough?—*Fruit.*—Could you arrange them differently?—*The pears and the other fruit.*—Suppose I add a banana?—*There are no bananas in* (1) *or in* (2), *so you'd have to find another box.*"

POUR (6; 4) puts the primulas in (1) *"because they're all the same thing"*, and the rest in (2). "Suppose that we have to write what's inside on these boxes?—'*Primulas*' here and '*A mixture*' there.—If we add snowdrops?—*In another box* (3), *because it's another flower.*—Would it be right to put it here (2)?—*No, there aren't any like it inside*—And this (a rose)?—*Yes, because there already are some like it inside.*"—Thus the mixture is relative to the initial set of objects only.

Fruit: *"Pears* (1) *and a mixture* (2).—And an apricot, there (1) or there (2)? —*No, there is no other fruit the same as it in there.*—And this (a cherry)?— *Yes, in the mixture* (because there already are some there).—Can you arrange them differently?—*Two cherries and a mixture.*—(etc.) Can one do this with any fruit one likes?—*Yes.*"

SIM (6; 6) divides the flowers into primulas and others. "What names?— '*Primulas*' here (1) and '*Daisies*' there (2).—But there aren't just daisies?— *No.*—Well, one word?—*The others.*—If someone gave us a snowdrop where should it go?—*There* (2), *because it isn't a primula.*"

Fruit: the apples in (1) and the rest in (2), *"I've put one of each here* (2) *and several which are like each other there* (1)." But he subsequently wishes to add a peanut to the apples, *"because there are many there* (2) *and few there* (1)", which is to abandon the initial classification in favour of numerical symmetry.

VUI (6; 6) puts the pears and bananas in (1) and the rest in (2), because *"they're all round in there* (2) *and those are fruits which aren't round* (1)".

HUNT (7; 6) divides the objects into apples and *"fruit".*—Does an apple go with the fruit?—*Yes.*—Well?—*They're apples there* (1), *and those* (2) *are other fruits, there aren't any apples.*—Can you arrange them differently?—*Yes, the pears* (1) *and the fruits which are not pears* (2)."

Flowers: *"The primulas and the other flowers.*—Try another way.—*Two roses and the other flowers.*"

There are two ways in which these subjects are more advanced than the first group. They accept the dichotomy from the beginning, and they realize that A' can only be defined as the elements of B which are not in A, i.e. by the negation of the property a which characterizes A. Thus Vui divides the fruit into those which are "round" and those which "are not round", and most of the subjects simply state that the A's are "the others". Pour defines the A's as "a mixture", while the As are "all the same", implying that the A's constitute a mixture by contrast with the homogeneity of the As. He too, in effect, defines A' by a form of "otherness'.

The evidence clearly indicates that both complementarity and otherness appear at an intuitive or pre-operational level, albeit in a simplified form. They do not come about only as products of class-inclusion. For it would be wrong to regard these children as precocious representatives of the final stage of concrete reasoning, stage III. There are several indications that they forget the whole B once it is divided, and that their conception of "otherness" is only partly a relative concept. Once the objects have become divided into the "(*A*s) and the others (*A'*s)" they often refuse to add objects to *A'* unless the variety is already represented. Thus Obr wants a third box for the bananas, because they are not represented in the pears or in "the other fruit"; Pour wants to put the snowdrops in a third box, although he accepts a rose (and, later, an apricot) in the second "because there already are some like it inside". When Sim is offered new elements, he forgets all about "otherness" and turns to numerical symmetry. These answers show that the concept of "otherness" is still weak, or that it is absolute and not relative, i.e. it is determined once and for all by the initial elements, and cannot be extended to any new ones. (Note that this error is not universal. Gub, the youngest of this group of subjects, does not make it.) Furthermore, these subjects often forget that the whole *B* is made up of *A* and "the others" (*A'*), and tend to identify *B* and *A'*. Hun, even at 7; 6, divides the collection into "apples and fruit", and Obr uses the same formulation for the total collection obtained by combining *A* and *A'*. These answers are a clear reminder of the non-conservation of the whole described in ch. IV, when subjects identified *B* with *A'*, and concluded that there were more *A*s than *B*s.

At stage III, however, complementarity is structured by inclusion. From this stage onwards, the secondary class *A'* has the precise meaning *B − A*, and both *A* and *A'* are understood as included in *B*.

BRA (7; 4) divides the flowers into "*primulas* (1) *and all the flowers excepting primulas* (2).—Could you arrange them differently?—*Yes, the roses here* (1) *and any flowers except roses there* (2)." Similarly with fruit: "*Apples* (1) *and the box of all kinds* (2).—Can one put mandarin oranges in it?—*Yes.*—Any fruit?—*Yes, except apples.*—Can you class them differently?—*Yes, the pears here* (1) *and all kinds of fruit, but not pears, there* (2).—Can one add a banana? —*Yes, any fruit you like, excepting pears.*"

FRA (7; 4). "*Apples* (1) *and here they're other fruits* (2).—Can you do it differently?—*Yes, the bananas here* (1) *and the fruit other than bananas there* (2).—Suppose that we put the two boxes together?—*Fruit.*"

FUR (8; 11). "*All the apples together and all the other fruit.*—And differently? —*The pears together, and then all the other fruit together.*"

SEI (8; 6). "*All the big ones here* (1) *and the others there* (2).—And differently? —*The pears and the others.*—Where would you put a quince?—*Here* (2), *because this is the box of fruit other than pears.*—And a fig?—*There* (2), *because it's all the fruit other than pears.*"

BEA (9; 4). "*The fruit without a skin and the fruit with a skin.*—And differently?—*The round ones and the ones which aren't round.*—What about this (putting the apples in 1)?—*Yes, the apples and the fruit without the apples,*" etc.

GRA (10; 1). "*One can put the small ones here and the others there.*—See if there are some which really belong together?—*The apples here* (1) *and all the different fruits, without the apples, there* (2)."

The very words they use show how these children have integrated complementarity and inclusion. Expressions like "all excepting" and "any you like except" (Bra), "all the others" (Fur), "the (Bs) other than the (As)" (Sei), "the (Bs) without the (As)" (Bea), and "all the different (Bs) without the (As)" (Grai), all indicate the existence of the whole B, and the relativity of the secondary class A' to the primary class A. Of course, although subjects of 7–8 years succeed in integrating complementarity and inclusion when dealing with such clear-cut and familiar classes as flowers or fruit, they will be less advanced in classifying vegetables or coats-of-arms (on which we have, in fact, carried out an experiment).

It is worth considering the precise meaning of such secondary classes; do they ever have a functional significance? In an experiment with 83 subjects of 6–14 years, we tried to compare ascending methods of classification (successive combination) and descending methods (successive subdivision). Initially, the material consisted of 4 inanimate objects and 20 living creatures, of which 4 were people and 16 were animals: 4 fishes, 4 wild animals and 8 tame ones (4 mammals and 4 birds). However, the tendency to associate inanimate objects with people in terms of their utility was found to be so powerful that we had to drop the objects.

We found that although dichotomies are not used by very young children, they show a steady rise from the time of their first appearance at the beginning of the level of concrete operations. Given the dichotomy, secondary classes take on their natural meaning which corresponds exactly to the integration of complementarity and inclusion. Younger subjects tend to be satisfied with a bare negation (the A's are the Bs which are not a). Later, the negation leads on to a search for some positive property to characterize the A's. Here are two examples:

GIL (8; 8) subdivides the objects into inanimate objects and animals, the latter into "*fierce*" and tame, and the tame into those that live in houses and those used on farms, etc. When a squirrel is added, his positive definition, not tame = fierce, makes him add it to the farm animals, and this leaves him unhappy. "*It is not fierce, but still it isn't as tame as the others.*"

HAS (10; 0) subdivides the objects into inanimate objects and living things, the latter into animals and people, the animals into "*anything walking and anything living in water*", and those that walk into "*anything which can fly and anything which justs walks*". The latter are then divided into "*wild and tame*".

Both subjects are combining negative and positive properties: not tame = wild or fierce, and not flying = only walking, etc.

4. NEGATION

We have just seen that complementarity precedes inclusion, and appears in an intuitive form at the level of non-graphic collections. Let us see what negation means to a child. Given a certain class A, does the expression "not-A" signify the complement of A with respect to "everything" (i.e. Z, being the most general class of the system), or with respect to B, the class immediately larger, or with respect to an intermediate class in the hierarchy, e.g. C or D? By putting the problem in this way, we are in fact appealing to relations of class-inclusion. But it is reasonable to ask what meaning is given to the extensional expression not-A, and the intensional one not-a, when those do not yet exist.

I. We started with an experiment on 78 children of 4–7 years, using 18 geometrical objects. These consisted of 3 large and 3 small squares, 3 large and 3 small circles, and 3 large and 3 small triangles. Each of these groups of 3 elements contained one blue element, one white and one red. The following questions were asked: I (descending order): (1) Give me all those which are not circles; (2) give me all those which are not blue circles; (3) all those which are not small blue circles. II. Give me those which are not large and red. III (1) Give me all except . . . and (2) the . . . except . . . . IV (ascending order): (1) Give me those which are not small white triangles (or "roofs"); (2) those which are not small triangles; (3) those which are not triangles. V. Give me a card which is not at all like (or "the same thing as") . . . . VI. If you give . . . to x and . . . to y, what will you be left with? VII. Give me all those which are not green. In addition, a classification is required either at the beginning of the experiment or at the end.

The following results were obtained when a single property had to be negated. (We limited the enquiry to two properties, "circle" and "triangle", in order to keep the interview reasonably short.)

Table IX. *Negation of a single attribute at ages 4–7* (%)

	Not a circle				Not a triangle				Average			
Age	4	5	6	7	4	5	6	7	4	5	6	7
(No. of subjects)	(20)	(24)	(21)	(13)	(20)	(24)	(19)	(13)				
Not-A	80	64	95	100	100	70	100	100	90	67	98	100
Part of not-A	5	0	0	0	0	20	0	0	2·5	10	0	0
No under-standing[1]	15	36	·5	0	0	10	0	0	7·5	23	2	0

Nearly all children who understand the question refer the negation to the entire set. The exceptions are the 20% at age five, who count only

[1] These subjects gave all the elements of A itself as not-A.

137

the circles as not-triangles and forget the squares, presumably because the circles were mentioned in the previous question. The 4-year-olds rarely make the same mistake, but this may well be an artefact of selection, since the subjects were all school-children and those 4-year-olds who are not too bright are probably not at school yet. However, it could be that performance does in fact deteriorate at 5 because the younger children would reason globally while the 5-year-olds would begin to analyse the various shapes, asking themselves what to include under "not-round" and what to exclude.

For the negation of a class $A_1 A_2$ defined by two attributes, e.g. blue (A_1) circles (A_2) or small (A_1) triangles (A_2) there are three types of response: (1) the negation is referred to the entire set (i.e. all except $A_1 A_2 = [A_1$ not-$A_2] + [A_2$ not-$A_1] + [$not-A_1 not-$A_2]$; (2) it is referred to an intermediate class (i.e. [not-A_1 not-$A_2] + [A_1$ not-$A_2]$; or (not-A_1 not-$A_2] + [A_2$ not-$A_1]$ which amounts to (not-A_1) or (not-A_2), e.g. all except the blues or all except the little ones (or all except the circles, or triangles); (3) it is referred to the nearest class in the hierarchy (i.e. [not-$A_1 A_2] = [A_1$ not-$A_2]$ or [not-$A_1 A_2] (= [A_2$ not-$A_1]$)), e.g. red circles or blue squares and triangles for "not-blue-circles".

The following table shows the results for questions I 2 and IV 2 in terms of the formal analyses only, i.e. irrespective of the particular attributes involved.

Table X. *Overall responses to the negation of two attributes* (%)

Age (*no. of subjects*)	4 (10)	5 (25)	6 (21)	7 (14)
(1) all except $A_1 A_2$	37	36	63	40
(2) not-A_1 or not-A_2	50	25	12	16
(3) A_1 not-A_2 or A_2 not-A_1	13	39	25	45
No understanding	—	—	—	—

These results may be compared with those obtained from question II ("give me those which are not large and red").

Table XI. *Negation of "large, red"* (%)

Age (*no. of subjects*)	4 (10)	5 (20)	6 (20)	7 (14)
(1) All except $A_1 A_2$	14	20	58	25
(2) Not-A_1 or not-A_2	72	30	21	8
(3) A_1 not-A_2 or A_2 not-A_1	14	40	21	67
No understanding	—	10	—	—

There are four possible ways of interpreting the negation of a class defined by three properties. (1) The negation may be understood with respect to all the objects, so that not-$A_1 A_2 A_3$ contains all but one of

138

the eight disjoint classes defined by A_1, A_2 A_3[1]; (2) not-A_1 A_2 A_3 may be taken as not-A_1 A_2 or as not-A_1 A_3 or as not-A_2 A_3, yielding 6 disjoint classes; (3) the negation is taken with respect to a class fairly far removed from A_1 A_2 A_3 and containing 3–5 of the eight basic disjoint classes (for example not-A_1 A_2 A_3 might be taken as not-A_1); (4) or finally the negation may be taken with respect to one of the classes next in rank to A_1 A_2 A_3 (for example not-A_1 A_2 A_3 might be taken as A_1 A_2 not-A_3, or A_1 A_3 not-A_2).

Table XII. *Negation of a class (A_1 A_2 A_3) defined by three attributes (%)*

	Small blue circle				Small white triangle				Average			
Age	4	5	6	7	4	5	6	7	4	5	6	7
(No. of subjects)	(10)	(25)	(21)	(14)	(10)	(25)	(21)	(14)				
(1) All but A_1 A_2 A_3	14	18	72	50	30	44	68	33	22	31	70	42
(2) 6 of the eight basic classes	14	22	4	17	15	5	17	42	15	13	11	29
(1 and 2)	(28)	(40)	(76)	(67)	(45)	(48)	(85)	(75)	(37)	(44)	(81)	(71)
(3) 3–5 basic classes	72	23	10	9	55	12	6	0	63	18	8	4
(4) 1–2 basic classes	0	37	14	24	0	40	9	25	0	38	11	25
									[0]	[18]	[9]	[25][2]

There are a number of uniform trends which run through Tables X–XII. (a) There is a steady decrease in negation with respect to a class of intermediate rank, i.e. one which is not the whole and not next in rank to the negated class (see row (2) in Tables X and XI and row (3) in Table XII). (b) Conversely, negation with respect to a class next in rank (with complementarity taking the form of a secondary class in the sense of §3), increases steadily with age (from 13 to 45% for the negation of a 2-attribute class, Table X; from 14 to 67% for the negation of "large red", Table XI; and from 0 to 25% for the negation of a 3-attribute class, Table XII (where the figure in square brackets showing strict secondary classes equals the unbracketed figure at 7, but not before). (c) Finally, negation with respect to the whole rises to a peak at age 6 and then begins to fall away. It increases between 4 and 6 years, because the fours and fives find it difficult to think of two or three properties at once. The subsequent decrease at 7 years, is due to the fact that subjects at this level are more bent on distinguishing the class under consideration from its nearest neighbours.

[1] These are $A_1A_2A_3$, $A_1A_2A_3'$, $A_1A_2'A_3$, $A_1'A_2A_3$, $A_1A_2'A_3'$, $A_1'A_2A_3'$, $A_1'A_2'A_3$, $A_1'A_2'A_3'$.

[2] The numbers in square brackets give those who took the negation relative to a class next in rank to $A_1A_2A_3$.

What these results suggest is that the development of negation depends on that of inclusion relations. The two types of negation which have a general meaning in a hierarchical or ordered system of class-inclusions are negation with respect to the whole (i.e. not-A in the absolute sense) and negation with respect to the next including class (which gives the secondary class $A' = B - A$). Negation with respect to a class lying between these two has a meaning only in terms of some particular problem that the subject has set himself. Thus, in the present experiment, where no indication of purpose is given, it is natural that interpretations should tend increasingly towards these two types of negation. The intermediate types, which are more frequent at 4–5 years, than at the operational level of 7 years, are simply an expression of the fact that young children cannot deal with ordered inclusions.

II. A second experiment, which was more delicate, can only be regarded as tentative. In this we used a variety of objects which were arranged to represent a farm. There were (a) people, (b) animals, including domestic quadrupeds and birds, (c) vegetables, including flowers, and (d) inanimate objects (tools, equipment, etc.). The following questions were asked (sometimes with the objects present, and sometimes in their absence):

(1) Show me (or tell me) which ones are not animals. Is it more true (or just as true) to say that a person is not an animal or to say that a ladder is not an animal? In order to induce the subject to provide justifications, we even asked: is it funnier to say that a person is an animal or that a ladder is an animal, and why? (2) Show me which ones are not birds. (As before, the subject is encouraged to amplify by being asked "Are there any more?") It is more true to say that a cat is not a bird or that a barrel is not a bird? Is it funnier to say . . . ? (3) Show me everything except the "things" (or everything which isn't an "object"). (4) Show me which ones are not tulips, etc. (cf. 1 and 2). (5) Are there more things which are not birds or more things which are not animals? (At this point, we also put the familiar problem of the quantification of inclusion: are there more animals or more birds?)

We shall not dwell on the results of questions 1–4, since these were similar to those obtained with geometrical objects, apart from the tendency for subjects to appear more backward in the present situation. This may be due either to the weaker structure of the inclusion relations involved, or to the fact that the subject has to think about the negation, instead of immediately carrying out a simple action. When we compare a group of 13 eight-year-olds with a group of 12 thirteen-year-olds, we find that the former tend to take the negation of a class in an absolute sense while the latter more frequently refer it to the next higher class. Eleven of the 13 eight-year-olds use the total set when asked to indicate which objects are not animals while 8 out of the 12 older subjects use the nearest class (living things). To indicate "not-birds", 9 out of 13 eight-year-old subjects bring in the entire set, and 11 out of 12 older subjects confine themselves to the class of animals. Here are two typical cases:

HAL (8; 11) indicates any person, vegetable or inanimate object as "not an animal". "A little boy told me 'the man isn't an animal', and another boy told me 'the ladder isn't'. Are they equally right, or is one more right than the other?—*The one who said 'man' is less right.*—Why?—*'Ladder' is more true. The ladder is made of wood. The man has legs; he's more like an animal than the ladder is.*" For non-birds, the corresponding choice is between a cow and a wagon (Hal having picked on both among his initial selection). "*The one who says the wagon is more right. The wagon doesn't have legs, it has wheels. The cow has legs, and birds do as well.*"

When asked to say which things are not tulips, without anything in front of him, Hal only mentions flowers and plants (i.e., elements of a class close to that of tulips). When asked whether it is more correct to say that a cow or an orchid is not a tulip (he mentioned orchids himself), Hal answers: "*A cow, of course. A cow has less of the shape of a flower. It has horns and ears. A flower doesn't. It has a tail (queue) . . . ah! but the flower does too![1]*—And an inkpot or an orchid?—*The one who says that it's the inkpot is more correct . . .* etc.*"

Ros (12; 3). Ros, on the other hand, provides an example of negation relative to a neighbouring class. "Is it more true to say that the man isn't an animal, or that the ladder isn't? Or are both equally true?—*Both are true. But, all the same, the one who says 'the man' is more right.*—Why?—*A man is a little like animals. He has legs. He has more or less the same body.*—Is it funnier to say that a man is an animal or that a ladder is?—*The ladder is an animal, that's funnier.*" "And is it more correct to say that a cow isn't a bird, or that a house isn't. Or are both equally correct?—*It's a little ridiculous to say that a house isn't a bird.*—And a cow?—*Well, it is an animal!*" When mentioning things which are not tulips, Ros names only flowers, adding: "*One can name all the other flowers which are not tulips.*—Which is more correct: that an animal is not a tulip, or that a rose isn't?—*Both are correct, but the second one is a little more correct, because it's also the category of flowers.*—Is it funnier to say 'the daisy is a tulip' or 'the dog'?—*'The dog' is funnier, because it's more* (!) *not a tulip.*—And isn't the daisy funny?—*Yes, but it isn't as funny as that.*"

These two examples, should suffice, since they are fully representative. They illustrate the way in which negation is understood. Hal and Ros are both agreed that negation includes many degrees of difference. A dog, says Ros, is "more not a tulip". And Hal explains that "a cow has less of the shape of a flower (tulip)" than an orchid. Now Ros, and indeed most of the older children, draws the conclusion that the most useful negations are those which indicate differences between neighbouring classes (i.e. not-$A = B$ not-A, or C not-A). Hal, on the other

---

[1] "queue" = "stalk".

hand, like the majority of 8-year-olds, thinks the strongest negation is the one which is most meaningful, because it points to a wide difference (i.e. not-$A = Z$ not-A).

This concern with neighbouring classes, which seems to increase with age, must be due to the development of ordered inclusion relations. We therefore considered it might be of some interest to pose the problem of the extension of negative classes to subjects aged 10–13 years. We shall discuss this in the next section.

5. THE INCLUSION OF COMPLEMENTARY CLASSES AND THE DUALITY PRINCIPLE

There is a duality between the ordering of classes and the ordering of their complements, which is expressed by:

$$(A) < (B) \rightarrow (\text{not-}A) > (\text{not-}B)$$

(for instance if the class of animals B includes the class of birds A, then the class of not-birds, not-A, includes the not-animals, not-B; it follows that there are more not-birds than not-animals, because the former include animals which are not-birds in addition to not-animals).

There are two reasons for introducing questions based on this implication to children of 10–13. The first is quite simply that the problem fills a gap in our study of complementarity and negation. But the second is more important from the standpoint of our general theory. We have argued elsewhere[1] that the structures which appear at the level of concrete operations are limited to elementary "groupings" of classes and relations. These groupings are actually only semi-lattices, and although in certain respects they resemble mathematical groups, the principle of associativity is only partially met. At the level of formal or proportional reasoning, we find that adolescent thinking begins to reveal the classical structures of lattices and groups—particularly in many instances where propositions are being combined in conformity with the four-group *INRC*. However, this should not be taken to imply a derogation of the logic of classes and relations as such. What it means is that only a part of this logic is available to a child so long as his reasoning is confined to operations involving the arrangement and rearrangement of concrete objects (level of "concrete" reasoning). The "groupings" of which we speak constitute that part of this logic which is available to him. Now such groupings do not include the duality which is our present consideration. The reason is that instead of being based on general negative classes (not-A, not-B etc.), they involve only the more limited relation of complementarity between adjacent classes (A and A', B and B' etc.).

[1] Inhelder and Piaget *The Growth of Logical Thinking*, 1959 and Piaget, *Logic and Psychology* with Introduction by W. Mays, Manchester Univ. Press, 1952.

Nevertheless, a complete logic of classes does include the principle of duality and therefore not only does it come nearer to a true lattice structure but it also involves the *INRC* group. It follows that we might reasonably expect children to grasp the law of duality in the logic of classes at the beginning of the stage of formal reasoning, just as we know they master the same principle in the logic of propositions: $(p > q) = (\bar{q} > \bar{p})$. This is what we wish to verify.

To make our point clearer we would add that the law of duality is itself an instance of the *INRC* group. In other words, the statement $A < B =$ not-$B <$ not-A combines an operation of inversion (N), which transforms A to not-A, with one of reciprocity (R), which reverses the order of the terms A and B. Now both these forms of reversibility are present in concrete "groupings", but the inversion occurs only in the grouping of classes while the reciprocity occurs only in the grouping of relations. At this level, we do not find a structure which is sufficiently rich to allow for both. The chief characteristic of formal reasoning is precisely that it reveals this synthesis of inversion and reciprocity. We know this to be true of the logic of propositions, and we shall now see that it applies equally to the logic of classes—because of the law of duality.

We carried out an experiment on 28 subjects aged 10–13. We used pictures of animals which had to be divided by successive dichotomies (e.g. into birds and other animals, and then into ducks and other birds). The following questions were asked: (1) "Show me all the things which are not ducks, all those which are not birds", etc.; (2a) "Are there more living things which are not ducks, or more living things which are not birds? (similarly with birds and animals); (2b) "Can one list more things which are not ducks, or more things which are not birds?" (similarly with birds and animals). The subjects who were asked question 2a, had started with straightforward questions on the quantification of inclusion ("Are there more birds or more animals?" etc.) Those who were asked 2b, had already been questioned on negation (§4). If a subject had difficulty with question 2a, he was helped by questions involving subtraction ("What is left if one removes all the ducks? Or all the birds? Or if a hunter kills all the ducks?" etc.). We saw in §4 that these are easier to answer than questions on inclusion.

The subjects fell into four groups: (1) those who fail with questions of the form $A < B$ as well as those of the form not-$B <$ not-A; (2) those who succeed with the first and fail with the second; (3) those who succeed with the first, and eventually succeed with the second after much preliminary groping; and (4) those who succeed with both without any difficulty.

There is no point in giving examples which clearly belong to group (1). But here is an example intermediate between groups (1) and (2):

Aud (11; 7). After carrying out the several dichotomies: "Are there more animals or more birds?—*Birds are animals; it's the same thing.*—But if one counted all the birds, and then counted all the animals, where would there be more?—*When one counts all the animals.*—And are there more ducks or more birds?—*The ducks belong to the birds; ducks are birds as well.*—And which way does one find more: when one counts only the ducks or when one counts the birds?—*It's the same thing, because the ducks are birds.*—How many ducks are there?—(He counts.) *Four.*—And birds?—*Eight.*—Are there more ducks or more birds?—*It's the same thing.*—Are there any birds which are not ducks?—*Yes.*—And ducks which are not birds?—*No.*—Well, are there more ducks or more birds?—. . .—How many birds are there?—*Eight.*— And ducks?—*Four.*—Is that more or the same number?—*Ducks are birds* (he counts them again). *It's the same thing.*—And, in the world, are there more . . . etc?—*You can't tell; you can't count them.*—When one counts the birds, does one find more or less than when one counts the animals?—*The same thing.*—How many birds do you have?—*Eight.*—And animals?—*Fifteen.*"

"Are there more living things which are not ducks or more which are not birds?—*I don't know.*—If you take the ducks away, what is left?—*The* (other) *birds and the* (other) *animals.*—And if you take the birds away?—*The* (other) *animals are left.*—Well then, compare them.—*It's the same thing, because the ducks are birds. One counted everything together* (in counting the birds).— Take away everything which is not a bird.—(He does so correctly.)—And (having replaced them) take away everything which is not a duck.—(Correct.) —When did you take away more?—*It's the same thing; the ducks are birds.*— And are there more living things which are not animals, or more which are not birds?—*Birds are animals, and so it's the same thing.*"

This case seems interesting. Although Aud is 11; 7, and although he can "read off" inclusions (he knows that there are birds which are not ducks, but no ducks which are not birds), so that he counts four ducks and eight birds, he still maintains that there are as many of the one as of the other! He cannot free himself from the incorrect symmetry given to inclusion (cf. ch. III), which interprets "all the *A*s are *B*s" as "all the *A*s are all the *B*s". This means, of course, that he also fails with the inclusion of complements, taking "the not-*B*s are not-*A*s" as equivalent to "all the not-*B*s are all the not-*A*s".

Following are three examples from group (2):

Duv (11; 6). "Are there more ducks or more birds?—*But the ducks are birds as well.*—Well then?—*There are more birds.*—And more birds or more animals?—*More animals, because birds are animals.*"

"And now show me all the things on the table which are not ducks— (Indicates those which are not birds.)—Is that all?—*No* (correct).—Show me all those which are not birds.—*The animals, those which don't fly.*—Are those all living things?—*Yes.*—Are there more living things which are not ducks or more living things which are not birds?—*The same thing, because a duck is the same thing as a bird.*—Suppose that one hunter wants to kill all the ducks and another one wants to kill all the birds. Would there be more left after

144

killing all the ducks or all the birds?—*More when I kill all the birds.*—Why?—*If one kills all the ducks and all the birds, the ducks are birds as well.*—Are there more living things which are not birds or more which are not animals?—*The same thing, nothing.*—What do you mean?—*Birds are animals. So there is nothing left.*"

AUB (11; 10). "Are there more living things which are not birds or more which are not animals?—*More living things which are not animals.*—Why?—*Because it's people who are not animals.*"

GER (13; 6). "Can one list more things which are not birds, or more that are not animals?—*More things which are not animals.*—Why?—*Birds are animals to start with.*—And so?— . . .*"

Finally, here is one example from group 3 and three from group 4.

ROC (11; 7) "Are there more ducks or more birds?—*More birds, because ducks are birds.*—And more animals or more birds?—*More animals, because birds are animals.*—And in the world?—*More animals, because birds are animals.*"

"Are there more living things which are not ducks or more which are not birds?—(Hesitates.) *More that aren't birds . . . They're equal.*—Suppose that a hunter kills all the ducks and another one kills all the birds . . . etc?— *There are more that aren't ducks, because there are all the birds which aren't ducks as well as the animals that don't fly.*—And more living things that aren't birds or more that aren't animals?—*There are more living things that aren't birds, because there are all the animals that don't fly. The ones that aren't animals, are not even birds; they aren't anything. As for the ones that aren't birds, that leaves all the animals that don't fly.*—And in the world?—(Hesitates.) *There are more that aren't birds.*—Why?—*The animals that don't fly and the human beings are left.*"

STU (11; 4). "Are there more ducks or more birds?—*More birds, because ducks are birds.*—And in the world?—*The same thing.*—More birds or more animals?—*More animals, because the birds are all animals.*—And in the world? —*It's the same thing.*"

"More living things which aren't ducks or which aren't birds?—*More which aren't ducks.*—And in the world?—*It's the same thing, because all the ducks are birds.*—And more which aren't birds or which aren't animals?—*All the birds are animals. There are more living things which are animals; there are more which aren't birds!*"

ROS (11; 8). "More ducks or birds?—*More birds; ducks are birds.*—Birds or animals?—*More animals, because birds are animals.*—More that aren't ducks or that aren't birds?—*More that aren't ducks. Among the birds, there are many kinds. The ducks are just one kind.*—More that aren't birds or that aren't animals?—*More that aren't birds, because birds are a kind of animals, and there are several different kinds of animal.*"

DRE (13; 4). "Can one list more things that aren't birds or more that aren't animals?—*More that aren't birds. Why?—Birds are a definite object* (= a sub-class) *and animals are many things* (= the whole class).—Try putting it better.—*For 'not a bird', one can say a cow and a horse. For 'not an animal', you can't say a cow and a horse!*—Are there more animals or more birds in

145

the world?—*More animals, because they're a whole group, and the birds aren't.*"

Not only do children solve the implication of the duality principle at the beginning of the level of formal reasoning, they formulate it in the clearest way possible. So when Stu says: "There are more living things which are animals; there are more which aren't birds", he is combining negation and reciprocity, showing his familiarity with the principle of duality. This means that the hierarchical ordering of classes is now complete. The direct inclusion of primary classes is the first phase and belongs to the level of concrete operation; the duality principle is the second and final phase.

6. THE NULL CLASS

The operations of classification are established during stage III, i.e. at the level of concrete operations. Such operations apply directly to objects, unlike formal operations which apply to verbal statements. The argument always proceeds from one term to the next, and the structure to which it conforms is always one of the "elementary groupings" of classes and relations. As we have just seen, these do not cover the entire logic of classes or relations, because the latter would include the principle of duality, one form of the *INRC* group (a group which applies to classes no less than propositions). That is why the implication: $A < B \rightarrow$ not-$A >$ not-B, is not understood until stage IV, the stage of formal operations. Nevertheless it is usually understood from stage IVA onwards.

There is another question relevant to the dividing line between concrete and formal operations: the question of the null or empty class. "Elementary groupings" of classes imply this notion, for if $A = B - A'$, then $B - A - A' = 0$ (or, more simply, $A - A = 0$). Also, $A \cap A' = 0$. In other words, a class becomes empty when subtracted from itself, and the intersection of two disjoint classes is empty. From a strictly operational point of view, the child of 7–8 years may be said to understand the operation $+ A - A = 0$, insofar as he knows that adding A, and then taking it away, is equivalent to doing nothing, i.e. $+ 0$. But, since concrete operations apply to objects and the empty class has no objects, we may well ask whether a child is likely to think of it as being on a par with other classes? This is not at all a question of operational manipulation. We know that zero was the last number discovered in arithmetic and that it was long after the invention of addition and subtraction (from which it results by virtue of the equation $n - n = 0$) that it was recognized as a true number. We might therefore follow up our study of complementarity and negation by finding out how children at different levels, will deal with a situation where a complementary class exists, as a class, but contains no objects and is therefore the null class.

An experiment was carried out in which this problem was posed in a perfectly natural form. We asked for a classification of a number of square, round and triangular cards, some of which had pictures of trees, fruit, houses, etc., while others were blank. The subject was first asked to classify all of these in any way he chose, and then instructed to make a dichotomy. The question was whether he would immediately accept the fact that some cards were blank, or whether he would limit his classification to positive properties, such as shape.

The children's reactions were very clear. It is only at 10–11 years that children adopt the classification which seems most natural to us: a division into blank cards versus cards with pictures. Until then we find three separate types of reaction, although these do not represent different levels of maturity: (1) the blank cards may be classified by a different criterion from the others, i.e. shape, instead of content; (2) they may be slipped in with the collections containing pictures; (3) they may be ignored and left in disorder while only the picture-bearing cards are classified. In all three cases, the subject is refusing to construct a null class. Here are a number of examples:

DEB (5; 8). Makes three piles: the cherries, the houses, and the trees, leaving the blanks in disorder (reaction 3). "What are you going to do with these?—*Nothing.*—Can one put them together?—*Yes* (he sorts them into three piles: squares, circles and triangles, reaction 1).—Now arrange all the cards using less space.—(Three collections of pictures and three of blank cards.)—Can you put them all into two lots?—(He divides the pictures into two collections and adds the blanks: reaction 2.)—Is that right?—*No, because there are no pictures on these and there are pictures on the others.*" (This amounts to a verbal recognition of the null class. But it does not enter into the actual classification.)

DAN (6; 5) classifies the cards both by their pictures and by their colours, which allows him to form a collection of white cards, being the blanks (reaction 1). "Can you make two piles?—(He puts the blank cards and the green ones on one side, and the red ones on the other.) *I decided to put all the green ones together, and all the red ones together.* (Note that there is no mention of the blank cards. Reaction 2.)—What about those (the blanks), are they green?—*No.* (He puts them aside. Reaction 3.)—But I asked for two piles.—*I've just had an idea. I'll turn them round* (the ones with pictures), *and then they'll all be blank.* (He does so, and then classifies them as circles and non-circles.)"

BON (7; 0) only classifies the cards with pictures. "And those?—*I can't put them in; they haven't any pictures on them* (3).—Arrange them all the same. The cards must all be used.—(She classifies them separately according to shape.)—But isn't there something that's the same about all of them?—*Yes, they're white.*"

JAC (8; 3) forms a pile of red cards and one of green cards. "And these?—

They aren't anything, they're all blank (3).—Can you put them together?—
Yes.—Tell me what you have now?—*A pile of red ones, a pile of green ones,
and a pile of nothing* (which seems to be the definition of the null class!).—
Well then, arrange them as you like.—(She classifies them according to their
pictures, leaving the blanks alone.)—Can you make two piles?—(She resists
this at first. Then:) *Yes, these have pictures, and these haven't.*—Would that
be all right?—*They're white. One can make a pile of white ones* (reaction 1
again, with the use of a positive property).—What else could one do?—(She
classifies the cards in a matrix arrangement, by pictures and colours, without
using the blanks.)—What about the blanks?—*I'm leaving them out* (3).—
Have you any other ideas?—*Yes* (classifying them separately by their shape.
Reaction 1).—But can't one do it like this (putting the picture cards in one
pile and the blanks in another)?—*Yes, the white ones together because they
don't have pictures* (which shows that she understands the possibility of the
null class). *But I haven't used the white ones, because they don't go with the
other pile.*"

DUR (9; 5). Dur likewise eventually yields to the suggestion of a dichotomy:
"*They all have pictures here, and there aren't any pictures there,*" but he too is
not quite satisfied. "How would you explain it, if you were asked why you
divided them like this?—*I'd say: if you like to put these together* (the blanks),
*you can. But that does not really make two piles, because there are three colours
here* (and none there)."

It is no exaggeration to say that there is a systematic resistance to
dividing the cards into those with pictures and those without, even
though there is an explicit instruction to classify all the elements. That
is why there is a tendency either to neglect the negative properties (reactions 2 and 3), or else to use the positive properties to the blank cards
(reaction 1). The best example of the last reaction, is that of Dan, who
decides to turn the cards round to make them all blank and then classifies
them according to shape.

One might object that the child is right, and that the empty class has
no place in a "good" classification. But we are not trying to find the
most logical procedure. We are merely comparing children with one
another. From the age of 10–11 years, their attitude is completely different:

HOF (10; 0). "Can you make two piles?—*Yes, by putting pictures together and
these* (the blanks) *apart.*"

JOB (10; 5). "You have three piles. How will you put them in the two
boxes?—*Those without pictures should go in one box, and those with pictures
in the other.*"

BRU (10; 8). "Suppose that they're all put in two boxes?—*A box with
pictures and a box with the others.*"

PIG (11; 4). "*All the ones with pictures in one box, to keep them together,
and those without pictures in the other.*"

We have to explain why this simple dichotomy develops so late. The reason must lie in the difference in attitudes which makes the level of concrete operations so different from the period of formal thinking and even from the preparatory phase which begins about the age of 10 or 11. Concrete operations are bound up with the objects to which they apply. This supposes that these objects do exist, and so the notion of an empty class is excluded. Formal thinking, on the other hand, deals with structures independently of their content, and this is true even in the realm of classification. Thus what seems natural to children of 10–11 years, or to us, may not seem natural at 5–7 or even at 7–9.

7. CONCLUSION

Although the results of this chapter are a little disconnected, there is a clear thread which runs through them all, showing how at every stage, the development of complementarity is related to that of inclusion.

First of all, a pre-operational form of "otherness" exists before inclusion is established (cf. §3). This is expressed by dividing a collection into the As and "the others" (A's). But since "the others" are not thought of in relation to the whole (i.e. $B = A + A'$), they frequently take on an absolute meaning (so that many subjects refuse to add new elements to A', even though they do not belong to A). In the course of time, "otherness" acquires a meaning which is relative to the whole B, which means an awareness of the inclusion in B of A and A'. It is only then that A' has the character of a true secondary class defined by the operation of complementarity.

As this mechanism develops, so the secondary class is generalized to include the case in which it contains just one element. At the pre-operational level, when "classes" are only foreshadowed by intuitive, pre-conceptual "collections", the notion of a singular class cannot be grasped, because it contradicts the very idea of a "collection" (cf. §2). A child of 5–7 years may, of course, solve the practical problem of singling out "the one that is different" in the course of a series of presentations in which its relationship with other elements is varied (§1). But there is no intensive classification involved, and it is only at 7–8 years, i.e., at the stage of operational complementarity, that a singular class is treated in the same way as other classes (§2).

The problem of the null class (§6) is a similar one, because the null class is also incompatible with the notion of "collection". But the order of difficulty is even greater, because a class without any elements is also incompatible with the logic of "concrete" operations, i.e. operations in which form is inseparably bound up with content. That is why the null-class is rejected right up to the time when the structure of inclusion relations begins to be separated from their concrete content, at 10–11 years.

Finally, in our analysis of negation, we were able to see that initially negation is undifferentiated (so that not-A may be taken to refer with equal force to any element which lacks the attribute a, §4). This lack of differentiation is akin to the intuitive understanding of "otherness" as opposed to the operational understanding which depends on inclusion. As time goes on children are increasingly prone to pick out the elements of a neighbouring class as peculiarly suitable objects of negation. Yet all the while they are well aware that differences are greater as between classes which are widely separated in a hierarchy. Indeed it is because children are aware of such a gradation of differences that they now distinguish between various shades of negation. The end of this development is the discovery of the law of duality, §5: $A < B \rightarrow$ not-$A >$ not-B. We pointed out that the law is one expression of the *INRC* group of 4 transformations, which is why it is not understood before the level of formal reasoning.

All this means that complementarity is closely related to the relation of inclusion in psychology, just as it is in logic. Indeed the former is elaborated in a succession of stages which exactly parallel the development of the latter, as outlined in chs. II–IV.

Chapter Six

MULTIPLICATIVE CLASSIFICATION
(MATRICES)[1]

So far this study has been confined to additive classification. We will now turn to double and triple multiplicative classifications, these being frequently represented by matrices, i.e. two or more entry tables.

As well as having a more complex logical structure, these pose an interesting psychological problem: while additive classification improves as the subject develops beyond graphic collections (in the sense of ch. I), multiplicative classification lends itself very readily to a certain form of spatial representation. No doubt such an arrangement eventually becomes purely symbolic, but to begin with it could easily be the equivalent of a graphic collection which happens to show an intrinsic correspondence with the relevant logical structure.

The situation is somewhat paradoxical. From a logical point of view multiplicative classifications are more complicated than additive ones. On the other hand, they are supported by a graphic representation which is very much in tune with the kind of thinking found in younger children (graphic collections). Now multiplicative and additive classifications are mastered at the same time, about the age of 7–8 years. The question we have to decide is whether the graphic factor compensates for the added logical complexity, or whether the fact that both systems emerge at the same time is due mainly to the interdependence of the two kinds of operation. In the latter event, we would regard the graphic properties of multiplicative structures as subordinate: initially, and up to a point, they help to make the classification possible, but the help soon becomes more apparent than real, and in time the representation becomes nothing more than a form of symbolism.

1. STATEMENT OF THE PROBLEM

Suppose that we have a set of elements (e.g. red and blue squares and circles) which can be divided into two classes A_1 and A_1' according to one criterion (e.g. A_1 = squares and A_1' = circles), as well as into two different classes A_2 and A_2' on the basis of a second criterion (e.g. A_2 = red elements and A_2' = blue elements). We may use the term B_1 to denote the union of the first two classes, i.e. $B_1 = A_1 + A_1'$ and B_2

[1] In collaboration with Y. Feller, F. Frank, E. McNear, F. Matthieu, A. Morf, G. Noelting, B. Reymond-Rivier, and W. Sears.

for the union of the second two classes, i.e. $B_2 = A_2 - A_2'$. Multiplicative classification consists of classing each element *simultaneously* in terms of the two additive orders B_1 and B_2. Such a classification yields four sub-classes:

$$B_1 \times B_2 = A_1A_2 + A_1'A_2' + A_1'A_2 + A_1'A_2' = B_1B_2.$$

If we wish to divide the elements into these four classes in such a way that the elements belonging to any one of the original sub-classes (e.g. A_1) are next to each other, then the only possible spatial form is that of a two-by-two matrix.

	A_1	A_1'
A_2	$A_1 A_2$	$A_1' A_2$
A_2'	$A_1 A_2'$	$A_1' A_2'$

In the diagram given here, A_1 and A_1' correspond to the two vertical columns and A_2 and A_2' to the two horizontal rows. Of course, multiplicative classification does not have to be presented spatially, and could be described in a purely abstract way. But multiplicative inclusions can be symbolized by matrices, and only by matrices, just as class-inclusion can be symbolized topologically by Euler's circles.

It is easy to check the two statements made at the beginning of this chapter: that a structure of this kind is more complicated than one of additive classification, but corresponds to a spatial configuration which subjects at stage I can interpret as a "graphic collection".

As far as the first statement is concerned, we recall that there are 10 criteria for additive classification (ch. II, §1), that all of them are observed by stage III, and that, with the single exception of class-inclusion (criterion 7), all of them begin to be applied during stage II. Now every one of these criteria applies equally to multiplicative classification (since it is a composite out of two or more additive classifications). But two new criteria have to be added. These, together with their consequences, will be numbered 11 to 14.

(11) All the elements of B_1 belong to B_2 as well, and vice versa. Thus all the elements of B_1 are multiplied by B_2. If there were elements of B_1 not belonging to B_2 (e.g. if there were black squares and circles as well as red and blue ones), then a new class B_2' (the black elements) would have to be added to complete the classification, and there would be six sub-classes.

$$B_1 \times C_2 = A_1A_2 + A_1A_2' + A_1B_2' + A_1'A_2 + A_1'A_2' + A_1'B_2'.$$

(12) All the elements of A_1 must also belong either to A_2 or A_2' (but

not to both, because $A_2 \times A_2' = 0$). Similar statements may be made for the classes A_1', A_2 and A_2'.

(13) A_1 and A_1' contain only elements belonging either to A_2 or to A_2'. Similarly, A_2 and A_2' contain only elements belonging to A_1 and A_1'.

(14) Each of the basic associations $A_1 A_2$, $A_1 A_2'$, etc. constitutes one, and only one, multiplicative class.

On the other hand, it is obvious that a matrix is the sort of spatial configuration that makes a special appeal to perception by virtue of symmetry. If A_1 and A_1' are squares and circles, and A_2 and A_2' are red and blue elements, then the squares in $A_1 A_2$ are balanced by those in $A_1 A_2'$, while the red elements in $A_1 A_2$ balance those in $A_1' A_2$, etc. The symmetry is twofold, corresponding as it does to the horizontal and vertical axes of the diagram, but it also corresponds to the two kinds of complementarity (by negation) in the logical structure.

This perceptual factor is so important that it facilitates, and even produces, solutions which appear to be operational but which are based on the methods of "graphic collections". This is true of the sort of test usually referred to as a matrix test, e.g. Raven's "Progressive Matrices". In tests such as these, the subject is given a multiplicative table with all the spaces but one already filled, and asked to complete it by filling in the last space. (A 2×2 matrix corresponds in our notation to the multiplication: $B_1 \times B_2$; a 3×2 matrix is simply an extended matrix: $B_1 \times C_2$.) Using our terminology, if $A_1 A_2$, $A_1 A_2'$ and $A_1' A_2$ are given, the subject must find $A_1' A_2'$. This means that the first ten criteria have been met in advance by the experimenter, while even criteria 11–13 have been met in part. Thus the three elements given are already classified simultaneously in B_1 and B_2; the two elements of A_1 already belong to A_2 or A_2'; the given element of A_1' belongs to A_2, and all that remains is to find an element of A_1' which belongs to A_2'; the sub-class A_1 contains only elements of A_2 and A_2', and the sub-class A_2 contains only elements of A_1 and A_1'. In short, for the elements already given, the conditions of operational multiplicative classification are met by the perceptual configuration of the matrix. To find the fourth element, the subject need only extend these graphic properties by following the vertical and horizontal symmetries in the matrix arrangement.

Thus, the conditions for operational multiplicative classification are already contained in the spatial lay-out of matrices. This means that such problems can be solved without one single logical operation, by following through the similarities and differences which are thrown into relief by the twofold symmetry of these diagrams.

What makes a psychological analysis so complicated is the fact that the subject can also complete these graphic structures by using more or less operational relations, i.e. pre-logical and logical relations, which arise as he progresses from stage I to stage III. It is very difficult to separate operational and perceptual factors, and their relative importance is likely to vary with the particular situation involved. We know that a child is dealing with his problem at an operational level, and not on the level of graphic collections, if he is reasoning in terms of classes and not in perceptual terms, and this in turn is simply a matter of attributing similarities and differences to the elements as such, without considering their spatial position. But it is very difficult to know when he is doing this and when he is not. One obvious solution is to ask subjects to construct their own classifications, and this we have done. Nevertheless, here again the subject may use multiplicative operations, or graphic collections, or intermediate methods.

However, although interpretation is bound to be difficult, the problem we have to solve is simple enough. We have to decide among the following three hypotheses:

(1) Operational structures are not developed out of graphic structures. This would imply that multiplicative operations appear quite independently of spatial configuration. We might still find occasions when the spatial configuration triggers off the operational insight, others where it blocks it for a time, and some where it renders the operations superfluous.

(2) Operational structures are foreshadowed in spatial configurations, and are directly derived from activity related to them.

(3) There is a phase in the development of operational classification, whether multiplicative or additive, when graphic collections play a predominant part. Nevertheless, their final form owes a great deal more to the co-ordination of such inadequate data as these may yield. The co-ordination is a matter of assimilating, and structuring, and generalizing whatever experience is relevant to classification as a whole. This would mean that we can expect a gradual progress in multiplicative classification exactly parallel to that in additive classification.

Hypothesis (1) implies a sharp discontinuity between the initial and final stages; (2) implies complete continuity, and (3) implies a relative discontinuity since the effects of spatial arrangements would be gradually being replaced by those of operational logical coherence. Comparing subjects' reactions to matrix tests with their spontaneous multiplicative classifications, hypothesis (1) would predict discontinuity in both situations, hypothesis (2) predicts continuity in both; and (3) should predict some relative discontinuities in the first situation, but continuity in the second.

2. MATRICES TESTS, I: RESULTS

14 matrices were used, each containing four or six objects of which one had to be determined. These were grouped according to shape, colour,

size, number or orientation (the last property arising in the case of animals whose heads were turned to the right or the left).[1]

The subjects numbered 14 at 4–5 years, 16 at 6–7 years and 17 at 8–9 years. All but two of the tests were answered correctly by 75% of the 8–9-year-olds.

The most interesting feature of our results was that some of the tests were answered better at 4–5 than at 6–7 years (cf. Table XIII, showing the results of a clinical study, which was later followed by a more standardized investigation).

Table XIII. *Results of matrix tests (percentage of answers correct)*

Sh = shape, C = colour, S = size, N = number, O = orientation, I = choice of three elements, II = choice of six elements (I being understood when no indication is given). The number of items is shown in brackets.

Age	ShC (3)	ShS (2)	CO (2)	ShN (2)	ShCO II (2)	ShCO I (1)	ShCS I (2)
4–5 years	46	43	45	76	26	60	53
6–7 years	76	89	67	74	55	46	44
8–9 years	84	89	80	95	86	64	61

The paradoxical result is that tests involving three qualities, which are more complex and difficult, are answered more successfully at 4–5 than at 6–7 years. The simpler tests show a regular improvement with age (except that the items involving number show no improvement between 4 and 7 years). Nevertheless, the 3-attribute items are less frequently solved even at 8–9 years, which confirms the assumption that they involve a more complex operational schema than do the 2-attribute items.

There is one exception to the rule that younger children do better at the harder tests. When there are six or seven elements to choose from, the 4–5s are worse than the 6–7s. This may well be due to a new factor in the situation, this being their limited span of apprehension.

To return to the 3-choice items involving 3 attributes, the figures show 53–60% answers correct at 4–5, 44–46% at 6–7 and 61–64% at 8–9. In other words, even the oldest subjects are hardly better than the youngest, and the middle group are far worse. The obvious inference is that the youngest age-group must be using a different approach, while the middle group are beginning to use the same approach as the eldest, and finding it difficult. Now we know that the youngest are at stage I

[1] The element which fits best in the empty space must be chosen out of an array of three or six elements illustrated on the same card. The subject is told to choose "to make it fit this way (horizontally) and that way (vertically)".

and naturally incline to thinking in terms of graphic collections. This explains why they are not at all handicapped by the third attribute: on the contrary, the symmetry in the arrangement is stronger when there are 3 attributes, and so we find that their percentage of success drops from 53–60% to 43–46% for the 2-attribute items. (Here again, the percentage of success rises when one of the two attributes is number, because this involves particularly sharp perceptual differences.) But from stage II onwards, children begin to think in terms of the objects as such and their definition by two or three attributes. Naturally enough, they find it harder to combine three attributes than two.

All this amounts to a very strong suggestion that 3-attribute matrices can sometimes be solved in perceptual or graphic terms before the subject has evolved an operational mode of attack. Now we might expect to be able to confirm the hypothesis by individual questioning, using our clinical method in order to find out just how the children set about finding the solutions they did. The difficulty is that usually younger children cannot justify their choice although they can describe the four elements accurately enough, once they have found the fourth. A study of the terms used in these *descriptions* tends to be misleading. It looks as if the method they used must have been identical with that used by older children, although in fact they are quite unable to analyse the way in which they *set about finding* the fourth element. However, to begin with, we shall merely compare the mistakes of the older children with the correct solutions of the younger ones. (In the next section we shall describe a more detailed experiment in which other choices are proposed to the subject, in order to assess the stability of his choice and his ability to justify it.)

We start with item 8. Logically there are three pairs of attributes: A_1 (squares) and A'_1 (circles); A_2 (large) and A'_2 (small); A_3 (plain) and A'_3 (striped). Three associations are given: $A_1 A_2 A_3$ (1) $+ A_1 A'_2 A'_3$ (2) $+ A'_1 A_2 A_3$ (3) $A'_1 A'_2 A'_3$ (4) remains to be found. (This means that the table contains only four of the nine possible combinations, because $A_2 A_3$ is a composite unitary attribute which is negated as a whole to give $A'_2 A'_3$.) Psychologically, in order to find an A'_1 element (circle) which is not $A_2 A_3$ (large and plain), the subject will now be thinking of both properties: A'_2 (small) and A'_3 (striped). What we want to find out is why young children can take both these properties into account, when subjects of 8–9 years often fail. Here are three examples:

Bab (5; 7) simply says "*You must put a round striped one here*." He does not mention the size, but unhesitatingly chooses a small one.

Chap (6; 0) chooses correctly. "Why that one?—*There* (1) *is a square without lines and there* (2) *one with lines. There* (1) *is a big one and there's* (2) *a small one* (mentioning all three properties). (He then adds spontaneously:) *If the large round one* (3) *were striped, one would have to put this one* (small plain circle) *there* (in 4). *If the large square* (1) *were striped, the small striped square* (2) *would have to be plain!*"

HEI (7; 9) first chooses the large striped square $A_1 A_2 A_3'$ for 4, thinking only of colour (A_3') and forgetting shape (A_1') and size (A_2'). He then chooses the large striped circle $(A_1' A_2 A_3')$, still forgetting size (A_2'). "Is that right?—*Yes, because this one has stripes* (4) *and this one has too* $(2 = A_1 A_2' A_3')$.—And does it fit in well horizontally?—*Oh, no! The small striped circle* $(A_1 A_2' A_3')$ *should be there, not the large one.* (He changes them.)—Does it fit now?—*Yes, you have plain and striped* (indicates 1 and 2), *and plain and striped* (indicates 3 and 4)."

Comparing Hei's difficulties with the immediate solutions of the others, it is difficult not to recognize that the two methods are different. When Hei forgets one or two of the three properties involved, he is probably trying to reason, and it is more difficult to think of three things than of one or two. When Bal and Chap immediately find the right element, they are probably not reasoning at all in the strict sense. Instead of thinking, they are perceiving. They are reacting to graphic symmetries instead of making conceptual transformations. Nevertheless, having made their choice, they describe the four elements in terms of appropriate verbal concepts. It is striking, for instance, that Hei does not recognize on his own that his choice $(A_1 A_2' A_3')$ does not fit in "horizontally", and has to be asked whether it does. It seems as though he is not aware of the configuration as a whole. The younger subjects start from spatial form and treat it as an incomplete pattern which helps them to fill the gap in terms of symmetries. Thus the apparent similarity of expression conceals a difference in approach. Hei is reasoning about objects by trying to co-ordinate three classes, while the others are reacting to a pattern, together with its perceptual symmetries.

We might compare these answers with item 5 which seems to have proved the most difficult of the three (5, 8 and 10), because the improvement at 8–9 is least marked (44% correct at 4–5, 35% at 6–7, and 52% at 8–9). The logical structure of test 5 is complicated because, in addition to the ordinary multiplication of classes, there is also an interchange as far as the third property $(A_3$ and $A_3')$ is concerned. We might think of A_1 and A_1' as anemones and tulips, represented by the two rows (item 5 being the same as item 9 in Fig. 10), and of A_1 and A_2' as large and small, represented by the two columns; A_3 and A_3' are the two colours, but the colour of each cell is opposite to that of its complement: if 1 is red, then 2 and 3 are blue, and 4 is red. That is why even stage III subjects find this item difficult, and do not solve it at the first attempt.

BAZ (7; 9) chooses a large blue anemone for cell 4 (instead of a small red tulip). "Does that fit across?—*No* (puts a small blue tulip there). *Like that!* —Look here (indicating the upper horizontal row).—*Oh! yes* (substitutes a small red tulip) *because it's the opposite both ways.*"

Now younger children use a much simpler method. They simply look at the symmetries of the pattern, and the diagonals help them.

BAB (5; 7). "*A small* (tulip) *one there, the red one* (correct).—Why?— *Because there is a blue one* (3), *there a red one* (1), *and there a blue one* (2)."

MEI (5; 10) first chooses a small blue tulip, and then exclaims spontaneously: "*Ah! This one must go there* (the red one) *because this goes like that* (indicating the diagonals)."

In the same way, in doing test 10 (shape, colour, orientation), older children forget the colour or the orientation. They are particularly inclined to forget orientation, because this is a relative property, and not a permanent feature of the object concerned. Younger children, on the other hand, spot the correct solution immediately, because they see that 4 must be symmetrical with respect to 3, as 2 is with respect to 1.

Thus there seems to be a graphic analogue to the structures underlying the multiplication of classes. It consists in neglecting the relations involved in these structures, and substituting simple spatial symmetries which are perceptually obvious and which may then be manipulated by visual images. That is why children of 5–6 years have a percentage of success that is not reached again until the age of 8 or 9.

But, although items involving three attributes indicate a certain discontinuity (since there is a decrease in the percentage of successful solutions between two of the stages), matrix tests on the whole show a relative continuity as between successive stages. So much is clear from the overall percentage figures for the 14 items.

Age:	4	5	6	7	8	9
Successes:	35%	55%	60%	82%	75%	90%

We can also look at first choices for each item, instead of crediting the subject with a success if he later corrects it. Once again, we find that the tendency to take more than one attribute into account when making this choice increases steadily with advancing years:

Age:	4	5	6	7	8	9
One attribute:	72%	67%	65%	50%	43%	35%
At least two attributes:	28%	33%	35%	50%	57%	65%

We see that the proportions pass through equality at about 7 years, that is about the beginning of the concrete operational stage.

The obvious inference is that, although younger subjects often solve an item in terms of graphic imagery, they only manage this after several attempts, without first understanding the importance of multiplicative intersections. Conversely, the older subjects start from the multiplication of properties more than 50% of the time.

Both the overall results and these first choices point to a relative continuity in development, and this is in marked contrast to the bimodal distribution of the 3-attribute items. We may deduce that there is a continuous development from the initial graphic structures to those of operational multiplication, analogous to a similar development of additive classification out of graphic collections. Nevertheless, it remains that the graphic structure is much closer to the operational structure in this sort of system, and the precise significance of this coincidence remains an open question. There is no doubt that the matrix type of test is one that is especially favourable to pre-operational solution in terms of graphic symmetries, and this militates against our making a categorical choice as between the middle hypothesis and the last of those we advanced in §1. The most we can say is that there is both continuity and discontinuity as predicted by hypothesis (3): the discontinuity is characteristic of 3-attribute items, and here we find it fairly easy to distinguish between graphic and operational solutions; the continuity features in the overall result and in the proportion of first choices based on more than one attribute. But we prefer to postpone a final decision until we have studied the spontaneous reactions of children to logical multiplication of classes, and this we will do in §§4 and 5. The immediately following section is a report of a more standardized investigation, still devoted to the matrix tests.

3. MATRIX TESTS (STANDARDIZED PROCEDURE)

The results of §2 were more or less clinical in character. We checked these by a more standardized series of tests. Some of the problems are slightly different, but they help to amplify what we have seen so far. In particular the evidence is mainly statistical.

We used 9 out of the 14 items of §2. The first was a practice item and these results have been omitted. That leaves 8 items which we shall refer to as I–VIII. Items I–IV are 2-attribute items (colour × shape, in I and II; shape × number in III; and colour × orientation in IV). Items V–VIII are 3-attribute items (colour × shape × orientation in V–VII and colour × shape × size in VIII).[1] We also used a shortened form of test, consisting of only two items (II and V) together with the practice item.

The practice item contains four possible choices; the three "distractors" duplicate the three items of the incomplete matrix. Items I–IV have 6 choices and once again 3 of the distractors duplicate the figures on the matrix itself. The latter condition is also true of items V–VIII, but each of these has a total of 8 choices. The multiple choices are presented one by one, on small cards, and the child is allowed to try each of them in the empty cell. The order of presentation for each item

[1] Cf. Fig. 10 (1–9).

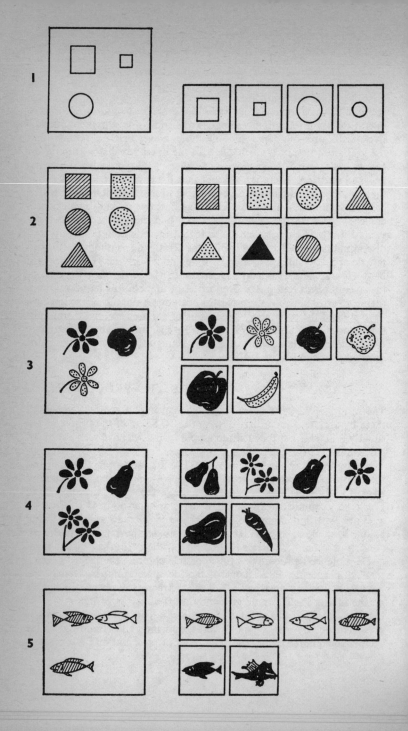

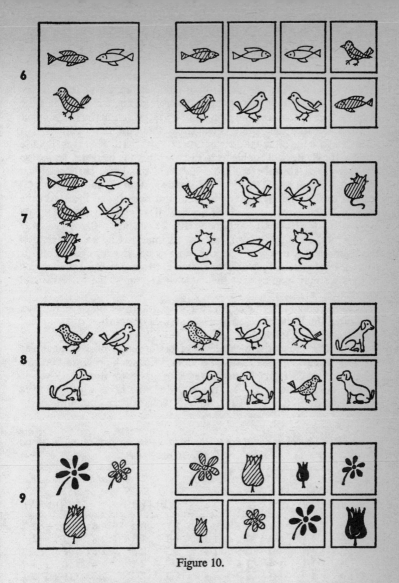

Figure 10.

is standard, although, naturally enough, the position of the correct card varies in random manner from one item to the next.

Each item involves three questions: (1) finding the correct picture; (2) justifying this choice; (3) stating whether one or two of the other pictures might fit in as well or better (the last question proved very enlightening because it showed the significance of the stability of choices).

We found that the results we obtained supplemented those of §2 in at least two ways. (a) The inclusion of pictures duplicating those in the matrix helps to throw some light on the role of abstraction. It has the disadvantage of reducing the number of correct solutions by the younger children, because they quite often chose these duplicate cards. As a result, we lose the bimodal distribution of Table XIII. However, the use of these duplicates did enable us to discover that the tendency to choose them decreases steadily (cf. Table XV), and this bears particularly on the development of abstraction. (b) Both question (2) and question (3) help us to distinguish between graphic and operational factors in the solution of these items. Question (3) is new. If the child gives an adequate explanation for his choice and then refuses to change it (these generally go together, but not always), we may assume that he has understood the relationships involved. On the other hand, if his initial choice is correct, but he cannot justify it and gives in to a suggestion for changing it, then we may assume that the choice was simply due to perceptual symmetries.

After showing the frequency of correct solutions, we shall also indicate how often duplicate cards were used, and the proportion of "graphic" to "operational" solutions.

Table XIV shows the mean level of performance of each age. The method of marking was to allow one mark for each criterion that had been observed correctly. Thus the range of marks for items I–IV was 0, 1 or 2, while for items V–VIII, it was 0–3. Those items which involved the same criteria (i.e. I and II, and V–VII) have been combined in the results.

Table XIV. *Level of solutions to the matrix test, as judged by the mean number of criteria observed*

| Age and no. of subjects | Complete procedure | | | | | | Abridged procedure | | |
	ShC (I–II)	ShN (III)	CO (IV)	Average	ShCO (V–VII)	ShCS (VIII)	Average	ShC (II)	ShCO (V)
4 (13)	0·4	0·4	0·2	0·3	1·1	0·2	0·8	0·9	1·2
5 (29)	1·1	0·7	1·2	1·1	1·9	1·3	1·8	0·8	1·0
6 (14)	1·4	1·0	1·5	1·4	2·3	2·8	2·5	1·8	2·0
7 (13)	1·1	1·4	1·6	1·3	2·7	2·2	2·6	1·7	1·9
8 (15)	1·8	1·7	2·0	1·9	2·7	2·8	2·8	1·9	2·3

Although there is a tendency towards improvement with age, the 6-year-olds sometimes do better than the 7-year-olds (particularly with the shortened form of test). It follows that more than one factor is involved. The correct answer may have an operational basis, but it may result from graphic symmetries instead of real understanding.

Our first clue as to which of these factors is operative comes from the choice of duplicate pictures.

Table XV. *Percentage of solutions in which duplicate pictures are chosen*

	Standard form			Shortened form		
Age	2 criteria	3 criteria	Average	2 criteria	3 criteria	Average
4	45	35	40	25	37	31
5	37	32	35	41	48	44
6	30	7	19	0	14	7
7	20	0	10	38	37	37
8	0	0	0	0	0	0

There is a certain amount of learning in the course of tests I–VIII, which explains why, with the standard procedure, duplicates occur less frequently in items involving three criteria than in those involving two. Not unexpectedly, this result is reversed for the shortened form of test. The frequency of duplicate choices decreases at 6 years of age, which fits in with the improvement at this age shown in Table XIV. However, with the shortened form at any rate, they reappear at 7, which suggests that we now have a hiatus: the 7-year-olds are less prone to rely on a perceptual mode of solution, but their operational understanding is still imperfect.

However, we can try to establish directly which of these two methods is being followed by reference to questions (2) and (3).

Table XVI. *Operational versus graphic solutions*
(All figures given as % of test items)[1]

	Graphic				Operational			
	Complete procedure		Abridged procedure		Complete procedure		Abridged procedure	
Age	2 crit.	3 crit.	2 crit.	3 crit.	2 crit.	3 crit.	2 crit.	3 crit.
4	20	20	35	25	10	0	0	12
5	19	23	29	18	19	10	12	12
6	36	36	28	28	25	18	57	14
7	0	19	12	0	45	29	62	37
8	0	4	—	—	68	64	88	22

Here are two examples of graphic solutions:

VUA (4; 5) correctly chooses the small circle for the practice item (large square, small square, large circle, . . .): "Why?—*Because there are two*

---

[1] Solutions not classed as graphic or operational are either incorrect, or correct only after intervention by the experimenter. This criterion is stricter than that used for Table XIII.

163

squares." But, when asked "Could one put anything else there?" she replies immediately "*Yes, the small square is better.*—Why?—*Because then it's the same* (identical to the element above it)."

In the same way Vua correctly chooses a yellow apple for item II (red flower, red apple, yellow flower). "Is that best?—*Yes, because there are two apples, one red and one yellow.*—Would a red apple do?—*Yes, that would make two red ones.*—And a yellow flower?—*Yes, because there is an apple* (already). —Which one fits in best out of the three (red apple, yellow apple and yellow flower)?—*The red apple.*"

FRA (5; 10) first chooses a large apple for item II, but rejects it and chooses first a red apple, then a yellow one (correct). "Why?—*That makes two apples, one red and one yellow.*—Is there anything that would fit in better?—*The banana.*—Does that fit well?—*Fair!*—You must choose one which fits in well. —(He chooses the red flower.) *It's the same colour* (as the apple above it).— Is it the best?—*No, the red apple is* (being identical to the one above)."

These subjects, who are representative of all those whose solutions are classed as "graphic", make the right choice even if they do not always find it right away. But they are generally unable to justify it.

Moreover, they immediately accept almost any other picture suggested by the experimenter, and they seem to prefer one which duplicates the picture above or to the left of the blank space. In other words, once they have to analyse relationships, they limit themselves to one attribute at a time, losing the advantage which they had in a global perceptual judgment.

Here, by way of contrast, is a typical example of operational solution:

GRA (7; 3). Item II. Chooses the yellow apple at once "*because these are the same, but of different colours* (indicating the vertical direction) *and these are the same colour* (indicating the horizontal direction).—Could I choose any of the others?—*The red apple, but it does not fit in very well, because there is a red flower and a red apple on top; you'll have a yellow flower and a red apple at the bottom. It's better to have a yellow flower and a yellow apple.*" Item V: chooses the green bird without any hesitation. "Is it the best of the lot?— *Yes, it's the best. There's a blue fish and a green fish, and then a blue bird and a green bird. They are turned in opposite ways on top, so they ought to be turned in opposite ways at the bottom as well.*"

Both of the criteria that we formulated are satisfied by Gra. The justification of choices shows how they depend on the two or three properties involved, and alternative suggestions are resisted.

Table XVI provides clear proof that the graphic and operational solutions are quite distinct. Whatever the item, operational solutions increase steadily with age while graphic solutions decrease after the age of six. The fact that they seem to reach a maximum at 6, is due to the presence of duplicate cards among the multiple-choice items, these being most attractive to the 4s and 5s. Without them, we should have had a larger number of correct solutions at 4 and 5 (cf. Table XIII), and the distribution would have been bimodal instead of reaching a maximum of 6.

These results confirm the hypotheses based on the clinical analysis and numerical distributions of §2. Although there is a continuous transition from graphic structures to operational structures in the multiplication of classes, just as there is in addition, there is also a relative discontinuity as between two types of solution, both of which lead to correct results. One is based on mere perceptual symmetries, the other on a true understanding of the relationships involved.

4. SPONTANEOUS CROSS-CLASSIFICATION

We shall first describe a method intermediate between completion of matrices (§§2–3) and classification into boxes (§5). We used a box which could be divided into four compartments by mobile partitions. Two kinds of classification were used: (I) one set of elements could be divided into four classes, each of which consisted of identical elements; (II) the other could also be divided into four classes, but no two elements were identical. A detailed description of these sets follows.

Ia: 16 pictures made up of (1) four seated black rabbits; (2) four seated white rabbits; (3) four running black rabbits; (4) four running white rabbits.

Ib: 16 geometrical objects consisting of (1) four blue squares; (2) four red squares; (3) four blue circles; (4) four red circles.

II: 16 pictures[1] representing (1) four men (a policeman, a clown, a football player, and a man in a morning coat); (2) four women (a skier, a woman with a hat, a woman carrying a basket, and a woman carrying a bucket); (3) four boys (two, not identical, carrying haversacks, one running and one playing with a kite; (4) four girls (one with a handbag, one running, one with a dog, and one playing with a doll).

The procedure with set II consisted of the following steps: (a) free classification ("Put together the ones that go well together, which are alike"); (b) the subject is asked to divide all the pictures into four piles, using a box with four compartments; (c) one of the partitions is removed, leaving two large compartments, and the subject is asked to "make only two piles" and to justify his division; he is then asked to repeat this "but differently"; (d) the partition is replaced: "You must make four piles again, but when this partition (vertical) is taken away, these two piles (which are then combined) must go well together, and when the other partition (horizontal) is taken away, these two piles must also go together."

(a) and (d) were also applied to sets Ia and Ib. But for steps (b) and

---

[1] Cf. Fig. 11.

(c) we used special boxes which were white or black and had openings in the shape of a rabbit, or which were round or square, etc.

This experiment differs from the matrix tests described in §§2–3 in several important ways: (a) the child is presented with a set of elements all of which are on an equal footing; he must classify them all and none

Figure 11.

are ready-classified to start with; (b) he must find the criteria of classification by himself (the boxes are empty, and they simply limit the number of classes allowed); and (c) the multiplicative sub-classes are not one-element classes.

There is no need to report the graphic collections found at stage I. These are not related to cross-classificatory tables by a continuous line of development, even if on occasion they have a similar appearance (cf. the example of Nel, ch. I, §2, under III). Turning to stage II, the stage of non-graphic collections, we observe a gradual transition from simple or successive classification (the two criteria being considered

166

separately), towards multiplicative classifications involving the simultaneous consideration of two or more criteria. Following are the main kinds of reaction. We will list the simplest of these first and go on to the most highly developed. Nevertheless, we should note that most of these reactions may occur in the same subject on different occasions. They cannot therefore be regarded as stable patterns of behaviour, and still less as distinct sub-stages.

I. The simplest reaction is to classify the pictures into two collections, without sub-classes, and without change of criterion once the two collections have been constructed.

BER (4; 5) constructs two columns of rabbits (sitting and running) without paying any attention to colour. Boxes and bags: idem. Compartments: he uses two only, still following the same subdivision. "Can you put them in all four?—*Yes*." But he puts the seated rabbits (both white and black) in spaces 1 and 4 (a diagonal), and the running ones in spaces 2 and 3. His reaction to the counters is of type II.

II. A second type of reaction consists in classing the elements in four collections, while still ignoring the simultaneous relationships.

JEA (5; 3) constructs a row of running white rabbits, another of running black rabbits, a third of seated white ones, and a fourth of running black ones, without any relationship between the four rows. Given the two boxes and the two bags, he puts the running white rabbits in the first and the seated black rabbits in the second, leaving the rest on the table. "Can you put the others in?— . . . —Do you think they can go in?—*No*," etc. After some suggestion, he switches to type I, and divides the elements into running and seated rabbits with mixed colours. He fails to respond to the box with four compartments. The four collections are then constructed in front of the child, and one of the partitions is removed. "What are these?—*They're running rabbits.*—And there?—*Rabbits playing* (seated).—(The partition is replaced and the other one removed.) And there?—*They're rabbits that are running and rabbits that are playing.*—And there?—*The same thing.*"

This subject distinguishes four classes on his own, but he cannot relate them to one another. What proves this in the first place is that, when he is told to make two classes, he retains two of these instead of constructing larger classes of which these would be subdivisions. In the second place, he recognizes these same classes, running and seated, in the box with partitions, but not those based on colour.

III. A slightly more advanced type of reaction is to construct two collections, of which one alone is divided into sub-classes.

DAN (5; 7) classes the rabbits as either seated (white and black mixed), or running and white, or running and black. Given the boxes and bags, he retains the division into three classes. With the box divided into four compartments, he first puts the seated rabbits on one side and the running ones on the other. Next he divides the latter into white and black, using two different compartments, but he still fills the remaining two compartments with seated rabbits of mixed colours.

On the other hand, Dan divides the counters correctly into four collections. But these are merely the four isolated collections of type II. When the first partition is removed, Dan recognizes "*squares and circles*". But when this is replaced and the other is removed, he does not recognize the two collections of red and blue elements, and says: "*They're squares and circles* (above) *and here they're circles and squares* (below)."

Type III is nearer the final solution, because one of the two initial collections is divided into two. But the subject is unaware of the symmetry which should help him to subdivide the second collection. When he turns to a type II division, he does construct four collections which are isomorphic to those of a matrix. But although the plan of construction lends itself to a cross-classificatory schema, Dan is unaware of it when his classification is complete and he fails to realize that the set as a whole can be split in two ways and not just one.

IV. Type IV is even closer to the final solution. We now find two successive dichotomies. But one seems more cogent than the other, so that the subject is inclined to resist the suggestion that they co-exist and therefore yield a multiplicative cross-classification.

Nis (5; 10) divides the counters into two collections (squares and circles), and then divides the same elements into two different collections (red and blue). She has no difficulty in arranging the two collections in the box with four compartments, by making four sub-collections. So far we would say that she has constructed a multiplicative matrix. But now she refuses to recognize the classes formed by the union of two sub-classes: "(The partition between the red and blue elements is removed.) What are they?—. . . —If we put them together, what are they like?—*Squares*.—Is that all?—*And circles too*.—Can one put them together?—*Yes*.—Why?—*I don't know*. (They are all blue, but she does not see this possibility of classification, even though she herself used it at the beginning)", etc. The reaction is similar when the second partition is removed.

With the rabbits, Nis constructs the matrix immediately in the subdivided box (dividing them into black and white, and seated and running). When one partition is removed, she recognizes the two classes of running rabbits and rabbits "*who aren't doing anything at all*". But when the other partition is removed, she refuses to recognize the two other classes (of white and black rabbits). "Are they the same colour (indicating the black ones)?— . . . —Can one put them together?—*No, yes, they all have pointed ears*."

In such cases, the spatial structure of a matrix seems to impose itself on the subject for perceptual reasons, before his understanding of the multiplicative operation is complete.

V. Type V also begins with a correct classification, based on successive criteria. But there is no interaction of the two criteria because the subject arranges the sub-collections diagonally in the box, instead of following its axes.

MYR (6; 5). "*Running rabbits and sitting rabbits; white ones and black ones!*" His verbal formulation is perfect, but Myr arranges the four collections in the box in such a way that the black rabbits are along one diagonal and the white ones along the other. When one partition is removed, he has the two classes of running and seated rabbits; but when the other is removed "*that will not do, they're all mixed*". He is then asked to rearrange them. But, although he makes numerous attempts, Myr always follows the diagonals.

VI. Here the correct solution is reached in the end by trial-and-error. This type evidently leads in to stage III.

ALA (5; 11). Counters: he first notices the blue ones. He then puts the squares on one side and the circles on the other, with red and blue counters alternating in each collection. Thus the two collections are still not divided into red and blue sub-collections. Ala only relinquishes this graphic arrangement (a relic from stage I) very gradually, but in the end he accepts a division into four sub-collections. However, as soon as these are constructed, he places them correctly in the box. (One of the partitions is removed.) What is this a box of?—*Circles and squares* (correct).—And like this (removing the other partition and jumbling the elements on one side)?—*That doesn't make any difference* (mixing squares and circles), *because they're both red.*—And on the other side?—*They're blue; squares and circles.*"

The reaction with rabbits is the same, the correct solution being reached after several attempts.

At stage III, we find that children immediately cross-classify.

FOR (7; 9) spontaneously classes the rabbits into the four possible sub-collections (without a box), and then places them correctly in the boxes and bags as well as in the subdivided box. When the partitions are removed, she accepts the classes so formed: "*Yes, because they are all white,*" then "*because they are all running*", "*because they are all sitting*", and finally "*because they are all black*".

There is the same immediate success with counters.

Neither the present technique nor the method described in §5 yields a spontaneous arrangement in matrix form at stage I. Stage II begins to pave the way for operational cross-classification. We suggest that the order of development is: first, types I and II, next type III, then types IV and V, and finally type VI. We will be in a better position to describe the process when we come to consider how children at stage II deal with the experiment of §5. For the present, there is little statistical evidence that these four groups represent distinct successive sub-stages. The simplest types of reaction (I and II) amount to a separate consideration of the two criteria, and there is no co-ordination between them even after the construction of the collections. Type III, which is more advanced, shows the beginnings of co-ordination. It consists in constructing three collections, in which the first is distinguished from the others by one criterion, and the last two are distinguished from one another by the other criterion. But the three collections are on the same footing, and the co-ordination remains incomplete, since we do not find the twofold dichotomy operating over the entire set. At the third level (types III and IV), we have two complete dichotomies, and the second modifies the first. But the effect is purely retrospective; there is no anticipation of an alternative classification, and as a result the subject does not elaborate a cross-classificatory structure. For this implies simultaneous awareness and not a mere succession of steps. In type VI we have anticipation and simultaneous awareness arising in the course of experimentation by the subject. Finally, at stage III, the relevant structure is reflected in an anticipatory schema, the application of which is immediate.

The classification of people (question II) gave similar results. We shall give just a few examples to illustrate the three main steps: division of the elements into sub-classes without real multiplication; gradual solution; immediate solution.

MAR (6; 6) begins by putting the two boys together because they "*are not quite in the same position; but they are both going to school*". Then he puts the two women together because they "*are in the same position*", then the man in evening dress and the policeman who "*are the same thing, but not quite*". He now goes on to make an alignment out of all the rest. When asked to construct four piles, he again fastens on the same four. For two piles, he forms "*little girls, ladies and little boys, daddies*".

In other words, he eventually arrives at the four collections of a possible matrix, but he has no idea of cross-classification. The following subjects either approach this conception, or actually reach it by degrees.

VAN (6; 3) starts with eight small piles, of which six are homogeneous (two boys with haversacks, etc.) and two are mixed (a woman and a girl, a clown and a skier). When asked to make four piles, she forms (1) a policeman, a man in evening dress and three women, (2) the clown, (3) two boys with haversacks and four girls, and (4) the lady skier and two running boys. When asked for two piles, she divides the people by age into children and adults. Asked for a division by sex, she puts "*All the gentlemen and the boys together, all the girls and the ladies together.*" Asked once again to make four piles, she succeeds in constructing a matrix, but one based on the diagonals; women and girls above, boys and men below.

CAT (6; 8) also starts with eight small piles. Then, asked to construct four, he forms: (1) three women skiers, (2) four girls, (3) the women, (4) the men. Asked for two piles, he first classifies the people by sex, and then by age. Asked once again for four piles, he constructs a matrix correctly; girls and women, boys and men.

The following subject is typical of those who succeed at once.

DUB (8; 6) starts with eight homogeneous couples. Asked for four piles, she at once constructs a matrix correctly. "And if one put them like this diagonally: (men, girls, women, boys), would that do as well?—*No, because there are girls and men over here.*" She proceeds to indicate clearly the multiplicative significance of her own matrix: across one direction there are "*children and grown-ups*", across the other, male and female.

We may fairly conclude that the construction of multiplicative structures is a spontaneous development, if a gradual one.

5. SPONTANEOUS CROSS-CLASSIFICATIONS CONTINUED

We carried out a number of other experiments based on the principle of presenting the subject with elements that can be classified according to two different criteria, to see whether he can apply both criteria simultaneously.

The best example was a set of eight pictures, representing a car, a lorry, a motor-bike, a motor-scooter, a wagon, a pram, a bicycle and a shopping basket on wheels. These can be classified as motorized or non-motorized, and as four-wheelers or two-wheelers. The child is asked to "put together the ones that go well together", first in four boxes, then in two (two or three times over), and then again in four. Finally, if he has still not discovered the matrix arrangement, he is given the four boxes arranged in a square (cf. Fig. 12).

We find that reactions increase in complexity, and appear to follow the stages found elsewhere. At stage I we find a mixture of similarity relations and functional association; at stage II, differentiated collections with complements; and at stage III, operational structures with inclusion and intersection.

There is no need to dwell on stage I. Here we find alignments or small lots, governed by the similarity of single pairs or by functional associations or simply by the requirement of putting some together.

BOU (4; 10) forms two alignments, each containing four elements but none of the resemblances extend over more than two elements (a bicycle and a motor-scooter).

NIC (5; 5). Four boxes: (1) "*They're bikes*," (2) "*They're cars*," (3) "*It's a wagon*" and (4) "*a pram*". Two boxes: (1) car, motor-scooter, motor-bike and shopping basket, (2) the others. The bicycle and the pram go together because they are often together in family garages, etc.

At stage I, then, there is no trace of spontaneous matrix constructions, even though subjects of this age solve matrix tests fairly easily (§§2–3) by simply reading off the double perceptual symmetries.

At stage II, however, collections are based on similarity alone. Moreover, they tend to give rise to complementary sub-collections. The division is not perfect to start with, and the sub-collections may not be completely disjoint. But later they are based on dichotomies. These are successive at first, but eventually they are combined in a single system of multiplicative intersections.

Figure 12.

Here are some examples to illustrate the beginnings of stage II.

GREI (6; 6) starts with four lots: (1) wagon, shopping basket, (2) bicycle, motor-scooter, motor-bike, (3) car and lorry, (4) pram. Then he puts the pram with the wagon *because the pram has four wheels.—And (2)?—Because they have two wheels.*

Given two boxes, Grei puts everything in a single box. *"I'm going to put everything with wheels here* (he starts with the total class).—How would you put them in two boxes?—*Here* (wagon, pram and shopping basket) *they're all wagons.*—And here (2, in which all the others are placed)?—*Because there's nowhere else to put them.*"

Given two boxes once again: (1) "*They're all the ones with two wheels*"; (2) "*They're all those with four wheels.*"

With four boxes, "Do it differently from the way you did it the first time": (1) lorry, car, "*They have a motor and they have four wheels*"; (2) motor-bike, motor-scooter "*They have a motor* (and two wheels);" (3) shopping basket and wagon; "*They're wagons. They have two wheels and four wheels*"; (4) bicycle and pram.

SAF (4; 6). (1) Car, lorry: "*These are two cars.*" (2) Motor-scooter and motor-bike: "*They're both electric* (= motorized)." (3) Wagon, scooter:[1] "*You have to walk and push with your feet.*"

With these beginnings of differentiation we also find a natural complementarity: four wheels and two wheels, the wagons and all the rest (Grei), motorized vehicles and those that need pushing, etc. But these subdivisions are neither complete (they do not cover all the cards) nor are they unified (there is usually a multiplicity of criteria), and this is why the subcollections are not disjoint. It is interesting to note that even when a matrix arrangement is suggested to these subjects, they cannot adapt themselves to it (although they might well have completed the fourth cell in a matrix test with three cells already given, as in §§2–3).

In the following examples, which illustrate the second half of stage II, the differentiations are generalized to the whole set of elements, and the subject can pass from one form of complementarity to another by switching the basis of his classification. But these classifications are still applied successively, instead of being combined in a single multiplicative system.

FER (5; 6) first puts two groups of two-wheeled vehicles and two groups of four-wheeled vehicles in four boxes, and then places them all in two boxes. "*Two wheels and four wheels.*—Can you do it differently (giving him two other boxes?)—*These take petrol* (= motorized) *and these don't* (correct)." But when he is given four boxes the second time, he reproduces his initial classification, which excludes the possibility of a matrix (the bicycle being alone in 1 and the scooter alone in 4).

GAL (6; 6) forms four piles and exclaims: "*I know it! They all have wheels.*" He puts four motorized vehicles together—"*They all have motors*"—in one of two boxes, and the remaining four—"*They all have wheels* (but no motors)" —in the other. Given two more boxes, he divides the same elements into two-wheelers and four-wheelers. But he does not succeed in constructing a matrix.

MAU (7; 5) constructs two successive classifications in the same way, one

[1] Replacing the wheeled shopping basket, which was unknown to this subject.

into two-wheeled and four-wheeled classes, and the other into those that have *"motors and no motors"*. But he does not succeed in combining them into a single system.

How does the child pass from two distinct classifications, applied in succession, to a multiplicative classification in which both are combined in the same system? As we shall see when we come to analyse the reactions of stage III, the transition seems to involve a retroactive action of the second classification on the first, which then induces an anticipatory effect allowing the two classifications to be combined. Before we can describe this complex process, we need to analyse one or two of the cases of successive dichotomy in greater detail.

SAC (7; 8) first classes the objects in four boxes without using any overall criterion, and then puts the lorry, the motor-scooter, the bicycle, the motor-bike and the car in one box, and all the rest in the other. *"They all have wheels here* (1).—And the others?—*Also*.—Well?—*They all have a motor except for the bicycle* (which he places in 2), *and here* (2) *they have wheels and no motors."* In a second trial, he divides the vehicles into two-wheeled and four-wheeled, without saying more than *"wheels"*. He is then given four boxes, and constructs: (1) motor-bike and motor-scooter; (2) lorry, car; (3) bicycle, shopping basket; (4) wagon, pram. "Why these (4)?—*They have wheels and no motor.*— (3) ?—*No motor.*—(2) ?—*A motor.*—And (1) ?—*Also a motor.*—Could one put the car with the motor-scooter and the lorry with the motor-bike?—*No, these* (2) *have four wheels and those* (1) *only have two."* We have the four multiplicative classes, although not arranged in matrix form.

One month later, Sac (7; 9) says that he remembers nothing of the experiment, but he immediately constructs the same classes in a row of four boxes. He is then asked to "arrange the boxes so that they go together in pairs". He constructs a pattern in which boxes (1) and (4) occupy one diagonal and boxes (2) and (3) occupy the other, describing the boxes as: (1) four wheels without a motor; (4) four wheels with a motor; (2) two wheels without a motor; (3) two wheels with a motor.

JAN (7; 1) starts on the basis of functional associations, using four boxes, but he then combines them into two on the basis of whether they have *"motors"* or *"no motors"*.—"Could you do it differently?—*Yes, some are made of wood and some out of iron."*

On a second trial with four boxes, he starts by dividing the vehicles into iron or wooden, and motorized or non-motorized. "Can you do it differently? —*Yes, I think I can, I have an idea:* (1) *wooden ones with four wheels* (wagon and lorry); (2) *wooden ones with two wheels* (shopping basket); (3) *iron ones with four wheels* (car, pram); *and* (4) *iron ones with two wheels* (bicycle, motor-scooter and motor-bike)."

KRO (7; 9) also starts with four collections that are not based on any overall preliminary criterion. He then divides the objects into the two classes of motorized and non-motorized vehicles, and again into the two classes of four-wheelers and two-wheelers. Given four boxes once again, he distributes the objects according to the four possible associations: motorized vehicles with two or four wheels, and non-motorized with two or four wheels.

The difference between these examples, which illustrate the beginnings of stage III, and those from stage II, is that the former testify to the presence of an anticipatory schema. Jan says, "I have an idea", before he proceeds to classify the objects according to his idea. Cross-classification is a matter of classifying objects in terms of two *simultaneous* criteria. It follows that unless a subject sets out with the prior intention of combining all the dichotomies which he has established in advance, he cannot cross-classify. But this anticipation cannot appear from nowhere, and the reactions which precede it must lead towards it. Now the cases which we have just given do not start with any anticipatory reaction. When they are first shown the four empty boxes, they begin by functional associations and go on to refine the classification by trial-and-error; there is no overall plan. It is only later that they discover first one general criterion (e.g. that of being motorized or not), and then a second.

Now even at stage II we noted that several subjects (Fer, Gal, Man) discovered these criteria one after another. But there is a difference which is crucial. At stage II they forgot all about the first criterion when they went on to the second; now we find a clear indication of hindsight. Even while they are engaged in following the second criterion, they tend to hark back to the first. So we see that a whole month after he has seen the material, Sac is still influenced by his former classification, and although he makes no explicit reference to the number of wheels, he still uses the criterion quite spontaneously. Here as elsewhere we find the same sequence of development. First, oscillation between two alternatives; then, with the beginnings of hindsight, the alternatives are seen almost simultaneously; finally the hindsight is accompanied by foresight and the two possibilities are combined to form an integrated system: in this case, it is cross-classification.

Unfortunately, in this experiment, there are a large number of possible dichotomies (Jan, for instance, introduced a classification into iron and wooden vehicles, instead of going by the number of wheels). For this reason, the reactions which we described at 7–8 years do not become stabilized at 8–9. Instead the subjects' reactions show a steadily increasing mobility.

BON (8; 3). Given four empty boxes, Bon immediately divides the vehicles into the four simplest multiplicative classes: motorized and non-motorized, four-wheeled and two-wheeled. But when asked to place the objects in two boxes, he discovers eight possible criteria: two or four wheels, with or without a roof, with or without a handle-bar, with or without a door, with or without a saddle, with or without a bell, with or without brakes, and with or without tyres. Their associations would engender 256 multiplicative classes! When he is given four empty boxes again, Bon tries several different combinations, all of which are incomplete. But when the boxes are arranged to form a matrix, he returns to the four initial exhaustive classes.

BEN (8; 6). Ben discovers six criteria: motor, number of wheels, saddle, spokes, lights, and load (persons versus things). These could give rise to 64 classes, and obviously he does not try to combine them in a single system.

Apart from these final complications, the experiments show clearly that once the subject has mastered the techniques involved in the addition of classes (cf. ch. II, §§1–2), he spontaneously tends to combine different criteria in a single multiplicative system. But, although he readily constructs four multiplicative classes on his own, he will not usually arrange them in the form of a matrix. All this confirms the notion that although cross-classification does involve an element of graphic intuition, it depends above all on the co-ordination of various insights. At the pre-operational level, the co-ordination is a matter of adjustments governed by hindsight together with a limited degree of foresight. These pass by degrees into the adequate anticipatory schema which characterizes operational thinking, and the development is relatively continuous (i.e. there are no leaps).

6. SIMPLE MULTIPLICATION (OR INTERSECTION)

What we have found so far seems to indicate that multiplicative structures do not develop quite independently of the earlier pre-operational and graphic structures (hypothesis 1 of §1). At the same time, they are not derived directly from these graphic structures (hypothesis 2). Although they pass through a graphic stage, they owe more to a progressive co-ordination which is partially dependent on the one that arises in class addition (hypothesis 3). This co-ordination passes through the following stages: at first there are one or two unconnected dichotomies, then the second has a retroactive effect on the first, and finally both are combined in an anticipatory schema.

We must therefore expect a marked difference between the complete cross-classification which we have been dealing with, and simple multiplication involving the intersection of only two classes. We say that there is "complete multiplication", when two classes $B_1 = A_1 + A_1'$ and $B_2 = A_2 + A_2'$ are composed of the same elements, and their intersections generate the four classes $A_1 A_2$, $A_1 A_2'$, $A_1' A_2$ and $A_1' A_2'$. There is "simple multiplication" when two classes A_1 and A_2 generate the class $A_1 A_2$, common to both, and the two classes $A_1 A_2'$ and $A_1' A_2$, each consisting of the elements of one that do not belong to the other. Simple multiplication is thus a partial operation which enters into complete cross-classification, but in simple multiplication A_1 and A_1' are not combined to form B_1, A_2 and A_2' are not combined to form B_2, and the class $A_1' A_2'$ is absent.

One might think, consistently with an atomistic logic or psychology, that simple multiplication should be more "elementary" than complete multiplication, and should therefore appear earlier in the subject's development: complete multiplication, being a system composed of simple multiplications must be a later development.

The opposite hypothesis, based on the notion that operational systems are more primitive psychologically and more fundamental logically, would predict that simple multiplication must develop later. For simple multiplication means abstracting a portion of the total system of complete multiplication. If this total system develops as a result of the interplay of co-ordinations which are first retroactive, then anticipatory, the fact that the subject is forced to classify all the elements in terms of the two classes B_1 and B_2, can only hasten the process. Simple intersection will be a later development, since the situations which call for it are less favourable to the co-ordination of the relevant classificatory criteria than those involving two possible dichotomies, each covering all the elements of the set.

We tried to analyse the development of simple multiplication in the following experiment.[1] The subject is presented with a row of green objects (a pear, a hat, etc.) and a row of leaves of various colours (brown, red, yellow, etc.) at right angles to it. An empty space is left at the point where they meet, and the subject is asked to fill this cell (the answer being in the form of a verbal description, or a free drawing, or if necessary a choice out of several alternative pictures).

He has to find an object that "fits in with everything" in each of the two rows, i.e. a green leaf. Before this, he is asked questions such as: "Why have all these objects been put together? Are they alike in any way? Are they a little like one another? They are all . . . ?" If the subject finds the problem difficult, the effect of intersection can be heightened by continuing the two rows so that they form a cross with an empty space at the centre. Sometimes further rows are added alongside the initial rows, to heighten the similarity involved. The same effect may also be achieved by using different elements for these new rows to contrast with the original row (for example, the fact that there is a property common to a row of leaves may be reinforced by placing a row of cats next to it).

This procedure is particularly interesting because at the same time as we study the intersection of classes as opposed to a complete cross-classification we can also learn something more about the relationship between the multiplication of two classes and the formation of the classes themselves.

[1] Cf. Fig. 13.

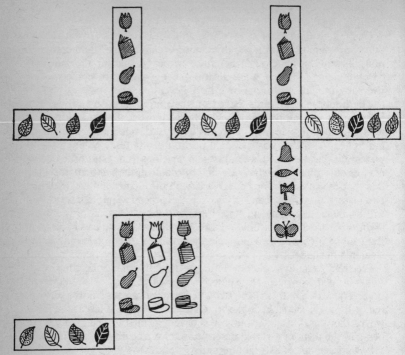

Figure 13.

The reactions fall into two groups: either the subject takes only one of the two rows into account when deciding on the element to fill the empty cell, or he takes both. If he takes both into account, he is making a choice which is consonant with class multiplication, although it does not invariably follow that his thinking is genuinely operational. The following table shows the relative frequency of each in a group of subjects ranging from 5 to 10 years of age.

Table XVII. *Intersection of two classes: Results* (%)[1]

Age	5–6	7–8	9–10
Choice matches one collection	85	42·5	17·5
Choice matches both collections	15	57	82·5

What is most striking about these results is that a 75% level of success is not reached until the age of 9 or 10, whereas the majority of matrix

[1] There were about twenty subjects in each age group.

178

tests (form, colour, number, direction, etc., i.e. whenever the criteria do not involve more complex causal functions) are correctly answered by 75% of 7–8-year-olds.

True, there is an important perceptual factor in matrix tests; but it is also present in this experiment, especially when the two rows form a cross, even if it is less compelling.

However, let us follow the stages of simple multiplication step by step, by describing the different types of reaction which go to make up these two broad subdivisions.

I. *The choice matches only one collection.*

(I 1) *Identity with a neighbouring element.*—This reaction, which is undoubtedly the most elementary, consists in filling the empty cell with an element identical in shape or colour to one of the two next to it.

FRA (5; 10). "What should I put here to go with all these and with all those?—*A hat* (the closest element in the row of green objects).—What else?— *A leaf* (choosing one which is violet like the leaf closest to it)."

MON (5; 10). "*A leaf* (the same colour as its neighbour).—(A red row is added parallel to the green.) And like this?—*A hat* (the same as its neighbour). —(The experimenter adds a row of apples to contrast with the parallel row of leaves.) And like this?—*An apple like this one* (coloured orange like its neighbour)", etc.

In this case the basis of choice is purely perceptual, since it always duplicates[1] an element situated next to the empty space. Neither the second collection, nor the other elements in the first collection, play any role whatever. This type of reaction occurs in more than half the cases of age 5. It still occurs in a third of the cases at 6, and only disappears at 8.

(I 2) *Identity with another element in one of the rows.*—This is simply an extension of I 1. It occurs with maximum frequency at 6 years, and becomes exceptional at 8.

COT (5; 9) starts with reaction I 1, then changes to I 2. "*A hat and a bell* (the two closest elements in one of the rows).—Just one thing.—*The pear* (further along the green row).—(The row of leaves is extended.) And like this?—*A leaf.*—What kind?—*Pink* (duplicating one some way away).—Could one put anything else?—*The book* (duplicating one of the green elements)."

CRI (6; 9). Flowers and yellow objects: "*A flower.*—How can we make it fit in with all these?—*A bug* (a yellow insect near the middle of the row).— (Cats and pink objects:) And like this?—*A pig and a little cat* (one element from each collection).—You must choose just one, which fits in well with all these and with all those.—*Well then a pig, because my sister and I love pink.*— Would a pig fit in with these (the cats)?—*No, you have to put a little cat there.* —But would it fit in with these as well (the pink objects)?—*The pig.*"

[1] Cf. the tendency for duplicate items to be chosen in matrix tests by the youngest subjects: §3, Table XV.

This second type of reaction occasionally gives rise to another which is intermediate between (2) and (3). This reaction leads naturally into (3), because it shows the beginnings of a relationship between the two collections. The object is always present in one of the collections, but it is chosen with an eye to the second collection (by virtue of a functional association or a possible complex object).

BER (5; 11). Leaves and green objects: *"The green pear, because that fits in with the leaves."*

The pear is chosen, not only because it is one of the green objects, but also because it goes with the leaves in that they all belong to the same object (a tree). This reaction is too exceptional to constitute a type of its own.

(I 3) *The element is not present in the original collections; it has a functional relationship with one or more of the elements in one collection, or it forms part of a possible complex object.*—What is new in this type of reaction is that the subject chooses an element which is not already present. But he cannot find an element belonging to either of these two classes, which is why he substitutes the more easily imagined relationship of partitive membership (relating part of a complex-object to the whole), for inclusive membership in a class. This is a return to a more primitive form of behaviour; but it is a return that occurs at an advanced stage, since it is most frequent at 7–8 and does not disappear until the age of 10. (Before the age of 7–8, children find it difficult to imagine objects that are not present.) But even though there is this resurgence of primitive reactions, it often goes with an attempt to establish some sort of a relationship between the two collections.

ELI (8; 9) starts by relating the two collections (leaves and green objects). *"A tree* (which is green and has leaves).—And like this (adding two extensions)?—*A tree-trunk* (green).—Would it go with these (the leaves)?—*Yes, because the leaf does go on a tree-trunk.*—(A pink row is added.)—*A tool for digging the earth; that would go well with the wheelbarrow* (one collection only is being used).—(Leaves and red objects.)—*Somebody to read the book* (one collection only).—Would it go with these (leaves)?—*No, there has to be a gentleman to look after the leaves."*

ANI (9; 6). Leaves and green objects. *"A plum.*—Why?—*Because the leaves are almost like a plum.*—Would it go with these (the green objects)?—*No, because it's blue.*—(Flowers and yellow objects.)—*A chestnut, because they're chestnut leaves.*—Would it go with these (leaves)?—*It doesn't go with the leaves. A vase* (would go) *because one can put the tulips in a vase, and the tulips are yellow."*

This type of reaction is in advance of the preceding ones, in that the subject chooses an element that is not present, and sometimes begins to relate the two given collections. It is a primitive reaction nonetheless, because the relation involved is either a part-whole relation or it is functional rather than classificatory.

(I 4). *The chosen element is not present already, yet it bears some degree of resemblance to the elements of one collection.*—This reaction marks a new advance in the direction of extending the given collection. But this is not a true class extension, because the subject is only relating one element to others, instead of thinking in terms of "all" the elements.

MIC (6; 2). Leaves and green objects. "*A leaf* (different from any already present), *or a bell-flower* (for the leaves), *or a green balloon.*"

PIE (8; 9) starts with reactions of type 3. "(Leaves and green objects.)— *A tree.*—(Flowers and pink objects.) And like this?—*Grass for the pig. No, we must have another flower.*—(Apples and yellow objects.)—*Some fruit.*"

LOU (8; 10). Leaves and green objects. "*Something pink.*—Why?—*Because there isn't any pink yet* (among the leaves).—(Two extensions are added, of which one consists of pink objects.)—*A cherry tree, because it has green and a little pink* (there is the beginning of a relationship between the two classes, although the reaction is still nearer type 3)."

CLAU (9; 5). Leaves and green objects. "*An apple*—Why?—*There is some fruit there already* (among the green objects). *So, when I choose an apple, I'm having more fruit.*—But does it go with these (the leaves)?—*No, a yellow leaf, because there aren't any yellow leaves.*"

In effect, each of these subjects is adding an element to one of the collections because it has a certain similarity to those already present. He is beginning to construct a logical class.

(I 5). *The chosen element is not present already, yet it clearly belongs to one of the two classes.*—What characterizes a class, as opposed to a collection, is the abstraction of the common property, determining its intension, together with the correct use of the word "all" to denote its extension. When a child can construct true classes, he can usually cross-classify as well, so long as both classifications cover the entire set of elements. Differences between items in tests like matrices or class-addition are fairly small and may occur in either direction. But this does not apply to simple multiplication. The intersection of classes continues to elude the child until he is a good deal more mature.

DAM (7; 0) suggests adding an apple to the row of green objects, "*because they aren't the same things, but they're coloured with the same colour*". She then suggests adding a leaf of a different colour to the row of leaves, because "*they're the same things, but with different colours*". For other rows, her answers are similar in that she considers only one row at a time. Finally, she arrives at the notion of intersection, and her reaction falls into type II 5 (and will be given under that heading).

This subject does not use the word "all", but it is obvious that expressions like "the same things" and "not the same things but the same colour" cover both the full extension of a class and its corresponding intension.

II. *The choice is a simultaneous function of the two collections.*—As soon as we have a schema which can be described by the word "simultaneous" we have some sort of a multiplicative relationship. In this general sense, a multiplicative schema usually appears long before it has acquired its final operational form. There is, after all, a rudimentary relation between the two collections in every one of the reactions which we have designated as types I 2–I 5. That is why it is important to follow the different stages that characterize type II reactions. For we shall see that operational multiplication is a schema in its own right which develops gradually, and in stages which parallel the growth of the additive schema. It is not a mere complication of the latter which is grafted on at the end of the developmental process.

We find that the same five stages occur in the development of multiplication and addition. There is, in addition, a type which we may call II 0, and represents a mixture of the two.

(II 0) *Juxtaposition of two elements.*—This reaction seems to bridge the gap between choices governed by one collection alone and those which are functions of both. The reaction is not very frequent, amounting to less than 10% at all ages from 4 to 9, perhaps because it usually passes over into a more effective kind of multiplication. Here is what we mean: instead of fastening on a single element to agree with both collections simultaneously, the subject insists on choosing two things, one for each collection.

BER (5; 11). (Ber has already been mentioned, as giving one reaction of type I 2 with a tendency to relate the two collections.) "(Pink objects and apples.) *One must choose something pink and an apple of a different colour.*—Which ones?—*Red or apple pink* (we see that he is on the verge of choosing a pink apple).—And here (cats and yellow objects)?—*We must have a very small yellow thing and a very small cat.*—(Flowers and purple objects.)—*A small purple thing and a small brown flower.*"

RIS (6; 9). "(Cats and pink objects.) *A pig and a little cat.*—(Apples and purple objects.)—*An apple and something purple.*—But I want just one thing.—*An apple, and we'll colour it purple.*"

Choosing a pair of objects is one stage nearer to co-ordinating the two collections. These children are trying to relate them by using one individual representative for each collection. Only one more step is required to make the two objects coincide, and Ris achieves it.

(II 1). *Multiplying the two nearest elements.*—When the two elements representing each collection are first combined, we find a tendency to consider only one element from each, usually the nearest.

JAC (5; 10) (whose other reactions are of type I 1). "(Leaves and purple objects.) *A cap* (like the nearest purple object), *but it must be the same colour as this* (the neighbouring leaf, which is blue)."

Jac derives the shape of his card from an element belonging to the collection characterized by colour, and vice versa. (But for this inversion, he might have chosen a purple leaf, and we should have taken his reaction as type II 5, unless we also took care to conduct a clinical enquiry!)

(II 2). *Multiplying two elements other than the nearest in each collection.*—This type of reaction is similar in structure to the last, because the two collections are still not considered as wholes. But there is some advance, since the child is no longer bound by the relation of immediate proximity.

DEN (6; 9) "(Flowers and green objects.) *A pear.*—Would it go with these (flowers)?—*No, then one like this* (the green tulip, which figures in the row of green objects).—And with these (flowers and yellow objects)?—*A flower.*—What kind?—*Like this* (pointing to an orange flower in the middle of the row).—Why?—*Because it's yellow.*—(Flowers and purple objects.)—*There isn't anything at all* (still looking for an object already in one of the rows).—Think of something in your head.—*The blue one, only coloured purple.*—(Apples and green objects.)—*I need red for the flowers . . . no, I need some green with the apples.*"

Here the subject is trying to find the intersection of two classes, but to begin with he fastens on one element which belongs to the row, even if later, when asked to imagine the common part, he starts thinking in a slightly more general way.

(II 3). *The choice is made in terms of a functional relation or, alternatively, in terms of a partitive relation subsisting within a single object.*—Type II 3 corresponds to I 3, and we have already noted cases which show an element of both (cf. Ani).

LEC (6; 2). "(Leaves and green objects, including an apple, a cap, etc.) *An apple, because you may have an apple on top of some leaves.*—Does that go with the green?—*Yes, because, sometimes, if you have an apple and a cap, you can put the apple inside the cap.*"

ALA (7; 11). "(Leaves and green objects, including an axe.) *A tree, because it goes with the axe and the leaves.*"

ELI (8; 9). "(Cats and yellow objects, including a pear.) *Some branches. The pear grows on the branch, and the cat climbs on to it.*"

PIE (8; 10). "(Cats and blue objects, including a bird.) *A tree with a little nest on top, and a cat climbing up.*"

ANI (9; 6). (Ani has already been mentioned under I 3.) "(Cats and purple objects.) *A ball of wool, because cats play with wool and because it's purple.*"

There is progress since these subjects are introducing objects which do not already figure in the diagrams. But the relations which bind them are either functional or partitive; they are not class relations. It is curious that such relations reappear at this late age, because by this time they have been superseded long since in spontaneous classifications, whether additive or multiplicative.

(II 4). *Multiplication of generic relations.*—This type corresponds to type I 4, with the essential difference that the subject now considers both classes in making a generic extension to one.

RIS (7; 6). "(Apples and blue objects.) *A suit-case. No, a pear.*—Why?—*Because it's the same fruit.*"

ONS (9; 6). "(Leaves and green objects.) *A plum* (green) *because the leaves are almost like a plum* (no doubt thinking of its shape)."

This is multiplication, but the equivalences are too weak. It is of a piece with the first logical definitions given by children, where genus alone is used and not differentia.

(II 5). *Multiplication of classes.*—This is the correct solution.

DAM (7; 0). (Dam has already been mentioned under I 5.) "(Flowers and pink objects.) *A pink flower.*—Would a pink ball do?—*No, because these* (the flowers) *are not balls.*—(Apples and yellow objects.)—A yellow apple.—*What about these* (cats and red objects)?—*A cat . . .* (silence). *A red cat! Because these are all cats, and those are all red.*"

Note that there is an explicit reference to the class ("all"), and not (as in II 1 or II 2) to any one particular element. What is more, the subject is prepared to invent a "red cat" although he knows they do not exist.

Reactions of type II 5 were found in the following proportions among children aged 5 to 10.

5–6	7–8	9–10
12·5%	30%	50%

This confirms that a simple intersection is more difficult that a complete cross-classification (§§ 2–4).

7. ADDITION AND MULTIPLICATION

The fact that simple intersection is more difficult helps us to a deeper understanding of the relation between the addition and multiplication of classes. For these partial situations must have some bearing on the easier problem of cross-classification.

All that we have seen so far, and particularly the close parallel between reactions of type I 1–5 and those of type II 1–5 (§6), favours hypothesis 3 of §1, i.e. the hypothesis that the schema of addition and the schema of multiplication develop together, and share a parallel progressive organization. But this hypothesis still leaves open the question whether addition precedes multiplication, or whether they both develop simultaneously.

At first sight, Table XVIII of §6 suggests that addition develops first, because 85% of subjects aged 5–6 years react to only one of the two collections, as compared with only 17·5% at 9–10. But this table does not take into account the degree of elaboration of the additive or multiplicative schema. It may mean that the child organizes additive schemata (involving reactions to one collection only) before multiplicative ones. But there is still the possibility that as the child progresses stage by stage through the structural organization of an additive schema, so he can transfer these successive insights to the problem of multiplication.

The results of §6 show clearly that it is the second possibility which holds. We find exactly the same forms and stages (1–5) in reactions of type I, where the problem is interpreted in terms of the single collection (i.e. an additive class), as in those of type II, where the subject shows his awareness of the multiplicative nature of the task. Thus Table XVII merely proves that the child finds it difficult to relate two collections, so long as his reactions to one collection are still elementary and far removed from real operational addition (types I 1–3). Conversely, when the additive schema is well-structured (types I 4–5, particularly I 5), the multiplicative schema is too (types II 4–5). There is but one common process of organization, and as this is accomplished, so it engenders stage by stage both the additive and the multiplicative operational schema.

Before we can accept this conclusion, however, we must be sure that the experimental situation did not retard the additive schema by suggesting an intersection of two collections, even in cases where the subject could not actually find the intersection. We therefore undertook an experiment in which subjects were simply asked to complete two collections considered quite separately.

In this experiment, a space was left blank at the end of each of two rows of objects, instead of one blank space being left in a zone of intersection. We asked the two following questions: (1) "Someone drew these pictures. Why did the gentleman who drew them put these pictures together? And those? Why do they go together? etc." (2) Several pictures were then presented, on separate cards. "You see that there is a blank space on each card. He forgot one of the pictures. You have to choose which of these pictures go with *all the ones* which are on the same card." In case of difficulty, the pictures were presented one by one.

The results were precisely the same as the reactions to one collection only in the preceding experiment, i.e. we saw the same types of reaction. I 1–5. The only difference was that type I 3 (partitive and functional relations) was more rare, because the question was given in the form of a multiple choice instead of being open-ended.

However, we will study a few examples because of the light thrown by this experiment on the ability of children to understand classes when these are presented ready-made. The problem is somewhat different from those which we considered in chs. I–III, all of which bore on spontaneous classification. From this new point of view, we see once more how gradually children overcome the difficulties involved in the relation of class-membership ("*x* is *A*"). In the main, these difficulties arise out of the operation of addition, being the characterization of a class *A* by the co-ordination of its intension *a* with its extension (the latter corresponding to the quantifier "all"). On the one hand: "All the *A*s are *a*"; and on the other: "All the *x*s which have the property *a* are members of *A*" (cf. ch. III). Here are some examples of reactions (1)–(3).

Ang (6; 2) gives a simple enumeration of the green objects, without formulating their common property. "Why are they together?—*Because the flower goes with the fruit.*" He chooses the green cap to complete the collection "*because it is just the same* (as another already in the row).—Anything else?—*The red cap. No, the colour won't go.*—Would the (green) shoe go?— *No, the shape wouldn't do.*" For the collection of leaves, Ang says "*some leaves.*—Can you choose a picture to put here (the empty space)?—*The blue leaf* (identical to the nearest leaf).—Why?—*The colour is the same, but the position isn't quite the same.*—Would the purple leaf do?—(He reflects.)— *Yes, because it has the same position as this* (the yellow one)."

Jun (6; 3) seems to formulate the common properties of the two collections correctly, since she says "*some leaves*" and "*it's the same green*". But, in completing the flowers, she suggests "*the blue pipe.*—Why?—*It's the same colour as this* (the blue leaf).—Anything else?—*The purple flower.*" And, for the green objects, "*the green cap.*—Why?—*Because it's the same as this* (the nearest object).—And would the red cap do?—*Yes, because it's also a cap.*— The green shoe?—*Yes, because it's green,*" but she also accepts a blue flower "*because one sometimes makes green out of blue*".

Ried (6; 6) simply enumerates the green objects, without mentioning their common property. He chooses "*the green book.*—Why?—*There is a book there.*—Anything else?—*The green cap.*—Anything more?—*The green leaf* (he removes it at once). *No, there aren't any leaves there.*—Would the green shoe do?—*No, there aren't any shoes.*—What goes best?—*The cap* (identical to the nearest element)." For the leaves, Ried says "*some leaves*", and he chooses the blue leaf (which is present already), and then the yellow one (id.). "Which is better: the blue one or the yellow?—*The blue, because it goes with this* (the nearest element).—But it must go with all of them.—*The blue leaf doesn't go with the yellow one . . . I don't know.*"

The definitions offered by these subjects are inadequate. They fail to recognize that "all" the elements in *A* share the common property *a*. At the same time, they cannot extend the collection in the correct way, which is to accept any *x* that has the property *a*. Instead, they look for something identical to the nearest element (cf. reaction I 1 of §5), or

186

identical to one of the others (cf. I 2), or else they invent partitive or functional relations (the flower with the fruit, the pipe with the cap, etc.). Now and again, they may look for broad similarities, which is properly type I 4.

Type I 4 consists in choosing the new element by virtue of a partial similarity with the elements of the collection. This similarity is often confined to some of the given elements and does not extend to them all.

BAS (5; 2) defines the two collections correctly as *"some leaves"* and *"green, green, green"*. This does not prevent him from wishing to add *"a pink apple because there is a pear there"* to the second collection, or *"a red cap* (because there is a red leaf)" and *"a blue pipe because there is a blue flower already"* to the leaves. In other words, the collection defined by shape is extended through similarities of colour, and vice versa.

NAD (6; 4). In the same way, Nad adds a red cap to the green objects, because these contain a cap, etc.

We see that the criterion is no longer that of identity (some subjects even refuse to add an element "because it is already there"). The criterion is a similarity, but one which would materially alter the definition of the given class, even though the definitions are given correctly.

We may conclude with two examples of correct reactions (corresponding to type I 5).

FRA (7; 6). For the green objects, he suggests: *"The pink apple, no, the green leaf because all the others are green. One can also choose the green shoe and the green cap."* For the leaves: *"The green leaf.*—And the green shoe?—*No, not with the leaves."*

BRU (7; 6) chooses correctly *"because that makes everything green"* and *"because they must all be leaves"*.

These examples are instructive from two points of view. One result, which may appear surprising at first, but which fits in with the conclusions of chs. I–IV, is that a new element cannot be recognized as a member of a given class until stage III. (Fra and Bru are examples of this stage. Note how the word "all" figures in their remarks.) We may therefore conclude that the close link between the development of an additive schema and that of a multiplicative schema was not peculiar to the experimental situation in §6. The additive schema of class membership and that of inclusion develop very slowly and gradually; as these develop so we find a parallel growth in the organization of multiplicative schemata. This conclusion is valid *a fortiori* for complete cross-classification as opposed to simple intersection, because the former is in fact an earlier development.

8. THE QUANTIFICATION OF MULTIPLICATIVE CLASSES

So far we have been studying the development of multiplicative schemata and this part of our analysis corresponds to the studies reported in chs. I, II and IV for the addition of classes. Once again, we can go on to consider the quantification of multiplicative classes, just as we studied that of additive classes in ch. III and in one section of ch. IV. As before, our chief concern will now be the use of "some" and "all" to quantify the relation of class-inclusion, the only difference being that the classes in question must form part of a cross-classification or a simple intersection.

However, we will confine ourselves to a problem of intersection. We chose a more active technique than that of §5. As a result we may expect to learn something more about simple multiplication. However, the main reason for adopting this technique was that it was expected to favour an understanding of the relevant quantification.

The material consisted of four kinds of counters: blue circles (*BC*), red circles (*RC*), blue squares (*BS*) and red squares (*RS*). Together with the counters, we used eight boxes. One box is covered with red paper, one with blue paper, one has a white circle pasted on a white lid, and one has a white square pasted on a white lid. The other four boxes correspond to the four types of counter, the appropriate one being pasted on the lid of each.

Finally, we had two sheets of paper both of which showed two large intersecting circles. One of the circles was black and the other yellow, so that they defined three areas to symbolize two classes and their intersection.

There are eight steps to the experiment. The child is first shown a small pile of counters mixed together, containing 5 *BC*, 5 *RC* and 5 *BS*. He is also given the four boxes with counters on the lids, each containing five counters matching the one on the lid.

(1) The content of the boxes is pointed out to the child and he is told what task he will have to perform (reproduce the pile of counters by memory). He is asked to look at the pile of counters closely. Then the pile is removed, and he is asked to construct a similar pile, using the contents of the boxes. If he fails the experimenter goes on to (2).

(2) The same fifteen counters are arranged on one of the sheets of paper, with the *RC* in the black circle, the *BS* in the yellow circle, and the *BC* in the area common to both. Thus the black circle symbolizes the circles, the yellow circle symbolizes the blue counters, and their intersection symbolizes the blue circles. Without mentioning the symbolism, the experimenter tells the child to look at this arrangement carefully. Once again the model is hidden, and the child is asked to

188

reproduce it on the second (identical) sheet of paper using the contents of the four boxes.

(3) A small pile is made containing all four kinds of counter. The child is then given the other four boxes, destined for the red counters, the blue ones, etc., their use is explained, and he is asked to fill them with the counters present. If he puts only one type of counter in each box (say BC instead of $BC + RC$), he is asked to do it differently. If he still fails, the experimenter does it with him.

(4) He is then asked to describe the contents of these four boxes (which are closed).

(5) The child is once again presented with the fifteen counters arranged on a sheet of paper as in (2). He is asked to describe the contents of the black and yellow circles, and to say why the BC are in their area of intersection, etc.

(6) Leaving this sheet of paper as it is, the child is given all the boxes, and asked to produce the same arrangement on the second sheet of paper, using only two out of the eight.

(7) Questions are then asked on the quantification of inclusion. "If a little girl could make a necklace with these counters (BC) or with these (all the blue ones), which way would it be longer?" This form of question is repeated to cover the following three comparisons. (I) BS and B (blue counters); (II) B and C (circles); (III) R (red counters) and S (squares). There are always five counters in each of the sub-classes BC, RS and BS.

(8) Finally, questions involving "all" and "some" can be asked in relation to the different classes involved.

We shall only describe the reactions to questions (5)–(8), in order to avoid lengthening the account unnecessarily. Questions (1)–(4) do not add anything to what we have already learned, apart from certain things we shall describe in ch. VII which deals with changes of criterion. (The problem of two criteria, raised by question (3), is usually solved by the age of seven.)

Question (5) shows the difficulties of intersection very clearly. Here are two examples:

CHA (6; 11). "What is there in the black ring?—*Blue squares.*—Show me with your finger (he does it correctly). What is there inside?—*Blue squares.*—Is that all?—*Yes.*—Show me again.—(He moves his finger round the circumference once more.)—*Blue circles.*—Is that all?—*Yes.*—And in the yellow one? —*Red circles.*—Show me (he does so). Well, what is there?—*Red circles.*" He is systematically ignoring the intersection.

CAR (7; 1). "What is there in the black circle?—*Blue and red.*—What?— *Circles.*—And in the yellow one?—*Blue squares* (forgetting the BC)—Would you show me with your finger?—(Traces the whole circumference of the yellow circle.)—What is there inside?—*Squares* (again forgetting the BC)."

189

The next few examples are transitional:

STA (7; 6). "What is there in the black circle?—*Blue.*—What?—*Circles and squares.*—And in the yellow one?—*Red circles.*—Follow it with your finger. —*Ah! Red circles and blue circles.*"

GUY (8; 3). "In the black circle?—*Blue squares and blue circles.*—And in the yellow one?—*Red squares and red circles.*—Show me with your finger.—*No, red circles and blue circles.*"

BAU (9; 6). "In the yellow one?—*Blue squares.*—Only?—*And circles*— Well?—*Blue squares and circles.*—And in the black one?—*Red and blue circles.*"

BOUG (10; 4). "In the black circle?—*Blue squares and blue circles.*—And in the yellow one?—*Red circles.*—Show me.—*Red circles and blue circles.*"

Finally, here are two solutions where the understanding is immediate.

ZAN (8; 2). "In the black circle?—*Five on one side and five on the other.*— What are they like?—*Blue circles and blue squares in the other circle* (in the intersection).—And in the yellow circle?—*There are five red ones and five blue ones.*—What sort?—*Circles.*"

BEG (10; 5). "In the black one?—*Blue and red.*—What?—*Blue circles and red blues, no, red circles.*—And in the yellow one?—*Blue squares and circles as well, blue circles.*—Is there anything that strikes you about these two circles?—*They cross.*—Could one have put the red circles in the centre?— *Yes, but then there would have been two different kinds in each circle* (= there would not have been any intersection)."

Question 6 (reproducing the classes *RC*, *BC* and *BS*, by using two boxes only) is solved more easily, because it does not depend on intersection. The 8 boxes include what amount to 4 unions (*R*, *B*, *C* and *S*) as well as the 4 intersections (*RC*, *BS*, *BC*, and *RS*), which means that the subject can find two boxes out of the former without realizing that the three collections make up two intersecting classes. Nevertheless, it is only at 7–8 years that the problem is solved, because it involves relations of inclusion. Here, to begin with, is an example of failure:

CAR (7; 1) takes boxes *RC* and *BC*, and tries to solve the problem. "What is missing?—*The squares.*" He goes on to try various other pairs at random. "If you take (*C*) and (*BS*), will that do?— . . . —And (*BC* + *RS*)?— . . . —What about (*R*) and (*B*)?—*Yes.*—And (*S* + *BC*)?—*Yes.*—Are you sure?—*No.*— What is missing?—*The circles,*" etc.

Here are two cases illustrating a groping solution.

PEL (7; 0) takes *BS* and *R* only to discover that the blue circles are missing. He then takes the box of blue counters and says: "*These are blue circles and blue squares.*" He takes *RC* as well, and succeeds. "Could you do it with (*S* + *BC*)?—*No* (correct)."

GUY (8; 3) succeeds at once with *C* and *S*, but he believes that there are no other possibilities, and does not succeed again until he hits upon *R* + *B*.

"Will $(S + BS)$ do?—*No, there are no circles* (correct).—And $(BC + R)$?—*Yes* (wrong).—What is there in (R)?—*Red squares and red circles.*—And here (BC)?—*Blue circles.*—Well?— . . . "

We conclude with three immediate solutions:

STA (7; 6) takes B and RC at once.

ZAN (8; 2) first takes R and B. Then tries other combinations such as B and RC, etc.

BAU (9; 6) takes S and C. "Any others?—*Yes, the blue ones and the red ones* $(B + R)$, etc."

Questions 1–4, bearing on the different ways of reproducing the collections present, prepare the subject for their quantification. So do questions 5 and 6, the first by showing what the intersections are, and the second by showing how three sub-classes may be derived from two classes alone. Let us look at the results of the questions on quantification. The questions fell into three types: (I) simple inclusion of the five blue squares in the ten blue elements, i.e. $BS < B$; (II) equivalence of the two intersecting classes of ten circles and ten blue counters, i.e. $B = C$; (III) inequality of the ten circles and the five squares, i.e. $C > S$. I is intensional (being independent of the actual numbers involved, provided that B and S are non-empty), while II and III are extensional. II involves the comparison of intersecting, and III of disjoint, classes. However, the fact that II and III involve number or numerical correspondence is comparatively unimportant. By the time that subjects come to deal with these two questions they know very well that each sub-collection consists of five counters.

First of all, here are examples of failure with questions 7 I and 7 II. 7 III may be solved.

VOG (6; 8). "Which necklace will be longer: the one made of the squares or the one made of the circles?—*Both the same length* (wrong).—And with the blue ones and the circles?—*The one made of circles is longer, because there are red circles and blue circles.* (Wrong, he is forgetting that the BC are part of the B.)—And with the blue counters and the blue squares?—*The one made of blue squares will be longer.*"

FER (6; 5). His answers are the same as those of Vog, except that his answer to the question on the blue and red counters is right.

CAR (7; 1). "Which necklace will be longer: the one made of the blue counters or the one made of the blue squares?— . . . *I don't know.* (He makes them and simply observes): *The one with the squares and the circles* $(= B)$.—And with the blue ones and the circles?— . . . *I don't know . . . both the same* (this could be right, but he remains hesitant).—Why?— . . . —What is there in the necklace of blue ones?—*Circles.*—Is that all?— . . . —And in the necklace made of the circles?—*Blue ones and red ones. The necklace of circles will be longer* (forgetting the blue squares)."

"And with circles and squares?—*Among the circles, there are red and blue*

191

ones; among the squares there will be blue squares. The one of circles is longer (right)."

The next group of subjects succeed with the extensional quantifications, even where they involve intersection, but they still fail the intensional:

PEL (7; 0). "Which necklace will be longer: the one of blue counters or the one of blue squares?—*The one of squares will be longer, because there are fewer circles than squares.*—Do you think so?—(He observes that $BC = BS$.) *Then they'll be the same length* (wrong).—And with blue ones and red ones?—*The same.* (He indicates the two collections correctly, which shows that he was not thinking only of $BS = RC$, disjoint.)—And with the circles and the squares?—*The one of circles will be longer. In the circles there are red ones and blue ones* (correct)."

GUY (8; 3). "The one of squares or the one of circles?—*Not the same. There are more circles* (right).—And with the blue counters and the blue squares?—*The same length.*—Try.—(He constructs them and sees his mistake.)—And with the blue ones and the circles?—*The same length* (indicates the collections correctly)."

Here, finally, are subjects who solve all three quantifications immediately:

STA (7; 6). "The blue counters or the blue squares?—*The one of blue counters is bigger.*—And with the blue ones and the circles.—*The same.*"

NIN (8; 9). "(B or BS)?—*The one of blue counters, because the blue counters are the blue squares and the blue circles.*—(S or C)?—*The one of circles.*—(C or B)?—*The same.*—(C or RC)?—*The one of circles, because the red circles are only half of the circles.*"

BAU (9; 6). "(B or BS)?—*One will be longer than the other: the one of blue ones.*—Why?—*Because it has all the blue ones.*—And with the circles and the blue ones?—*It will be the same.*—Why?—*Because one will have the red and the blue circles* (among the C), *and the other will have the blue circles and the blue squares* (among the B).—And with the red ones and the blue ones?—*The one of blue ones will be longer. In one there will be circles and squares, but in the other there will just be circles.*"

It seems then that the quantification of inclusion (I), already studied in ch. IV, is the most difficult of the three questions. Question III is, of course, the easiest, because it applies to two disjoint classes. Question II, involving a comparison of two intersecting classes, is no more difficult than the one involving inclusion (although we have to check that the child really is comparing $BS + BC$ with $BC + RC$, when comparing B and C, and not merely BS with RC!). The fact that it appears to be easier may be due to the practice effect of questions 1–6, or it may have something to do with the fact that the common part BC is being related to two larger classes, B and C (which is intuitively a more obvious way of proceeding), instead of to one only, B.

We may now turn to question 8 which deals with "all" and "some". The configuration $RC + BC + BS$ is exactly parallel to that of ch. III, §1 (except that all the squares are blue while some of the circles are red).

In other words the configuration of ch. III itself implied the various relations inherent in the intersection of two classes. However, whereas previously the fact of intersection remained implicit, the present experimental technique is specifically designed to bring out the relation. Questions 1–7 prepare the ground for question 8. The question is whether such training accelerates the relevant understanding. In point of fact, the results are entirely negative.

Cou (5; 8). "Are all the squares blue?—*Yes*.—Are all the blue ones squares? —*No, because there are circles as well* (correct).—Are all the circles red?— *Yes* (forgetting the intersection).—Are all the red ones circles?—*Yes* (which is the right answer, but carries the wrong implication of reciprocity)."

Fer (6; 5). "Are all the squares blue?—*Yes*.—Are all the blue ones squares? —*Yes* (wrong).—Are all the circles red?—*No, because there are blue ones as well*.—Are all the red ones circles?—*Yes* (right).—Are all the blue ones squares?—*Yes* (wrong).—Are all the squares blue?—*Yes* (right)."

Vog (6; 8). "Are all the circles blue?—*No* (right).—Are all the blue ones circles?—*No* (right).—Are all the red ones circles?—*No* (wrong).—Why?— (Indicates the blue circles.)"

Mal (7; 2). "Are all the squares blue?—*Yes* (correct).—Are all the blue ones squares?—*No, because there are circles and squares* (correct).—Are all the red ones circles?—*No, because there are some like this* (blue circles).—Are all the circles red?—*No, because some of them are blue* (correct)."

Hes (7; 5). "Are all the blue ones squares?—*No, there are blue circles as well* (correct).—Are all the blue ones circles?—*No, because there are some red circles*. (This inversion is typical of the way in which the question is misunderstood as meaning: "Are all the blue ones all the circles?").—Are all the circles red?—*No* (right, but the same misunderstanding may still be present)."

Zer (7; 6). "Are all the red ones circles?—*Yes*.—Are all the circles blue?— *No, because there are squares as well* (! cf. Hes).—Are all the circles red?— *Yes*.—All?—*Yes* (forgetting the intersection BC)."

Chu (7; 10). "Are all the blue ones squares?—*No*.—Are all the circles red? —*No*.—Are all the red ones circles?—*No, because there are blue circles as well* (!)"

We find the same answers here as in ch. III. Very often we find one and the same subject giving right and wrong answers to different questions of the same type. This variation may be due to the graphic properties of the collections (for example, the contrast between red and blue elements may be clearer than that between squares and circles). Or it may be due to the fact that the child sometimes considers the predicate intensionally ("all the As are b" where $b =$ the property of being red, etc.), and sometimes extensionally ("all the As are Bs" ="are some of the B"). The intensional point of view facilitates the solution, while the extensional one poses the problem (raised by Hamilton) of quantifying the predicate. However, when the reasoning is extensional, the errors seem to follow the same pattern as in ch. III. The question "Are all the Bs As?" is usually answered correctly, because the misinterpretation "Are all the Bs all the As?" still leads to the right answer. When the question takes the form "Are all the As Bs?" a similar misinterpretation leads to the wrong answer. This is what is happening when Mal and Chu deny that all the red counters are circles, because there are some blue circles as well.

However, what is new in the present experiment is to find the same kind of error being committed for questions of the type "Are all the Bs As? (Where $A < B$.) The reason may well be that all the questions which went before (1–7) tend to bring out the intersecting classes. Hes, for example, denies that all the blue counters are circles, not because there are some blue squares, but "because there are red circles". Zer denies that all the circles are blue, not because there are red circles, but "because there are also (blue) squares". (In both cases what the child is saying amounts to "All the Bs are not A, because there are some A_2 not-B" instead of ". . . because there are some B and A'".)

At stage III both the answers and the explanations are correct:

SEI (7; 0). "Are all the blue ones squares?—*No, there are circles and squares.*— Are all the circles blue?—*No, they are red and blue.*—Are all the blue ones circles?—*Not all.*—Are all the circles red?—*No, only one lot is* (*RC*).—Are all the red ones circles?—*Yes.*—Are all the squares blue?—*Yes.*"

CAR (7; 3). "Are all the squares blue?—*Yes.*—Are all the blue ones squares? —*No, there are some blue circles.*—Are all the circles blue?—*No,*" etc.

HEY (7; 3). "Are all the squares blue?—*Yes.*—Are all the blue ones squares? —*No.*—Are all the blue ones circles?—*No.*—Are all the circles red?—*No, there are blue circles as well.*"

GRA (8; 6). "Are all the squares blue?—*Yes, because there aren't any red squares.*—Are all the blue ones squares?—*No, there are circles as well.*—Are all the circles blue?—*No, there are also red ones.*—Are all the blue ones circles?—*No, there are squares too.*—Are all the red ones circles?—*Yes.*"

Here there is a strong suggestion that the ease of solution is due to the practice in intersection that went before. Indeed this is bound to be the case when the child can use "all" and "some" correctly without making a false quantification of the predicate. But we have to remember that before he can do that, the accent on intersection makes for added difficulty with questions of the type "Are all the Bs As? (when $A < B$). Now we know that the use of "all" and "some" depends on a correct appreciation of inclusion and of additive classification in general. It follows that this is yet another example of the close link that obtains between the construction of multiplicative schemata and that of additive schemata.

9. CONCLUSIONS

What this chapter brings to light, more than anything else, is the way in which the additive and multiplicative operations are parallel and inter-connected in their development at every stage.

In §1, we asked whether multiplicative structures or matrices were directly derived from graphic structures, whether they were independent of them, or whether they developed from them in successive stages in the way that additive structures develop out of graphic collections by way of non-graphic collections.

The results of this chapter allow us to give the following answer. In the first place, multiplicative structures do not spring directly from the corresponding graphic configurations, for in §§2 and 3 we found discontinuity as between perceptual and operational solutions of matrix tests. Moreover the two techniques led to precisely the same result although they were quite different. In the second place, they do not depend on a belated co-ordination which is simply superposed on those earlier structures that derived from graphic arrangements, for in §§4 and 5 we showed that spontaneous multiplicative classifications start from graphic collections, and then develop step by step, just as do additive classifications.

Thus the third possibility is the only one left. We were able to confirm this directly in §§6–8. The study of intersections (§6), the relations between addition and multiplication which appear in the course of this study (§7), and the use of "all" and "some" in regard to multiplicative classes (§8), all show how closely the construction of additive operations and that of multiplicative operations are bound together. It is wrong to think of additive structures as being established first and then generalized, so producing multiplicative structures of two or more dimensions. In point of fact, at every level we find children using some form of classification, however rudimentary, and each of these can be applied to several criteria simultaneously as well as to one alone. In the first case the structure is multiplicative, in the second it is additive, but there is no essential opposition between the two.

That these two structures develop through parallel stages, and in close mutual dependence, shows that they constitute a single operational organization, in spite of differences in graphic power and in complexity. We shall come to the same conclusion when dealing with the additive and multiplicative operations of order relations (chs. IX and X). Indeed we also find a genetic relationship between the system of ordering and that of classification. In our opinion, this sort of genetic connexion constitutes one of the weightiest arguments in favour of an operational conception of intelligence.

Chapter Seven

FLEXIBILITY IN HINDSIGHT AND FORESIGHT[1]

THE main difference between the operational classifications of stage III and the imaginal or graphic classifications found at stage I is that the child who is more mature is very much more flexible in the way he handles the elements. This applies both to his mental perspective and to the actual shuffling and reshuffling of which he is capable. He shows flexibility in hindsight when he can change the criterion, either because he notices some property which he failed to take into account when he started, or because the experimenter brings in additional elements to add to an existing classification. He shows flexibility in foresight when he can mentally anticipate a classification before putting it into practice, and particularly when he is able to choose the best classification out of a number of possible alternatives without overt trial-and-error.

At stage I (graphic collections), the subject does not really anticipate the classification. He establishes it in the course of constructing the collection, which he does one step at a time. Once the collection has been constructed, he is tied to it, which is roughly what is meant by perseveration. He lacks the necessary flexibility in hindsight to change the criterion and offer an alternative construction. Conversely, at stage III (operational classifications), the subject does not act at all until he has an anticipatory schema. At the same time he is far more ready to change his criteria or to incorporate his initial constructions in larger and more general ones.

We have every reason to suppose that this flexibility of hindsight and foresight provides the psychological mechanism for the elaboration of those fundamental structures which are characterized by operational reversibility. Indeed we may well anticipate that for every stage in the development of operational structures (beginning with the irreversibility of action and ending with the reversibility of logic) there must be a corresponding development in flexibility. This should include those intermediate stages when the structure is first semi-reversible, then quasi-reversible. The aim of the present chapter is to analyse the growth of this twofold flexibility.

However, it would not have been easy to carry out such an analysis without a working knowledge of the development of additive and multiplicative structures, because we shall be trying deliberately to provoke changes of criteria (e.g. by introducing additional elements), and this

[1] With the assistance of Vinh-Bang, G. Noelting, M. C. Reymond and I. Taponiez.

procedure very easily leads either to two-way or many-way classifications, or alternatively, to fairly complex structures which are part-additive and part-multiplicative. Now that we already have a working understanding of the two main structures, we are in a far better position to study the development of flexibility in classification.

The first investigation deals mainly with hindsight. The second is devoted to anticipation. The material is such that several alternative classifications are open; we want to find out how far subjects can bear in mind these several criteria in the course of their arrangements or even anticipate them beforehand. In particular we want to know how such anticipation links up with the levels we have discovered in earlier chapters. Once again, the structures concerned are neither purely additive nor purely multiplicative.

Finally, in ch. VIII, we shall go on to compare the classifications made by children in regard to material presented visually with what they do when their perception is restricted to kinaesthetic and tactile perception. These two chapters conclude our study of classificatory behaviour.

However, the importance of flexibility in hindsight and foresight extends to the remaining structures studied in this book: simple seriation and serial multiplication. We will therefore return to the problem when we come to deal with the elaboration of these structures (chs. IX and X). Again, we can use analogous techniques: asking the subject to anticipate the series, restricting the seriation to haptic perception, and introducing additional elements after the initial seriation has been completed.

1. REARRANGEMENTS CAUSED BY THE ADDITION OF NEW ELEMENTS

All cognitive structures (and affective processes as well) are subject to temporal effects. Any structure, whether perceptual or conceptual, tends to affect any of those that succeed it, provided there is a sufficient degree of relationship between the two (e.g. analogy, nearness in space or time, etc.). We might consider such instances as perseveration, carry-over following an interval (here the effect can be one of contrast or of identification), various kinds of transposition or transfer (with or without anticipation), and, last of all, generalization. Such effects are limited to one temporal direction at the perceptual and sensori-motor levels: for instance, perception is modified by previous perceptions but it cannot alter these in turn. However, as soon as we move away from mere transposition or sensori-motor transfer and consider the many intermediate forms of behaviour which lead into conceptual generalization at the operational level, we begin to find new possibilities, their main feature being a reversal of temporal direction. The simplest way of generalizing is to assimilate what is new to what is old. Later the assimilation is coupled with hindsight, which is an active process and may eventually lead to a remodelling of the system as a whole, both new and old, following on the assimilation of the former to the latter. Earlier concepts and earlier information may therefore be revised in the light of what comes after. Many different combinations then become possible. The most stable is one in which the rearrangement does not do away with part or all of the previous structure, but integrates it into a new structure containing two sub-systems: the old and the new.

Our investigation of the development of operational structures out of the more primitive perceptual and imaginal structures cannot be complete without an analysis of such temporal effects. In particular, we want to know how far existing structures are conserved or modified when new elements are incorporated.

We adopted the following techniques:

I. (Apparatus *A*): classification restricted to two boxes, making a change in classification necessary each time new elements are added. (0) The initial elements are flat green circles and crosses, all of the same size and made of smooth card. (1) The first additions are yellow stars (of the same size and same card). (2) The second are two large rhombi and semi-circles, mauve instead of green. (3) The third are triangles and ovals in corrugated cardboard.

II. (Apparatus *B*): no rearrangement is necessary, although the classification is still restricted to two boxes. (0) Large and small circles of one colour. (1) Addition of large and small circles of a different colour. (2) Addition of squares of the two preceding sizes and colours. (3) Addition of squares and circles of both sizes, but with jagged edges.

III. (Apparatus *B*): with successive partitions provided one at a time so that the child can arrange them inside the two boxes as new elements are added.

IV. (Apparatus *A* or *B*): the child is asked to name all the possible classifications each time new elements are added (no boxes being used).

I and IV tend to favour repeated changes in classification while II and III tend to favour the retention of the first. We tried all of them because together they help to indicate what children incline to do naturally, be it to forget about what went before and rearrange everything in the light of the last additions or to cling to the initial classification. These are the principal tendencies to look for in the illustrations which follow.

The first few examples are from 3- and 4-year-olds:

RUD (3; 6) (II, apparatus *B*). He puts large blue squares in I, and the small blue circles, the large orange circles and some more large blue squares in II. He then removes them all, and places the small squares and circles together with some large squares in I, with the large squares below the others, and some large squares together with the large circles in II. When new colours

198

are added, he continues to put the small elements together (in I) and the large elements together (in I below the others, and in II).

TIL (3; 6). (II, apparatus *B*.) After several attempts, he puts the blue elements in I and the red ones in II. He is asked to classify the elements into large and small, but he continues classing them as red or blue. The experimenter then starts the classification by size, and he continues it correctly. He also completes a classification of the elements into those with jagged edges and those without. But when he is left free and new elements are added, he classes them exclusively by their colour, as he did at the beginning.

ARG (4; 5) (II, apparatus *B*) puts the large red circles in I and the small red circles in II, these being the only elements presented at first. When the blue circles are added, he puts the large ones with the large red ones in I, and says "*This blue goes here. Now these small ones* (blue circles), *where do they go? I've put the blue ones here* (I), *so these must go there too.*" This amounts to a change of criterion without any rearrangement, which means that the classification is contradictory (blue circles, large and small, and large red circles in I, small red circles in II). The circles with jagged edges are added: "*These are stars. They're better over here* (II). *I'm putting them like this with the small ones* (a new contradiction).—Look carefully.—(He changes them.)—*Well, I've put the blue ones* (large and small, with jagged edges and without) *over here* (I). *Here* (I) *they're all blue, and there* (II) *they're all red.*—(Jagged squares and small circles are added. He rearranges everything, starting with the new elements.) *These are stars. Now these* (jagged squares), *what are they?* (He puts them all in I and II in a way which argues an ever-increasing jumble among his criteria; then he simplifies, which, for him, means reverting to the dichotomy between blue elements, in I, and red, in II.)—Can you do it differently (putting everything back on the table)?—*I could put the red ones here* (I) *and the blue ones there* (II).—And in any other way?—*No, I can't.*"

PRIM (4; 0) starts by putting the large red circles in I and the small red circles in II. He retains this criterion when the blue ones are added: "*These are the big ones* (I: red and blue) *and these are the small ones* (II: red and blue).*" Jagged circles, large and small; he tries to fit these in, but the division now ceases to be based on size alone. After a few rearrangements, it tends towards a dichotomy into jagged elements (I) and others (II), but there are some exceptions. "Is that all right?—*Yes, very good.*—Can you do it differently?" Once more he begins to separate the whole into two lots, but he cannot help shifting his criterion and veering between size and type of edge. Finally, he gives up the attempt to classify the elements by their qualities, and simply puts them in alternately in the two boxes.

We might sum up these reactions as follows:

(1) The first characteristic is perseveration: a child starts with size and continues with it; adding a new colour fails to induce an alternative dichotomy or a sub-classification by colour (Rud). If he starts with colour he goes on classifying by colour. He can make two collections by an alternative criterion if he has an example to follow; but, left to himself, he goes on ignoring such criteria.

(2) When the effect of perseveration ceases, so does the temporal

effect as a whole. In other words, the subject forgets all about the old criterion and is taken up with the new one. This can happen in either of two ways. Sometimes the new criterion is tacked on to the old, which makes for contradictions. So we find Arg starting out by dividing circles into large and small, and then switching when he does the blue circles: first he puts large blue circles with large red circles, which is perfectly reasonable, then he puts the small blues with the large. Here the criterion of colour replaces that of size. Alternatively the new criterion simply takes over altogether. Once again, Arg provides a good example of this when he finally decides to divide the elements into red and blue.

(3) In addition to perseveration and forgetting we may find a mixing of criteria. But this sort of thing is very far from reconciling the new elements with previously existing structures. It is more of an arbitrary incorporation of the new in the old, based on rather fluid relations of belonging which cannot be analysed in terms of "all" and "some"; the child merely says that "these go well together". Arg, for example, having classed the ordinary circles as red and blue, puts the large jagged circles, both blue and red, among the small red ones, saying "They're better over here". Prim also incorporates the jagged elements in a way which suggests the same sort of confusion, and eventually he gives up altogether.

These incorporations, which are difficult to understand, arise from the fact that a child of 3–4 years does not try to extend the properties of "all" the elements of an existing collection to the new element. He simply looks for some kind of a relationship between this element and one of those which is already in the collection, which becomes a sort of plenipotentiary representative (!) (cf. ch. VI, §7). The relationship that he finds may not be consistent with the original dichotomy, and may introduce a new criterion, bringing us back to reaction (2).

We may say, then, that (3) is not a new type of reaction, but a mixture of perseveration (1) and forgetting (2). These little children are doing precisely what they did when constructing alignments (cf. ch. I, §2): perseveration and/or change of criterion. Instead of retroaction (or hindsight), there is either assimilation in one direction, incorporation of the new in the old, or else accommodation to the new. Where there is assimilation, there is insufficient accommodation for a restructurization of the schema to which the assimilation occurs, and where there is accommodation, it happens at the expense of assimilation to the previous schema. In either case, the new schema has no retroactive effect.

We can now pass on to examples taken from 5- and 6-year-olds.

CAR (5; 6). Here there are the beginnings of successive organization. She is given the red circles, and divides them into large (I) and small (II). When the blue circles are added, she puts the red circles together in I and the blue ones together in II. The circles with jagged edges are then added: "*Hey! These are stars!*" She first takes the small jagged circles and classifies them by their colour in the two existing collections. Then she takes everything out, and constructs a sort of matrix (with one mistake): jagged circles on the right, smooth on the left, large circles above, small below. (Colour is now ignored.) Squares are added, with and without jagged edges: "*Oh! This will be long!*" She first divides them into sub-collections within the existing system. But she becomes confused, and ends with a new dichotomy: "*I'm putting all the stars there* (in I, with the squares included) *and the circles there* (II)." She then sub-divides them by colours and so constructs a second matrix. She has indeed constructed a multiplicative classification correctly, but she has done it empirically, without anticipating the result.

GET (5; 8). Get eventually produces what is no more than a series of successive differentiations, but he can incorporate new elements correctly in his existing arrangements. The red circles are divided into large and small. When the blue circles are added, he divides these likewise into large and small: "*There, I've done it.*" He puts all the large elements together in I and the small elements in II: "*The biggest ones in this room, the small ones in the other.*" The circles with jagged edges are added: "*These prick! I'm doing the same again*" (continuing to classify by size): *the biggest ones stay in this box, the smallest ones go in the other.*" Squares, with and without jagged edges: "*Different again!*" He divides these again into large and small, and starts to divide the main collections into sub-collections. But there is no evidence of an overall plan and there are no spatial symmetries. Large jagged red squares form one lot, large jagged red circles another, large jagged blue squares yet another, etc.

SAB (5; 8) first divides the red circles into large and small. When the blue circles are added, she constructs two successive matrices, both arranged diagonally: blue elements above and red below, with the small circles along one diagonal and the large ones along the other; then blue elements on the left and red on the right, without changing the arrangement of sizes. Circles with jagged edges are given next, and Sab constructs a true matrix with these: small elements above, large below, red on the left and blue on the right. But when she tries to incorporate the smooth circles in this matrix, she puts the smooth blue ones with the jagged red ones and the smooth red ones with the jagged blue ones. She then corrects this mistake, and obtains a matrix that is correct as far as colour is concerned, although there are smooth and jagged elements in each of its four classes and she ignores the size of the smooth circles. Finally, the smooth and jagged squares are added. First she puts these in at random, mixing up the criteria, then she starts a new matrix classification in which all but two of the criteria are ignored: circles above and squares below, red on the left and blue on the right.

FAN (5; 8). He first divides the red circles into large and small. When the blue circles are added, he classes the elements as blue (I) and red (II), without taking size into account. When the circles with jagged edges are added, he puts the large smooth blue circles in I on the left, and the large jagged blue circles in I on the right. The small jagged blue circles are piled together near the upper edge of box I, and the small smooth ones are piled near the left-hand edge. The red circles are arranged in the same way in box II. The smooth and jagged squares are added next, and once again Fan constructs a new series of subdivisions in I which he tries to reproduce in II. But towards the end he grows tired, and simply piles the elements in at random.

BAE (5; 10) (procedure I, apparatus A) divides the red circles into large and small. The blue circles are added, and he puts the blue in I and the red in II, with the large circles at the top and the small ones at the bottom (this is a matrix, however intuitive in origin). The squares are added; he introduces subdivisions in I and II. When the elements with corrugated surfaces are added, he places them next to the smooth shapes which correspond in shape and colour (there are some mistakes which he corrects). There are also subdivisions according to size, but without symmetry as between boxes I and II.

RIC (5; 10) (procedure II, apparatus B). Ric gradually succeeds in constructing a pattern based on three criteria: the large elements are in I, with red above and blue below, circles on the left and squares on the right; the small elements are similarly arranged in II. But he finds procedure III difficult (this involves the use of boxes which can be partitioned to give successive dichotomies), because he cannot form an overall plan. This proves the empirical nature of his initial success.

NID (6; 1) (II, apparatus B) classes the red circles as large and small. When the blue circles are added, he puts the red circles in I and the blue in II, with the large circles on top and the small ones at the bottom. The circles with jagged edges are added next, and he fits these into the previous classification, red circles on the left and blue ones on the right, large jagged circles above and large smooth ones below. So far the matrix is correct. But the symmetry is incomplete insofar as all the small circles are grouped near the large smooth ones, the jagged immediately above and the smooth immediately below. When the squares, both smooth and jagged are added, Ned starts an entirely new classification. He carefully sorts out the sub-collections, and then arranges them in such a way as to suggest an approximation to a four-entry table: large versus small, red versus blue, jagged versus smooth, squares versus circles. This appears spatially in the form of two main collections, each subdivided into four quarters, representing three dimensions. The bottom layer has large elements only, so that by putting the corresponding small ones on top, he can show the fourth dimension vertically. However, the beauty of his representation is somewhat marred by failures of symmetry: what forms the upper half in I is the lower half in II, while the dimension smooth versus jagged is shown diagonally in I and not in II. In other words, the classification is complete, but unco-ordinated as a whole.

MYR (6; 2) classes the red circles into large and small. When the blue circles are added, she divides the circles into red and blue, without taking size into account. The jagged circles are then added, and she puts the red circles in I, these being divided into sub-collections of smooth versus jagged and large versus small. She puts the blue circles in II, without any subdivisions. Finally, the squares are added, and she puts all the red elements in I and all the blue in II, with the different kinds all mixed in together.

HUG (6; 4) first divides the red circles into large and small. When blue circles are added, he divides all the circles into red and blue. This simple dichotomy persists when jagged circles are added. But when all the squares

are added, he says "*Oh! This time I have a lot, I've got to work really hard.*"
Nevertheless, he simply puts the blue elements in I and the red in II, without
differentiating further. "Can you do it differently?—*No, I can't.*—What about
this (putting two jagged elements together)?—*No, that won't do; (yes) I could
put the little stars over here.*" He attempts this, but becomes confused, and
ends by constructing two large classes without subdivisions: large elements
versus small.

JAC (6; 7) first divides the red circles into large and small. When the blue
circles are added, he constructs a matrix. When the circles with jagged edges
are added, he separates out the large ones and divides them into red (I) and
blue (II). He adds the large smooth circles of the same colours, and puts them
beneath these, which gives him a new matrix. But when he goes on to add
the small circles (which he places on top of the large ones, making a vertical
third dimension) he puts the small jagged circles on the large smooth ones,
and the small smooth circles on the large jagged ones. When the squares are
added, he begins by dividing the elements into squares versus circles and
smooth versus jagged. But when he comes to deal with colours and sizes, he
proceeds to make up a series of subdivisions without planning and without
symmetry, so that he ends up with several new inversions.

PIE (6; 8) first divides the red circles into large and small. Once the blue
circles have been added, he constructs a blue-red dichotomy and maintains it
to the end, ignoring any further distinctions. When he first sees the jagged
circles, he does comment: "*Oh! That's funny: like stars!*" but he still mixes
them with the others.

KEC (6; 10) maintains nothing but a large-small dichotomy from beginning
to end. When procedure IV is tried, which means asking him to suggest the
different possibilities each time new elements are added (starting from the
beginning, without any boxes), he divides the elements on the basis of the
following dichotomies in turn: circle-square, blue-red and large-small. But he
still fails to distinguish any subdivisions.

The behaviour we are observing at 5 or 6 is very different from what
it was at 3 or 4. There is less perseveration and less forgetting. In other
words, where previously we saw either no temporal effects or forward
effects only, we now find considerable evidence of hindsight. Many of
these children are going over all the material again and trying to
reconcile the new elements with the existing system:

(1) To begin with, there is less perseveration in the true sense. At 3
or 4, children were often unable to shift their criterion spontaneously
and even a suggestion to try another way proved unavailing. We had
to start the new division for them. Now we see them holding on to the
first criterion but adding subdivisions to take care of the new dimensions. True perseveration means that the subject simply cannot see the
new possibilities or else ignores them because he cannot construct an
alternative dichotomy. We may easily find a subject who can construct
different dichotomies, but still prefers to stick to the original division so
long as it holds good. But very often such a preference does in fact argue

perseveration. Get clings to the first dichotomy (large versus small) right up to the introduction of squares at the end: only then will he try subdivision; when he does, he is not particularly successful (the symmetry is far from perfect, etc.). We may rightly conclude that he does find it difficult to free himself from the effects of his first systematization. Myr shifts from size to colour, but she holds on to this dichotomy right up to the end; here again, the fact that she tries a subdivision for size and colour, and then gives it up when new dimensions appear on the scene shows that in her case perseveration is still stronger than retroaction (or hindsight). Pie and Kec are two more who cling to the first or second dichotomy and fail to introduce subdivision, but Kec shows us that he can at least think of alternatives.

(2) Forgetting the first criteria (or simply ignoring them when faced with new possibilities) is rather more common than perseveration. Yet this too is less frequent than at 3 or 4. We begin to find it unusual for this to happen as soon as we bring in the second differential: but Fan and Pie are both cases in point. Myr and Hug are two more who ignore size when faced with differences in colour, but they do eventually return to the first criterion. However, what is far more common is to forget the first and second criteria by the time we reach the third and fourth.

(3) We still find mixed collections of a contradictory nature, but they occur less and less frequently. Sab, for example, constructs a matrix of jagged elements (red + blue, small + large), then, when she tries to add the smooth elements to this, she inverts the colours. This type of reaction seems to disappear at 6 years.

(4) What is new and important about this stage is the attempt to reconcile new elements with the existing system. The simplest way for such hindsight to be manifest is for the subject to differentiate each of the original collections into sub-collections by taking the various elements as they occur, without regard for symmetry (cf. Get and Myr).

(5) A slightly more advanced form is seen in unsuccessful attempts to subdivide the original collections so as to make the two boxes symmetrical. The subject is often satisfied with partial symmetries which fail to embrace the system as a whole (cf. Fan, at the end, Bae, Nid and Jac).

(6) When the symmetry is successful, the arrangement takes the form of a true matrix. Such an arrangement solves the problem by subdividing existing systems on the basis of new criteria. But we should emphasize that, at this stage, a child builds up a matrix as he goes along, if at all: he does not as yet construct an anticipatory schema before beginning to group the material. Each one of our examples is an instance of successive subdivisions arranged symmetrically (cf. Car, Sab, Nid, Jac, at the beginning). When more than two criteria are reached, most of our subjects fall back on one of the preceding reactions.

(7) Nevertheless, we do find occasional patterns based on three (Ric) or even four (Nid) criteria. Even now, by trying procedure III (Ric), or else by noting failures of symmetry (Nid), we can still detect the empirical character of these constructions.

Both the simple two-by-two matrix and patterns based on more than two criteria occur earlier than they do in the experiments of ch. VI. We should point out that the present procedure, involving successive additions, leads far more naturally to the construction of matrices than simultaneous presentation. When all the elements are introduced together, the subject is compelled to take all the possible dichotomies into account at the same time, and he cannot do so without an anticipatory schema. But when the dichotomies are presented successively, he can imitate operational multiplication by dealing with each differentiation separately as and when it occurs.

However, what these results do show clearly is that there is a retroactive process whose influence increases. We see it in the various rearrangements which follow on the introduction of new elements.

Finally, we come to the reactions of stage III (7–8 years), when there is anticipation as well as hindsight.

STE (7; 1) classes the red circles into large and small. When blue circles are added, he subdivides the two classes of red and blue circles into large and small (forming a matrix). With the addition of jagged circles, he subdivides the classes of large and small circles into jagged and smooth in box I. He does the same in box II, with an inversion which he afterwards corrects, so achieving a 3-way matrix. With the addition of squares, he arranges the smooth squares in box I by size and colour and similarly with the jagged squares, in box II. This gives a pattern based on three criteria. He then puts the circles on top of the squares of the corresponding colours and sizes, thereby adding a fourth dimension to his arrangement.

BAR (7; 6) divides the red circles into large and small, then, with the addition of the blue circles, he subdivides the two classes according to colour. When the jagged circles are added, he maintains the division into large and small circles, but groups the large jagged circles at one end of box I, with the red above and the blue below, and the large smooth circles likewise, at the other end of box I. The small circles are arranged in box II in exactly the same way (so yielding a pattern based on three criteria). When the squares are added, he retains this framework, and simply divides each existing sub-class in two (squares and circles), so forming a pattern based on four criteria.

GOL (8; 0) also starts by dividing the red circles into large (I) and small (II), and then subdividing the collections into red and blue. With the addition of the jagged circles, she gives up the division based on colour, and arranges the large circles in box I with the smooth ones at the top and the jagged at the bottom, repeating for the small circles in box II. When squares are added, she subdivides the large elements into smooth and jagged squares and smooth and jagged circles. She does the same with the small elements, thereby producing a pattern based on three criteria in which colour is neglected. When she is asked for other classifications, she constructs alternatives but this child goes no further than patterns based on three criteria.

RAU (8; 2) starts with a division into large and small circles. With the addition of the blue circles, he divides the elements into red and blue circles, these being further subdivided into large and small. With the addition of the jagged circles, this framework is maintained, the blue circles being divided into smooth and jagged in box I, with a further subdivision by size, and the red circles likewise, in box II. With the addition of the squares, he subdivides the blue elements into squares versus circles, jagged versus smooth, and large versus small, and the same for the red elements, thereby producing a pattern based on four criteria.

BAR (8; 8) proceeds in the same way as Rau until the squares are added (3-entry table). But instead of constructing a pattern based on four criteria, she now produces three successive two-by-two matrices according to the three possible combinations: jagged versus smooth elements, squares versus circles, and red versus blue, with size serving as the second criterion for each.

HAG (8; 9) maintains the same system of two classes (large and small elements) until the end. However, when she is asked to arrange the elements differently, she constructs the same 3-entry tables as Bar.

HEN (9; 3). Hen confines himself to two-by-two matrices until the squares are added, using the criterion of size and a variable second criterion. Following the addition of the squares, he retains the same framework but subdivides his classes into squares versus circles, and again into jagged versus smooth. Finally he puts the blue elements on top of the red (thereby forming a pattern based on four criteria). "Could you do it differently?—*Oh yes, all the jagged ones on one side and the others on the other side. There have to be three of each kind* (= three pairs of properties). *That comes to quite a lot* (he produces another pattern based on four criteria)."

These examples illustrate a number of features which are distinctive of stage III:

(1) There is no perseveration. Occasionally a subject like Hag reproduces the same dichotomy time and again, but one can tell that he is simply making things easy for himself because when he is asked to produce an alternative he has no trouble in making 3- and 4-entry tables. So the repetition cannot be due to the sort of rigidity associated with lack of hindsight.

(2) We find little or no forgetting of earlier criteria. The only exceptions are cases of momentary distraction or deliberate neglect, as in the instance of Gol, who produces a variety of 2-entry and 3-entry tables but refuses to take any account of colour (which would imply 3- and 4-entry tables).

(3) There are no contradictory subdivisions, and none of the arrangements show the lack of symmetry associated with a purely empirical approach.

(4) There are two ways in which the subject can take care of a new dimension when we produce additional elements. He can leave the

original framework unchanged and simply add further subdivisions, or he can change one of the first subdivisions—or even the first main division. Bar is a good example of this sort of flexibility: he holds on to the same main division right the way through (large versus small) but his first subdivision changes from red versus blue to jagged versus smooth (colour being retained as a rank 3 classification); finally, he keeps this classification when the fourth dimension is introduced (squares versus circles) and simply adds a further set of subdivisions (of rank 4). Ste prefers to regroup: he alters the main division twice and the subdivisions repeatedly.

(5) But the order in which the different subdivisions are constructed is unimportant (because the relations are multiplicative, we have a set of intersections instead of a fixed order determined by relations of inclusion). What *is* important is whether the subject tries to reconcile the new criteria with the old, or whether he has to sacrifice one for the other. Here we now find retroactive integration, as shown by the generality of true multiplicative responses: the first set of additional elements almost invariably results in a two-by-two matrix, and those that follow either lead to spontaneous 3-way and 4-way matrices ($2 \times 2 \times 2$ or $2 \times 2 \times 2 \times 2$), or else the subject prefers to stick to the 2-way or 3-way classifications, but with this important difference, that he can change his criteria at will.

(6) Logical multiplication, involving two, three or four criteria, includes anticipatory reactions. The presence of an operational anticipatory schema may be obvious from the subject's remarks. Hen, for example, says "There must be three of each kind; that comes to quite a lot", when speaking of the three subdivisions that have to be introduced after the first dichotomy. More often the anticipatory nature of the multiplicative schema is shown only by the subject's flexibility when asked to rearrange his pattern (we shall be making a separate study of the degree of anticipation at the various stages in §3).

To sum up: the present results provide a vivid illustration of the mechanisms which lead from stage I to stage III:—At the level of graphic collections there is neither anticipation nor even hindsight, so the subject cannot reconcile new dimensions with an existing classification: each classification in turn is dominated by the graphic properties of the material, very often modified by the perseveration of what seemed most salient earlier on. As development goes on, so the possible rearrangements become increasingly systematic in character. They do so because there is hindsight, and then anticipation. The first enables what is new to be integrated with what is old, and the second makes the framework of classification a good deal more flexible.

2. CHANGES OF CRITERION REQUIRING THE REARRANGEMENT OF EXISTING CLASSIFICATIONS

In the preceding experiment we introduced the several dimensions one after the other. In effect we were asking for the modification of an existing classification. This might take the form of new subdivisions, although it could amount to an entirely new basis for the various groupings. In the following, somewhat similar, experiment we introduced all the elements from the start: we allowed the subject to make up his own form of classification, and then asked him whether he could suggest some other way (or even more than one), which means changing the first criterion. The actual material we used was the same (squares and circles, red and blue, large and small, although none were tooth-edged), but, from the child's point of view, the problem is considerably harder. In the first place, by introducing the possible dichotomies one at a time (A_1 and A'_1, then A_2 and A'_2, then A_3 and A'_3, etc.), we were in fact helping the child to realize the multiplicative nature of the required classification; conversely, when we produce all the elements together, he cannot tell immediately whether they fit in to a multiplicative cross-classification or an additive structure (made up of successive inclusions: $A < B < C$, etc.). In the second place, it is easier to alter an existing arrangement when there are fewer classes involved and the problem can be solved by simply adding a new subdivision; what we are now demanding is a completely new arrangement, either by using a new criterion or by changing the rank-order of criteria. In any case, the problem is bound to be different, which is why we thought it worthwhile to find out how children would respond to this situation. By taking both sets of data into account, we should be in a better position to say just how much flexibility in hindsight there is at each of the stages I, II and III. In order to complete the picture we went on to introduce three new dimensions after the subject had been asked for changes of criteria based on the three he had to start with (colour, shape and size). For this purpose we had a number of very large or very small shapes, some shapes with holes in the middle, and a few large yellow squares (similar to the large red and large blue).

The experimental procedure may be summed up as follows: The subject is first shown the main group of objects comprising squares and circles, red and blue, in two sizes: 25 mm. and 50 mm. (side or diameter respectively). He is first asked for a verbal description of these objects. Then he is told to classify them as he sees fit. Next he is required to make a dichotomy using two large boxes; he can make further subdivisions inside the boxes but he is not compelled to do so. We go on to ask for alternative classifications up to a maximum of three. Finally, for certain subjects, we went on to introduce shapes measuring 13 mm. or 75 mm.

(as well as a 50 mm. yellow square and a number of cards with holes in them, wherever this seemed to be indicated).

To begin with, here are the results based on 60 subjects of 5 to 8–9 years, using a standard set of questions[1] (some 40 additional subjects took part in a clinical enquiry involving greater variation in the questions). Table XVIII shows the number of criteria discovered by these subjects.

Table XVIII. *Number of criteria at ages 5–9*

Age (*no. of subjects*)	5 (*12*) %	6 (*17*) %	7 (*18*) %	8–9 (*13*) %
Criteria: 0[2]	27	12	5	0
1	46	12	11	0
2	27	47	56	31
3	0	29	28	69
2 or 3	27	76	84	100

Even though, as we explained above, multiplicative constructions occur later than in the experiment of §1, 75% of the six-year-olds still succeed in using two or three criteria. This is rather earlier than the operational level of 7–8 years. Now once a child can divide the same objects according to two or three complete dichotomies, it is but a short step to being able to cross-classify them in accordance with a multiplicative schema.

But we do not wish to return to the development of additive and multiplicative classifications. The purpose of this chapter is to elucidate the factors of retroactive and anticipatory flexibility which explain their development. The table given above provides a clear quantitative index of the extent to which hindsight proves effective at these various ages, because it shows whether a subject was able to change the basis of his dichotomy once or even twice over, or, whether, as was common enough at 5, he did not succeed in making so much as one initial dichotomy. However, the qualitative descriptions that follow enable us to go one step further. We want to know whether the child's retroactive and anticipatory mobility are related, the first being measured by the way in which he rearranges existing collections, and the second by the way in which he undertakes his initial classification and carries out the first dichotomies for which he is asked.

[1] When the criteria are colour, shape and size, young children always choose colour and shape. The use of size only appears later, even when differences in size are very large.

[2] 0 means that there has been no classification which resulted in a complete dichotomy of the elements.

Here are some examples of stage II (5–7 years). We already know that such children have little flexibility in hindsight; we want to know how this relates to their capacity for anticipation.

BLA (5; 0) starts with the sort of composite pattern (or collective object) which is so characteristic of stage I: large red squares are put together with small red squares to form a repetitive pattern. "Can you put them in piles?" He constructs five small collections: large red squares, small red squares, small red circles, small blue squares, and blue circles of both sizes. Given the two boxes, he puts all the squares in one, together with some blue circles (both large and small). The red circles go in the other, together with some more blue circles (large and small). "Do these go together?—*No* (he takes the small blue circles from the first box and puts them in the second).—What about these (large blue circles)?—*They have to go there* (he takes a third box).—But suppose you have to put everything in two boxes?—(He succeeds in putting all the blue elements in the third box and the red ones in the second.)"

Everything is mixed together again, and a new classification is called for. He constructs a number of small collections: large red squares, small red squares and circles, small blue squares, small blue circles and large blue circles. He then puts all the red elements in the first box and the blue ones in the second. He does not find an alternative criterion. When a large yellow square is introduced, he puts it on its own in the first box, with all the other elements in the second. Once again, he finds no way of improving on this arrangement. But when the experimenter puts all the squares in the first box and all the circles in the second, he accepts the distribution "*because they're all circles there, and all squares here*".

NYF (5; 0) first constructs small piles, and then puts the small squares, red and blue, in box I, the circles in separate piles (large and small) in box II, and the large red squares in box III. Everything is mixed together again, and he is asked to put the elements in two boxes. He puts the large red squares and some large blue circles in I, and the small blue circles and some large blue circles in II (thus collection I contains only large elements, and collection II only blue ones, but there is no dichotomy). Eventually, he puts all the circles in I and all the squares in II. The elements are mixed together once more and the experimenter asks for a new classification. Nyf starts by making small piles, and putting them together on the basis of shape or colour. He ends by putting all the blue elements in I and all the red ones in II. The large yellow square is shown next, and he puts it with the red elements "*because it's the same size* (pointing to the large red squares)".

JAE (5; 2) begins by examining the elements one by one, and ends by dividing them into squares and circles. "Can you divide them into two piles differently?—*Yes* (he takes the elements one by one and slowly groups them together, but he still finishes with the same division into squares and circles).—Haven't you done this once before?—*Yes*.—Can you find another way to arrange them differently?—*Yes* (once again finishing with the division into squares and circles).—Well, will this do (dividing the elements into red and blue ones)? Are these alike (I)?—*No, because there are circles and squares*."

When elements with circular holes are added, Jae merely says: *"They are circles and squares, and some of them have a circle* (= the hole!)"

DUC (5; 3) "What can you see?—*Circles, squares, big circles, small squares.* —Anything else?—*No.*" He then constructs six small piles, dealing with each element as he comes to it. When he has finished, he puts them in the two boxes with the small red squares in I and the other collections in II. The elements are mixed together again and a new classification is called for. This time he puts the large red squares in I and the remaining five collections in II.

ROH (5; 3). Roh also ends with six small collections. He puts the red squares in I, large and small, and all the rest in II. "Why did you put these (I) together? —*Those ones are small* (the small red squares).—*And these* (the large squares in I)?—*They're large.*—Well then, what are all these (I)?—. . .—Well, arrange them.—(He simply changes the positions of the sub-collections inside each of the boxes.)—What are these (I)?—*They're all squares* (correct).—And there (II)?—*They aren't squares* (wrong).—All of them?—(He puts the blue squares in I.)—Try to do it differently (mixing everything together).—(Puts the squares in I and the circles in II.)—Didn't you do this last time?—*Yes.*— Well, can you do it differently? (No reaction. The experimenter starts to classify the elements by colour.) What have I put in here?—*Red ones.*—And there?—*Blue ones.*—Go on then.—(But he reverts once again to the criterion of shape.)"

LIE (5; 5) divides the elements into three sets: (I) the small squares, blue and red; (II) the large blue circles and the large red squares; (III) the small circles, blue and red. He then corrects this, and obtains: (I) small blue squares; (II) large and small red squares; (III) circles. "Do these go together (III)?— *They are all circles.*—And these (II)?—*They are all squares.*—And these (I)?— *All squares as well.*" Given two boxes, he divides the elements into squares and circles, and repeats this at every attempt. The experimenter then divides the elements into red ones (I) and blue ones (II). "Do these go together (I)?— *No.*—Are you sure?—*Yes.*" When the large yellow square is introduced, he simply classes it among the squares.

ROS (5; 5) forms six small collections, and divides them between the two boxes on the basis of colour. A new classification is asked for, and he starts by putting the small red squares in I and the small blue circles in II. He continues by taking each element as he comes to it, and oscillating between the criteria of shape and colour. He ends with the squares in I and the circles in II. A third classification is asked for, and it looks as if Ros is going to use the criterion of size. He takes the cards one by one and puts the small elements in I and the large ones in II. But he then corrects this *"because there are more red ones than blue ones* (in I)", and falls back on the criterion of colour.

KUN (5; 6) ends with a dichotomy into red and blue elements, and repeats this twice when new classifications are asked for. The large yellow square is introduced, and he adds it to the blue elements. "Will this do (II)?—*Yes* (=all red).—And here (I)?—*No, because some are blue and some are yellow.*" The experimenter starts to class the elements into circles and squares, and Kun continues this correctly, but justifies it by saying *"It's because they're red and blue"*.

The present experiment, like the previous, provides ample testimony of the limited flexibility in hindsight to be found at stage II. We base this conclusion on the fact that all of these children seem to have a systematic difficulty in altering a given arrangement to meet with an alternative criterion. In other words there is a good deal of perseveration. Forgetting an old criterion because of a new one is much less common, since all the possible criteria are there from the start and what we are asking for is a change in the arrangement of what is still the same set of elements. (It was more apparent in §1, when new elements suggested different criteria.)

Can we analyse the lack of hindsight more closely, to see if it carries some suggestion that lack of foresight will prove to be a closely related phenomenon? As a matter of fact, the present technique should throw some light on the question, because we can always study how a subject sets about making his first classification, with all the elements in front of him.

Our first pointer consists in deciding which of the two possible modes of classification is preferred by these children: an *ascending* method or a *descending* method. Using an *ascending* method means starting out with a multiplicity of sub-collections corresponding to the lowest rank of an ordered classification, and then combining them step by step until one reaches one or more possible dichotomies. Using a *descending* method means starting from a more general classification which may well take the form of a broad dichotomy, and then subdividing these classes in terms of further dichotomies. Now when a subject uses the second method, it usually means that he is anticipating, and as a result he tends to have less difficulty in using hindsight later on in order to change his criteria. Conversely, using the ascending method generally means that the subject deals with each element as and when he comes to it: there is no anticipation, and consequently, when we tell him to change the criterion, we tend to find rigidity, instead of the flexibility associated with hindsight.

The striking fact is that all these children of stage II use the ascending method. Bla makes a pattern of complex objects, then he makes up five small collections and cannot reduce them to a dichotomy without trial-and-error. The behaviour of Nyf is very similar. Jae eventually divides the material into squares and circles, but he too begins by studying the shapes one at a time. Duc and Roh start with small piles and fail to find any satisfactory dichotomy. Lie has three collections to start with; when he manages to discover that the material can be dichotomized into squares and circles, he hangs on rigidly to this one idea. Ros and Kun have less trouble in finding the dichotomy of red versus blue, but they too start from a multiplicity of smaller collections. In other words, not one of three children begins with a systematic survey of the material, formulates a plan, and then carries it through. What they do is to make up little collections right away, which means setting about the actual classification without any anticipation whatever, and discovering the contents of the inventory as they go along. Yet they were all asked to describe the material first, before classifying it, and the verbal description was designed to help them form an anticipatory schema. However, the descriptions they did offer were no more than incomplete enumerations in random order, and they show little relation with the behaviour which follows. For example, Duc seems to start with a dichotomous description ("circles, squares"), but he then gives an inadequate account of the relations of size ("big circles, little squares"), and he makes no mention whatever of the fact that there are two colours. When he comes to classify the material, he makes six little collections and eventually sorts them into the two boxes in a manner which bears no relation to the verbal description.

If there is little flexibility in hindsight when children use the ascending method, the reason is not far to seek. We have only to look at the lack of anticipatory mobility which springs from the same causes. Using an ascending method means looking for the *maximum similarity* among elements which go to form a class, and the effect is of course that the *extension* of such classes is correspondingly reduced. So the child begins with little collections and then goes on grouping these step by step until he finally reaches the widest classes in the system. Using a *descending* method means looking for the most general properties, i.e. the *extension* is *maximal* and the *intension* is therefore *minimal*. Only then does the child go on to subdivide in terms of specific properties. But he must have anticipated these subdivisions beforehand because he could hardly have found the most general properties without considering the various criteria and choosing the divisions in the light of these criteria. The fact that he has to make this choice beforehand explains why he finds it easier later on to alter the criteria, for he must have been aware of these possibilities when making the first choice. Now it is true that an ascending order *can* go hand in hand with anticipation and with flexibility in hindsight. But it *need* not do so. Instead the child may very well set about the task empirically, taking just one step at a time. In that case, he makes up every one of his little collections of elements which share a maximum of intension without regard for any of the others; then he groups them into larger collections on the basis of the chance influence of one property or another, usually one that happened to strike him in the last of his smaller collections. At no point will he be making a conscious selection. This explains why, when he is asked to try to find an alternative classification, he is rather more likely to hit upon the same property as the one which struck him before than he is to discover a new dichotomy. Unlike the child who uses the descending method, he has not made a systematic inventory of the material and he has never made a conscious choice.

However, the ascending method and the descending methods are two extremes and between them we may find a wide variety of intermediate reactions. These again, fall into two groups. Either the subject begins the classification using the ascending method which means tackling the problem piecemeal, but then starts looking ahead, and these belated anticipations may still help him when he is asked for alternative classifications. Alternatively he may start with a dichotomy without anticipating all the possibilities, and then find himself reduced to trial-and-error at some later stage. Both types of reaction are especially common about the age of 6 to 7. The following are examples:

DES (6; 9) starts with a dichotomy: "*Squares and circles.*—How many boxes will you need?—*Two for the squares and the circles.*—Can you do it differently (mixing them together)?—(He puts the large red squares, the small red circles and the small blue circles in I, and the large blue circles, the small red squares and the small blue squares in II. Each collection is divided into three sub-collections, so that the grouping as a whole shows a kind of balance.)—Do they go well together?—*Oh, no!* (he puts all the red elements in I and the blue ones in II).—Will that do?—*Yes, because these are the colours.*—Can it be done differently?—(He starts separating the squares and circles, as in the beginning.)—And differently?—*I really don't know . . . All the small ones with the small ones, and the large ones with the large ones.*" The yellow square is then introduced, and he reclassifies the elements by shape.

MAR (6; 10) starts with eight piles, which he arranges in four boxes in such a way as to observe the three criteria of size, shape and colour. When he is asked to put the elements in two boxes, he divides them successively into blue versus red, squares versus circles, and large versus small.

ART (7; 0) starts with three collections: the large squares, the large circles and the small elements (subdivided according to shape and colour). "Can you divide them into two boxes (the experimenter does not mix the elements together, as he is looking for a verbal anticipation)?—*Squares and circles.*—And differently (again without mixing the elements)?—*One could put the blue circles with the blue squares, and the red with the red.*—Is there yet another way?—*No.*—(The cards are mixed again.)—(He divides them according to size.) *Here they're big and there they're small.*"

Finally, we come to cases of clear-cut anticipation, where the child begins with a dichotomy, following the descending method, and has no difficulty in changing the criterion:

PER (7; 1). "What are these?—*Squares and circles.*—How many boxes will you need?—*Two. The large squares in the first, large circles in the second . . . four altogether* (foreseeing the same dichotomy for the small elements).—Can you sort them using two boxes only?—*Squares and circles.*—Can one do it differently?—*Yes, all the red together and all the blue together.*—And differently still?—*All the big ones together and the small ones together.*" When the large yellow square is added, Per foresees the two possible classifications, one by shape and one by size.

MOU (7; 6). "What do you see?—*Squares and circles, small ones and large ones.*—How many piles will you make?—Three, no, four (forms a two-by-two matrix and subdivides according to colour).—Try using two boxes only—*The squares and the circles.*—Can you do it differently?—*Yes, the blue ones and the red ones.*"

GIL (8; 0) first divides the elements into red and blue. When they are mixed together again, he classes them as squares and circles. "Can you do it differently?—*Yes, all the big ones together and all the little ones together.*"

These replies suggest a quite different attitude from those we saw earlier. Instead of dealing with the problems of classification piecemeal, first seeking out which elements have most in common and then combining these little groups by trial-and-error, children at stage III go straight for the most general characters and only then do they subdivide the major classes. They know what it means for a characteristic to be general, one which applies to all the elements in the set (shape, colour and size) and they can therefore anticipate these several dichotomies. All this suggests that the anticipatory flexibility is what accounts for the flexibility in hindsight when a change of intension is called for.

We can prove the point only by studying anticipation as such, and this we shall be doing in the next section, where the subject is required to say how he would classify the objects before actually doing so. All we can show now is that these children, who can alter the basis of their classifications by shifting their criteria, can also preserve the integrity of the classes they construct even if we mix up the sub-classes of which they are made up. Now this might seem self-evident and therefore not very instructive. But in fact it is a sure sign that a child is freeing himself from the actual overt behaviour of making piles and subdividing them, and is substituting the mental operations of union or dichotomy, which imply the conservation of the whole through any transformation in the spatial arrangement of its parts:

Our first example may be taken as an illustration of stage II:

DEI (5; 5). When the experimenter jumbles the circles together, after Dei has subdivided them into red and blue, he reacts as follows: "Do they still go together?—*No, they don't go together, because they've been disarranged.*—But what are they?—*Circles.*—Well then, do they go together?— . . ."

Statements like this, of course, leave some room for doubt because the child may simply think that he is being asked whether the elements are properly arranged. But it is significant that at stage II he cannot dissociate the notions of "going together" and being "well arranged", while he can at stage III.

PHI (7; 2) classes the elements by shape, and divides the squares into large and small ones. The box is then shaken so that everything is jumbled together. "Is it still right?—*It isn't the same, because they aren't all in line any more. But they are all squares, and they do go together.*"

CHE (7; 3) divides the elements into red and blue, and then subdivides them into squares and circles. The blue elements are disarranged: "Do they still go well together?—*No, because they're circles and squares . . . Yes, because they're blue!*"

NEM (7; 5) puts the squares together, and divides them into the sub-classes of large and small ones. "*They go together, but they're all untidy.*"

HER (7; 6). Id.: "*They're arranged differently.*—But do they go together or not?—*No . . . yes, one can put them together. They aren't the same size, but they're square just the same.*"

It seems then that there is a close relationship between the ability to rearrange the criteria of classification, anticipating the classes beforehand, and handling classes conceptually independently of their spatial configuration. In order to say just what this relationship is, and in what order these different forms of flexibility develop, we have to proceed to a further refinement in method.

3. ANTICIPATION, EXECUTION AND CHANGE OF CRITERION IN PARTLY SPONTANEOUS CLASSIFICATIONS

The preceding results seem to indicate that flexibility in hindsight is a direct function of flexibility in anticipation. We have also suggested that anticipation can be recognized by the fact that a child can put into operation a plan which is more or less complete, instead of feeling his way as he goes along. Our estimate of the degree of hindsight was based on the ease with which he could shift from one criterion to another. We have to verify the hypothesis that the latter depends on the former, and there is a very simple way of doing so. We simply ask the child to state what he intends doing, and we then compare his verbal formulation with the actual classifications and subsequent changes of criterion. We shall describe an experiment in which this is done. The objects used are similar to those of the preceding experiments, but there are three shapes, three colours and two sizes. The classifications to be carried out are partly spontaneous. The child is not obliged to construct any dichotomies; he is simply asked to reduce the initial collections to a smaller number (and this is followed by a request for other possible classifications).

Eighteen cards were used and these were arranged in a standard way on a large sheet of paper so that they were completely jumbled. There were 6 circles, of which 3 were large (6 cm. in diameter) and 3 small (3 cm.); 6 squares, of which 3 were large (of side 6 cm.) and 3 small (3 cm.); and 6 right-angled isosceles triangles, of which 3 were large

216

(the equal sides being 6 cm.) and 3 small (3 cm.). Each set of three consisted of one red, one blue and one yellow element.

We also had a set of empty envelopes and the subject was asked to envisage the distribution of the cards in the envelopes, and to write on each envelope what its contents would be: "You have to try and put everything in order. All the things which are the same will go in one envelope, so that we can write on the envelope whatever will be inside. You must take as few envelopes as possible." Once the child had examined the objects to be classified, he was asked the following questions, always in the same order: (1) How many envelopes are necessary? (2) What must be written on these envelopes? (3) Point out what will go in each envelope.

If the child suggests using six different envelopes for his first projected classification, he is asked to use a smaller number.

Once the first project has been completed and the child has succeeded in finding a general criterion, he is asked to class the elements differently. This means asking the same questions as in §2, involving a change of criterion. But all this is still at the level of verbal anticipation. If a second criterion is discovered, we go on to ask for a third.

We now ask the subject to do the classification and he is free to carry it out in any way he chooses. He may put one or other of his projects into execution, or he may even execute all of them at once, in the form of a pattern based on several criteria.

For several groups of subjects, we introduced a number of variations in the experiment. These do not figure in our numerical results, although they did provide useful supplementary evidence. The main variation consisted in presenting the elements one by one, in a fixed order which was deliberately made random, and asking the subject to describe each one. We then hid the material and asked him how he would classify it. Strangely enough, the anticipation seems to be facilitated by the preliminary enumeration more than it is retarded by the fact that the things are hidden. In other cases, the subject was told that another child had taken two envelopes only (or three only), and was asked to say how the child had managed to classify the elements. If necessary, two objects would be placed on the envelope, to see whether he could complete the suggested classification. Finally, some of the subjects were asked questions bearing on the quantification of extension.

Before proceeding to the results we would like to put in two words of caution. In the first place, we can only speak of anticipation when the subject produces a preliminary project without verbal trial-and-error. A child who has to feel his way when saying what he might do, and then feels his way when he actually does it, can hardly be said to have anticipated. All we can say is that he lacks the necessary anticipatory schema to dispense with both kinds of trial-and-error.

In the second place, we should not exaggerate the significance of this sort of evidence. What we really want to know is how far the subject can form the sort of anticipatory schema that goes with operational classification. In other words we are interested in the *form* of classification, which should be an ordered system of inclusions, which means that the whole set is broken up into disjoint classes and these are then subdivided. In addition the child may realize a number of alternative schemes, involving shifting criteria, so that main criteria can become subordinate and vice versa. In practice the kind of anticipation we get deals simultaneously with *form and content*; in other words, the subject tells us what will happen to the actual objects. It is not easy to study the anticipation of form directly without introducing some kind of abstract symbolism which would take us far beyond the level of our subjects' understanding. (We can separate form and content more easily in seriation than in classification: in ch. IX we show how young children can often draw the general form of a serial arrangement without being able to anticipate the seriation of the actual things; but one conclusion is then unavoidable: the form in question is not an operational structure but a "graphic" structure.) It follows that we are interested not only in complete anticipation, which would mean being able to tell in advance just how many envelopes will be needed, anticipating the various classes and sub-classes, and above all faithfully carrying out exactly what was anticipated; we are at least as interested in partial anticipation, because partial anticipation helps to reveal the structure as such, or at least shed some light on the various levels through which that structure is achieved.

Table XIX shows the degree of anticipation as revealed in the initial classification, without taking changes of criteria into account. These results are based on 93 subjects, with the standard method used throughout (as opposed to prior enumeration):

Table XIX. *Anticipation of the first classification by age* (%)

Age (no. of subjects)	4 (12)	5 (20)	6 (18)	7 (16)	8 (14)	9 (13)
A. No anticipation	75	65	22·2	12·5	7·2	7·7
B. Partial anticipation	25	25	22·2	43·75	42·8	30·8
C. Complete anticipation	0	10	55·6	43·75	50	61·5
B + C. Partial or complete anticipation	25	35	77·8	87·5	92·8	92·3

If we look at row C, we note the fact that there is no progress in complete anticipation between the ages of 6 and 8. Indeed, there may be regression. Looking at the last row of the table, we find a steady improvement with increase in age. Nevertheless, the important point is that even at 6, 75% of our subjects show either partial or complete anticipation. At the ages of 7–8 a child who is capable of changing criteria, and seeing two or three possible classifications from the beginning, may hesitate in choosing the content of his classification and confine himself to anticipating its form. Such a child would figure in Table XIX as showing only partial anticipation.

When we look at the ability to change the initial criterion, we find that it appears a year or two later. Table XX shows the frequency of such changes of criterion. These results were obtained with 86 of our 93 subjects (7 did not complete this part of the test). The first classification could be based on colour, shape or size (although, in fact, none of the subjects started with size, a number used the criterion of size for the first sub-classes). This means that there were two ways of changing the criterion.

Table XX. *Changes of criterion obtained after the initial classification given in Table XIX (%)*

Age (no. of subjects)	4 (8)	5 (20)	6 (17)	7 (17)	8 (12)	9 (12)
A No change of criterion	87·5	40	35·3	11·7	16·7	8·3
B One or two changes by trial-and-error	12·5	60	58·8	70·6	8·3	33·3
C One or two changes made immediately	0	0	5·9	17·7	75	58·4
B + C	12·5	60	64·7	88·3	83·3	91·7

Immediate changes of criterion do not reach the level of 75% until 8; and even allowing for trial-and-error (B + C) the changes do not reach this level until 7 years.[1] Evidently systematic changes of criteria demand an operational level of thinking, even though partial or complete anticipation of the first classification, which occurs at 6 years (Table XIX), did not. Let us go on to consider the reason for the difference in level. We need to know exactly what it means when a child shows anticipation or semi-anticipation without operational reasoning. This should elucidate the true role of these various levels of anticipation in the construction of an operational schema of classification.

We can find out the answer by studying each stage of development from each of the three relevant standpoints: anticipation of the initial classification (Table XIX), changes of criterion (Table XX), and relations between large classes or collections (properly definable by a single criterion: shape *or* colour *or* size) and smaller ones (definable by a combination of two or more criteria).

[1] The results obtained in §2 (Table XVIII) were better because we were using 2 colours, 2 shapes and 2 sizes, instead of 3 colours, 3 shapes and 2 sizes.

During the first stage (4–5½ years), the subject cannot find a general criterion for the projected classification or if he does it is only after fairly prolonged trial-and-error. The actual classification is not much better,[1] and although it may at times be rather more rapid, it does not necessarily agree with the anticipation. As for changing the criterion, some fail this outright (perseveration, etc.), while others do modify their first classification, but only to jumble the various aspects instead of discovering a stable alternative criterion. The actual collections are a mixture of large and small collections, with the latter predominating. They also show a lack of homogeneity within the behaviour of any one subject.

A second stage (6–7 years), shows three related developments. In the first place, we now find a sort of semi-anticipation (which may be partial or complete in the sense of Table XIX). This is not a graphic anticipation like that we find from the age of 5 (55%) or 6 (73%) in seriation (ch. IX, §2, Table XXIV), nor is it the anticipation of transformations, which is a later development related to the formation of inclusion. What is anticipated are the actions involved in combining elements and piling them together on the basis of their similarities. In other words the anticipation refers to the collections as such, i.e. as so many static combinations. In the second place, the anticipation is limited to the first classification, subsequent criteria being found by overt trial-and-error, if at all (in contrast to what we found in §2 where the possibilities were restricted, $2 \times 2 \times 2$ as opposed to $3 \times 3 \times 2$). Altogether, there is little flexibility in changing criteria, and hardly any such changes are "immediate", in the sense that the new criterion creates a fresh anticipation. In the third place, the first anticipations (which start at this stage) bear on the larger collections only, i.e. red, blue and yellow, or squares and circles, not on the smaller ones, e.g. large red squares. But when the subject proceeds to the execution of his plan, he starts with the small collections and builds from these, using the "ascending" method. Towards the second half of this stage, we tend to find some kind of "mixed" behaviour, with alternation of the "ascending" and "descending" methods. The differentiation of the large collections now leads to changes of criteria through trial-and-error. However, it is essential to note that the descending process which occurs in this mixed type of behaviour is still far from being the exact inverse of the ascending process: the sub-collections constructed by differentiation remain separate instead of giving rise to immediate combinations; conversely, the actual combinations are performed with little awareness of the inverse

[1] This stage corresponds to that of graphic collections. But the construction of these is excluded by the procedure itself (the use of envelopes). It often happens that a subject ignores the envelopes, and starts to construct complex objects on the table.

relation connecting collections with their sub-collections (there is as yet no inclusion).

The third stage (starting at 7–8 years) is marked by a new type of anticipation, one that refers to transformations as opposed to static collections, as well as showing an understanding of inclusion. The schema of inclusion may begin as a mere form in search of content. This is what happens when the very diversity of possible criteria makes it difficult for the subject to decide on his first classification without trial-and-error. Alongside this development in anticipation, we find a correspondingly greater flexibility in changing criteria: sometimes an alternative criterion is adopted immediately, while at others the new classification may be preceded by trial-and-error, but even the trial-and-error shows that the subject is aware of the different possibilities. Finally, children now show equal facility with the two methods, ascending and descending. Indeed the two have now become one, since each is the inverse of the other when the classification is seen as a set of possible transformations governed by the reversible operations of combination and dissociation.

Here are examples of these different stages, starting with stage I:

JUL (4; 9). The situation is first explained. "How many envelopes will you need for putting all this in order?—(Takes the large yellow square.)—*This one*.—But how many envelopes for all of them, when the same ones are put together?— . . . —A few or a lot?—*A lot*.—Well, what will go into the first envelope?—(He again points to the large yellow square.)—And what else?— *That* (the large red circle).—Is it the same thing?—*Yes*.—Why?— . . . —If it's the same envelope, you must put in things which really are the same.—(He points to the small blue circle.)—What else?—(Large yellow square.)—*With the square* (he also points to the large blue triangle).—Are these four the same?— . . . —Show me which things are alike.—(He points to the large yellow square and the large red circle.)—Are they really the same?—*Yes*.— Why?—*This and this* (pointing to the large yellow square and the large blue triangle).—Why?—*Because they have to go together in the envelopes*.—But look at all these, there are a lot of things. Are there any which are alike?— *Yes* (points to the different squares, of various colours and sizes).—Good. Well, what will one write on the envelope with all these things?—*Whatever is inside*.—Well, what should one write?—*A square*.—One or several?—*Several*. —How many more envelopes?—*These* (he points to the six circles, indicating the small blue one twice).—What should be written on the envelope?—*Several circles*.—And now, how many more envelopes are needed?— . . . —How many to put everything in order?— . . . —What will be put in the new envelope?— . . . *That, that, that* (pointing out some of the triangles).—What shall we write?—*Several roofs*.—And how many more envelopes?— . . . — Well, what shall we put in this?—*The circles*.—And here?—*The squares*.— And there?—*The roofs*."

"Now try to put things in order differently, by putting different lots in the envelopes. Do you have any idea?—*Yes*.—How many will you need?—*Three*.

—What will you put in the first?—(He points to the three small circles, which seems to suggest a classification by size.)—What will you write on it?—*The circles.*—And on the other envelope?—*The roofs*—(pointing to the six triangles).—And on the other?—*The squares.*—Are any more envelopes necessary?—*You need more.*—Is it different from before, or the same?—*Not the same.*—Why isn't it the same?—*Because the roofs . . .*—Well, how is it different?—*The circles.*—Why are they different?—*They have to be arranged.*" The anticipation is discontinued at this point, and Jul arranges the circles to form a sort of collective object, made up of three pairs two of which have a large circle on the left and a small one on the right, while the third is the other way around. The first pair consists of blue circles, and the others consist of one red circle and one yellow.

A third classification is attempted, but Jul returns to the criterion of shape. Some questions on the use of "all" are asked, and the answers are wrong every time. For example, Jul states that all the squares are large. "And are all the large ones squares?—*Yes.*—Look carefully.—*No, squares and circles* (forgetting the triangles)," etc.

FEL (5; 0). This child is asked to put "the same ones" together, and to say how many envelopes will be necessary. She points to the small yellow triangle. "And what else?—(Points to the large blue triangle).—Why?—*It's just like that.*—And next?—(She points to the small red square and then the large blue circle.) *No.* (Points to the small yellow square.)—Next?—(Points to the large blue circle and the large red one, then to the large red and yellow squares.)— Have you pointed to all of them?—*Yes.*—How many envelopes will be needed? —(She points to two large squares, two small triangles, two small squares and two small circles.)—And then?—*Nothing at all.*—Is that really everything?— *There are still two small circles.*—Is that all?—*Yes.*—How many envelopes does that make?—*Three.*—What will you put in the first one?—*Two circles, square circles.*[1]—Which?—*These* (large blue and yellow squares).—And next? —*And then these* (two small circles).—In the same envelope?—*No.*—And next?—The two circles (already pointed out).—We've already written them. And next?—*That* (small yellow triangle).—All on its own?—*No, with this* (small blue triangle).—Why?—*Because it's the same*—Are there any others which are the same?—*No, yes these two* (large triangles), *because they're bigger.*—Are there any others which are the same?—*Yes, there's still this one* (large blue triangle)," etc. Helped by the questions put by the experimenter, Fel finally describes three envelopes headed: "*The circles*"—"*The square circles*" and "*The roofs of houses*".

The experimenter then tries to induce a change of criterion by starting again. She points to two large squares and then a small one, and says "*This one is smaller. This one too. They're smaller.*" She notices the same difference of size in the circles and triangles, and decides to take "*seven envelopes* (of which six are actually described): *the large house roofs and the small ones.*—And next?—*The large circles and the small circles.*—And next?—*The small squares.*

---

[1] This nice way of describing them, "square circles", corresponds to an intuition which is intermediate between the topological notion of a closed figure (= a circle, taken as the genus), and the Euclidean notion of a square (being the species).

—And next?—*The large squares.*—Could one do it with less?—(She removes the seventh envelope.)—And with three?—*No.*"

In the actual construction, Fel manages, by trial-and-error, to make up three collections of large circles, squares and triangles. She places the small circles, squares and triangles on top of these.

These two examples of the first stage show why any anticipation is impossible at this level. The initial failures are revealing; but so also are the partial successes due to the experimenter's questions.

The child completely fails to foresee a classification, although he can construct graphic and even non-graphic collections, based on similarities and differences. The reason is that when he is merely thinking of a collection, he forgets what he said a moment before. On the other hand, when he is actually building one, the results of previous actions remain perceptible and guide his subsequent choices. In order to anticipate we have to remember, because all but the first choices have to be based on those that precede. This is precisely what our subjects cannot do on their own. The experimenter's questions, however, taken together with the child's answers, provide a verbal context which is just enough to allow some co-ordination between the immediate past and the immediate future. Without it, there can be no anticipation. Once again, we may note the tie-up between anticipation and hindsight. But at stage I the co-ordination is not yet spontaneous, as it will be at stage II.

We may begin to analyse the process in detail by starting from the successive assimilations which we find at the outset. The child sees the material for the first time, he has no idea how he will arrange it inside the envelopes, and he does not know how many of these he will require. Now Jul happens to fasten on the large yellow square. His next choice is the large red circle, either because of its size, or because both are closed figures. For all we know, the assimilation is based on some kind of belonging. But now we insist on similarity. So Jul goes on to a small blue circle (because it is a circle), and then to a large blue triangle (because it is blue). Jul cannot think back to the reasons which governed his choices as he made them; *a fortiori*, he cannot choose one out of several possible schemata in order to guide his future assimilations. In other words, where there is no hindsight, anticipation is out of the question. But when the experimenter goes on to say: "You look at all this lot. There are lots of shapes. Are any of them similar?", he manages to find all the squares after starting with one, and he now sees that they might all go in a single envelope. On being encouraged to continue, he mentally collects "several circles", followed by "this and this and this", i.e. "several roofs". We see very much the same sequence in the interview with Fel. First she assimilates in pairs, without considering more than one pair at a time: two triangles, then two squares, then two circles, then two more squares, and, last of all, two small circles. Yet she too manages to sort out the three shapes and choose three envelopes when she is helped by the experimenter's questions.

We can now see the principal obstacles to anticipation, and we can also see what must be the necessary conditions for anticipation to occur at all. There can be no anticipation so long as the child deals with each item as he comes to it. The paradox is that the failure to anticipate what comes next is the sure result of not being able to go back over the steps which took him where he is. He starts from *A* and moves through *B* to *C*; but since he cannot reconstruct the reasons which led him from *A* to *C*, he can hardly be expected to know where to look for *D* and *E* which lie ahead. Conversely, as soon as there is retrospection there is hindsight in the sense of a conscious awareness of the schema which governed the actions in the immediate past ("the squares", etc.); and as soon as there is hindsight there is anticipation. To begin with the hindsight is limited to this sort of awareness of the assimilatory schema as it actually operated, but very soon after the hindsight leads to some kind of restructurization: having found the schema, the subject will begin to systematize it, or to subdivide it, and so on. When the hindsight is active in this sense, the anticipation also takes on an increasing measure of precision and detail, and this is what we begin to find at stage II.

Now at stage II there is a measure of spontaneous anticipation, while at stage I there is no anticipation whatever unless the experimenter draws it out by repeated questions and answers. Even at stage II we still find that the less mature reactions are confined to the semi-anticipation of static collections, and the only difference is that they are spontaneous. When he is telling us what he thinks he can do, the subject mentions large collections first and does not think of subdivisions until later; but when he actually does it, he begins with small collections and feels his way bit by bit in order to group them together. The anticipation tends to conform to what we called the descending method while the actual classification is nearer the ascending method: the two processes are not synthesized, which means that there is no reversibility. We begin with some of these earlier examples, and the reader will find that they also show a certain lack of flexibility in changing criteria:

Wut (5; 10). "How many envelopes are needed, few or many?—*Few*.—Three, four?—*Four*.—Four or eight?—*Four*.—What will you put in these envelopes? —*Some circles* (pointing to the first envelope).—And in this one?—*Some squares*.—And in this one?—*Some triangles*.—Will you want another envelope or is that all?—*That's all*.—Can't we put anything in these envelopes over here?—*Yes, some circles*.—Show me.—*These*.—Is that all?—*These* (two large and two small circles).—And in this envelope?—*These* (a large and a small square).—Is that all?—*Yes*.—Show me again.—(She points out five.)—And in another envelope?—*These* (the triangles)."

"Could one do it in another way with more or with fewer envelopes?—*With more.*—(There are several attempts, but they all end with the three collections: squares, circles and triangles.)"

The actual classification, however, starts from small collections: the three large squares and the three small ones, the three large circles and the three small ones, the three large triangles and the three small ones. Then she starts again on the basis of colour, but also taking shape and size into account. In this way, she constructs two patterns in succession. These are based on three criteria, and but for a number of asymmetries, they would constitute a correct matrix. The first consists of three rows one above the other, made up of the triangles, squares and circles respectively. Each row has three small elements on the left and three large ones on the right, and each triple is arranged according to the three colours (but the arrangement of red and blue is inverted in the row of squares). The second pattern consists of three pairs of columns, one pair being red, one yellow and one blue. The left-hand column of each pair contains the small elements and the right-hand column contains the large ones, but here the arrangement of the red columns is inverted. The elements in each column are arranged vertically in the order: squares, circles, triangles; but there are some inversions.

RAP (6; 10). "How many envelopes are needed?—(He looks at the set of objects.) *Two.*—Are you quite sure?—*Yes*—What will be written on the first one?—*The circles.*—And on the second?—*The squares.*—Will everything be in order then?—*No.*—How many more envelopes are needed?—*One.*—And what will be written on it?—*The roofs.*—Will everything be in order?—*Yes.*—There will be enough envelopes?—*Yes.*"

In the actual construction, however, Rap forms six small collections by distinguishing the large and the small elements of each form. He even hesitates before combining them into larger collections. For example, to the large and small triangles, we have this sequence: "Can you put them together?—*No, one can't. I have to take the small ones away.*—But are they alike in some way? —*They're the same but some of them are smaller.*" When asked for changes of criteria Rap falls back on the same six solutions. He finally agrees to combine these in three collections, which he calls *"large and small squares, because they're all squares,"* etc. But he fails our questions on the quantification of inclusion, arguing that there are as many small squares as squares, because he compares the small squares with the large ones instead of with all the squares.

GRA (6; 10). "How many envelopes are needed?—*To put all the squares, the large ones and the small ones, in the same envelope?*—As you like. How many envelopes do you need?—*Three.*—What will be written on the first one?—*Triangles.*—And then?—*Circles.*—And then?—*Squares.*—Is that all? —*Yes.*" Gra then turns to the actual classification and remarks: *"There are three of each colour."* She arranges the elements in sub-collections consisting of the large and small squares, triangles and circles. The experimenter points to the large and small squares: "Can one mix them?—*No.*—Will they go all right together?—*No . . . yes, because they're all the same shape.*"

The objects are put back in their original positions, and a new classification is asked for. "Do you think you can put them in order in a different way?— *Yes, with six envelopes.*" She foresees the six small collections that have already been constructed in the actual classification.

"Try to find a different way.—*Yes, I know, with eighteen envelopes* (one for each element)." She then falls back on the six previous collections: "How many envelopes for these?—*Six.*—Do you think that you could use less?—*Two.*—How?—*Like this and like this* (indicating all the large ones and all the small ones).—What would one write?—*Large circles, triangles and squares, and small circles, small triangles and small squares.*—In one word?—*Small surfaces and large surfaces.*" The questions on the quantification of inclusion are nevertheless answered wrong.

Finally, we come to cases showing greater facility in passing from sub-collections to collections and vice versa, although still short of the complete reversibility characteristic of stage III.

MAR (6; 11) starts by foreseeing the need for five envelopes: the large circles, the small ones, the large squares, the large roofs, and the small roofs. She then adds the small squares, making six. "Could one put these things in order with fewer envelopes?—*Yes, One could take the large squares and the small squares* (together), *the large roofs and the small roofs, the large circles and the small circles.*—How many envelopes does that make?—(She counts.) —*Three.*—And what would one write?—(Same long formula.)—Just one word?—*Squares, roofs, and circles.*"

Asked to anticipate a different classification, she describes the large squares, circles and roofs separately. "What does that leave?—*The small roofs, the small circles and the small squares.*" (This would appear to be the same classification as before. But there is a significant difference in that the preceding classification started with six sub-collections and then combined them into three collections based on shape, while this one starts with two collections based on size, and then subdivides them.)

The actual classification results in three collections based on shape, each being subdivided into two sub-collections according to size "*because I've separated the small ones and the large ones*".

CRO (7; 9). "How many envelopes?—*Four.*—The first one is for?—*The squares.*—The second?—*For the triangles.*—The third?—*For the circles.*—And the next?—*The next one is for the small squares.*—Is that all?—*No, there are two more for the small triangles and the small circles.*—How many envelopes does that make?—*Five, no six.*—Can you put things in order with fewer envelopes?—*One can take one and put everything in it, or take two and divide everything up.*—But you must have the same things in one envelope.—*One can put them all together, all the circles together, all the squares together, all the triangles together. Or else the large circles with the small circles, the large triangles with the small triangles, and one only takes three envelopes.*—What does one write on the first one?—*Large squares and small squares: the squares, of course.* If one just writes "squares", would one know what was inside?— *Yes, all the squares: big squares and little squares.*"

The actual classification follows this prevision: collections based on shape, divided subsequently into sub-collections according to size. Cro cannot find any other criterion. But after being questioned on "all", he returns spontaneously to the problem of finding new criteria and exclaims: "*Now I've got the idea, I know what to do: one can put all the big ones in a single envelope,*

and all the small ones in a single envelope too.—What would one write?—
'*All*' and '*all*', '*small things*' for all the small ones, and '*big things*' for all the
big ones."

Nevertheless, only half the questions on "all" are answered correctly. Some
of the answers are correct: "Are all the blue ones circles?—*No! Oh no,
because this one is blue and it's a triangle,*" etc. But sometimes they indicate
an incorrect quantification of the predicate: "Are all the red ones triangles?—
*No, no, there aren't only red among the triangles. There are blue ones and
yellow ones.*"

The quantification of inclusion also causes systematic difficulties. "Are
there more squares or more large squares?—*Small ones or large ones?*—More
squares altogether or more large squares?—*The same.*—How is that?— . . .
—How many squares are there altogether?—*Three. But with the large ones
and the small ones there are six.*—The squares together, does that mean the
large and the small ones together or just the small ones?—*Just the small ones.*
—Does "all the squares" mean just the small ones?—*No.*—How many squares
are there altogether?—*Six.*—And small squares?—*Three.*—And large ones?
—*Three.*—Well then, are there more squares altogether or more large squares?
—*They're both the same, the large ones and the small ones.*—What did I ask
you?—*Whether there were more small squares than large ones.*—No, I am
not asking whether there are more small ones than large ones, but whether
there are more squares altogether than large squares.—*There are more
altogether, because that makes six.*" (But we note that he is still using numbers
instead of simply comparing the part with the whole.)

To begin with, we may look at the progress achieved in relation to
stage I. What stands out is that the anticipation is spontaneous, even if
it is imperfect. Typically, these children are unable to foresee the details
of a classification (most of them do not even know how many envelopes
will be required), but they can at least adumbrate a project, because they
do manage to name one or two of the proposed collections: Wut and
Rap start off with one envelope for "the round ones", and then go on
to the squares and the triangles, etc.

What this means is that we are no longer dealing with a series of *ad hoc*
assimilations. Once a subject has assimilated a number of "round" ones,
each to its predecessors, he can go back on his moves and so discover
the assimilatory schema which he has been using and which corresponds
to the common property of these things.

Moreover, the hindsight is something more than a matter of remembering a set of connexions. There is also a beginning of systematization
about its working inasmuch as the objects are continually being sorted
throughout the process of scanning itself. There are several possibilities
but the subject abstracts one of these. This sort of re-appraisal is of
course of the very nature of hindsight; it goes on alongside the successive
assimilations, and eventually gives rise to an anticipatory schema. To
begin with anticipation is simply a matter of looking for other "round

ones", but inevitably the child is then led on to look for other shapes like squares and "roofs". All this is new at stage II.

Now it is no accident that the youngest of our subjects, even though they are at stage II, tend to anticipate in one way and classify in another. When they are actually grouping objects they start from small collections and gradually build up larger ones, but before they begin, many of them (like Wut, Rap and Gra) think of the bigger collections first, and they may then be unable to subdivide these further. The actual classification follows the ascending pattern, while the anticipation suggests an abortive descending pattern.

True, this sort of thing is by no means universal. The true measure of the level of a subject is the flexibility he shows in shifting from small to large or from large to small, not which kind of collection he starts from. The children we mentioned are less advanced because they cannot synthesize the ascending and descending methods, not because they think of large classes first. Nevertheless, we are bound to ask why they do so. One possible answer might be that the anticipation itself follows the ascending method, just as the actual grouping, but that the subject does not become aware of the intermediate steps. But we have to rule this out, because a child who did just this would hardly find it so difficult to anticipate subdivision. The only answer that remains is that, unlike the actual classifications of these children, their mental classification can sometimes hit on the most general properties right away—because they are mentally considering similarities covering the collection as a whole rather than taking each element as it comes. In other words the interaction of hindsight and anticipation as we described it is still the one thing which allows the subject to start from large classifications. Before this time the only possible method was to take each element separately, which is why this method was universal at stage I, while even at stage II it is usually the one favoured in the actual classification.

As to the limitations to the anticipation found at stage II, these are once more a matter of limited flexibility. Near the beginning of the stage it is easy to tell that our subjects find it difficult to switch from one method to another: they cannot anticipate subdivisions when using the descending method, yet a moment later they start with these when actually classifying—and now they find it difficult to get back to the major collections they anticipated (Rap for triangles and Gra for squares). Inability to shift from one criterion to another is yet another corollary to the failure to combine the two methods, because changing the criterion means taking the smaller collections as the major ones and vice versa, which is easy enough, but only if one can pass freely from the ascending method to the descending method and back. (The only *prima facie* exception to our analysis is Wut, who seems to have mastered all these transformations and manages to construct two three-entry tables one after another, apparently changing her criteria for the second: but a closer study of the protocol as a whole shows quite clearly that the success is intuitive and not a case of true anticipation.)

As we come to study subjects who are more advanced (beginning with Gra) we begin to see greater flexibility in the transitions between small collections and large ones, and this argues a measure of synthesis between the ascending method and the descending method: these children anticipate the subdivisions and they can also re-group sub-collections to find the original collection (cf. Cro, "the squares, of course!"). Nevertheless, they are still unable to discover all the possible changes of criteria and tend to omit one of the three possibilities: shape, colour, or size. More significantly, they still make systematic errors when answering questions about "some" and "all" (see ch. III); and in spite of the fact that they have just handled the material involved, they still fail to quantify inclusions (see ch. IV). A striking example of this last is the resistance shown by Cro to the suggestion that the large squares must be fewer than the squares "as a whole".

In conclusion we might say that children at stage II show spontaneous hindsight and even foresight, but both processes apply to the configurations as they stand (i.e. to the actual collections, which remain pre-logical even though they are no longer tied to a graphic image). They cannot bring these same processes to bear on the transformations. The criterion of this must be the ability to pass freely from the ascending method to the descending method and vice versa. In other words, children at stage III will be in a position to anticipate simultaneously both the several unions ($A + A' = B$) and the corresponding subdivisions ($B - A' = A$). When this happens, retroaction and anticipation reach a level of operational reversibility, and it is this which finally allows the subject to master inclusion. We have already seen, on many occasions, that inclusion is based on an understanding of the relation $A = B - A'$ and what this means is that the interplay of anticipation and hindsight must bear on transformations.

At the beginning of stage III, many subjects do not anticipate more than two of the three possible criteria, although every one of the following subjects illustrates operational reversibility. By the age of 9 or 10, children usually anticipate all three criteria right from the start.

Vui (7; 6). "How many envelopes will be needed?—*The same colours or the same shapes?*—Just as you like.—*The triangles, the squares and the circles.*— You mentioned another idea, didn't you?—*Yes, three envelopes: the red ones, the yellow ones and the blue ones.*—Is there a third way?— . . ."
In the actual classification he places three rows on top of each other, these rows consisting of the large circles, the large squares and the large triangles respectively. These are arranged so that the column on the right is yellow, that in the centre is red, and that on the left is blue. He then arranges the

small elements in the same way, thus achieving an entirely symmetrical pattern based on three criteria.

NIC (8; 10). "How many envelopes?—*Does it matter if they aren't the same colour?*[1]—As you like. How many envelopes then?—*Three.*—What shall I write?—*The circles, the squares and the triangles.*—Now put everything in order in a new way. How many envelopes will you need?—*Six.*—Good. What will you put in them?—*One for the large circles and one for the small circles, one for the large squares and one for the small squares, one for the large triangles and one for the small triangles.*—That is a second way of doing it. Can it be done in yet another way?—*Yes, the large squares, circles and triangles together, and the small squares, circles and triangles together.*—What would one write?—*The large shapes here and the small shapes there.*—Is there yet another way?—*Yes.* (She starts to suggest that the circles and squares be put together, with the triangles apart, and then she thinks of colour.) *All the things coloured yellow, all the blue things and all the red things.*"

The actual classification is unnecessary, because all the possibilities have been exhausted. The subject is asked instead to say which of her projected classifications seems the best. Nic prefers the first (shape) "*because all the things which are small are not triangles together*" etc.; in other words, because size and colour are less important than shape. The experimenter then asks the questions on "all", which are answered correctly, and on the quantification of inclusion: "Are all the red ones squares?—*No, there are two squares, two triangles and two circles.*—Are there more red ones or more red squares?—*More red ones.*—(The two red circles are removed.)—More red ones or more red squares?—*More red ones!*"

ZBI (9; 0) "How many envelopes?—*Three: the squares, the circles, the triangles.*—Can one do it in another way?—*Yes, but one would need more envelopes.*—How many?—*Six: the large squares, the small squares, the large circles, the small circles, the large triangles, the small triangles.*—And in another way?—*Yes, a large one, a small one, etc. . . . all the little things together, all the big things together. That makes two envelopes.*—And in still another way?—*All the blues, yellows and reds. That makes three envelopes again.*" He is then asked to repeat his projected classifications, and remembers them easily. He changes from one to another without any difficulty. For example: "*The envelope with all the red ones could be divided into three: the red squares, the red circles and the red triangles*". In the same way, he can go from classes based on shape to sub-classes based on colour, and from classes based on colour to sub-classes based on size, etc.

"Are all the squares blue?—*No, there are also two red and two yellow ones,*" etc. "Are there more squares or more large squares?—*More squares. There are three large squares, and adding the small ones makes six.*—More red ones or more red squares?—*More red ones, because there are also red triangles and red circles.*"

There are several new features in these reactions:

[1] This question shows that the reason for ignoring the criterion of colour (which is common) is that colour is generally thought to be less important, not that the subject is unaware of these differences.

(1) The choice of criteria is no longer based on an implicit abstraction, but involves an explicit decision. Thus Vui asks: "The same colours or the same shapes?" and Nic: "Does it matter if they aren't the same colours?"

(2) It follows from this that, once the subject has finished a classification, he can return to a criterion which has been provisionally laid aside. The whole classification can then be rearranged on the basis of this immediate retroaction (which is what constitutes genuine "shifting").

(3) On the other hand, the deliberate choice of the first schema strengthens its anticipatory character. Both hindsight and anticipation are thus reinforced, and this ensures complete flexibility when changing criteria, together with the possibility of anticipating multiplicative operations (cf. Vui's pattern based on three criteria, etc.).

(4) This complete flexibility is particularly evident when the subject can not only substitute one type of collection for another when changing his criteria, but can also combine the collections, then divide them and recombine them so there is complete reciprocity between the ascending and descending processes. Cf. Zbi's reactions to the questions on inclusion ("one could divide . . ." etc.).

(5) Anticipation becomes an anticipation not merely of configurations, but of transformations. This amounts to saying that collections and sub-collections have become classes and sub-classes. The chief sign is that the combination $A + A' = B$ is anticipated whenever B is divided into A and A' (and, conversely, their dissociation is anticipated whenever A and A' are combined). It is this advanced form of anticipation which allows the extension of a sub-class to be compared with that of the entire class, and which therefore establishes inclusion relations of the type $A < B$. (We might add that we prefer to consider this as the only true anticipation; what we saw at stage II was really only a first beginning.)

It is very obvious that the development of the operational schemata which we analysed in chs. I–VI is intimately related to these retroactive and anticipatory processes. It is the interplay of these processes which gradually leads to the reversibility on which additive (inclusion) and multiplicative relations are based. That is why a study of anticipation was essential to a complete analysis of the development of operations themselves. We can now see the causal mechanism involved.

Chapter Eight

THE CLASSIFICATION OF ELEMENTS
PERCEIVED BY TOUCH[1]

THERE are two central ideas which emerge from the preceding chapters. The first is that the origin of classification is to be sought in graphic collections, where the role of spatial configuration is less overriding than it is in perceptual structures, but is nonetheless far from insignificant, as is the case with operational structures governed by relations of inclusion. The second is that the development from graphic structures to operational structures depends on a complex interplay of retroactive and anticipatory activities. These may be grouped together under the heading of "representative regulations". We now know that they prepare the way for operational reversibility.

Both these findings suggest the relevance of an experiment designed to compare the classification of elements perceived visually with the classification of elements which can only be perceived by touch. Tactile perceptions can only occur successively and not simultaneously. The first question is therefore whether we will find any configurations corresponding to the visual graphic collections when the elements are perceived by touch, and, if not, what replaces them. We should also expect that the fact that perception is successive should systematically impede the process of hindsight. If so, we may ask how the corresponding anticipations will arise and whether they will appear rather later.

1. EXPERIMENTAL PROCEDURE

In order to have as many different experimental combinations as possible to elucidate these problems, we used two types of object and two distinct methods of procedure. (The experiment was sometimes preceded by a verbal enumeration of the objects in each case, which constitutes a third experimental variable.)

The two sets of apparatus differed in that the first contained elements identical to one another, while the second did not.

Set I: 8 curved objects and 8 rectilinear ones. The curved objects consisted of two small circles (discs 2 cm. in diameter and 2 mm. thick), two large circles (diameter, 4 cm.) two small spheres (diameter, 2 cm.) and two large ones (diameter, 4 cm.). The rectilinear objects consisted of two small squares (side, 2 cm.; thickness, 2 mm.) two large squares

[1] With the collaboration of H. Niedorf and E. Siotis.

232

(side, 4 cm.; thickness 2 mm.) two small cubes (edge, 2 cm.) and two large ones (edge, 4 cm.).

Set II: 16 wooden objects consisting of:

(1) two spheres (diameter, 2 cm. and 4 cm.);
(2) two cubes (edge, 2 cm. and 4 cm.);
(3) two cuboids (3·5 × 3·5 × 7 cm. and 1 × 1 × 5 cm.);
(4) two ellipsoids (one having semi-axes of 3·5 and 7 cm., and the other of 2·5 and 3·5 cm.);
(5) two squares (one 4 cm. and the other 2 cm., both 2 mm. thick);
(6) two discs (diameter, 2 cm. and 4 cm., both having a thickness of 2 mm.);
(7) two rectangles (6 × 3 cm. and 3 × 1·5 cm., both having a thickness of 2 mm.);
(8) two ellipses (with axes 6 cm. and 3 cm., as compared with 3 cm. and 2 cm., the thickness being 2 mm. for both).

The objects were placed inside a framework representing a little house, with walls and roof made of cloth. The child puts his hands "under the walls" to handle the objects. When a visual control experiment is carried out afterwards, the cloth is simply removed. A further control group was questioned using visual perception alone.

Procedures.—The first consisted of asking for a spontaneous classification, and then for a dichotomy (assisted by a partition). Once this had been obtained, changes of criterion were asked for. One group of subjects was asked to make a project of classification in advance, after first examining all the objects (without any time limit).[1]

This preliminary exploration could be entirely free, but occasionally we asked for a verbal enumeration. The verbal enumeration tends to make the classification somewhat easier, and more often it was omitted. But, of course, it cannot be assumed that language played no part. Even in an entirely free examination, the child may name the objects if he wishes; and, if he does not, there may still be internal language.

The second procedure consisted of imposing a dichotomy without the spontaneous classification. At the same time, we invariably asked for a classificatory project immediately after the objects were examined. Once again, the experimeter went on to look for changes of criterion. A few subjects were asked for an enumeration during the preliminary examination, but here, too, these were a minority.

Subjects.—More than 350 children were examined, their ages ranging from 4–12 years, with the majority between 5 and 10.

Stages.—The stages we observed corresponded with those found in

---

[1] If the subject fails to touch all the elements, they are placed in his hands one by one. Alternatively they are put on the left of a partition, and he is asked to transfer them all to the right.

visual classification, although we did find some slight differences: some tasks were more difficult, but others were easier!

We found two interesting reactions at stage I. In the first place, there was a tendency to make graphic collections in spite of the fact that the subject could not see the objects. They are less frequent than when he can see them, but they still have the same familiar properties. The second reaction is a more primitive one, and is a residue of what might be called sensori-motor classification. It is analogous to the reaction of children of 2-3 years, mentioned in ch. I, when they seize objects one after the other and recognize that they are "the same": the child puts the elements which he recognizes during his exploration on one side, and ignores all the others. A classification begun in this way may still end with a collection containing a class criterion, but this criterion is not formulated. What is more, the classification cannot be continued, nor can it be recognized as being a classification.

Stage II is analogous to the corresponding stage observed with a visual field. But anticipation of the first classification seems easier, and this may be because it now corresponds to a functional need due to the fact that the perceptions are successive instead of simultaneous. On the other hand, contradictions between anticipation and execution are frequent. In addition, the discovery of a second criterion seems slightly more difficult than in the visual set-up, and quite often, in trying to find one, the subject falls back on the graphic collections of stage I.

Stage III is similar to the familiar corresponding stage, except that there may be a slight advance in flexibility when changing criteria.

2. STAGE I: CHOICE OF KNOWN ELEMENTS AND GRAPHIC COLLECTIONS. NO ANTICIPATION AND NO COMPLETE CLASSIFICATIONS

Here are some examples:

Ros (4; 8). He is asked to enumerate the objects, and he names them one by one as he touches them. "Do you remember?—*A heart* (= square!), *a small ball, a small brick, a large brick.*" When he has to divide the objects into two compartments, he puts "*the bricks and the balls*" in one. "Are they alike?— *No.*—(He moves every object from the left-hand compartment to the right-hand one, naming some of them as he does so. He then says:) *These two balls are alike. The two bricks are alike.*" He puts "*the balls and the bricks*" on the left, leaving jumbled together on the right all the other objects which he does not recognize so easily. "And are they alike on this side?—*I don't know.*"

The experimenter then puts the large elements on one side and the small ones on the other, simply saying that another little boy arranged them like that. Ros cannot find a reason for doing so. The curved objects are then put on one side and the rectilinear ones on the other, this distribution also being attributed to another child: "*Yes, because he has put the small balls and the large balls over here.*—And on the other side?—*There are hearts* (= squares), *and bricks.*—And where should this one go (a cube)?—*I don't know.* (He places it among the curved objects.)"

GAL (4; 10). There is no enumeration. She examines the objects and says: "*Yes, bricks and flat ones.*" When the instruction to put together the ones which are alike is repeated, she constructs a sort of diffuse complex object. The various pairs of identical elements are invariably put close together. The large cubes are near the large spheres, but these are separated from the small spheres; the ellipse is near the cubes; the small cubes are near the large ones; etc. Gal cannot say why these objects are near each other, except for the bricks: "*The small ones are with the big ones. They're bricks.*—Show me which objects go well together.—(She points to the cubes and the spheres.)—Do they go well together?—*Yes.*—Why?—*Because.*—Are they more or less the same thing?—*No.*—Are there any others which go well together?—(She points to the two small spheres.)"

The objects are then uncovered, and Gal is asked to classify them visually. She constructs much the same complex object, making it a little more regular.

CHRI (5; 1). Asked for an enumeration, she distinguishes the balls, the bricks and the "*bits of wood*". She then constructs a complex object which is a double alignment with certain correspondences based on similarity and others based on more general relations of belonging: large cube—large square, large sphere—small ellipse, large square—large circle, large ellipse—small ellipsoid. The other objects are placed in disorder in the second compartment (these being the "*bits of wood*"). "Are the balls and the bricks alike?—*No.*—Well, should they be together?—*No.*—What should you do?—*The balls should be together and the bricks should be together.* (She places the curved objects on the left, again in a double alignment, and the rectilinear ones on the right, together with a few curved ones.)—What have you done?—*I've put the balls on this side; then I've put the little wooden things and the bricks on this side.*— Why are they different from the balls?—*There are round and square wooden things.*" When a new classification is asked for, she puts two spheres and two ellipsoids on the right and all the rest on the left: "*The balls are on this side. The little wooden things and the bricks are on the other side.*—Are the little wooden things and the bricks alike?—*No.*—Well?—*I'll put them with the balls.*"

The experimenter puts all the rectilinear objects on one side and all the curved ones on the other: "Will this do?—*No* (putting the circles and squares together again)." The visual classification also leads to the "*rounds*" on one side, and the rest on the other side.

BLA (5; 3). After an enumeration, she constructs an alignment in one compartment, consisting of a large cube, a large circle, a large square and a cuboid with a circle on it. In the other compartment, she makes another alignment starting with the large sphere and the large ellipsoid and ending with the large ellipse, with two rows of small cubes, spheres, cuboids and ellipsoids in between. She is asked to find better similarities, and starts to construct two new alignments in which it is easy to see a number of partial resemblances between neighbouring elements. Nevertheless, the juxtaposition is quite often arbitrary (for example, the small circle and the cuboid). The three-dimensional figures are then placed in one compartment and the two-dimensional ones in the other. She senses that there is some similarity between the members of each collection, but cannot express this better than by saying: "*It's because they've been cut like that.*" The visual classification is similar in type, but rather more regular.

GEO (5; 3). He enumerates the elements using such words as ball, field, square, roller, stick, circle, etc. "You try making two piles by putting together the things which go well together. Do you understand?—*Yes, I'll put a ball with a square.*—What will you put in one pile?—(He puts a large and small ellipsoid, a large cube and a large sphere in one compartment, and arranges the rest in the other compartment with a few unexpected juxtapositions.)—Do the squares and the small rollers go well together?—*Yes.*—Why?— . . ." The experimenter starts a classification based on shape, by putting the squares together. Geo cannot continue this. The complete classification based on shape does not suggest anything to him either, nor do those based on dimensionality, size, or rectilinearity versus curves.

KUN (5; 6). He starts the spontaneous classification by putting "the bricks and the square bricks" together. He then indicates the large spheres "*and the others which are big like that, and then the little ones together*". In this way, he manages to construct eight pairs of similar elements which he arranges in two alignments. One contains the two large spheres and two large cubes, but the spheres are followed by two small circles. The other contains two large circles, two small squares, and some cubes and spheres. "Could you make fewer piles?—*A square and a thin square! The fat ones and the thin ones! Then it's the same for the others afterwards.*" He constructs a long alignment of cubes and spheres, etc., putting the corresponding two-dimensional object after each one. "What have you put together?—*I've put two and two together.*"

The visual classification is of the same type: one long alignment of which the first half is formed of three-dimensional objects and the second of the corresponding two-dimensional ones. The two halves are: (1) cube, sphere, cube, sphere, two small spheres and two small cubes; (2) two circles, two squares, two small circles and two small squares.

By way of comparison, we follow with two examples taken at the same level with subjects who were allowed to look at the elements throughout the testing.

SRY (4; 11) aligns the large cube, the large rectangle and the small square in one compartment. He then places the two ellipses at the beginning of the alignment, and the two circles at the end. He continues with the two ellipsoids and the two cuboids, the whole alignment being shaped like a horse-shoe. The experimenter tries to persuade him to divide his pattern into two collections, one for each compartment; he now constructs another alignment in the right-hand compartment made up entirely of similar pairs (two circles, two squares, two cubes and two spheres). "Are all the things in this room alike?—*Yes, because this and that* (in each couple) *are the same.*" He constructs the same arrangement in the second compartment.

He does not accept the experimenter's division of the objects into curvilinear versus rectilinear, or three-dimensional versus two-dimensional.

236

GUY (4; 2) also starts with a single large alignment, but his is more advanced in that the first eight objects are all three-dimensional (large and small ellipsoids, large sphere, large cube, large and small cuboids, small sphere and small cube), while the other eight are two-dimensional (but not associated according to any further similarities). He is then asked to arrange the set in two different compartments, so that there is a "family" in each. In spite of his age, the answer he reaches belongs to stage II. He puts all the curved elements together and all the rectilinear ones together, saying: "*In this room there is the ball and the balls . . . mother, father, children, parents, it's a family of rounds. Over here is the family of squares: this is an enormous tubby, and this is a little tubby, etc.*" (He groups them like people in a living-room.) But when the experimenter tries to persuade him to change his criterion, he falls back on the dichotomy into round elements and square ones four times in succession, and each time he uses the same make-belief names.

These reactions are very similar to those of children at the same level when the classification was visual. What small differences there are are not specific, but simply point to the difficulty of making tactile comparisons. These have to be successive. But this method of comparison occurs in the visual field as well in the early stages, so that the fact that it is bound to occur all the time in the tactile field does not lead to any new phenomena peculiar to this modality. Instead of leading to new facts, these experiments merely serve as an additional check on our hypotheses concerning the role of retroaction and anticipation.

The most primitive response is to pick out a number of pairs made up of identical elements, or alternatively to select a few objects which seem significant and forget about the others (cf. Ros). But this is no more than a further instance of successive assimilation which we already know to be typical of very young children. We found it in ch. I, §3, when we asked them to find objects similar to a given object ("Give me one like this", etc.). However, because tactile comparisons are always successive, we find the same sort of behaviour persisting to a later age.

As soon as the subject tries to create some kind of a collection, his behaviour corresponds to what we know of graphic collections of stage I. The constructions are naturally less detailed than in the visual field, and the proportion of little piles to graphic collections is rather greater (but this kind of collection shades into the graphic collection in any case). The most usual construction is a simple or double alignment, with varying degrees of relationship between its elements. But we also find graphic configurations, both two-dimensional and three-dimensional, and we find all kinds of variations of the two. The surest indication that an arrangement really is a graphic collection or a complex object is that the subject tries to reproduce it when he is eventually asked to classify the objects visually. The fact that graphic collections are still found even when the mode of apprehension is tactile is highly significant, for it confirms our interpretation of the phenomenon as a product of the failure to co-ordinate extension and intension. Graphic collections must represent something more than the imitation of perceptual configurations. They are not like decorative drawings, the sole purpose of which is to produce a pleasing picture. For if that were all, we fail to see why they should appear in these attempted classifications of elements perceived by touch. To say that the child is arranging objects so perceived in such a way as to conform with an interiorized visual image hardly explains why he should want to build such configurations when he cannot see them. The interpretation we have already given is that the relations of similarity which form the starting-point are intensive, and the only way these children can structure the extension to which they give rise is in spatial terms. From the child s point of view, a sensori-motor schema has no extension, and the only kind of extension is that which belongs to perceptual groups, being either spatial or temporal. If this interpretation is correct, we must expect graphic collections to occur even when the objects are known only by touch and kinaesthesis, and this is what we find.

The main difference between visual classification and tactile classification is that the second condition militates against an early discovery of general classificatory criteria. At stage I children never do find these by themselves, because the essence of these graphic collections lies in the use of limited similarities (between successive terms) together with irrelevant associations of a functional or spatial character, instead of the generic similarity of a true classification. However, so long as the subject can see all the elements, the experimenter can quite often provoke a search for common properties either by using some such word as "family" (see Guy), or even by simply asking for a verbal enumeration. When he cannot see the objects, the resistance is greater. Nevertheless, the difference is comparatively slight and not difficult to explain: because the comparisons have to be successive, the successive assimilations take place less rapidly, and the kind of hindsight we spoke of in the last chapter is more difficult. As a result the child also finds it harder to achieve the anticipations (or semi-anticipations) which eventually lead to his discovery of common properties (see ch. VII, §3).

3. STAGE II: NON-GRAPHIC COLLECTIONS; DISCOVERY OF A SINGLE CRITERION FIRST BY TRIAL-AND-ERROR, THEN BY SEMI-ANTICIPATION; DIFFICULTY IN FINDING OTHERS

Stage II is the stage of non-graphic collections and starts as soon as the subject can construct collections based solely on similarity relations without regard for a particular spatial configuration (at about $5\frac{1}{2}$ years).

Nevertheless, we can single out a succession of steps or intermediate stages in terms of the degree of anticipation. The first of these represents a transition from stage I to stage II, when all that the child can do is to discover one criterion by trial-and-error.

Following are examples of this transitional stage:

REM (5; 6) touches the objects one by one and explores them carefully with his finger-tips. Then he groups them in pairs, some made up of identical elements (two cubes, two squares, two spheres, etc.), and others of a three-dimensional element together with a two-dimensional one (a cube and a square, etc.). In the end, he places all the rectilinear objects in one compartment and all the curved ones in the other. But he cannot explain what he has done, and when the experimenter points to the curved objects and asks: "Are they a little bit the same?" he answers: *"Because they are smaller and bigger* (the difference strikes his consciousness before the similarity!).—But are they a little bit the same?—*Yes, two balls.*—And over here (the rectilinear objects), is there anything which makes them all alike?—*Yes, two bricks.*—But why did you put them together?—*They're alike.*—Why?—*They're a large and a small card. Yes, they're bricks.*" He is given some of them to touch again, and says, "*A large ball, a square,*" etc., and finally: "*Over here I've got the round ones.*— And the others?—*The others are squares.*" Each time the experimenter tries to make him change the criterion he ends up with the same division into round and square elements. Curiously enough, the final visual classification is less adequate than the tactile one: he has a set of pairs some of which are identical and others similar, but the pairs are all mixed up without regard to the criterion of rectilinearity.

HOF (5; 6) examines the objects very carefully, without classifying them at first. Then she exclaims: *"The large squares! The large balls!"*, and puts two cubes on one side and two spheres on the other. She touches a small circle and puts it "*with the other round ones*", and then a small square: "*I'll put it with the big squares.*" She continues in this way, taking the objects one at a time, ending with two large collections which are not subdivided: "*The large and the small squares, and the balls, large ones and small ones together.*" Various attempts to make her change the criterion always end in the same dichotomy, although different alignments emerge (all of which show the alternation of large and small elements). The visual classification also results in a division of the objects into curved versus rectilinear, but each of these collections is further subdivided into large and small.

CHE (5; 6) constructs three piles, the first consisting of two spheres, one large the other small, and one circle; the second of large and small squares; and the third of large and small cubes. "Can you divide them in two piles?— *The squares over here and the round ones there.*" Che fails to find a second criterion. The experimenter puts a large sphere on one side and a small one on the other: "*The big things on one side and the small ones on the other.*— Could you do it differently?—*No.*—(The experimenter starts with a sphere and a disc.)—*The thick things on one side and the small ones on the other.*"

GOS (5; 6) starts by constructing six piles each of which consists of a pair of elements: large spheres, small cubes, large cubes, large squares, large circles, small spheres, small squares and small circles. "Can you make two piles of things which are alike?—(He puts the cubes on one side and the spheres on the other, and then puts the circles with the spheres) *because they're round also*," etc. He fails to find a second criterion. When the experimenter then starts one or two classifications, either he cannot continue them, or else he falls back on the division into curved versus rectilinear.

Sto (5; 6) follows much the same principle: *"Yes, the round ones with the round ones.—What are you doing.—The balls with the balls, the circles and the balls are round.—*And on the other side?—*The squares. They're all square on the other side."* Another criterion: he divides the objects into three collections, these being the squares, the circles and the bricks (cubes). "But can you put them in two piles?—(He falls back on the collections of 'squares' and 'round ones'.)" His visual classification is similar.

Dro (5; 7) states that he is going to form three piles, but cannot say what these are except for the first pile of *"round ones"*. In fact, he constructs four piles: the spheres, the cubes, the squares and the discs. "How many piles have you made?—*Three.*—Touch them to see.—(He touches all four:) *Three.* Touch them again.—*That makes three piles.*—What have you put in the first one?—*Balls.*—In the second?—*Squares* (= cubes).—In the third?—*Squares as well* (flat ones).—And in the fourth?—*Circles.*—I want you to make two piles in the two rooms. What will you put in the first one?—*The squares.*—And in the second?—*The round ones* (he does divide the elements into curved and rectilinear ones)." He fails to find a second criterion. The experimenter starts a classification based on size: *"It's a small one and a large one.*—Go on then. —*The round ones must go there and the square ones there."* He is presented with a complete classification into three-dimensional and two-dimensional elements: "How have I put these?—*Fat ones and flat ones."*

There are two interesting features in these examples. In the first place, several subjects (Rem, Hof, Sto) begin the actual classification in terms of large collections (rectilinear versus curvilinear) instead of building these up gradually from smaller ones, which is what they would do if they saw the material. We have already noted in the last chapter (§3) that when children can see the material but are asked to anticipate the arrangement, they do the same: they anticipate the major collections. It looks as if once a child has grown out of the stage of graphic collections, the fact that the perception is tactile forces him to try to abstract the relevant properties: the interplay of hindsight and semi-anticipation follows as an inevitable consequence of the difficulty of this set-up, where simultaneous comparisons are ruled-out. In the second place, we should draw special attention to the fact that the hindsight is apt to appear much earlier than when the subject can see the material. So also are the occasional anticipatory glimpses which figure in the course of trial-and-error behaviour. Thus, when Hof finds the contrast between thick squares and the thick balls, he goes on to think of a wider project and puts it into operation. Sto is another example of this.

A second group of subjects do achieve a real semi-anticipation, i.e.

they anticipate the first criterion immediately after touching the objects, even if they cannot change this criterion afterwards. For the reasons we have discussed, this semi-anticipation can occur fairly precociously.

FRI (5; 2) first touches each of the objects. "What are you going to do now? What will you put in the first room?—*Round ones.*—And in the second?—*Squares ones.*" When he has done this he is asked for a second classification, but he does not succeed in carrying it out. He is then asked to describe the objects which he has just classified: "What were they?—*Square ones and round ones.*—What else?—*Large squares and small ones.*—Could you make two piles differently?—*No.*—Try.—(He falls back on his first dichotomy.)" But when the experimenter starts a classification based on size, he understands: "*The small ones must go here and the large ones there.*" He still cannot discover any other criterion, but when the experimenter starts a classification into three-dimensional and two-dimensional elements, he understands this as well: "*The thinner ones and the thicker ones.*"

ALE (5; 3). After an enumeration: "What will you put in the first room?—*The round ones.*—And in the other?—*The square ones.*—Suppose that I ask you to make two other piles, not like the ones before. What would you do?—*The round ones and the square ones.*—You've done that already. But think of the things that you touched. What were they like?—*Small, medium and big.*—Well then, try to make two piles once more, but different from before.—(He falls back on the round and square elements.)" On the other hand, he too understands the dichotomy into large-small elements and the dichotomy into "thick" and "thin" ones, once the experimenter starts these without further comment.

A third group of subjects is made up of children who do not reach real semi-anticipations, but only arrive at partial semi-anticipations through trial-and-error, like Hof, Sto, etc. but who are nevertheless able to change the criterion subsequently. This type of reaction is much less frequent. We give just one example:

WEB (5; 9) examines each object with one hand, without saying anything. "I want you to put together the things which are alike. Do you have any ideas? —*Yes, the balls together, the bricks, the bricks . . .*" In actual fact, she puts the three-dimensional objects on one side and the two-dimensional ones on the other, repeating: "*I am going to put the balls together and then the bricks together. But that's the high balls* (= spheres).—That's good. Now I'd like you to put them together in a different way. Can you think of one?—(She begins to divide the objects into curved and rectilinear ones.) *Yes. I'm going to put the bricks together and the balls together.* (She manages a complete dichotomy, as she did before.) *This time I've put the flat ones and the tall ones together.*" She cannot find a third criterion (and finishes up with one collection of three-dimensional objects and two collections of two-dimensional objects, the first made up of circles and the second of squares and circles mixed together). The visual classification only results in pairings.

Here, to end with, are subjects belonging to a fourth group. These

241

are the clear-cut examples of stage II. They show a semi-anticipation of the first criterion, and they then arrive at others by trial-and-error:

Ris (6; 3). "What are you going to do?—*A rectangle, then a square, a square, etc.*—And on the other side?—*All the rest.*—What are they?—*An egg and then round ones.*" He succeeds in carrying out a complete dichotomy into recti-linear and curved objects. Asked to find a second criterion, he spends a long time groping, but he finally succeeds in grouping the small elements on one side and the large ones on the other. But he cannot formulate this division, and simply says: "*I've put the round ones and the square ones together so that it won't be the same* (as the first time).—And can you make three piles?—(He divides the objects into circular, square and oval shapes.)"

Gal (6; 3). After touching the objects, he anticipates: "*Balls, bricks.*" The actual construction results in one collection of rectilinear elements and another collection containing a mixture of curved and rectilinear objects. "What have you done?—*I've put the balls here and the bricks there.*" When a second criterion is asked for, he says "*I don't know*", but he makes the attempt and ends with a dichotomy into three-dimensional and two-dimensional objects. The visual classification repeats this.

Bru (6; 6). "How many piles will you make?—*Three: square ones, round ones and small round ones.*" In his actual construction, he starts this way and then subdivides the squares into large and small ones: "But do you want three or four piles?—*Four.*" Then, in continuing his construction, he discovers the difference between the two-dimensional and three-dimensional objects, and subdivides the four piles into eight. Thus he almost constructs a pattern based on three criteria. "How many piles were there?—*Eight*—What were they?—(He enumerates them correctly from memory.)—Suppose I ask you to make just two piles, how would you do it?—*The square ones and the round ones.*" When first asked for other possible dichotomies, he does not think of using his previous subdivisions. Then he does: "*There are small ones and big ones.—*What else?—*Flat ones and thick ones.*"

Mea (7; 3) envisages four piles: squares and cubes, circles and spheres. But in the actual construction he ends with three collections: cubes, spheres and two-dimensional elements. "Can you put them all in two piles?—(Trial-and-error, then:) *There they're all thick and here they're all thin.*" Asked for a second criterion, he eventually ends with a division into large and small elements. He does not succeed in finding a third (straight edges).

There is very little difference between these reactions and those that occur at the same level with the help of vision. The first criterion is apparently discovered rather sooner, and the second somewhat later. Once a subject can change the criterion, he usually shows considerable flexibility right from the start, as compared with the usual type of experiment. We will return to this last point when discussing stage III. Finally, at stage II, the criterion of shape is by far the most popular. There are one or two exceptions, such as Weg who first finds the two-dimensional–three-dimensional dichotomy; but he does not anticipate that criterion.

242

4. STAGE III: ANTICIPATION OF TWO OR THREE CRITERIA. CONCLUSIONS

From the age of 7–8 years, and in a few instances even at $6\frac{1}{2}$, our subjects anticipate the first two criteria, usually the dichotomies large-small and three-dimensional–two-dimensional. From the age of 8–9 they readily anticipate all three criteria.

AUG (6; 7) examines the objects and says: "*The ones made of thin wood will go together. The surfaces are of thin wood.*—And then?—*Everything made of thick wood together* (the three-dimensional objects) *and everything of thin wood together.* (He does so.)—Could one arrange them differently?—*Yes, the squares with the squares; then the bricks with the squares and the balls with the circles.*"

He cannot find a third criterion. He is given a large and a small rectangle: "*I have two squares, no, two bricks. Oh, that's an idea! All the little things together and all the big things together.*"

FAB (6; 8) says immediately: "*Round ones and square ones.*—Could one do it in a different way?—*The little ones with the little ones and the big ones with the big ones.*" He cannot find the third criterion. He is given a cube and a square: "*This one is thin. One could put the thin squares on one side and the thick squares on the other.* What about the rest?—*You have to put the thick round ones and the thin ones in another room. That will make four piles.*"

RAM (7; 8). "*The round ones, the square ones.*—Could you do it differently?—*A flat square and a flat counter.*—And in the second room?—*A thick round one, the thick ones.* (He carries out the classification into two-dimensional and three-dimensional elements.)—And in still another way?—(He cannot find one.)"

SAN (8; 5) succeeds in anticipating three criteria: "*I'll put the small ones on one side and the big ones on the other.*—Can you see another way?—(She touches the objects again.) *I'll put the flat ones on one side and the thick ones on the other.*—And in a third way?—*The circles and squares on one side, and the rectangles and ovals on the other.*"

STA (8; 11) says: "*Two piles, square ones and round ones.*" But he immediately distinguishes between the large and small elements, and divides the material on the basis of two criteria. Then he subdivides it further according to the third criterion of dimension. "Can you do it differently?—*Yes, four piles: I can put the flat squares with the flat circles, then the balls and the bricks go together.*—Can you see a third way of doing it?—*There are small ones and large ones.*"

ROS (9; 7). "*First the big things and the little things*—Can you do it differently?—*The things which are round and the square things.*—And differently still?—*The round ones on one side, the square ones on the other.*—You've just said that. Do it. (She does so.)—Can you do it differently still?—*Yes, the flat things and the thick things.*"

HUN (9; 10). "*The round ones and the square ones.*—And differently?—*All the flat ones on one side over against those which aren't flat.*—Tell me another way.—(He scratches his forehead while he enumerates first the circles and

243

squares, then the balls and bricks.)—And differently still?—*Oh, now I know! All the large ones and all the small ones.*"

These examples of stage III need to be seen in the light of the whole course of development in this sort of experiment. The following figures are significant. The first set of results refers to the easier material in which the different objects are duplicated:

Table XXI. *Classification by touch using the easier material, I (%)*

G = graphic collections; 1, 2, 3 indicate the number of criteria used correctly

Age (no. of subjects)	G	1	2	3
4 (10)	80	20	0	0
5 (26)	15	77	8	0
6 (30)	5	**82**	13	0
7 (20)	5	25	**50**	20
8 (20)	0	15	40	45
9 (24)	0	12·5	30	57·5
10 (20)	0	5	35	**60**

Classifications in terms of one criterion reach a maximum at 6 years, those involving two are modal at 7 years, and those involving three, at 10 years. Shape is the first criterion chosen in 80–90% of cases. There is little to choose between size and dimensionality but neither appears very often before the age of 7.

The next table refers to the more complex set of objects, which does not contain any identical elements. The last column shows the extent of anticipation.

Table XXII. *Classification by touch using the complex material, II (%)*

G = graphic collections, the numbers 1–4 indicate the number of criteria, A = anticipations

Age (no. of subjects)	G	1	2	3	4	A
4 (8)	90	10	0	0	0	0
5 (22)	54	41	5	0	0	9
6 (14)	21	**71**	7	0	0	21
7 (15)	20	33	27	13	7	40
8 (20)	15	20	**35**	30	0	55
9 (15)	13	0	33	53	0	87
10 (17)	0	6	27	53	23	82
11–12 (18)	0	0	16	53	31	93

The fourth criterion would oppose elongated shapes like cuboids and ellipses to squares, circles, cubes and spheres. It turns out to be difficult to find.

The main conclusion is that classification as a whole is an *operational* development. Both classification and seriation could be considered as different kinds of perceptual "Gestalten", the first involving a nesting series of inclusions while the second represents asymmetrical transitive relations. This interpretation turns out to be false. If either or both were a matter of perception, we should find that the limitation of perception to the successive modalities of movement and touch will systematically retard the development because a simultaneous apprehension of the whole is ruled out. In point of fact, tactile classification turns out to be easier in some respects, if not in all. Much the same is true of seriation (see ch. IX).

There is one striking feature about this kind of enquiry which would be very obvious if we could show film sequences as well as presenting written protocols. Children rarely refer back to the objects they have already explored to compare them with the ones they are investigating: they behave as if they actually "saw" all the things together. There are two reasons for this. In the first place, they have already been through them one by one before we ask them to classify them. During this initial exploring, most children feel compelled to enumerate the objects. Often enough, their verbal descriptions are rather vague, but they do use language (both overt language and no doubt internal speech), so that there is little difference between children who are specifically asked for an enumeration and those who are not. In the second place, although they rarely go backwards in the actual manipulation, the backward movement, or retroaction, does occur mentally. Both memory and verbal symbolization undoubtedly play a part in this, but the whole process is one of continual re-organization, with an ever-present re-systematization of the relations in the light of successive perceptions.

In other words, the very fact of its limitations means that tactile comparison brings out a more active organization on the part of the subject. The actual comparisons are always made separately, as they must be, but the subject now fills in the lacunae by bringing in an even more adequate hindsight to take the place of the simultaneous perception he might have enjoyed, had the comparisons been visual. The importance of such hindsight is therefore especially clear in this kind of experiment, even though its existence was already noted in our discussion of visual classification.

All this explains why anticipation occurs earlier and seems relatively easier. Even children of 5 may begin to anticipate the first criterion (as do Fri and Ale in §3), although what is more frequent is the kind of semi-anticipation which seems to arise in the course of a child's trial-and-error behaviour but which is also the true forerunner of the eventual operational response. Earlier on we had occasion to suggest that hindsight and anticipation are closely related, and the present findings confirm that conclusion: an assimilatory schema becomes anticipatory in relation to the comparisons which lie in the future when it has undergone a sufficient degree of re-moulding and re-adaptation in the light of hindsight.

The interplay of hindsight and anticipation is what lies behind the most remarkable feature of these observations: the fact that our subjects can abstract qualities which are common to quite a large number of elements (and even at stage I, we find them doing this, with a certain degree of experimental prompting). The abstraction itself affords as clear a proof as one could wish of the fact that classification is an active process and not merely a perceptual one. These children are not dominated or overwhelmed by the whole complex of relations which would be present in visual perception, which is why they are all the more able to undertake a genuine kind of construction by using hindsight and anticipation. True enough, the qualities which they abstract (first of all shape, then, at stage III, size and dimensionality) correspond to certain perceptual variables, and the critic might therefore argue that the abstraction is made out of a perceptual given, or out of the object as such. But, here as elsewhere, the (abstract) notion is richer than what is given in perception. In other words abstraction means not only taking relations out of a perceptual given but adding relations to it. To recognize the existence of common characteristics like squareness and roundness, or large and small, or "flat" and "thick", means to construct so many schemata in terms of the actions of the subject as well as the properties of the object: a square (even a material square) is a figure whose four sides and four angles are comparable; they are in fact equal, but they only take on this property when it is conferred on them by the activity of the subject (by measuring, and so on). More generally, a classification depends on common properties, but these properties cannot become "common" without the activity of a subject, even though the latter would be of no avail were it not for the fact that the objects lend themselves to such bracketing. The abstraction is the fruit of activity, and that is why the very lacunae of tactile comparison tend to favour it instead of hindering it, as they would do if only perception were involved.

To sum up, both the similarities and the differences found as between visual and tactile classification point to their operational character. The argument becomes even stronger when we come to compare classification with seriation (tactile and visual) because there the opposition of perception and operation is even sharper.

Chapter Nine

SERIATION[1]

IN chs. I–IV we found that the difficulty of operational classification is largely due to the fact that young children cannot co-ordinate extension and intension. This sort of co-ordination is foreign to perception; nor does it play any part in sensori-motor organization. As a result we find a considerable time-lag between graphic collections, which are dominated by perceptual and sensori-motor configurations, and hierarchical classifications, which rely on the relation of class-inclusion. Multiplicative classification (as in matrices or multiple-entry tables) is somewhat nearer on the surface to the corresponding perceptual organization, since the logical interference of two or more properties is closely mirrored by an intuitive, symmetrical arrangement of objects. Nevertheless, we found that the operational organization is not a continuous development out of the perceptual organization, but that it relies on its own structurization—without which the correct solution of matrix problems tends to be misleading. Let us now see whether the development of seriation shows any parallel to what we have found in classification.

1. STATEMENT OF THE PROBLEM

There are two main differences between seriation and classification. The first is that a relation can be perceived while a class as such cannot, and the second is that a serial configuration constitutes a "good form" perceptually, which is apparently simpler and more elementary than the structure of a matrix. If perceptual structures are to be regarded as the sole source of operational structures, seriation ought to appear long before classification. It does not. It is a little earlier, but neither develops much before the age of 7 or 8.

The two main problems which arise are the following:

(1) Does the perceptual configuration of a series constitute the initial datum from which operational seriation is abstracted?
(2) In what way does operational seriation differ radically from perceptual seriation, and is this sufficient to account for its relatively late development?

The first problem really calls for an analysis of perception, and such a study lies beyond our terms of reference. All that we can do is to

[1] With the collaboration of M. Zanetta.

remind the reader of a few facts which are of obvious relevance to the solution of the second problem.

Seriation exists at the sensori-motor level even if the relevant behaviour is unsystematic. A necessary condition appears to be that the difference between the elements of the series must be fairly sizeable so that the child can pick them out just by looking at the material. The kind of thing we have in mind is the way a child builds a tower at eighteen months by using bricks of decreasing size, or the way he manages the Montessori nesting boxes a little later. These are examples of seriation, and although they depend on the perception of relations, they also imply a sensori-motor schema which is not merely perceptual. It is legitimate to ask whether this sort of schema really lies behind the awareness of the perceptual configuration of a series rather than vice versa.

One investigation relevant to this question was that of Piaget and Morf.[1] We presented children aged 4–10 with a variety of serial arrangements of sticks of different lengths. Some of these had equal differences so that the series went up in a straight line, while others had unequal differences. But these were still regular: when the sticks were ordered along a straight line, the tops of the sticks described either a positively accelerated or a negatively accelerated parabola, i.e. the differences increased regularly from left to right or they decreased regularly. The operative question is to ask the subject to compare the differences between two pairs of adjacent elements. The first pair is near the beginning of the series while the second is near the end. Now younger children (5–7 years) need to compare the two differences by measuring one pair against the other, while older children (9–10 years) can tell at once whether the differences are equal or unequal by taking the configuration of the series into account (i.e. by referring to the shape of the line across the top). Now this experiment seems to prove that children do not use the configuration of the whole until a comparatively late age. A control-experiment which is unambiguous is to ask them to compare the differences between neighbouring pairs of adjacent elements. The results prove to be similar.

In addition, we recall that Lambercier's study of the effect of serial arrangements on size-constancy showed that the transposition of equal differences increases with age. This confirms that the total shape, i.e. the serial configuration, plays only a secondary role.[2]

The known facts seem to indicate that the perceptual schema corresponding to a serial configuration is not a primary datum but is itself

[1] Cf. J. Piaget and A. Morf, "Les préinférences perceptives et leurs relations avec les schèmes sensori-moteurs et opératoires" in *Etudes d'Epist. Génét.* (Paris, P.U.F.), Vol. VI, *Logique et perception*, 1958, ch. III.

[2] M. Lambercier, "La Constance des grandeurs en comparaison sériale", *Arch. de Psychol.*, Rech VI. Cf. Rech. VIII, *ibid.*

influenced by the subject's activities. These would include perceptual activities, but they would also include the actions involved in ordering objects, which are sensori-motor. In other words, even when a subject has this immediate perception of a serial configuration, it is because he recognizes the structure as one which he himself can construct or reconstitute. Serial operations are simply an interiorized result of previous activities. Their origin must therefore be sought in sensori-motor schemata rather than in a purely perceptual schema.

The second problem can now be reformulated as follows. We take it that the schema which underlies the recognition of serial configurations is a sensori-motor schema, i.e. one that arises from activity as a whole and not from perception alone. We should therefore be in a position to trace the intermediate steps leading from graphic to operational seriation. This will help us to determine what the second adds to the first, as we did in the case of classification. The present situation is different in that perceptual serial configurations correspond more closely to the relevant operational organization than do graphic collections to classifications based on inclusion. Since operational seriation does not, in fact, occur appreciably earlier than operational classification, we have to study those intermediate stages where the serial configuration is more advanced than operational seriation. In so doing we should be able to bring out the differences between the two, and this might help to explain why operational seriation does not appear earlier.

Intermediate steps of this type can be observed. Because of their graphic character, series tend to be recognized as good perceptual forms. Therefore serial configurations give rise to a sort of semi-anticipation at 5-6 years which has no equivalent in the domain of classification, since classes cannot be perceived as such.

We have already seen something of the relation between anticipation and the operations involved in the addition and multiplication of classes. Now we propose to study the semi-anticipation of a serial configuration in order to find out how and why it arises at a pre-operational level. But we shall also see why the semi-anticipation is not enough to permit the operational organization of the mental actions involved in seriation.

There is one way of separating aspects of seriation which arise from graphic factors from those which are bound up with operations as such. Once again, we can analyse the seriation of objects which are perceived by touch alone, and then compare these "tactile seriations" with ordinary visual ones. Even in tactile seriation, we can ask the subject to touch the sticks and then draw a picture of the configuration that he intends to construct. We can then compare the graphic anticipations that arise in tactile tests with those that arise in visual ones.

2. SERIATION AND THE ANTICIPATION OF SERIAL CONFIGURATIONS WITH ELEMENTS PERCEIVED VISUALLY

Many years ago, Piaget and Szeminska studied the development of seriation in an experiment using 10 small rods ranging from 9–16·2 cm. together with a set of rods of intermediate lengths for subsequent insertion in the completed series.[1] We found three distinct stages. In the first, the child cannot arrange the ten initial elements in order. He arranges them in sub-series of 2, 3, or 4 elements, which he cannot then put together. At the second stage, he manages the initial seriation empirically by a process of trial-and-error. He can only insert the additional elements by further trial-and-error, and he usually has to start again from the beginning. At the third stage, which starts at 7–8 years, the child proceeds systematically by looking for the smallest (or largest) element first, then for the smallest among those remaining, etc. This procedure, and this alone, may be regarded as properly operational, because it implies an awareness that any given element is both larger than the preceding and smaller than those that succeed it (e.g. $E > D$, C, etc. and $E < F$, G, etc.). This operational reversibility is accompanied by the ability to insert the new elements correctly, without trial-and-error.

We repeated this experiment in order to confirm the age at which the final third stage is reached and the order of succession of the three stages. B. Oxilia and E. Schircks have standardized the tests, with a number of statistical controls based on Kendall. Their results will appear in a work by B. Inhelder and Vinh-Bang on standardized tests of development. The following table is taken from this work, and provides a useful starting-point for the studies which follow. (The results of the intercalary series are omitted because they are not directly relevant to our present purpose.)

Table XXIII. *Development of seriation* (%)

Age (no. of subjects)	4 (15)	5 (34)	6 (32)	7 (32)	8 (21)
Stage IA. No attempt at seriation	53	18	7	0	0
Stage IB. Small unco-ordinated series	47	61	34	22	0
Stage II. Success by trial-and-error	0	12	25	15	5
Stage III. Success with operational method	0	9	34	63	95

Systematic seriation is not reached until 7–8 years, at least with this set of objects. This age is dependent in part on the particular experiment.

[1] Cf. J. Piaget and A. Szeminska, *The Child's Conception of Number*, ch. VI.

As we noted elsewhere,[1] the seriation of weight develops about two years later than that of length. Again, we might have found a marked improvement in the seriation of length had we used fewer elements, or if there had been greater differences between the elements. But either of these variations would mean that we were measuring a perceptual adjustment to an intuitive whole instead of operational reasoning. In point of fact, this sort of perceptual adjustment is a fairly early development, as we shall soon see.

On the other hand, had we increased the number of elements without altering the difference between elements (i.e. keeping it small enough to make the child compare the rods by actually measuring one against the other) it is probable that the average age by which stage III is reached would still be the same: once a systematic method is found, it can be generalized.

Knowing that seriation is not operational until about the same age as classification, we can now turn to the anticipation of seriation, in order to try to separate the intuitive and operational factors relevant to the formation of this logical schema.

We must first emphasize that the operational schema of seriation is necessarily anticipatory. The subject knows in advance that by choosing the smallest element among those that remain, he will eventually build a series in which each term is larger than the preceding ones, which is why he is able to avoid any errors or inconsistencies. The anticipatory nature of the seriation schema is confirmed in a neat experiment by A. Rey.[2] Rey showed his subjects a square sheet of paper measuring 10–15 cm.[2] with a small square drawn on it, some 2–3 cm.[2], asking them to draw the biggest possible square and the smallest possible square on the same paper. Children aged 7–8 immediately drew one tiny square (1–2 mm.[2]) and another square along the edges of the paper. Younger subjects, however, simply drew other squares near the model, trying to make them slightly bigger or slightly smaller. Strangely enough, they did not even succeed in doing this, and oscillated about the dimensions of the one they could see. Since they have no anticipatory schema, they cannot envisage the limiting sizes of squares drawn on the given sheet of paper. Needless to say, Rey also found a wide variety of intermediate reactions in between these two extremes: anticipation following on a step by step approximation, with insights occurring at various points in the enquiry.

Our own problem is rather different. In Rey's experiment, the subject is shown one single element and he has to imagine the two extremes of

[1] J. Piaget and B. Inhelder, *Le développement des quantités chez l'enfant*, Delachaux and Niestlé, 1941.

[2] A. Rey, "Le problème psychologique des 'quantités limites' chez l'enfant", *Revue suisse de psychologie*, 1943, Vol. II, pp. 238–249.

an entirely imaginary series. In our experiment the subject perceives all the elements of the series, and is then asked to imagine (or to draw) the serial arrangement before constructing it. The only thing which he has to work out is the form of the series, for he can actually perceive every one of its constituent elements, whether visually, as in this section, or by touch, as in the next.

The first question is whether children cannot anticipate the series until the operational level at 7–8 years, or whether there is a stage at which they can anticipate the framework of the series, (e.g., by drawing an ordered set of elements), but cannot then seriate the elements themselves so as to conform with it. If indeed this does prove to be the case, we shall want to find out how this sort of semi-anticipation arises, and why it is not enough to give rise to an operational organization. There is a certain paradox in admitting that children can construct a seriation in a drawing, but cannot carry it out in fact, since ordering abstract graphic symbols can hardly be easier than ordering material objects!

In point of fact, the paradox does exist, for the second hypothesis proves to be right. Our method of experiment is as follows. First of all we show the subject four dolls of different sizes, and ask him to arrange them in order. This is to give him an idea of what is required. He is then given ten small coloured rods 0·5 cm. in cross-section and increasing in length from 9–16·2 cm. (the differences being 0·8 cm.). These are in jumbled order, and the child is asked to arrange them in the same way as the dolls. Before he does so, he is asked to "guess" what the arrangement will be and to make a drawing of it. There are two ways in which the drawing can be done. We may ask for a drawing in colour; each rod has its own colour, and the child is given a crayon to match each one, as well as additional crayons in other colours. He is allowed to touch the rods to check the correspondence between each rod and the crayon used to represent it, but the rod must then be put back in its place immediately afterwards. He is not allowed to rearrange the rods at this stage. If the coloured drawing is incorrect, he is asked for a drawing in ordinary pencil. This is particularly useful for younger subjects. When the drawing is done, he tries the actual seriation. This means that we can compare the level of his graphic anticipation with the level of his performance.

Here are the results for 88 subjects. We found three levels of anticipation in the drawings: (1) complete and analytic anticipation, i.e. an exact correspondence of colours and sizes together with a correct seriation of the latter; (2) a global anticipation, i.e. a correct pencil drawing or a correct seriation of size in the coloured drawing, but without correspondence between the colours and those of the real objects; (3) failure. In the actual seriation, we distinguish between a correct solution achieved operationally, a correct solution achieved by trial-and-error, and an incorrect solution.

Table XXIV. *Anticipation and performance in seriation* (%)

Age (no. of subjects)	4 (19)	5 (33)	6 (19)	7 (10)	8–9 (7)
I. Failure in anticipation	89	42	5	0	0
Global anticipation	11	55	73	20	0
Analytic anticipation	0	3	22	80	100
II. Failure in seriation	84	54	42	0	0
Success by trial-and-error	16	40	36	20	14
Operational seriation	0	6	22	80	86

It is well to bear in mind that the graphic anticipation provides a certain amount of practice for the actual seriation. That is why the results of the latter are slightly better here than in Table XXIII for subjects of 4–7 years. There is no appreciable difference for subjects of 8–9 years, but we saw only 7 subjects in that age-group. However, the important point is that the graphic anticipation is clearly in advance of the actual seriation at 5–6 years. At the age of 5, the figures for correct anticipation are 55% and 3%, while those for the actual seriation are 40% and 6%. At six, they are 73% and 22%, as against 36% and 22%. These results are all the more striking when it is remembered that, although "analytic" anticipation corresponds obviously enough with operational seriation (with one exception, these occurred together), "global" anticipation bears little similarity to seriation by trial-and-error. Global anticipation means drawing the serial configuration quite correctly, and without trial-and-error, although the individual lines do not match the colours of the rods to which they should correspond. So it looks as if children of 5 or 6 can anticipate the form of a series well before they can seriate objects in an operational manner, and, at least at six, the anticipation is ahead even of correct solution by trial-and-error.

Before trying to explain the discrepancy, we may well study a few protocols to bring out the qualitative differences between these stages.

Stage I: no anticipation.—At this stage, children cannot anticipate the series in their drawings, nor can they construct it later on. Neither the drawing nor the action can be said to be more advanced: each results in small unconnected groups of two or three elements.

FRA (4; 0). Given colours, Fra draws seven lines of the same length going from one edge of the paper to the other, and two small lines which are more than ten times smaller than the others. The pencil drawings are: (1) a long line and a short one; (2) five lines, three short alternating with two long. The actual seriation is a set of unco-ordinated pairs.

GIL (4; 8) draws nine coloured lines which are alternately long and short, the long ones varying in length, sometimes by several centimetres, while the short ones are all more or less equal. The pencil drawing contains seven lines but is otherwise similar, and the actual seriation is no better. Gil was also asked to copy a correct seriation made by the experimenter, using the coloured crayons. The first three lines she drew were decreasing, the fourth and the fifth were equal, the sixth was smaller than the seventh and equal to the eighth, and the ninth was smaller than all the others.

CAL (5; 5). In spite of his age, Cal does not succeed in the preliminary arrangement of the four dolls, and these are placed in order for him. Presented with the rods, his first drawing consists of three equal lines followed by a small one, in arbitrary colours; and his second of 9 black lines and 1 yellow one, all equal. His third drawing consists of lines in the order 2, 1, 9, 3, 8, 2, 1 (the numbers corresponding to sizes). His actual seriations are, first 2, 4; then 2, 3; and then 1, 2, 7, 5, 3, 6, 4, 9, 8, 10 (these being the numbers of the rods).

HIL (4; 5) orders the dolls correctly. "And now I'd like you to draw me the sticks, but in order, starting with the smallest, then one that's a little bigger, then a little bigger, till you get to the biggest one of all.—(Pencil drawing: 2, 1, 4, 10; then 10, 2, 6, 8, 7. Actual seriation: 1, 3, 7; then 8, 7; then the two unco-ordinated series 1, 3, 7, 10 and 2, 4, 8, 9.)"

CHA (4; 5). The dolls are arranged correctly. Drawings: 1, 3, 9, 7, 4; then 5, 8, 6, 2 on the left of this, so that the whole is in the order 5, 8, 6, 2, 1, 3, 9, 7, 4. Actual seriation: 2, 8, 9, 3, 4, 10; then 2, 4, 7 (unco-ordinated).

JOS (5; 6). The dolls are arranged correctly. Pencil drawing: 2, 4, 5, 6, 8, 7, 3, 9. Actual seriation: 1, 9, 10 (and stops).

There is no anticipation in these drawings apart from small unco-ordinated sequences of two or three elements. The actual seriations are of the same type. The partial series in the drawings might be thought of as anticipations, but in actual fact the same simple type of activity is at work both in the drawings and in the arrangements of the objects themselves. Neither is more advanced than the other. That is why it sometimes happens that at stage I children establish a better correspondence of length as between the rods and the colours used to represent them than at stage II. For they are only copying two or three of the elements at a time. Later on, when they begin to anticipate the total structure, the drawing depicts a configuration which is ahead of actual performance, and this leads to a dissociation between colour and size.

Stage I raises a curious problem. In the case of classification, stage I is the stage of graphic collections, while the pre-logical collections of stage II are no longer tied to a particular spatial configuration. In the case of seriation, however, stage I is the stage of small unco-ordinated sequences, while it is only at stage II that we find a graphic anticipation of the total serial configuration. In other words there are apparently no graphic serial structures at the stage which corresponds to the graphic collections in classification, and the graphic anticipation of a series arises only when classificatory collections begin to lose their graphic character. However if we pose the problem in terms of "intension" and "extension", the "intension" of a series being its order and the "extension" being the set of its elements, the paradox disappears. We know that graphic collections arise out of a lack of co-ordination between intension and extension, due to the fact that the intension is based on relations of similarity which are only constructed through successive comparisons, while the extension depends on the actual spatial perception. Now this is also true of the small unco-ordinated series of elements constructed at stage I. The subject fails to anticipate a complete seriation, just as he fails to carry it out, for the very good reason that both would involve building up a spatial totality out of a sequence of successive comparisons. What he does is to make isolated comparisons yielding tiny series of two or three elements. Then he simply puts these together in a line. There is the same lack of co-ordination between intension and extension as we found in classification. So these little series do correspond to the graphic collections and the "complex objects" with which we are familiar. Conversely, in order to anticipate the serial configuration, as children do at stage II, they have to achieve some co-ordination between intension and extension, however incomplete. Once again, the same is true of non-graphic collections in classification.

Stage II: semi-anticipation. Sub-stage IIA: no correspondence between the colours in the anticipatory drawing and those of the actual objects. Actual seriation is by trial-and-error and may be unsuccessful.—Stage II is extremely interesting. At this stage the child can depict the correct seriation in his drawing, occasionally after one or two shots, but sometimes immediately. But at the same time his actual performance is usually only approximate, and even if it is entirely correct, he still requires a good deal of trial-and-error. We shall first describe a sub-stage *IIA*, during which there is no relation between the colour and size of the lines in the drawing. There are a good many individual variations, depending on the regularity or irregularity of the differences between the lines and on the extent to which the colours interfere with the accuracy of the form. We do not propose to insist on these shades, but they are fairly clear in the individual protocols.

BAD (5; 2). (In the early stages of this investigation we used 9 rods of the same colour.) "You try to arrange them from the biggest to the smallest. Can you guess what they will be like?—*Yes.*—Well draw these sticks.—(Draws a house.)—No, these sticks.—(Draws eight elongated rectangles.)" The drawing is a good series with the rectangles increasing in height: 7, 11, 19, 27, 57, 65, 82 and 91 mm. The differences are irregular, but the increase is consistent. Bad looked at the objects after each drawing, although it was impossible to tell whether he was trying to copy each object or merely to gain a global impression. The experimenter now points to the first and the last elements in the drawing, and asks him to show the corresponding rods. Bad puts these on top of his drawing, and continues by placing the others on his drawing, so that eventually he obtains a correct seriation of all the objects.

He is then asked to repeat the seriation without the drawing, and this time he finishes with 1, 5, 2, 6, 3, 9, 4, 7, 8! "Is that like the drawing you made?—*Yes*.—Have you arranged them from the smallest to the biggest?—*Yes*.—(The experimenter corrects the first two choices by placing 1, 2 at the beginning.)—(Bad continues and ends with 1, 2, 3, 5, 4, 8, 7, 6, 9.)"

DOM (5; 3) arranges the four dolls correctly. The first coloured drawing, "from the largest to the smallest", is: 7, 1, 2, 4, 10, 3, 6, 5, 8, 9. "How can you tell whether you've drawn them all?—(Places several on the drawing.)—Show me with this black pencil what they will look like when they're in order." The second drawing is a good seriation of lines ranging from 185–90 mm., with the differences fairly regular. The first actual attempt at seriation is 1, 2, 3, 4, 6, 5 but in the end he arrives at the correct solution by trial-and-error.

BAR (5; 3) says she will put the small ones on one side and the large ones on the other. The first drawing, which is coloured, is a good seriation with regular differences between the elements. But there is no attempt at representing the real objects (by looking at them), and there are twelve of them instead of ten. The actual seriation results in short series of the smaller elements only. She cannot seriate all ten.

MAN (5; 6) also draws a regularly ascending series at the first attempt, which does not correspond with the objects themselves. He is then presented with five elements only and asked to choose the right colours: He can only do so at the expense of the seriation. The actual seriation results in small unco-ordinated series.

BOR (5; 9) first tries to make his drawings correspond in size and colour to the objects. He achieves this approximately, but without any seriation. The second drawing is a regularly decreasing series, but does not correspond with the objects (there is one element too many and green is used three times). When asked once again to keep to the right colours, he produces them like the first time, without the seriation. The actual seriation results in 1, 7, 2, 8, 6, 3, 4, 5, 9, followed by 1, 3, 2, 6, 4, 5, 7, 9, 8, 10, which he now proceeds to correct bit by bit until the seriation is right.

PLO (6; 0) starts by drawing coloured lines which do not have a common base, and are not seriated either. His black pencil drawing, however, is a regular series. The actual seriation results in small unco-ordinated series.

ANG (7; 0) first draws coloured lines of equal length, in an arbitrary order. "*I'm going by the colours. The green is here, the red is here*, etc.—I'd like you to draw the sticks arranged in order of size (repeating the original instruction), using a black pencil.—(He looks carefully at the objects.) *The green one is the first*. (Draws a line, and looks at the objects each time he draws a new line.) In this way, he constructs a perfectly regular series. "Could you make a drawing without looking at the sticks?—*No* (draws three lines and then stops)." The actual seriation: 1, 2, 4, 3 (corrected) (6), 6, 5 (corrected), 7, 8 (he compares them), 9, 10.

In spite of considerable individual differences, these reactions have a great deal in common. Every one of these subjects can draw a perfectly good series of nine or ten elements, but when it comes to the actual seriation he fails outright or else he has to resort to trial-and-error. Yet he draws the seriation correctly at the first attempt when all the objects are of one colour (Bad), or when he is using a black pencil, or again, when he does use colours but is not concerned that these should correspond with sizes (Bar and Man). When the correct anticipation of the series is not produced at once, we invariably find that the subject has been trying to take the colours into account, and could not do both together (Dom, Bor, Plo and Ang). As soon as he neglects the colours, he succeeds in drawing the seriation right away, using a black pencil (Dom, Plo and Ang) or using colours at random. But, although the anticipation is both immediate and correct, the actual seriation is inadequate or far from immediate. In other words, there is a sharp contrast between the systematic nature of the drawings and the total lack of system in the actual seriations. The problem is that we know that it is not the colours of the rods which prevents children from actually arranging a series of rods in order of increasing size. The seriation is often incorrect at this stage, and always halting, even when we use rods of the same colour (see Table XXIV).

The solution of this problem is really very simple. We have seen that the systematic method of carrying out a seriation implies reversibility: finding the smallest element, and then the smallest among those that remain, etc., means bearing in mind that a given element, say E, is both longer than those already in the series ($E > D, C$) and shorter than the ones yet to follow ($E < F, G$). Now a drawing does not require anything of the sort. A child draws the lines one after another simply following one direction of the size variable, and he has no need to make any comparisons between pairs. The relation he imposes is one-directional and therefore irreversible. The anticipation expressed in these drawings is an incomplete anticipatory schema because it is pre-operational. There is no anticipation of the comparisons involved in the operational seriation of the actual objects (which implies the co-ordination of the two directions $<$ and $>$). The only anticipation is that of the global result, and the child cannot anticipate the steps which are necessary to obtain it. This is a *semi-anticipation*, in a very precise sense, because it applies to one direction of variation only instead of to both. It is very natural that this semi-anticipation should be a whole stage in advance of operational seriation and of the complete anticipatory schema which this implies.

But although our first problem has been solved, there is still a second one: the problem of explaining the formation of this semi-anticipation. It is not there at stage I. This is where we come back to the relation between the "intension" and the "extension" of series which, as we have seen, remain unco-ordinated at the stage I level, since the "intension", or the order, involves a sequence of successive comparisons while the extension corresponds to an actual spatial configuration. As the ability to relate objects to one another develops (and this sort of development depends on the progressive co-ordination of actions which is going on all the time) so a stage is eventually reached when the child finds it easy to envisage the indefinite repetition of the same relationship, in particular the relationship $<$, $<$, etc. *or* $>$, $>$, etc., and to represent this repetition by drawing a spatial pattern. But one thing that is very obvious is the fact that the co-ordination of intension and extension is fairly easy only because the intension can be fashioned by the subject as he chooses. When he has to take the actual objects and arrange them, the attempt at co-ordination is brought up against the resistance of real things with all their multiplicity of relations in both directions ($<$ *and* $>$). That is why the co-ordination of intension and extension is far from being complete at stage IIA when real objects have to be arranged, even through there is anticipation to the extent of a simple graphic representation.

When we have finished our description of the different stages, we shall come back to the nature of these graphic images and the mental imagery behind them.

Stage II. Sub-stage IIB: beginnings of correspondence between graphic anticipation and individual objects. Actual seriation is by trial-and-error, but successful.—There is some advance in that the subject tends to take the colours and sizes of the actual rods into account in his drawing, instead of being satisfied with an entirely abstract design. The actual seriation, too, is always correct, but the method is trial-and-error and not systematic or operational.

RAC (5; 2) draws a series of coloured lines decreasing regularly from 15–7·5 cm., and with colours corresponding to the rods in the order 2, 1, 4, 3, 6, 10, 7, 5, 9. He is trying to make colours and sizes correspond, but he cannot help making a number of inversions. This case is intermediate between stages IIA and IIB. Actual seriation: first 2, 1, corrected to 1, 2; then 1, 2, 4, 3 corrected to 1, 2, 3, 4, etc. The correct solution is eventually achieved.

POS (5; 4) draws 1, 4, 6, 8, 10, 9, and then adds 2 in front of 1. Thus the elements are increasing in size, but there are two inversions and three elements are omitted. The actual seriation: 2, 6, 9 and then 2, 6, 7, 8, 5, 9, 10, without a uniform base-line. The correct solution is achieved eventually, after further errors have been made and then corrected.

WAL (6; 10) draws 1, 3, 5, 7, 9, 10, 8 (8 being drawn as the smallest, so that its size and colour do not correspond). There is a regular seriation from 5·5–1·7 cm. "Have you forgotten anything?—(Only looks at the elements of the drawing, one by one.)—*No.*—Why is this one (8) after this one (10)?—*I don't know* (corrects it).—Is that what the sticks will look like when they are arranged?—*Yes*—Are you sure?—*Not altogether.*" The actual seriation: 1, 3, 5, 7. He then measures 4 against 7, and puts 4 aside. He eventually constructs 1, 3, 5, 7, 6, 2, 4, 8, 9, 10 (i.e. two separate series), and finally corrects this to reach the correct solution.

The advance in sub-stage IIB is that the graphic image is no longer a semi-anticipation only, for it is more than a global one-directional schema. Although imperfect, it is an anticipation in the true sense, since it bears not only on the result of the seriation, but also on the details of its construction. The graphic anticipation and the actual seriation of these subjects should therefore be at the same level, as indeed they are.

Stage III: Anticipation correct in detail, together with an operational method in the actual seriation.—At this stage, the anticipatory graphic image is completely correct (when mistakes occur they are due to distraction and not to any error in method), and the actual seriation is entirely operational. There is a remarkable correlation between these two properties (cf. Table XXIV). Nearly every subject who shows one of them shows the other. (There are only two exceptions, one at 5, the other at 8.) This agreement is not surprising, because both the analytic graphic anticipation and the correct performance depend on one and the same method, which is the culmination of this developmental process.

Here are three examples, starting with an intermediate case:

MIL (6; 2) starts with 2, 3, 1, 4, 5, . . . , 10, so that the sizes of the first three elements do not correspond with their colours. The actual seriation: he starts by copying his drawing, and then corrects the first elements to 1, 2, 3. "*It was wrong, the green one should have come before the red one.*" He then continues correctly, without looking at the drawing any more.

POU (6; 1) draws without error, and inserts additional elements correctly when these are introduced. His actual seriation is operational.

BEN (7; 1). His drawing and actual seriation are immediately correct. The latter is disarranged, and a new element is added to be inserted in the series. Ben compares it systematically to the smallest elements, and places it between 5 and 6, without reconstructing the series. "Why there?—(Reconstructing the series to prove his point.) *There!*"

At stage III, the graphic anticipation and the actual seriation are at the same level, just as they were at stage I, but for the opposite reasons. Both are incorrect at stage I, because there is no co-ordination of intension and extension. Both are analytically correct at stage III, because these two aspects of the series have been co-ordinated. At stage II, and particularly stage IIA, there is a semi-anticipation applying only to the global schema of the series, because extension and intension are more easily co-ordinated in an "abstract" drawing than in the real arrangement of objects.

There is one question we have yet to consider, and that is the precise nature of this sort of anticipatory graphic image (whether global as at level IIA, or analytic as at level III, or transitional as at level IIB). In particular, how is this sort of image related to mental images as such, or, in general, to perceptual schemata. The reader will no doubt recall (§1) that although classes are not perceived as such, relations are often perceptible. In particular a regular seriation constitutes a "good form". For the reasons given earlier, we would not allow that this sort of perceptual schema is a primary datum from the start, but it is nevertheless probable that the marked differences in the development of anticipation, as between seriation and classification, are bound up with the fact that only the former is perceptible. What we need to know are the relations between anticipation and imagery, or between imagery and perception. One possible solution would be to explain the early anticipation of seriation by arguing that this global sem-anticipatory schema is abstracted from the "good" perceptual form, or, it might be, from a child's perceptual experiences, and the same would no doubt apply to the operational schema itself. The alternative solution is that not only the operational schema but the anticipatory image which precedes it are both abstracted from the subject's own actions in relation to seriable objects instead of being directly abstracted out of his perception. This means recognizing imagery as an interiorized imitation of actions, while operations are then regarded as extended forms of interiorized actions with the added richness that comes from a more or less complete structurization. Now to accept this second solution does not entail denying the role of perception altogether. We may quite well agree that perception influences actions reciprocally, just as actions influence perceptual schemata. In other words, where the relations have an obvious perceptual correlate, the subject will have less difficulty in evolving a corresponding schema based on his actions (both at the level of semi-anticipation and at the operational level): so the anticipation of seriation is easier than that of classification. But it still remains that the "good form" of an ordered series only becomes perceptually apparent because of the corresponding sensori-motor action schema and its development as a whole. (It is true that classes never do become perceptible as such, but this is because they are outside the spatio-temporal framework of perception; on the other hand, actions do influence one's perception of objects as belonging to a particular class, or their "categorization" in Bruner's sense, and this is a matter of perception.)

Now we do not accept the first solution. In the first place, there are good experimental reasons for maintaining that the perception of serial configurations is something which develops in line with activity as a whole, including operational reasoning, so that the relation between perception and action (including interiorized action) is a two-way relation. The evidence has already been summarized briefly in §1. But in addition to these general grounds for rejecting the first solution, we would like to refer to the results of a small side experiment carried out in conjunction with the investigation described in this section. We asked a number of children at the lower stages to do a drawing of the series when the experimenter had built it for them correctly. (This came after the anticipatory drawings.) The result was that none of the 3-year-olds, and only a third of the 4-year-olds managed to produce a drawing with a regular increase or decrease in the height of the lines. This makes it difficult to argue that the graphic image is abstracted out of the perception: in order to draw the series, the child has to make a graphic reconstruction based on a succession of imitative movements; and these have to be seriated themselves. The perception of the model may help the seriation but it does not fully determine it. Conversely, the perception itself is easier when the child can order his actions in such a way as to arrange real objects in series (cf. §1).

We therefore accept the second hypothesis, and we may now turn to a study of tactile seriation which will help us to amplify it.

3. TACTILE SERIATION AND ITS ANTICIPATION IN DRAWINGS

In order to clarify the role of perception, we went on to study seriation of objects when their perception was limited to tactile exploration. We started by using rods of the same dimensions as in §2, but found that the tactile discrimination involved was too near the threshold for the results to be comparable. We therefore decided to use 10 rods from 10–19 cm. long but with the same square cross-section of 0·5 sq. cm. The difference in length between each rod and the next was now 1 cm. We had 43 subjects ranging from 4 to 8–9 years for this experiment. In another experiment, with 50 subjects of similar ages, we used 5 rods of 4–16 cm. in length and 1 cm.[2] in cross-section. This time, the difference between each rod and the next was 3 cm.

There were four steps in the experiment: (1) Tactile examination. The child is encouraged to examine the objects until he is convinced of their inequality. For the group using 5 rods, these are given one by one so that the subject can "feel how long they are", in the order 3, 4, 2, 5, 1. (2) Anticipation of the seriation: the subject is asked for a pencil drawing of "first the biggest one of all, then the one which is just a little less big, then the one still less big, and so on down to the smallest one of all". If the drawing is not clear, a second or third drawing is called for. (3) Actual seriation by touch. The subject is asked to state what he is doing and later to see whether it was correct. (4) When the child fails to carry out a seriation by touch, he is asked to do it visually. He may correct the series obtained by touch or start again, as he prefers. A drawing of the rods arranged in order was sometimes asked for to allow for difficulties in the actual drawing.

261

The following results were obtained:

Table XXV. *Graphic anticipation and actual seriation using tactile perception* (%)

Number of elements			10			5	
Ages	4	5	6	7	8–9	4	5
(no. of subjects)	(3)	(10)	(7)	(9)	(9)	(15)	(30)
I. Failure in anticipation	66	50	43	11	0	53	23
Approximate global anticipation	33	20	14	0	0	20	20
Correct global anticipation	0	30	43	89	100	27	57
II. Failure in seriation	100	90	71	89	11	67	40
Success by trial-and-error	0	10	29	0	56 ⎫	33	60
Operational method	0	0	0	11	33 ⎭		

If we compare these results with Table XXIV,[1] we find that most of the tactile results lag behind the visual ones, although the difference is smaller than one might have imagined. We also find that the greatest difference between the two results is in the actual seriation. The graphic anticipation is affected less, and after the age of 7 or 8 it is as good as it was using visual perception.

In assessing the significance of these facts, we might begin by introducing a few qualitative results of the experiment with ten rods. These results are again divided into three stages corresponding to the stages of visual seriation, but allowing for the systematic age lag shown by the two tables. During stage IA, there is no anticipation of the global schema and no seriation, even by trial-and-error.

PIL (4; 9). 10 rods are arranged fairly close together, in the shape of a fan, beneath a screen. "Put both your hands under it, and tell me what you can feel.—(He takes two rods.)—*Wood.*—Feel them all.—(Takes them without examining them.)—Are there any which are the same length?—*Yes.*—What are they like?—(Still without any examination) *Small.*—All of them?—*Yes.*—Are they all as small as each other?—(He compares two.) *No.* (He takes 3, and then 1 and 9, and examines their length separately. Then he does the same for 10.)—Are they all different?—*Yes.*—Feel them again to see if there are two the same size—(He takes 1 and examines the ends.)—That one? And which other?—(Indicates 10.)—What are they like?—*They're big.*—The same size?—*No.*—Are there two big ones which are the same?—*Yes* (indicates 10 and 2). *These ones.*—Touch them carefully (he examines the lengths of the

[1] There are two reservations to this comparison: (a) there is no tactile equivalent of analytic anticipation, which is based on the use of colours; (b) in the tactile experiment with five rods, it is almost impossible to distinguish between operational seriation and seriation by trial-and-error.

rods). Now do you understand? There aren't two which are the same size. If you find any, give them to me.—(Indicates 10 and 5.)—Touch them carefully. Are they the same size?—*No.*—Well then, they are all different, large, medium and small. You try putting them in order, starting with the largest, etc. (Usual instruction.) But first I want you to draw what they will be like when they are in order." Drawing I consists of seven lines, of which one is short, three long and two are intermediate. There is no seriation and no common base-line. Another drawing (II) is asked for. This time the lines start from the lower edge of the paper: there is one long one, a short one and then three long ones: still no seriation. Actual seriation (the instruction being repeated): he takes 10 and 1, which happen to be next to one another, and proceeds to align them as he comes to them without even examining them: 1, 10, 4, 5, 2, 3, 7, 8, 9, 6 (the small sub-series being due to chance). "Are they properly in order?—*Yes* (putting his fingers on the rods).—Draw me what they're like now (drawing III).—(He draws 11 lines, starting with large ones and finishing with small ones. There is a seriation of a kind although there are several inversions)." We now throw out five rods, leaving 1, 3, 5, 7 and 10, and Pie is asked to arrange them in order. He touches them without examining them, and constructs 10, 3, 1, 7, 5. "I would like you to put them in order, starting with the biggest one." He looks for the biggest, and constructs 1, 5, 7, 3, 10. Then he starts again and constructs 1, 5, 10, 7, 3, without attempting to check his progress. Finally, the screen is removed, and he constructs 10, 7, 5, 3, 1 visually.

Cor (5; 4) examines the elements a little more, but unsystematically. She thinks that 8 and 9 are the same length at first, so she is asked to "feel them better". Now she touches their ends and realizes that they are unequal. She touches two others, but does not examine them. She compares several of them with 9, by touching the ends, and agrees that no two are equal. Drawing I consists of 1 (large line), 2–5 (smaller equal lines), 6–9 and 10–12 (very slightly larger, and equal). There are 12 lines in all (because Cor has not counted) and the base-line slopes upwards instead of being horizontal. Actual seriation: examines four rods successively without any comparison, and then takes them all and puts them down in the order 8, 5, 4, 2, 6, 7, 10, 1, 9, 3. "Have you finished? Did you really start with the biggest one? (etc.)—(Takes 3 and 9, and puts them back again, without any examination.) *That's right.*—Have you touched them carefully?—(Takes them up one by one, without examining them, and constructs the following series, which still has no common base-line:) 8, 5, 4, 7, 10, 9, 1, 6, 3, 2.—Draw me the way you've arranged them.—(Drawing II: 1 large, 2–4 smaller and decreasing, 5–7 smaller and equal, 8 slightly larger, but then decreasing from 8–12, with 13–15 small and equal.)" When the screen is removed, Cor constructs the series 1, 2, 3, 6, 4, 7, 5, 8, 9, 10 visually, and draws it approximately (1–3 decreasing, 6 larger and 8–10 equal).

It is fairly obvious that failure is inevitable because these subjects are not examining the objects. The child at this stage remains passive (as we already know from our work on "haptic" perception):[1] instead of

---

[1] J. Piaget and B. Inhelder, *The Child's Conception of Space*, (1956) ch. II.

following the edge of the rod with his fingers, he simply touches one end and neglects the other; he never compares two rods unless told to do so, and he has no idea how to compare one rod with all the others; finally, he makes no effort to ensure that he has felt all the elements. This of course, makes seriation impossible. The reason that this stage lasts longer than it does with visual perception, is that simultaneous perception of all the elements is impossible in the tactile field, and this makes comparisons more difficult, so that greater activity is needed from the subject.

The graphic anticipation can hardly be much of an improvement, when the initial examination of the elements is so inadequate. But it is remarkable that when the child has carried out what he believes to be a seriation, he can produce a drawing which is appreciably better than the preceding ones (cf. Pil's drawing III and Cor's drawing II). This shows that anticipation is slightly in advance of actual seriation even at level IA: although the child has failed in carrying out the actual seriation, he thinks he has done better than he really has.

At level IB, the anticipation is considerably better, and the subject now produces a global schema which is approximately right, and may be absolutely right after several attempts. But the actual seriation is still at the same level as it was.

RAE (4; 7) puts his hands on the rods, without moving them about, and says: "*There are large ones and small ones*," all unequal and all "*black*" (which must mean that he cannot see them!). "You must touch them carefully so that you can tell.—(He continues to rest his hands on the rods without moving them.)—Take them in your hands to feel them better.—(He takes half the rods in his hands.)—Are there two which are the same size?—*Yes, two* (5 and 7).—Touch them carefully.—(He puts them on the same base-line and examines the ends.) *No.* (He compares 4, 5, and 9, then puts 6 and 9 on one another, and compares 8 and 9 on the same base-line.) *Maybe I've felt them already.* (Compares 8 and 10.) *One has to feel the end.* (Compares 8 and 9.)—They are all different. We're going to put them in order of size, that is . . . etc. But first you are going to make me a drawing to show me what they will be like when you have put them in order." Drawing I is a set of very small lines (1 cm. to 1 mm.), very approximately seriated. Drawing II contains 6 lines, 1 being large, 2–4 decreasing and 5–6 small and equal. The actual seriation results in unco-ordinated pairs of large and small.

MON (5; 9) examines the rods in the same way as Rae: his hands are motionless at first, then he touches one end, etc. The first drawing contains five lines only: $1 > 2 < 3 < 4 > 5$ (1, 3, and 5 being about the same). "Have you finished?—*Yes.*—Tell me what it's about.—*A small one, a large one and a small one*, etc.—(The instruction is repeated.)—(Drawing II: seven lines on an inclined base-line, with a fairly adequate seriation, although there are one or two equalities.)" The actual seriation results in 8, 7, 4, 9, 2, 5, 1, 6, 3, 10. "Do you think you'll manage?—*One of them won't go!*" He continues till he thinks they are in order. Drawing III is similar to I. The screen is removed, and Mon succeeds in seriating the rods visually after several attempts. Then the rods are hidden again, and he draws the seriation that he has just constructed, producing a drawing similar to II.

BLO (6; 3) examines the rods in the same way as the others, and then produces a drawing (II) consisting of five elements: $1 = 2 = 3 > 4 > 5$. "Tell me what you've done.—*A large one, a medium one, a very little one.*— Have you drawn them all?—*Yes.*" Before carrying out the tactile seriation he re-examines the rods. This time he puts them all on the same base-line and follows the length of each rod instead of just feeling the two ends. As he seriates them, he runs his finger along the top line: the order he reaches is 2, 5, 6, 4, 7, 3, 8, 9, 1, 10. He examines the line of summits once again. The inclination seems right to him, and he does not feel the gaps. He is asked to draw the result, without lifting the screen, and produces $1 = 2 > 3 = 4 > 5 = 6$. He succeeds in the visual seriation, after some errors, and draws this (without seeing it) as a regularly decreasing series of six elements.

The slightly improved anticipation goes with a more thorough examination of the objects. The best performance includes examining the line of summits with the bases along a straight line. Now this method of examination ought to be sufficient to solve the problem, but it remains no more than an intention because the subject fails to perceive the irregularities which persist. Once again the semi-anticipation is in advance of the actual seriation, which still remains at the level of IA.

During stage IIA, the subject anticipates the global schema correctly. But he still cannot carry out the seriation, even by trial and error:

AGU (5; 3) first touches the whole collection of rods, and then examines them all together to see whether they are equal. He then touches them half-way down with his finger-tips, without any systematic examination. Nevertheless, he is able to say: "*There is one which is big, and there's a small one.*" He takes 2 and says: "*One which is quite small; this one* (5), *is a little smaller.*—Are they all alike or different?—*One is big, then one is small, then one is smaller, then another is very small* (this being the principle of seriation, which he is formulating in advance of the instruction).—Well, you are going to arrange them. But first do me a drawing to show what they will be like when they're in order.—*Yes, I'll first make the biggest, then a smaller one, then a small one. It isn't difficult.*" His first drawing (I) consists of nine rectangles, all on the same base-line and in perfect descending order.

In the actual seriation, he takes the rods one by one at random and assesses them by holding them in one hand and measuring them against the other. Finally, he puts 10 aside, and then 6, and tries to put them on the same base-line. He replaces 6 by 7, and then puts 3 next to 7. He takes 3 away and puts 6 in its place, then assesses 9 and substitutes it for 7 alongisde 10. He continues in this way, estimating lengths on his hand, and ends with 10, 9, 7, 8, 6, 5, 2, 4, 3, 1. He then feels the line of summits and, realizing that 2 is small, he substitutes 4 for it, placing this between 6 and 5. After further corrections, he ends with 10, 9, 7, 8, 6, 4, 5, 3, 2, 1. He is asked to draw this, and he draws a neat staircase of 11 rectangles arranged very regularly.

JAN (5; 10) touches the rods by putting his hands on them, and says straight away that they are all different. His drawing consists of 7 rectangles decreasing in length from 10–1·5 cm. His tactile seriation is irregular. The subsequent visual seriations are by trial and error, but eventually correct.

DRA (6; 0) examines the rods globally and says: "*All the same.*—Look at them carefully.—(He examines them more carefully.) *No.* (He compares 8, 4, and 2.)" Before his first drawing, he examines some of the elements again by touching their ends, and compares 4 and 9, 8 and 3, 5 and 4, 5 and 10, and 4 and 9. "*No, they aren't all the same size. I want to feel the biggest, then the smaller one, then the medium one.*" He continues his examination, saying "*It will soon be finished.*" He then draws a neat staircase with very regular steps, formed of rectangles next to one another on the same base. He stops after the tenth, and then adds another six.

In the actual seriation, he puts 7 next to 1 and then adds 6, saying "*There are more than two big ones.*" He looks for "*the very little one. One like that is missing* (the last one on the drawing)." He constructs 1, 10, 3 and then substitutes 2 for 10. After further trial-and-error: "*I can't go on to the end any more.*—But you are doing very well." He continues and ends with a series which is irregular except for the elements 1, 2, 3 at the beginning. The screen is removed and he corrects his seriation, then produces a new drawing identical to the first one.

There is an obvious improvement in the examination of the elements, and the anticipation is correspondingly more adequate. Thus Agu, although he appears to be taking a global view, understands the situation sufficiently to state the form of the seriation before receiving the instruction. Jan's thinking is similar, even though he is less explicit, and Dra compares the elements in pairs before proceeding to the drawing. The anticipation gives rise to a regular global schema, which is as much a guide to the examination of the rods as its result. In spite of this double advance, the actual seriation is little better than it was at stage I. It is better conceived, and also better carried out in some respects (there are small sub-series, the child examines the line of summits, etc.); but it is still inadequate because each element is not related to a sufficient number of others.

At stage IIB, however, the anticipation and the seriation are both correct, even though the latter is the result of trial-and-error.

TOM (6; 8) takes three rods, puts them on the same base, and examines their ends. He continues in this way, and answers the usual question by: "*There aren't two the same.*" He is asked for a drawing, and tries to arrange the rods first: "*I am putting them from the smallest to the biggest.*—No, do a drawing before you arrange them." He then draws seven lines in descending order. In the actual seriation, he starts with couples and constructs 6, 8, 5, 7, checking the bases each time. He then constructs 3, 2, 1, and brings the elements close together, feeling the line of summits and keeping the base-line constant. He separates 8 and 6 and places 7 between them, then he separates

4 from 5 and places it next to 3, 2, 1. In this way, he completes the seriation correctly, and draws it as before. When the screen is removed, he is satisfied with his seriation, and does a third drawing similar to the preceding ones.

CHA (5; 9) starts by a most cursory examination of the ten hidden elements, and soon states that they are all different. She has doubts about 1 and 2, but she compares them and realizes that they are different. Drawing I consists of a regularly decreasing series of 9 rectangles. In the actual seriation, she looks for the largest rod 1, and then puts 6 in place and puts 2 next to it. She begins to feel the ends, always careful to check that the bases are in line. She arrives at 1, 2, 3, 6, 10, 4, and then inserts 4 between 3 and 6, etc. She feels the ends of the rods once more with one hand, using the other to keep them on the same base. Finally, only 3, 5, and 7 are missing. She succeeds in inserting two of these, and leaves the third aside. She does a drawing (II) of ten elements arranged in a regular series, with an eleventh element apart from the others! The visual seriation is also by trial-and-error.

There is systematic progress which results in a successful seriation through trial-and-error. It consists in checking both ends of the rods so that the problem can then be solved by successive rearrangements and insertions. Table XXV shows that this method persists for a long time. The reason is that in this situation it is more practical than the operational method, because the elements cannot be perceived simultaneously. More precisely, this method is a way of making the tactile perception of the elements more nearly simultaneous, which is why it succeeds.

Nevertheless, there is a third stage which starts at 7–8 years, and which is characterized by the operational method. This means looking for the largest of all the elements, then the largest among those that remain, etc.

ELI (8; 2) examines the elements very little before her anticipatory drawing, which is a series of ten rectangles, decreasing very regularly. In the actual seriation, she collects all the rods together, and looks for the largest, 1. She puts this in place, and arranges all the others on the same base and then looks for the largest among them. After hesitating over 3, she finds 2 and puts it next to 1. By proceeding in this way, she completes the correct seriation.

HAN (9; 3) examines the rods for an instant, says: "*There are smaller ones and bigger ones*", then draws eleven rectangles in decreasing order. In the actual seriation, she takes 3, 4, and 1, examines them, and then leaves them. She takes 2 and finds 1 once more. "What are you looking for?—*The big one.*" She continues by standing the others on the table and feeling their tops, in order to find the largest. In this way, she arrives at a correct seriation. "Do you agree with your drawing?—*No.*—Would you like to make another?—*Yes, a bigger one* (draws seventeen rectangles in a regularly decreasing series). —Why are you drawing so many sticks?—*I know that there are ten, but I've drawn them a little too big, so I have to make more.*"

Compared to the method of examining the line of summits by trial-and-error with the rods on a common base, the operational method means sacrificing a quasi-simultaneous perception in favour of successive comparisons. No doubt that is why it is not generally used at an age when it is universal in visual seriation.

Coming back to the question of the relation between seriation, anticipation and perception, after comparing tactile and visual seriation together with the corresponding graphic anticipations, we are convinced of the correctness of our second hypothesis in §2. The advance of anticipation over actual seriation is as clear in the tactile field as it is in the visual (even though both are slightly retarded). What is more, the relative retardation of tactile seriation is due only to the successive nature of tactile perceptions. The pre-operational (correction by trial-and-error) and operational procedures are the same for both. From this point of view, the comparison of tests involving ten rods with those involving five, is highly instructive. If the size of the series is reduced by half, while the differences between elements are increased, the anticipation and the actual seriation obtained in the tactile test with subjects of 4–5 years are not only better than in the tactile test with ten rods, but better than in the visual test with ten rods. We will give only one example to illustrate the experiment with five elements, because the qualitative results are similar to those of the main experiment. The only systematic difference is that a seriation carried out by trial-and-error can no longer be distinguished from one carried out by the operational method, since the nearly simultaneous perception is so much easier.

BAD (5; 8) examines the ends of the rods, after having collected the five elements together and drawn a regular series of five rectangles. In the actual seriation, she takes all the rods together and indicates 1, which she puts aside. She then chooses 2, followed by 4, which she takes back again and replaces by 3. Finally, she puts 4 and 5 in place.

Once again, it is wrong to say that serial structures, whether in anticipation or in actual construction are abstracted from perceptual forms which exist independently of the subject's actions.

Anticipatory structures grow out of the progressive organization of actions, and that organization also structures perception, adapting it to its own needs. This is neatly illustrated by the way in which successive comparisons are translated into a simultaneous figure.

Chapter Ten

MULTIPLE SERIATION[1]

WHEN we compare the development of class structures and that of asymmetrical transitive relations we find a paradox. On the one hand, it seems that seriation (which is an additive arrangement of asymmetrical transitive relations) is more intuitive than an additive sequence of class-inclusions, because it corresponds to a far simpler perceptual configuration. On the other hand, the multiplication of classes seems to correspond to a fairly simple perceptual configuration, so that matrix tests can be solved independently of any operational methods, while the multiplication of asymmetrical transitive relations (involving a matrix with series ordered along the horizontal and vertical axes) may well be much more complicated because it involves a double asymmetry. However, without proceeding to an actual experiment, we cannot be sure of this. We do know that serial correspondence, as opposed to serial multiplication, is just as easy as simple seriation. In other words, a child who can build a single series can also build two or three: $A_1 < B_1 < C_1 \ldots$; $A_2 < B_2 < C_2 \ldots$; $A_3 < B_3 < C_3 \ldots$; and he can tell that C_1 corresponds with C_2 and C_3, etc.[2] But the correspondence between series is symmetrical in this structure. It does not involve a new asymmetry in a different dimension. What we need is an investigation on the *multiplication* of asymmetrical transitive relations, so that we can properly compare its development with that of multiplicative cross-classification. We have in fact carried out such an enquiry on 52 subjects.

1. EXPERIMENTAL PROCEDURE

The child was presented with 49 drawings of leaves, cut out of cardboard. These could be ordered according to size and according to colour intensity. There were seven sizes, which we shall number I–VII, and seven shades ranging from yellow green to dark green, which we shall number 1–7. Each size was represented in every one of the seven shades, and each shade in every one of the seven sizes. We sometimes used 98 elements consisting of 49 identical pairs, to test the child's reaction to identical elements. Also, with the younger children, we sometimes used a smaller collection of 4 × 4 identical pairs with greater differences of size and colouring. The subject was asked to arrange these elements as

[1] With the assistance of A. Morf.
[2] Piaget and Szeminska, *The Child's Conception of Number*, 1952, ch. V.

he wished. If he did not succeed, the experimenter might arrange one series in a line along one of the dimensions of the table shown (see diagram), or two series along both dimensions, leaving the rest of the table to be filled in by the subject. Once the table had been constructed, whether spontaneously or with the experimenter's help, the subject was asked to find an element according to two simultaneous criteria. It sometimes happens that a subject constructs a complete table by himself, but still fails to understand its true multiplicative significance.

I 1	I 2	I 3	I 4	I 5	I 6	I 7
II 1	.	.	.	.	.	.
III 1	.	.	.	.	.	.
IV 1	.	.	.	.	.	.
V 1	.	.	.	.	.	.
VI 1	.	.	.	.	.	.
VII 1	.	.	.	.	.	.

We shall distinguish three stages, corresponding to the usual three levels. During stage I, there are no seriations in the strict sense. The child's constructions are intermediate between classification and seriation, and are usually based on graphic collections (alignments, etc.). During stage II, there is seriation, but only according to one of the criteria, or else the child switches from one criterion to the other, without achieving a multiplicative synthesis of the two. Finally, during stage III (starting at 7–8 years), the child reaches a multiplicative arrangement based on the twofold seriation of the set of elements.

2. STAGE I: NO TRUE SERIATION

We begin with a few examples:

HEN (5; 5). The small set of 32 elements: he starts by aligning the 32 leaves, with the identical elements next to one another. He also has the 8 largest leaves together but the remaining 24 are dispersed irregularly. "Can you do better still?—(He arranges them again, and ends with four collections based on size, but these are not in serial order; he ignores colour altogether.)—Can you put them together so that one can see which are dark, less dark, light and very light?—(He attempts a seriation, but this remains approximate because he is distracted by the sizes.)—Try to arrange them now so that the large ones are together and the small ones too, but so that the same colours are together as well.—(He constructs a large circle by combining the leaves by their colour, and then subdividing these collections according to size.)—The experimenter then fills in the top row and the left-hand column of the 16-cell matrix and asks Hen to place two or three leaves in the right cells. He can do this by trial-and-error: *"because it's the same colour and the same size"*.

Ver (5; 7). 32 elements: he classes them in four unseriated collections based on size. "Do you have any other ideas?—(Forms two piles, the large elements and the small ones.)—Any more?—*No*.—Could one put the dark ones together and the light ones together?—*No, that wouldn't do. There are large ones and small ones*.—Do it all the same.—(Forms three piles: the light, the medium and the dark leaves.)—What about these? (the third pile)? You have very dark ones and less dark ones.—(He subdivides them, to obtain 4 collections based on colour.)—Could one arrange them so that I can put my hand on, say, the big ones straight away?—(He forms four collections based on size, paying no more attention to colour.)—Could you do it so as to find the size and the colour at the same time?—(He forms a single pile subdivided into light ones, small ones, etc., without the multiplicative system.)" Finally, the experimenter fills in the upper row and the left-hand column of the table, and Ver completes it by trial-and-error.

Bur (5; 9) divides the 49 elements into a number of collections some of which are based on size and some on colour. When given a hint how to seriate the elements by size, he continues the series without paying any attention to colour. With the set of 32 elements, he forms a collection of large dark leaves, another of large light ones, and a third of small leaves, both dark and light, and then stacks these three collections to make three separate rows, without any seriations or any multiplication.

Vus (6; 0) makes separate stacks for the different colours. But these columns are not seriated, and each one contains various sizes mixed together at random, except for a few sub-series of three elements. "Could you do it differently so that one could know where to find any size?—(Now she produces similar vertical alignments based on size, with the colours jumbled together.)" She then tries to pile together leaves of the same size, without seriation or consideration of colour.

The general characteristic of these reactions is that the subject constructs graphic collections (alignments, circles, columns, etc.), which can develop into classes as easily as into series. He does not construct any real seriation spontaneously, even though he may be capable of carrying one out through trial-and-error (cf. Hen). Furthermore, his graphic classifications are based on one of the two properties involved, or he may alternate between the two without achieving a multiplicative synthesis (cf. Bur). If the experimenter then reminds him of the property which has been forgotten, the subject can take it into account by subdividing the collections which he has constructed already. But this is not multiplication in the true sense. Nevertheless, he does succeed in using a matrix based on the multiplication of relations, when the experimenter fills in the upper row and the left-hand column (cf. Hen and Ver). But this is done by trial-and-error and it is a graphic, rather than an operational, solution of the problem.

3. STAGE II: SPONTANEOUS SERIATION OF ONE OF THE TWO PROPERTIES, BUT FAILURE IN THE MULTIPLICATIVE SYNTHESIS OF BOTH

Here are some examples:

SAN (6; 0). With the 32 elements, San spontaneously constructs a square table with 16 cells, the identical elements being superposed. The horizontal rows are formed of the four different shades, and they are seriated from the lightest to the darkest, but the sizes are distributed at random. "What have you done? —(She points to the four columns!) *The light ones, the less light ones, the dark ones, the darkest ones.*—And where are the big ones and the little ones.— (Indicates them.)—Can you do it to help find them quickly?—(San constructs a new table with the horizontal rows chosen according to size and seriated from the smallest to the largest. This time the colours are jumbled together.)— But, you know, one can't find the colours now!—(San takes the light leaves and orders them vertically from the largest to the smallest.)—Can you do the same with the dark ones?—(She does so, and then inserts the intermediate colours, also seriated by size.)" Thus San has succeeded, with the help of the experimenter's suggestions, in constructing a table which is graphically iso-morphic to a matrix based on the multiplication of relations. But San has not done this spontaneously and she does not grasp its full meaning. When she is given the table for 49 elements, with the upper row and left-hand column filled in by the experimenter, and is asked to place additional leaves on it, she can only find the row corresponding to the colour; she cannot find the column corresponding to the size unless the correct cell happens to adjoin one that is already filled in.

STEC (6; 3). With the 32 elements, Stec also constructs a square table whose four columns correspond to the four colours and are arranged in order of decreasing darkness from left to right. The sizes are jumbled together within these columns. "It's still mixed up. Can you arrange it so that I can find the sizes more quickly?" Stec then carries out an approximate seriation of each column by size. She goes on to construct four piles each of which is seriated according to size (the largest leaf being at the base and the smallest at the summit), and she then seriates the piles according to colour. Then she spon-taneously spreads the elements in her piles to form columns, so that she reaches a square matrix which is complete and correct. But, like San, Stec does not understand its full meaning. When presented with the key to the table for 49 elements, she places additional leaves correctly for size, but not for colour— unless one of the nearest cells is already complete.

CAT (6; 2) seriates the dark leaves among the 32 elements according to size, but in cyclic order, i.e. the smallest is next to the largest. She constructs another three circles in the same way, first using the less dark leaves, then the light ones and then the lightest ones. Identical elements are always superposed. The four circles are then arranged in a line in order of decreasing darkness. This configuration is really a complete and correct multiplicative system. But there is no convenient way of connecting an element in one circle with a corresponding element in another circle. Cat then tries another system: she transforms one of the circles into a column, with the leaves partially super-posed as though they were tiles. She does the same with the other circles, forming a square matrix with 16 cells. She then replaces these columns with vertical piles, the largest leaf being at the base and the smallest at the summit. Finally, she rearranges everything, laying the large leaves in a horizontal row (I) seriated in order of decreasing darkness. She places a second row (II) formed of leaves of the next size, and also seriated according to colour, immediately below this. But, instead of the colours of row I and row II corresponding, row II is shorter, and so the correspondences are oblique instead of vertical. She constructs another row (III) of leaves of the next size, seriated by colour, making it even shorter than row II. She does the same for row IV. She now has a two-entry table, but a table which is not square. Only the first column, consisting of elements I 1–IV 1, is vertical. The other columns are more and more steeply inclined.

Asc (6; 4) classes the 32 elements according to the four different colours, and then takes the collection of the lightest elements and seriates it by size. He does the same with the other collections, and thus constructs a complete multiplicative system. But because the collections are not exactly super-posed, he remains unaware of the correspondence of leaves of the same size scattered in different collections. In other words, although he understands the seriation of the four colour-collections and the seriation of size within each one, he does not find the correspondence between elements in different collections.

There is a gradual development throughout this stage and its cul-mination comes very near to the multiplicative seriation matrix. Taking this evolution in order, we have first of all subjects like San who merely seriate one of the two variables and are content to ignore the other until they are specifically reminded of it by the experimenter. Initially the reminder is ineffective because all they do is to seriate on the basis of this second criterion, forgetting about the first, but later on they do try to reconcile the two, although they do not become aware of the multiplication as a whole. Next we have subjects like Stec who also begin by seriating one of the variables, but who can introduce a seriation of the second variable within the collections so formed, when prompted by the experimenter: they therefore end up with a set of seriations within a seriation. Nevertheless, even where this configuration is identical with a representation of a multiplicative matrix, they still fail to appreciate its full significance. Finally we have subjects like Cat who start out to construct some sort of double seriation. However, although the inten-tion is clear enough, as it is on the colour series of Cat, where each colour grouping is ordered on the criterion of size (in cyclic order), the result is often imperfect because the two seriations are on separate planes, one being a seriation of collections (circles, columns or piles), while the other is a set of seriations within these collections. The ar-rangement as a whole therefore fails to establish a one-one correspon-dence between individual members of different collections. Cat himself reaches a quadrilateral arrangement where the correspondences are practically correct, but the very fact that his matrix is not square, which it should be in view of the multiplication involved, shows that he is still thinking of the two seriations on heterogeneous planes instead of co-ordinating them. What Asc does is similar, but he does it right away. Asc is therefore quite close to an operational insight.

Responses to the set of 49 elements confirm the hypothesis that the two seriations are thought of on separate planes at stage II. Although we always fill in the top row and the first column, so that the subject has only to place various leaves in the right cells of the skeleton matrix, children at stage II never manage to find the correct intersection unless they are helped by neighbouring elements, but they do find *either* the correct row *or* the correct column immediately. The difficulty can hardly be attributed to perceptual factors. What they find hard is to follow the two seriations simultaneously, which is after all the essence of multiplication. When there are only 32 elements, these same children can take both seriations into account, but because they fail to see the multiplicative essence of what they are doing, the two variables are not seen as homogeneous.

4. STAGE III: SUCCESSFUL MULTIPLICATION

We shall first give three examples which are intermediate between stage II and stage III, and then go on to examples of stage III proper.

KRO (6; 6) immediately arranges the 32 elements according to size and colour. She gradually constructs a pattern with four columns seriated from left to right according to decreasing size, and 4 rows seriated from the darkest shade at the top to the lightest shade at the bottom. She understands that only one of the two properties varies along a column or a row, and when she is asked to find an element both lighter and smaller than another, she follows the diagonal or a line parallel to it.

However, her arrangement of the 2 × 49 elements, is a good deal less than perfect. Nevertheless, when the experimenter proceeds to fill in one row and one column, she fills in the remaining elements with only a few errors, and these she corrects spontaneously.

At 7; 1, the same subject immediately arranges the 32 elements in a matrix. She starts correctly, but then tires, when given 98 elements. When given the table with the upper row and left-hand column filled in, she completes it without mistakes.

JUN (7; 6). With the 32 elements, he starts by forming 8 horizontal rows arranged in order of decreasing size, with colours jumbled together. He arranges the rows in groups of four, forming two juxtaposed tables. He then orders the colours in the interior of each row, and thus constructs two matrices formed of identical elements. The second has a systematic inversion with respect to the first in the seriation of colour, while size is seriated in the same way in both.

SUT (7; 2). In the same way, Sut starts a seriation of size with the colours jumbled together, and then seriates each colour in order of decreasing intensity. She thus constructs a matrix correctly, with each element occurring twice.

With the set of 2 × 49 elements, she immediately starts to construct a matrix by following the same method. She completes it correctly, except for a few small errors where the differences in hue are only slight.

MAR (7; 4). "Tell me what you see.—*There are some which are darker and some which are smaller than others.*—Can you put them in order?—(He takes the darkest leaves and seriates them by size.) *It's the darkest ones which I've put first. Does it matter?* (He places leaves on one another to assess their sizes, continuing with the less dark ones, etc., until the matrix is complete.— How did you arrange them so well?—*I kept looking at the smallest ones and the lightest ones.*"

WES (7; 5) first constructs rows of 3–4 elements in which size and darkness decrease simultaneously. This means that he thinks that he can avoid constructing series in which one quality changes while the other remains constant. But he realizes that he cannot seriate all the elements in this way. "Is it possible to do it differently?—(He now constructs rows of the same size and decreasing darkness, and columns of the same colour and decreasing size.)"

DUB (7; 11). With the 32 elements, Dub first seriates the large leaves in order of decreasing darkness. Then he seriates the next largest leaves in the same way, etc. But he arranges these series in one long line. "What if you wanted to find the darkest ones or the lightest ones straight away?—*Oh, I know!* (he superposes his series, forming a matrix)."

He does the same for the 49 elements, and this time he superposes his series immediately.

GUY (8; 3), on the other hand, seriates the dark leaves in the order of decreasing size, etc., again leaving his series in juxtaposition. "Can you do something to make it easy to look at everything at once?—*Oh, of course!*" (He superposes the four colour-collections to obtain the matrix.)

PAR (8; 6). Like Wes, Par starts with a row along which size and darkness of colour decrease simultaneously (and which thus corresponds to the diagonal; I 1, II 2, III 3, IV 4). He then constructs a column of elements of fixed size, and decreasing darkness (I 1, I 2, I 3, I 4). Naturally, he cannot complete this table, having started by taking the first sequence as the upper row and the second as the left-hand column: so he switches to the second method.

Comparing this stage with stage II, we find two features which are new, although they are not independent.

The first point to note is that these children realize they will have to seriate in terms of two variables as soon as they see the material. A typical reaction is to say, like Mar, "Some are darker and some are smaller". What is more, although a child may begin by seriating in terms of one variable, he always realizes from the start that the eventual outcome will take care of both.

Secondly, the two seriations are always seen as being homogeneous

275

and equal in importance, and this is true even when one seriation is made first. So the second seriation does not become subordinate, as it did at stage II. We are no longer being presented with a series of seriated collections, one set of series being within collections, the other series obtaining between collections. In other words, the end-result is always a seriation by colour *and* size, not a seriation by colour *or* size, even though the child usually starts with one or the other. When a subject like Dab constructs a series of classes decreasing by size and also seriates the elements in each class by their colour, he is already establishing a mental correspondence between the colours in the different size-classes (which is the reverse of what we saw at stage II). That is why both Dab and Gay need only a word of prompting on the part of the experimenter to superpose the classes so as to arrive at a matrix which faithfully represents a systematic co-ordination of both variables.

However, it is worth noting that the anticipatory schema is limited to the idea of twofold ordering and of two homogeneous seriations. In other words, the schema includes the idea of multiplication which is essential; but the subject does not always know in advance the precise spatial arrangement which will best represent it. This is not what we found in the multiplication of classes, where the majority of subjects seemed to anticipate the spatial arrangement (as a matrix) as well as its multiplicative essence. Yet we saw in ch. IX that when only one seriation was involved, there is a semi-anticipation of the graphic arrangement as early as stage II! This is the crux of the problem with which we set out at the beginning of this chapter.

Now a seriation is a "good" perceptual form for two reasons. First, the same qualitative difference reappears between successive terms, and, second, these differences may be quantitatively equal (but they need not be so). Moreover the difference relations themselves can be perceived directly, and this is not true in classification.

Conversely, a classification is not a "good" form because of the perceptual complexity of the relations of which it is composed. An ordered system of classes has the form $A < B < C$ and is governed by the operations $A + A' = B$, $B + B' = C$; etc. It contains two types of relation: (1) Equivalence relations, e.g. a for all members of A, b for all members of B, etc. (these relations are perceptible, but the classes which are unions of members so related are not, or if they are, it is only in terms of some graphic disposition which is imposed on them); (2) difference relations or "complementarities" as between members of A and members of A' or members of B and members of B', etc. The latter relations are not repeated; i.e. the difference between members of A and those of A' is not the same as that between members of B and B'. Nor, in general, are they seriable. Because of this mixture of equivalences and complementarities, the configuration of a classification is much more complex than that of a seriation. It has neither its simplicity nor its regularity, and therefore it is not a "good" perceptual form.

$A_1 A_2$	$A_1 A_2'$	$A_1 B_2'$
$A_1' A_2$	$A_1' A_2'$	$A_1' B_2'$
$B_1' A_2$	$B_1' A_2'$	$B_1' B_2'$

When we come to the multiplication of classes we find the following difference relations or complementarities for the 9 elements shown on the above table: between A_1 and A_1'; between $(A_1 + A_1')$ and B_1'; between A_2 and A_2'; and finally between $(A_2 + A_2')$ and B_2'. These difference relations parallel those which figure in an additive classification. But the fact of multiplication, far from adding confusion to the perceptualization of such a system, has the effect of making it easier by virtue of the symmetries to which it gives rise. Thus the same characters reappear in each row or in each column, which makes for a twofold symmetry in the arrangements. The net effect is that although there are as many difference relations as equivalence relations, the equivalences dominate in the graphic presentation. We therefore find that a multiplicative matrix of classifications yields a more convincing "good form" than a simply additive structure, whence the paradoxes in development which we considered in ch. V.

Now the same ought to be true of the multiplication of asymmetrical and transitive relations as illustrated. The only difference is that instead of complementarities we are dealing with serial differences.

I 1 $\rightarrow$	I 2 $\rightarrow$	I 3
$\downarrow$	$\downarrow$	$\downarrow$
II 1 $\rightarrow$	II 2 $\rightarrow$	II 3
$\downarrow$	$\downarrow$	$\downarrow$
III 1 $\rightarrow$	III 2 $\rightarrow$	III 3

Seriation, as we know, is a "better" form than classification; so the multiplication of seriation should be easier than multiplying non-seriable classes. But the fact is that the very equivalences which make cross-classification easier than simple classification also make multiple seriation harder than simple seriation. The reason for this paradox is that the subject is looking for equivalences when he is classifying because a class is a union of elements based on an equivalence relation. Difference relations (i.e. complementarities) which inevitably occur in an ordered system of classes run counter to this mental "set", making the task more difficult. Now such differences are attenuated by the symmetries which occur in a multiplicative arrangement, and the subject is able to focus more easily on the equivalences. Conversely, when he is trying to seriate, he is looking for differences, because a series is simply a chain of asymmetrical and transitive differences. The fact that in multiple seriation there are two sets of seriable differences makes this "set" all the stronger. Now unfortunately you cannot make up a table to represent a twofold seriation without introducing equivalences. If you try it, then all you discover are the diagonals of the complete matrix. In other words, you cannot limit the combinations to $<<$, $>>$, $><$, and $<>$; you have to foresee the additional possibilities $<=$, $>=$, $=<$, $=>$, and $==$ (whether or not they actually occur). These partial equivalences, which do not occur in simple seriation, act as a hindrance to the graphic solution of a multiple seriation. This, surely, is the explanation of the paradoxical finding that cross-classification yields a "better" form than simple classification while multiple seriation corresponds to a "worse" form than simple seriation.

There is an interesting pointer to this in the fact that several subjects (like Wes and Par) start out by trying to construct a double seriation by ordering the elements in terms of both variables at once $<<$ or $>>$ (e.g. larger and darker). What they are doing is to construct the diagonal, but they do so under the misapprehension that they are building the table itself, or at least one row or one column. This sort of attitude is exactly what we should expect—on condition that the subject is aware that there are two relations. That is why we do not find it at stage I when the child tends to classify in terms of graphic collections, and we do not find it at stage II, when he thinks of one seriation only or of one seriation as dominant.

It is all the more striking that, in spite of these difficulties in graphic translation, subjects do spontaneously arrive at ordered classes like the long alignments of Dub and Guy (I, 1–4; II, 1–4; etc.) which are a one-dimensional way of representing the multiplication, or even at a matrix in two dimensions.

By way of conclusion, we would answer the problem we raised at the beginning of this chapter in the following terms: (1) Children reach an operational level in the multiplication of series about the same period (7–8) as cross-classification. (2) Nevertheless the first of these schemata does entail a problem of its own, a problem of spatial symbolism and not one of logical structure. From the age of 7 or 8, on average, they show that they understand the need to observe the equivalences as well as the differences involved (and this is true even of those who start out by looking for combined differences, $>>$ or $<<$). Indeed they cannot solve the problem without at the same time constructing sizeclasses seriated for colour and colour-classes seriated for size. But they do not all hit on a two-dimensional symbolism right away; some do, but others use a one-dimensional cyclic order (I, 1–4; II, 1–4, etc.).

Finally, there are four principal "groupings" in the logic of classes and relations, corresponding with simple and multiple classification and simple and multiple seriation. It is a most remarkable fact that, in spite of the differences just noted in respect of ease of perceptualization, all four structures become operational at roughly the same period. There are certain minor differences depending on the extent to which the content of a problem lends itself to imaginal representation, but they do not invalidate our main thesis.

CONCLUSIONS

THERE is a fairly extensive literature which deals with the development of classification and a number of published works deal specifically with seriation. Some of the most outstanding work in the field has been that of Goldstein and his collaborators, notably M. Scheerer. Goldstein and Scheerer[1] analysed behaviour in "categorization" from the point of view of the abstractions involved. It is to these workers that we owe the notion of the opposition between flexibility or ease of "shifting" and rigidity in categorization. Goldstein and Scheerer's "sorting-test" consists of 33 common objects which the subject is asked to arrange in as many ways as possible; he may also be asked to define classes as constructed by the tester. Reichard, Schneider and Rapaport[2] studied this sort of behaviour in children, as also did Thompson.[3] As early as 1937, Hanfmann and Kasanin,[4] basing themselves on the work of Ach (together with certain modifications introduced by Sacharov and Vigotsky), were able to devise a test of classification using 22 blocks. The objects differ from one another in colour (5 shades), in shape (4), in height (2) and in width (2). The subject is told to divide them into four groups: the solution demands flexibility and persistence; fluidity of thinking is essential, while rigidity hinders the correct solution. The ideas of Goldstein led Wallon to posit a "pre-categorizing" level in children's thinking, which is one manifestation of pre-operational thinking in general. A former collaborator of ours, G. Ascoli, also carried out a study of children's classifications under Wallon's direction.[5] In addition, the ideas of Gestalt psychology inspired R. Meili in his work on classificatory structures.[6]

It is not surprising to find that a large number of studies deal with the relation between classification and language. The work of Oléron[7] and

[1] K. Goldstein and M. Scheerer, *Abstract and Concrete Behaviour, an Experimental Study with Special Tests*, Psychol. Monogr., LIII, 151 pp. (1941).
M. M. Bolls and K. Goldstein, "A study of the impairment of 'abstract' behaviour in schizophrenic patients", *Psychiatr. Quart.*, XII, 42–65 (1938).

[2] S. Reichard, M. Schneider and D. Rappaport, "The development of concept formation in children", *Am. J. Orthopsychiatr.*, XIV, 151–161 (1944).

[3] J. Thompson, "The ability of children of different grade levels to generalise on sorting tests", *J. Psychol.*, XI, 119–126 (1944).

[4] E. Hanfmann and J. Kasanin, "A method for the study of concept formation", *J. Psychol.*, III, 521–540 (1937), and *id.*, *Conceptual Thinking in Schizophrenia*, New Mental Dis. Monogr., No. 67, 115 pp. (New York, 1942).

[5] G. Ascoli, "Comment l'enfant sait classer les objets", *Enfance*, 1950, No. 3.

[6] R. Meili, "Experimentelle Untersuchungen über das Ordnen von Gegenständen", *Psychol. Forsch.*, 1926, Bd. VII.

[7] P. Oléron, "Etude sur les capacités intellectuelles des sourds-muets", *Année Psychol.*, 1949 (XLVII–XLVIII), 136–155, and "Pensee conceptuelle et language", *ibid.*, 1951 (LI), 89–120.

Vincent[1] might be mentioned here, both of these dealing with the behaviour of the deaf. Special attention might also be given to a remarkable recent study by Slama-Cazacu,[2] also dealing with the role of language in classification. The subjects were normal children, but an outstanding feature of this work is the way in which the experimental situation mirrors that of ordinary life. Slama-Cazacu uses a "cupboard-game": the subject is asked to arrange the material in a real cupboard, which means that the classification has a genuine functional significance.

The outstanding contribution to the field of multiplicative classification is, of course, Raven's "progressive matrices".[3] We know of no systematic investigations on seriation, but the problem is frequently discussed in the literature on perceptual structures.

In view of the extent of the work that has already been done and its high quality, we cannot be sure how far the actual results of our own work are entirely new. However, we would like to stress the fact that the questions we asked ourselves are rather different, because our own point of view is also somewhat different from that of our predecessors.

It is natural that the psychologist should study the behaviour involved in classification and seriation. But classification and seriation are also logical structures with precise laws as formulated by logicians and mathematicians. As the child develops, so his behaviour tends increasingly to conform with these logico-mathematical structures. Now the majority of psychologists who deal with classification and seriation have been concerned with purely functional problems, e.g. why a particular group of individuals lacks the flexibility to "shift" from an unsatisfactory classificatory criterion to one that might be more fruitful, or how language furthers the construction of some classes but not of others, etc. The exceptions are those "Gestaltists" (Goldstein, Meili, etc.) who try to reduce every structure to the very general terms of "Gestalten". We believe that such an attempt does violence to the specific properties of operational structures.

The main problem with which we have been concerned stems from our interest in genetic epistemology, and it is very different. We want to know why the organization of behaviour in classification and seriation takes the forms that it does. In particular we want to know why later forms tend to approximate more and more closely to logico-mathematical structures. (Neither the logician nor the mathematician can

[1] M. Borelli-Vincent, "La naissance des opérations logiques chez les sourds-muets", *Enfance*, 1951 (IV), 222–238. Cf. also, *Enfance*, 1956, 1–20.

M. Vincent, "Sur le role du langage à un niveau élémentaire de pensée abstraite", *Enfance*, 1957, No. 4, 443–464.

[2] T. Slama-Cazacu, *Relatiire dintre gîndire si limbaj in ontogeneza* (The relations between thinking and language in development), Acad. Rep. Popul. Romîna, 1957, 508 pp. (with French summary).

[3] C. Raven, *Progressive Matrices*, Lewis, 1938.

impose these models *a priori*, but it is a fact that the subject, without knowing these models, tends to construct forms of organization which are increasingly isomorphic with respect to the models.) For instance, one of the main questions with which we dealt is the way in which children gradually build up the structure of class-inclusion. This structure is not a primary *datum* (it is not genetically given, nor is it a Gestalt, etc.): it is elaborated by a process of gradual construction whose very existence we should hardly have suspected had we set out by thinking only of the finished product as reflected in adult linguistic behaviour.

The question of how structures are elaborated is not one with which psychologists in general have been much concerned. The majority of psychologists are not interested in logic, and this means that they have a tendency to accept what they regard as logically necessary as somehow "given", instead of posing a problem. We have to ask ourselves what precisely is the process whereby we come to construct or admit this kind of "necessity", and this entails analysing our development as children and adolescents. All our previous investigations have convinced us that classifications and seriations are essentially operational forms of behaviour. It is for that reason that we set out in the present work to enquire into the genesis of these operations, and in particular, to analyse the relation between their underlying structures and the corresponding mechanisms in perception and sensori-motor behaviour. We may now attempt to summarize our results:

1. There is a very close relation between the development of logical operations, and prior to this, of pre-logical actions and that of sub-logical operations and actions. The difference between what is logical (or pre-logical) and what is sub-logical is simply that the former deals with the relations between discontinuous elements while the latter relates to elements forming part of a spatial continuum. The "graphic collections" of stage I (see ch. I) are a pointer to the complete lack of differentiation at the outset between the logical and the sub-logical. At stage II, there is partial differentiation (see ch. I, §4); at stage III they are completely differentiated (see ch. II, §3). The two sorts of behaviour develop in parallel. We begin by making this point, because it shows that we should be wrong to confine our search for the origins of these operations to the symbols and concepts of language. Instead, we must look to any sort of action which involves either a bringing together (union) or an ordering of elements, irrespective of whether these elements form part of a larger spatial continuum or are discrete members of a set.

2. The fact that classificatory unions and subdivisions reach back to a primitive origin in actions, where they are in no way differentiated from sub-logical union and subdivision, means that the child has a very long way to go from these early and ill-differentiated functional

aggregates to arrive at true classificatory concepts. The latter, as we know, form a part of the semantic content of language and lend themselves to mental manipulation through the medium of language. Such concepts have both an extension (to define the members of the given class), and an intension (being the properties common to its members). Now the intension is based on relations of similarity, which means that it harks back to sensori-motor assimilations: even at the sensori-motor level there is assimilation by similarity; it derives both from the perception of common qualities and from an elementary kind of abstraction which is intimately bound up with functional ends. On the other hand, the extension of concepts can only be developed with the aid of a precise symbolism. Nor is it enough to possess the appropriate verbal signs: they must enter into an adequate system of quantification.

We therefore believe that the only adequate explanation of the phenomenon of graphic collections is that little children have difficulty in co-ordinating intension and extension. It is not enough to try to account for the generality of this kind of behaviour by pointing to the lack of differentiation between the logical (or pre-logical) and the sub-logical. The lack of differentiation helps to account for the strange way in which little children tend to confuse relations of qualitative similarity with mere spatial contiguity, both in their alignments and in their complex objects. It also helps to explain the tendency to introduce functional relations of belonging alongside those of similarity. So long as the union itself is partly spatial in essence, the principle of union need not be homogeneous, for it is only a logical set which constitutes a union based solely on relations of similarity. But the real problem is why there is this lack of differentiation and why it persists: why is it that when little children set out to classify a group of objects they end up with spatial and graphic wholes, and why does this sort of behaviour go on for so long? We now know that the reason is that whereas there is some appreciation of intension right from the start, based on sensori-motor assimilation, there is only one kind of "extension" available to children at this level, and that is the spatial or graphic extension of a perceptual whole. This sort of extension may be adequate to construct a sub-logical whole, but it is very far removed from the extension of a logical class of discontinuous elements, because that extension is independent of spatial arrangement.

3. We therefore see the co-ordination of extension and intension as the central problem in the development of classificatory behaviour. Accordingly, we set out to examine the growth of such co-ordination by studying the actions and operations of the subject himself. In other words, we accepted from the outset that it is not enough to study the ways in which intension and extension are as it were pre-figured for the child in the system of verbal concepts which is incorporated in common

language. As a matter of fact, the results of our investigations on the use of "all" and "some" and on the quantification of inclusion (chs. III and IV) showed very clearly that children only reach a proper understanding of the extension of verbal concepts (and also, for that matter, of perceptual configurations) in the measure that they can themselves re-structure the content. In other words, the starting-point for the understanding, even of verbal concepts, is still the actions and operations of the subject. But by taking this as our starting-point, we automatically come up against the paradoxical and circular character of the relations between extension and intension. We have in fact a vicious circle which can only be resolved by a genetic analysis.

On the one hand, we cannot determine what properties are common to a set of elements (i.e. the "intension" of the class) by studying individual members in succession; if we try to do so, we are liable to omit one of the elements, so that the properties we ascribe to the class will not be truly "common". Therefore we must compare "all" the members of the class; in other words, we base our decision on its "intension" on an analysis of "all" and "some" of its members, so that the intension cannot be known unless the extension has been elaborated previously or is elaborated simultaneously. On the other hand, we cannot construct the extension without qualifying the elements in the grouping. Once again, we cannot decide what are the "all" and what are the "some" without referring to more and less common properties, and that is the intension of the class. In other words, extension presupposes intension, and *vice versa*. We can understand a situation like that of stage I, where the two are entirely unco-ordinated, and we can understand a situation like stage III, where every concept has these two aspects but they are fully co-ordinated and interdependent. But the transition from one to the other appears rather mysterious.

(4) The mystery begins to clear when we examine the results of our investigations. The gradual formation of intension and extension is more than a matter of increasing co-ordination between the two: the co-ordination itself is only possible insofar as they are differentiated from one another. To begin with, both aspects are ill-defined, and because of this, they are relatively undifferentiated. In particular, the extension of a collection, which governs the use of the words "some" and "all", is not a purely quantitative notion even at the level of non-graphic collections, let alone the level of graphic collections, because both "some" and "all" are used as if they somehow described an object, that object being not the individual elements but the collection as a whole, or total object. In other words, the force of these words is part-extensive and part-intensive (see ch. III, conclusion). The reason is that even though a non-graphic collection is not tied to a particular spatial configuration, it is still an aggregate of elements having a definite

location in space, as opposed to a true class defined only by its intension. Nevertheless, there is always something which corresponds to intension, because even at the sensori-motor level, the child perceives certain relations and assimilates what he perceives to various functional schemata. In the same way, there is something which corresponds to extension at every level, even though for a long time this something is very much dominated by topological and other spatial characteristics. It follows that if one simply asks how intension or extension come to emerge, be it *ex nihilo* or out of one another, one is posing the problem incorrectly. The question should be how they come to be differentiated, and hence co-ordinated.

(5) Obviously, we want to know in particular what governs the transitions from stage I to stage II and from stage II to the equilibrium of stage III. Why is it that children who were continually building aggregates on the basis of a variety of considerations (graphic collections) eventually finish up by considering nothing but similarities and differences (i.e. intension), which is what they do when making non-graphic collections (stage II)? Secondly, how do we explain the transition from these collections, which are simply juxtaposed, or perhaps subdivided, to hierarchical systems of inclusions (stage III)?

Now here again, the question is not one of sudden appearance, as if these things appeared *ex nihilo*, for here again there is growing differentiation and co-ordination. Thus although it is only at stage II that similarities dominate the classification entirely, they are by no means absent at stage I; indeed the similarities are there beginning with the earliest sensori-motor assimilation, and they play a considerable part in the detail of graphic collections (the relation between couples or within a small sub-group of elements inside an alignment or a complex object). Their predominance at stage II may be new, but this is a matter of being freer from graphic considerations and more sharply differentiated from extension. Similarly, hierarchical inclusions are prepared by the differentiations and subdivisions of non-graphic collections. The latter are so impressive that we would be unable to distinguish between non-graphic collections and genuine classifications without the experiments of chs. III and IV.

(6) It now seems apparent that the transition between stages I and II is governed by the beginnings of hindsight and anticipation, just as, in a more developed form, these processes lead to the reversible operational structures of stage III.

If we try to analyse the course of behaviour and thinking at stage I, we are inevitably struck by the fact that the child is taking each step as he comes to it, forgetting what went before, and not foreseeing what must follow. One example is the alignment where he is continually altering the criterion which determines the juxtaposition of one element in the collection to the next; another is the collective object, or the complex object, when the child is simply putting elements together without any consistent plan (indeed, he may actually say half way through "I'm going to build a house", but although in a sense this is a plan, it means that he has now forgotten the original intention, which was to classify, because he has drifted into a play attitude). What we saw in ch. VII (§3) was that children only begin to abstract a common property when they abandon this kind of successive assimilation and when they show some sign of a retroactive process by remembering the way in which they started a collection. This enables them to achieve some coherence between the beginning and what comes after, and it may even lead them to alter what they have already done in the light of what followed. In other words, as soon as an assimilatory schema becomes retroactive, it also takes an anticipatory character, because one cannot be consistent with the past without eventually making choices and forming intentions as to the future. At first this is no more than a semi-anticipation, partly in the sense that the child cannot foresee what follows as a whole, but also because the anticipation only arises in the course of his ongoing trial-and-error. Yet even this semi-anticipation makes for some beginning of a method which is far better than successive assimilation. The key experiments in this connexion are those in which we compared visual classifications with classificatory behaviour where the perception was limited to touch and feel, because they showed the importance of these early hindsights and semi-anticipations in the construction of non-graphic collections, i.e. in the transition from stage I to stage II.

Of course, neither retroaction nor anticipation can create something which is entirely new. In other words, the present argument is not circular or tautological, which it would be had we said: "Sooner or later, the child is able to discover a property which is common to a set of elements and he can put these together in one collection on the basis of that criterion—because he can now go over his own moves and anticipate their common property!" As a matter of fact, there is a common property between any two elements whenever they are united by a common action. What we want to know is not how common properties arise, but how an assimilatory schema, being a feature which is common to all behaviour, can begin by functioning in a purely successive manner, and then become an instrument of thinking or representation which is applicable to any number of elements instead of just two or three (perceived successively and then forgotten). We know that the n elements are then united by a stable interiorized action. Now the interest of retroaction and anticipation is that these two notions help us to specify the conditions for the interiorization, the permanence and the coherence, by showing that these are not a matter of a sudden illumination by an unexplained consciousness. Instead we can see that they arise as a result of a growing co-ordination between successive actions which eventually overcomes the one-directionality inherent in a succession and takes the form of a shuttling from the present to the past which very soon begins to impinge on the future. Once we are aware that this kind of shuttling is essential to the comparison of elements in a set taken as a whole, we begin to understand why these regulations are likely to end up in the form of operations, since the shuttling is itself a primitive form of reversibility.

(7) Because his behaviour now includes some measure of hindsight and anticipation, a child at stage II will begin to construct non-graphic collections. But there are two ways open to him, and they lead to opposite methods of construction. He may start with small collections, using properties common to small groups of elements as his criteria, and then unite these collections to form larger collections with more general properties in common: this is the ascending method. Alternatively, he can start from the larger collections with the general properties, and then subdivide them to form smaller collections; this is the descending method (the subdivision may or may not be dichotomous at every stage).

Naturally enough, we found ourselves asking whether there might be some way of discovering an order in the application of these two methods, and one that would be universally applicable: e.g. would it be true to say that children always start with the ascending method before they turn to the descending method? However, we found no general solution to the problem when put in this form. One reason is that one can never separate the form of a classification from its content, and the actual method does depend in part on whether the material to be classified incorporates differences of size, or of colour, or of shape, etc., and how marked are the differences, as well as on the relative distribution of these properties and the absolute number of elements. But there is another reason which is even more important. It stands to reason that, on the whole, where a child begins with successive manipulation of the objects, he is naturally led to apply the ascending method; and, conversely, when he tries to anticipate a result without arranging the objects (and, oddly enough, even when he begins to classify, if the classification is by touch), he tends to hit upon the descending method first. One consequence is that there is bound to be a good deal of variation between individuals (and much of this variation may well be due to differences of character rather than cognitive differences): one child may want to manipulate the objects right away and postpone a precise formulation of his projects until he has done a little preliminary exploring; another will hesitate before acting, and the anticipation may well come at an earlier stage (which may not mean that the anticipation is better). As a result, we find that there is no regular sequence and the two methods can be mixed or combined in all sorts of ways.

But there is another question which we now know to be more important than the chronological order. Suppose we ask how far the two methods can be co-ordinated at any given stage: the answer to this is that in spite of the fact that both the ascending method and the descending method are liable to appear at any point in stage II, the one thing which is most characteristic of the stage as a whole is that they are never fully co-ordinated. A child who is actually using one of these methods finds this little help in anticipating what would be the result of using the other. For instance, he can subdivide a collection, say B, and form two sub-collections, A and A'; now this ought to tell him that both A and A' are contained in B. But at stage II, a child does not realize this fact without reviewing the matter afresh from this new standpoint, and sometimes not even then. In other words, although he is anticipating, he is anticipating only the bare results of doing this or that, and not the transformations as a whole. This is why he cannot understand class-inclusions or, indeed operations in general.

We can now see why extension and intension are still not fully differentiated and co-ordinated at stage II, in spite of the considerable advance over stage I. An accurate use of the quantifiers "all" and "some", which is what the co-ordination implies, entails the presence of a schema of inclusion. But the schema of inclusion in turn means simply that the ascending process $(A + A' = B)$, and the descending process $(B - A' = A)$, which is its inverse, have become fused to form a single operational whole.

(8) Following this line of explanation, the transition from stage II to stage III is exactly what one would expect once the anticipation and the hindsight are more developed. When they first appear on the scene, they are only partial (one example being the semi-anticipations of ch. VII), and what this means in particular is that they do not bear on transformations as such, but only on their isolated or static results. But we already know that anticipation and hindsight constitute a shuttling back and forth, and we are therefore entitled to expect that sooner or later the process will reach a state of equilibrium. This equilibrium is bound to be a "mobile" equilibrium. Such a state exists if and only if a subject, when confronted with a set of elements which he has to classify, can anticipate the several stages involved in the complete classification and can also at the same time anticipate these stages in reverse order. In other words, he must anticipate both the unions and the subdivisions. Thus there is equilibrium when the ascending method and the descending method together form a unique system of transformations, as they are bound to do when the subject anticipates the transformations as such instead of their static results. Both the anticipations and the hindsights

enter into such a system, but because they are so integrated, they have the additional character of direct and inverse operations.

We found that the best single test as to whether a child has reached this stage of equilibrium or not is to find out whether he can quantify the relations involved in an inclusion (ch. IV). It sometimes happens that a child can construct a hierarchical classification before he can answer these questions correctly, and we have to make quite certain that he understands exactly what it is that we are after: very often, when one asks a child whether there are more As or more Bs (with $B = A + A'$), he starts off by comparing A and A'. Nevertheless, it is fairly easy to separate the verbal misunderstanding from the inability to hold on to the actual relation, and when a child can hold on to it, we can be certain that he is in fact anticipating both the operations at once: the direct $(A + A' = B)$, and its inverse $(A = B - A')$. The net result is that he can understand the relation of inclusion.

(9) Still following the same line of interpretation, a change of criterion or a "shifting" is simply another expression of operational, and therefore reversible, mobility, this being the hallmark of a complete classificatory structure. Given the same set of elements, changing the criterion means "shifting" from one mode of classification, say C, to another mode, say C' or C''. But there is more to the process than mere substitution, because the two classifications are necessarily related. In other words, the "shifting" expresses a new set of operations, being a system of "vicarious" relations. By this we mean relations of the type $A_1 + A'_1 = A_2 + A'_2$, where A_2 includes part, or all, of A'_1, and, similarly, A'_2 includes part or all of A_1. These vicarious relations form an operational "grouping" on a par with others, and it is in terms of this kind of grouping that we can translate one mode of classification into another. A simple example of this sort of translation is the equivalence: Frenchmen and others (i.e. non-Frenchmen) = Englishmen and others (i.e. non-Englishmen). Consequently, one is not suprised to find that children can change criteria when they reach the level of operational mobility in general.

(10) We may well remind the reader that we found a continuous parallelism in the development of additive classifications and multiplicative classifications, and this is so in spite of the fact that the latter lend themselves more readily to an intuitively acceptable sort of configuration. The fact that they do does not mean that their development is largely a matter of perception. But at the same time, these multiplicative structures are not a secondary development from additive structures, depending on some kind of generalization. What actually happens is that children discover little by little how to classify in terms of one criterion by constructing hierarchical systems of inclusion, and at the same time, they gradually learn to classify on the basis of two or three

criteria at once by making up a cross-classificatory matrix. The two processes are synchronous because they express one and the same general operational mode of organization.

(11) Nevertheless, the most striking instance of parallelism in development is that between classification as a whole and seriation as a whole (regardless of whether they are additive or multiple). This finding is all the more remarkable because there are two reasons which might well lead us to expect the development of seriation to follow a different course. Seriations correspond closely to a highly acceptable "good" perceptual form, unlike classifications which do not. Conversely, classificatory structures are constantly being reinforced by the syntactical structure of language.

The fact remains that, apart from changes of criteria which have no counterpart in seriation, the development of classification and seriation is marked by similar turning-points, at ages which are roughly parallel. In both cases we find a stage I where the establishment of relations is successive, a stage II, where the problem may be solved, but the method is pre-operational, and a stage III, where the ascending method and the descending method are co-ordinated. What is more, we can make a similar distinction in both cases between the anticipation of a static configuration and the anticipation of a transformation. The first sort of anticipation is reinforced in the case of seriation by the intuitive felicity of a serial configuration, but it still appears at much the same age, i.e. 5 or 6, as pre-operational anticipation of classifications. In both cases, this sort of "semi-anticipation" is insufficient for immediate and operational success in performance. Similarly, the second sort of anticipation appears round about the age of 7 or 8 in both cases, and it is invariably linked with operational performance.

The developmental parallelism between classification and seriation is just as evident in cross-classification and multiple seriation. From a theoretical point of view, the parallelism is most important because it constitutes the strongest argument possible in favour of the thesis that the development of operational behaviour is an autonomous process rather than a secondary consequence, depending on the development of perception or of language. We are far from denying that language is a contributory factor in operational development, but what this parallelism proves is that operations do not arise directly out of language, nor is language the central factor in their development.

(12) Leaving aside for a moment this crucial point of the autonomy of operational development, we would remind the reader that nearly all the structures whose development we have been studying in the course of this work are in fact completely formed at the level of concrete operations. This means that they correspond to the elementary "groupings" of classes and relations, and do not cover the whole of the logic

of classes and relations. In particular, these structures do not include classificatory structures which are isomorphic with respect to propositional structures, like the various expressions of the "law of duality". We have in fact touched on the way in which children later discover this sort of transformation, one which implies a fuller structure than these "groupings". The question was: when can a child understand the transformation $(A < B) \rightarrow [(\text{not-}A) > (\text{not-}B)]$? Not surprisingly, we found that the transformation is not understood until the level of formal operations, because it implies the combined application of negation (or complementarity) and reciprocity, which is precisely the structure of the 4 transformations of propositions forming an $I \, N \, R \, C$ group (see ch. V, §5).

(13) To come back to the autonomy of operational development as revealed throughout this research, we should point out that this by no means implies that logical operations are somehow divorced from mental life as a whole, like some kind of "state within a state". The very reverse is the case. Operations are a continuation of actions; they express certain forms of co-ordination which are general to all actions; whether or not the co-ordination is complete, operations and pre-operational co-ordinations enter into the most diverse kinds of behaviour. That is why we find that their development is largely autonomous, and not subordinated to this or that factor which is more specific, be it perception, learning, or language. In other words, what we are saying is that operations are autonomous because they are general in application, and this is the very reverse of what is very often maintained, that they are autonomous because the field in which they apply is highly restricted.

What we have seen once again is that logical operations (i.e. in particular, classification and cross-classification, and seriation and multiple seriation) are closely linked with certain actions which are quite elementary: putting things in piles, separating piles into lots, making alignments, and so on. The development is astonishingly continuous: after the actions we have various adjustments to these actions and these in turn become increasingly complex so that in time the entire process is interiorized and generalized. The principal kinds of adjustment are of course those retroactive and anticipatory processes which figure so prominently throughout these pages, both in the behaviour of our subjects and in our interpretation of that behaviour. By following their development, we could see almost step by step how reversibility first begins and how it then grows until it reaches the form in which it is most familiar to us: that of the most general characteristic of operations as a whole. First of all, there is a beginning of co-ordination between segments of overt behaviour; next the adjustments become sufficiently far-reaching to make the actions increasingly internal; finally, they take the form of mobile and reversible operational structures. This is essentially the same order of development as that which we have found in our previous investigations of development involving logico-mathematical processes, and the definition of these stages is if anything more precise than in any of those others.

(14) When we speak of the autonomy of this development, we wish to be understood in the very precise sense that the development can be explained without necessary reference to various factors which undoubtedly do play a part in its concrete realization, e.g. maturation, learning and social education, including language. For the key to its explanation lies in the concept of equilibration, which is a wider notion than any of these and comprehends them all. The reason that we would insist on this point is not (only) because we are interested in a systematic formulation, or because we are trying to cling to a particular set of hypotheses, but quite simply because all our investigations make this conclusion inevitable.

To take the case of classification: at stage II, which is when the child is gradually coming nearer to an operational mode of solution, we find him oscillating between an ascending method and a descending method, but still not achieving that stable synthesis of the two which would make him understand the nature of inclusion. But how is the stabilization achieved at stage III? The answer is by a system of compensations which is such that for every transformation in an ascending direction the subject will find a corresponding transformation in a descending direction, and *vice versa*. In other words, the operational structure which brings this development to an end (and which is itself but the culmination of all the retroactive and anticipatory adjustments of previous levels), represents a state of equilibrium, both because it is a stable state, and in the further sense that its stability is the outcome of compensatory forces (which in turn express the reversibility of these particular operations).

In seriations, there is equilibrium when the subject is able to follow both directions of the series at the same time. In particular, there is equilibrium when he can set about the business of constructing a series by comparing each element from the outset both with its predecessors and with its successors (e.g. $E > D$, C, and $E < F$, G). Here too the stability is a function of compensatory operations, and the reversibility merely expresses their compensatory character ($<$ and $>$).

The value of being able to reduce this kind of development to a series of phases each of which possesses a higher degree of equilibrium than its predecessors lies in the fact that the process itself is essentially one of equilibration. It is a process of equilibration because of the very close link between the reversibility of operations and certain kinds of compensatory forces which define their equilibrium. Once the process is understood as being of this kind, one can begin to explain why it takes the form that it does by simply translating the succession of phases into probability terms.[1] It then becomes apparent that each successive phase is the most probable given the results of the preceding phase. What this means is that the movement towards an eventual equilibrium is not fully determined by the mechanics of, say, the human brain, but is guaranteed by the nature of the sequential process itself, the reason being that the behaviour peculiar to each phase in the series gains in probability of occurrence throughout the completion of the preceding phase, as a function of such antecedent behaviour and its results.

Needless to say, it still remains a reasonable question to ask what are the psycho-physiological mechanisms underlying the co-ordination of actions, the retroactive and anticipatory adjustments and the operations themselves. But this would be a matter of explaining how these things become possible. What we have attempted to do is something very different, and that is to give a detailed account of the reason why, given the fact that they are physiologically possible, they assume these particular forms as and when they do.

(15) The time has now come to reconsider the various points which we raised in our introduction. First of all, we would take the role of language. We are still prepared to admit that some kind of language is essential for the completion of the structures under discussion, i.e. classification and seriation. This is because the operations involve a symbolic, and therefore a representative handling of objects, inasmuch as they go beyond what could be done in terms of overt behaviour. But the point upon which we would insist is that language alone is not enough. On the contrary, whether a child understands words like "all" and "some", or any other form of words used to refer to the concept of class-inclusion, and similarly, whether he understands the sort of language we use to refer to the asymmetrical and transitive relation of a series, these are questions which are mainly dependent on the level which he has reached in the development of operational behaviour—and that development is relatively independent of any other, because it is governed by its own laws of equilibration. We therefore say that language is not a sufficient and necessary reason for the process.

As for maturation, we have already agreed that without maturation it would hardly be possible for a subject to reach the successive co-ordinations with which we have been dealing. But we have also shown that, granted the possibility of a given co-ordination in terms of maturation, that co-ordination will still not occur unless there is a tendency for its occurrence, and that tendency depends on a process of equilibration governed by sequential probability. In other words, maturation is not a sufficient cause either, because it is not maturation that can decide what degree of equilibrium will attach to this or that form of behaviour.

[1] Cf. J. Piaget, "Logique et équilibre", *Etudes d'épistémologie génétique*, Vol. II, 1957, pp. 27–113.

We might add that maturation is itself subject to laws of equilibration insofar as there is bound to be an interaction between maturation and experience, both social and material.

Finally, we may turn to consider the part played by perceptual and sensori-motor factors. As was indicated in the introduction, each of these plays an important role, yet both have their limitations. As the reader will no doubt recall, they recur continually in our interpretations of the earlier stages of classification and seriation. For instance, it would be difficult to account for the graphic collections of stage I without mentioning successive assimilation, to which we must look for the origin of "intensive" similarities; and such assimilations are typical of sensori-motor schematization in general. Similarly, the extension of these precursors of true classes invariably took a spatial form, and therefore owed a great deal to perception. What this means is that sensori-motor and perceptual factors combine to give these collections their positive character. Nevertheless, it is to the above factors that graphic collections also owe their limitations: these are essentially due to the successive character of assimilations and the spatial specificity of this primitive form of extension. Likewise, in the case of seriation, the early stages up to and including the global anticipation of the form of the series, which we saw was a remarkably early development (ch. IX), can only be accounted for in terms of the perceptual configuration of series and of certain elementary behaviour patterns which are essentially sensori-motor in character, yet constitute an early attempt at ordination.

Nor were these by any means the only ways in which we found that perceptual factors play an important part in the development of classification and seriation (they were especially prominent in the solution of matrices, ch. VI). But in every case, irrespective of whether the perceptual factor seemed to constitute a help or a hindrance, the development of operational behaviour was shown to transcend the merely perceptual. Operational behaviour has its origin in sensori-motor activity as a whole, and perceptual structures have a similar origin, because they too undergo a certain development, so that the various perceptual structures which are characteristic of any given stage are best understood as a sort of crystalline sedimentation which is the residue of all the activity that went before. It is therefore hardly surprising that the operational activities of classifying and seriating eventually transcend any sort of perceptual configuration. In fact they eventually take the form of sets of transformations which have their own characteristic operational structure, and are governed by their own laws of equilibrium.

Such, then, is the origin of these elementary groupings of classification and seriation, which arise long before the more complex "groups" peculiar to formal reasoning. This brings us to the end of the present enquiry. It only remains to say that we are very much aware that much remains to be done. In particular, we have by no means exhausted the question of the relation between active thinking and imagery. We feel that we are beginning to know a good deal about the former, since this is a matter of the development of operational mechanisms. But we cannot dismiss the whole topic of mental imagery with a few references to perceptual configurations. From the very beginning of symbolization, all mental activity, whether pre-operational or operational, is invariably accompanied by a sequence of mental images, i.e. by representation in the form of images. Now mental images have their own laws which are different both from the laws of perceptions and from those of operations. We need to understand these laws in order to complete our picture of the mechanism of anticipations, and the latter were shown to be of the utmost significance to our interpretation (particularly in chs. VII–IX), because they are so closely related to operations. This whole subject of anticipation and imagery will therefore form the topic of a new series of studies, one upon which we have been engaged for some time, and which we may expect to complete in the not too distant future.

Piaget, Jean. *Play, Dreams and Imitation in Childhood.*

Piaget, Jean and Bärbel Inhelder. *The Child's Conception of Space.*

Piers, Gerhart and Milton B. Singer. *Shame and Guilt.*

Ruesch, Jurgen. *Disturbed Communication.*

Ruesch, Jurgen. *Therapeutic Communication.*

Ruesch, Jurgen and Gregory Bateson. *Communication: The Social Matrix of Psychiatry.*

Schein, Edgar et al. *Coercive Persuasion.*

Sullivan, Harry Stack. *Clinical Studies in Psychiatry.*

Sullivan, Harry Stack. *Conceptions of Modern Psychiatry.*

Sullivan, Harry Stack. *The Fusion of Psychiatry and Social Science.*

Sullivan, Harry Stack. *The Interpersonal Theory of Psychiatry.*

Sullivan, Harry Stack. *The Psychiatric Interview.*

Walter, W. Grey. *The Living Brain.*

Watson, John B. *Behaviorism.*

Wheelis, Allen. *The Quest for Identity.*

Zilboorg, Gregory. *A History of Medical Psychology.*